REPRODUCING THE STATE

REPRODUCING THE STATE

Jacqueline Stevens

PRINCETON UNIVERSITY PRESS PRINCETON, NEW JERSEY

Copyright © 1999 by Princeton University Press
Published by Princeton University Press, 41 William Street,
Princeton, New Jersey 08540
In the United Kingdom: Princeton University Press, Chichester,
West Sussex
All Rights Reserved

Library of Congress Cataloging-in-Publication Data
Stevens, Jacqueline, 1962–
    Reproducing the state / Jacqueline Stevens.
        p.   cm.
    Includes bibliographical references.
    ISBN 0-691-01713-1 (cloth : alk. paper). — ISBN 0-691-01714-X
(pbk. : alk. paper)
    1. Ethnicity—Political aspects.   2. Race relations.   3. Sex role.
4. Kinship.   5. Political anthropology.   I. Title.
GN495.6.S74   1999
305.8—dc21   98-55312

This book has been composed in Janson

The paper used in this publication meets the minimum requirements
of ANSI/NISO Z39.48-1992 (R1997) (*Permanence of Paper*)

http://pup.princeton.edu

Printed in the United States of America

10   9   8   7   6   5   4   3   2   1

(Pbk.)
10   9   8   7   6   5   4   3   2   1

Contents

Acknowledgments

As a graduate student I had the privilege of being taught by Hanna Pitkin, who provided comments on the Introduction and Chapters 4 and 5. Pitkin, along with my colleague Don Herzog, pressed me early on to reflect on the parallels between the uses of 'race' and other words for concepts that express gradual and not categorical understandings of the world. I also want to thank Mary Dietz, Philip Green, Michael Rogin, and Jeremy Waldron, for their early and long-standing support, advice, and inspiration.

The manuscript benefited enormously from various institutional and personal commitments to interdisciplinary scholarship at the University of Michigan. The faculty-graduate workshop Comparative Studies in Social Transformations (CSST), sponsored by the International Institute, enabled me to meet literary theorists, historians, anthropologists, and sociologists here and elsewhere whose ideas and enthusiasms permeate this book in ways too numerous to recount. I especially want to thank Ann Stoler, who provided comments on the Introduction and Chapter 4, and who has been a helpful interlocutor on questions of race and Foucault. I am grateful, also, to the other members of our writing group, which has included Julia Adams, Sonya Rose, Margaret Somers, and Katherine Verdery. One of Somers's typically useful suggestions was the notion of an "iconographic Foucault," which appears in the Introduction. Along with F. Trenholme Junghans, Verdery provided valuable assistance on various sources in anthropology.

I also want to thank Elizabeth Anderson, Nicholas Dirks, and Sally Haslanger for their comments on Chapter 4, and Martha Ackelsberg, Kathleen Jones, and Joan Tronto for their comments on Chapter 5. And thanks to Jennifer Widner who, in addition to comments on the Introduction, gave me a copy of the Unity Dow citizenship case in Botswana, discussed in Chapter 2. Zvi Gitelman has my appreciation for his reading of portions of Chapter 2 and for passing on some of the information relevant to the discussion of Jewish identity in Chapter 6.

Two people have assisted me with translations. I want to thank Christine Schoefer, for her advice on my interpretations of idiomatic and philosophical German phrases. Also assisting me was Arlene Saxonhouse, who provided translations of various phrases from Latin and Greek. I do not read Latin or Greek, so any errors are due to my misunderstandings of what Saxonhouse told me.

I want to gratefully acknowledge the support of the Robert Wood Johnson Foundation, which funded my research at Yale University from

1997 to 1999, and that of the University of Michigan Rackham University Distinguished Faculty Research grant. The New School for Social Research has my appreciation for funding Rebecca Musselman, who compiled the index. Amy Heibel read the page proofs.

Marek Steedman tracked down numerous journal articles, as well as statistics on immigration to and from Mississippi, with equal efficiency and good cheer. The University of Michigan's Research Opportunity Program provided me the research assistance of Jill Durocher and Ellerie Weber in 1995–1997. And my thanks to Gordon Adams, who kindly allowed me access to the computer facilities at the University of California at Berkeley's Department of Political Science in the summer of 1997.

Portions of Chapters 2 and 5 appeared in "On the Marriage Question," in *Women Transforming Politics*, Cathy Cohen, Kathleen Jones, and Joan Tronto, eds. (New York: New York University Press, 1997). Sections are republished here with the permission of New York University Press. An earlier version of Chapter 4 was published in *Theory & Event* Issue 2:2 (1998) and appears here with their permission.

Ann Himmelberger Wald, Editor-in-Chief at Princeton University Press, also has my gratitude, for her early interest that proved sustaining. And I want to express my appreciation to the Press's readers, for their conscientious and lengthy comments that significantly informed my revisions.

Finally, I was fortunate to have the assistance of Samantha Frost, who provided instant, thorough, and terrifically useful readings and suggestions for the Introduction and Chapters 1 and 2. My arguments have again benefited from the astute and thorough comments of Laura Green, who read the entire manuscript. For her indefatiguable support and attention to my work I will always be in her debt.

Preface

I.

The newly built Croatian National Library on the outermost corner of Zagreb—far from the Parliament and other buildings that attracted Serbian strafing during the early 1990s—stands out as a hyper-modern government building in the nine hundred-year-old city. The immense structure echoes many of the design motifs of the sleek, imposing Berlin Staatsbibliothek, and the resemblance between the two state libraries may not be coincidental. Germany and Croatia have long-standing affinities. Croatia offered broad support for the Nazi-installed regime during World War Two. In 1991 Germany was the first country to grant Croatia recognition as a sovereign political society—in opposition to the wishes of the United States and the United Nations. It was this action that officially transformed the skirmishes within the fractious Yugoslavia into a full-blown war. If the Croatian state architectural firm were to look to any European national library for inspiration, it would be that of Germany. (The coldness of the library's stone, concrete, and glass materials betrays an affinity with another Zagreb building designed by the same architectural firm: the state crematorium.)

In the summer of 1996, a Croatian colleague, Maria, and I mistakenly entered through the rear of the Zagreb library, where we were met by the state militia, armed with sub-machine guns and ensconced behind a bullet-proof window. Our reception in the public entrance was not all that different. The catalogues and other reference materials are separated from the lobby by locked turnstiles. In order to gain access, one must answer various questions about one's nationality, for purposes of a bar-coded card that is issued for 20 kunas (about $4).

The allusive overlapping themes of nationalism, genocide, war, state knowledge, and state secrets implied in this rendering of Croatia's library instantiate the paradoxes of the state form as simultaneously one of rationality and insanity, tidy rules and the messy triumph of blood—in the particular, as in "my people's blood must survive at the expense of your people," as well as 'blood'-s more general significations, as when there is a consensus that, say, "blood is thicker than water." The immaculate library staffed by vacant-faced bureaucrats above the basement-level army personnel was hundreds of miles from Mostar, where a Croatian general had led the eviction and slaughter of hundreds of Muslims, but the places were not so distant after all. As was the case in the Nazi extermination of

Communists, Jews, Gypsies, and homosexuals, the state's assembly-line approach to mass killing was the means to the very personal, particular, and obviously embodied experiences of, if not killing, then dying.

The misleading quality of my narrative is that by referencing a place of such recent and horrifying violence the implications of the same routinized expressions of the state that occur in so-called liberal political societies—which also strictly regulate the movement of populations and the reproduction of national symbols—may be elided or appear harmless. The political constitution of adversarial forms of being is not the work of a few zealots in the Balkans but is ubiquitous.

Reading off my passport, which was issued by the United States government for the purpose of requesting that access be given me to other countries—access that most likely would be denied if not accompanied by a passport—the library clerk recorded my surname as "A. Stevens," printing my middle initial as the first letter of my last name. A Stevens? Yes and no. 'Stevens' is the name now on my California state-issued birth certificate, which is the source of information for the passport, but my birth certificate at birth revealed a different last name. 'Stevens' is the Anglicized name that my mother's second husband's father used when he immigrated to the United States from Germany during World War Two, after rejecting as "ethnic-sounding" the "Jewish" last name he had in Germany and adapting his middle name 'Stephen' for United States official documents.[1] This son of the name-changing Stevens was not my own biological father. Details of the above are confusing, prompting attention to the particular ways they seem hard to follow. It is important to realize that the disjuncture between the models of biological, genetic ancestry and the patterns of political ancestral genealogies do not mean the birth certificates or other legal documents that assign identity perform simple nominalist mistakes. Rather, it is the discursive possibilities of such ongoing political kinship systems that are the foundation for the apparently material, biological laws of nature.

Nine years after I was born, my birth certificate was purged and amended, to indicate 'Claude Stevens' as my father. My photocopied white-on-black

[1] Following the conventions of ordinary language philosophy, I use single quotation marks to denote a word. Double quotation marks indicate reference to a concept. To put this in the idiom of the Sausserian signifier/signified = sign relation, by "concept" I mean a sign *qua* sign, a sign that is being attended to as such. For instance, a 'word' is a signifier; a "word" reflects on that signifier; and a word is the thing we write down without reflecting on it being a 'word'. Saussure's image of a piece of a paper with the signifier on one side and the signified on the other is a wonderful metaphor for the way that the word and the concept are intrinsically joined. It is as impossible to have a word without a concept, or a concept without a word, as it is to have a one-sided piece of paper (Ferdinand Saussure, *Course on General Linguistics* [1911], tr. Wade Baskin [London: P. Owen, 1960], p. 113. See also J. L. Austin, *How to Do Things with Words* [Oxford: Clarendon Press, 1962] and Paul Ziff, *Semantic Analysis* [Ithaca: Cornell University Press, 1967].

reproduction includes Claude's age at the time of my birth, even though he and my mother had not yet met. The birth certificate also states that both of my parents are Caucasian, that my mother was born in California, and that Claude was born in Germany. When I was in college, Claude legally changed his name to 'Klaus' and changed his last name as well, so that the father indicated in the birth certificate no longer exists as such. Under the heading "Maiden Name of Mother," it says 'Barbara', and of course her last name, Moskowitz, appears under "Maiden Surname." This brief history of my name has the aura of a bureaucratic oddity strictly because of the prevalent myth that biological ancestry determines who we are. What I've described is nothing more complicated than a dominant pattern of immigration and marriage practices that has existed since ancient Athens, if not longer. The truth is that, in the United States and elsewhere, political societies constitute and assign one membership to these intergenerational groups.

The passport revealed none of the conventions underlying the reproduction of my personal name, but rather made possible the sleek identity cards that my colleague and I swiped through the magnetic lock to release the turnstiles. Our entrance was recorded by an elaborate computer system that was well beyond the means of President Franjo Tudjman's bankrupt government.

Not physical appearance, but one's first and last names on official documents are regarded as the best evidence of "who one is" in that region, for purposes of what the Serbians referred to as "ethnic cleansing" and for the discriminations that underlie other harms as well. Official documents become a second, or even a first, nature. Realizing that signs such as personal names are never "only" or "merely" signs, I was in Zagreb to attempt to find books and articles that would explain how various regimes in the former Yugoslavia had instituted and enforced the use of certain names to determine and distinguish the nationality of inhabitants within political borders. Just as my mother's name 'Moskowitz' prompted people to think her Jewish, the governments and people in the Balkans have long used first and last names to ascertain the identities of individuals as Serbian (Orthodox Christian), Croatian (Roman Catholic), or Serbian or Croatian Muslims. I had hoped that by documenting the political production of these names I might demonstrate that the materiality of personal names is actually a matter of political, not biological, laws and forms, and to learn more about the conditions under which this occurs.

As we began our search of the catalogues, a man in his fifties approached. Maria whispered that she recognized him "from television," where he frequently opined on behalf of Tudjman's government. He asked who we were and what we were looking for. He and I proceeded to speak in German, with Maria translating among Croatian, German, and English during the rough spots. The man showed me a large reference text that indicated the presence of the inhabitants with every family name in various parts of Croatia, along with brief histories of their origins.

The official asked where I was from. I said the United States. He left and fifteen minutes later returned. I inferred that he had been checking on my recently entered biographical information. He was not satisfied. "What is your mother-tongue?" he asked, "Italian?" I said that it was English. "Ah," he smiled condescendingly, "I guess you do not understand what mother-tongue (Muttersprache) means. Where is your grandmother from?" Thinking first of my maternal grandmother, I said she was born in the United States. He became hostile, "No, before that. Where is her family from?" I told him they were from Germany. "No, that is not right," he said, "you are not from there," and then I began to realize what he was after. Somehow he grasped that none of my relatives from these places were simply German. In response to his skepticism and severe tone, I confessed that my family was Jewish. He relaxed and smiled, "Yes, yes." And then: "Ashkenazi or Sephardic?"

II.

This book attempts to clarify the sources of the paradoxes that emerge repeatedly in accounts of certain group affiliations, namely, those of family, nation, ethnicity, and race. How is it that certain affiliations that may have a tenuous, or even no, relevance to one's daily practices and worldviews are experienced (by oneself as well as others) as immutably part of one's being—who one is—while other forms of group membership do not exert that effect? How is it that my grandmother's relatives' presence at some point in Germany—and her ancestors' presence thousands of years earlier among the Israelites—could be used to make inferences about who I was that summer in Croatia?

The tie of intergenerationality is what distinguishes the objects of the official's questions—family, nationality, race—from his lack of interest in my membership in the American Political Science Association, for instance. Rather than accept his special interest as indicative of a biological disposition to preserve his lineage and people, it seems important to reflect on the political practices that produce the kind of attachments that motivated his queries.[2]

A focus on intergenerationality highlights the insistence of the state and

[2] Wendy Brown calls such concerns about identities "wounded attachments" and attributes them to oppressed groups unable to overcome feelings of ressentiment (*States of Injury: Power and Freedom in Late Modernity* [Princeton: Princeton University Press, 1995]). It is also, however, the case that those who hold power often experience themselves as weak and indulge in exercises that enhance the status of their particular ancestral group. It is that these activities, e.g., state libraries, are seen as universal ones and not statements or enactments on behalf

other kinds of political associations (ranging from communist regimes to emergent democracies to Native American tribes) on invoking terms of ancestry for purposes of reproducing their respective groups. The appeal to intergenerationality is always paradoxical, depending on naturalized rules of kinship that are produced by political societies. How can we understand the juxtaposition of the heavy-handed bureaucratic technologies of Croatia's reproduction of its identity—ranging from declarations of war to intense scrutiny of state-issued identity papers to the monitoring of researchers in the state library—with the man-from-television's facile, yet utterly idiomatic assumption that one simply possesses a nationality the way one possesses brown hair—through an ancestral route of inheritance? The Croatian national library is not a gene pool, and its preparations for the next generation's identities as Croatian seem at odds with the notion that one's ancestors produce one's identity.

III.

In brief, the laws productive of the Croatian library's power/knowledge nexus emerge from the form of political societies themselves, which all entail kinship rules. I want to invoke a critical, neo-Hegelian view of these kinship rules, to suggest that it is the rules, a matter of 'law' in its various meanings, that constitute various forms of being, including heterosexual and lesbian, girlfriend and prostitute, married and single. These kinship laws also constitute nationalities, ethnicities, and race as forms of being. I use 'being' here and not 'identity' or 'subjectivity' because the gerund of "to be" disrupts the commonplace intuition among non-Hegelians—I have in mind some post-structuralists and all liberals—that a person might or might not have a particular "identity" as one might or might not have an overcoat. My use of 'being' is similar to the use of 'Dasein' (being-there) by Hegel. 'Dasein' connotes the dialectics of various tensions within the self-consciousness of an age, a political society, or an individual, for instance. 'Being' as a gerund provides a similar sense of movement, between one's certainty of a thing and its elusiveness to being named, between self-consciousness as to the ways categories may fail us and the awareness of them as still useful, and for purposes of this study, between frustrations over certain conventions of naming affiliations and the idiomatic uses of these conventions nonetheless.[3]

---

of a particularly Croatian, or other, national affinity that leads critics of "identity politics" to focus solely on the contexts in which weaker groups make these statements.

[3] Hegel refers to 'Sein' (being) to describe conditions that are static. I do not follow this convention because the word 'being' is sufficient to convey a sense of movement and because the phrase 'being there' is not idiomatic. Also, non-English words are not italicized unless they are from languages that are no longer spoken, i.e., transliterations of ancient Greek

According to Hegel, one's oneness or individuality (Einzelheit or Individualität) develops in tandem with the psychological internalization and institutional externalization of a particular political and spiritual order. The *Phenomenology of Spirit* and the *Philosophy of Right* describe how both individuals and nations are free when their individualities are fully developed, which is to say, when political institutions are not experienced as separate from the self-conscious will of each individual, when one believes that the laws of the Croatians are thought good laws because they are objectively right, and not because each person has actually or in principle offered her endorsement of them:

> [T]he ethical order ['valid laws and institutions'] is the freedom or the absolute will as what is objective . . . To these powers individuals [das Leben der Individuen] are related as accidents to substance, and it is in individuals that these powers are represented, have the shape of appearance, and become actualized.[4]

One's free will develops not as a subject externally shaped by the laws, nor as an individual erratically choosing to obey or to elude laws, but through a process whereby each individual actively joins one's mind, sentiment, and soul to the state.

One's fully developed subjectivity is always a specifically national one, according to Hegel. It is the distinction of one's nation-state from others that makes possible its individuality, and hence the individuality of its members:

> Individuality [Individualität] is awareness of one's existence as a unit in sharp distinction from others. It manifests itself here in the state as a relation to other states, each of which is autonomous vis-a-vis the others. This autonomy embodies mind's [Geist] actual awareness of itself [Dasein] as a unit and hence it is the most fundamental freedom which a people [Volk] possesses as well as its highest dignity.[5]

Rather than opposing each other, the state subject and the individual's will coalesce, through a political society's institutions of kinship and citizenship. Finally, though the link between state laws and institutions and individuality may appear overstated, since people have subjectivities of, say, ethnicity, race, religion, sex, and sexuality that appear to have little to do with their citizenship, a more careful analysis of these forms of being reveals that they too are inseparable from the rules of political society.

---

and Latin. The difference between languages that are and are not spoken calls for the sort of notational attention that when applied to contemporary languages insidiously establishes a border between the familiar and the foreign.

[4] Tr. T. M. Knox, *Philosophy of Right* [1921] (Oxford and New York: Oxford University Press, 1952), p. 105; *Grundlinien der Philosophie des Rechts oder Naturrecht und Staatswissenschaft im Grundrisse* [Grounding of the Philosophy of Right, or Natural Right and State Knowledge-Making in Sketches, 1821] (Frankfurt am Main: Surhkamp, 1970), p. 294.

[5] *Philosophy*, p. 208; *Philosophie*, p. 490.

The kinship forms constituted by political societies comprise a variety of ancestral communities of members and aliens. In addition to the forms of opposition among politically established ancestral communities (of nation, ethnicity, and race), political societies constitute abject forms of being within themselves—those consciousnesses that are relatively weak, rejected from that which they, by virtue of their relation to that particular political society, seemingly desire to be or to have. Marriage laws make outlaws of same-sex partners, for instance, and alienate their forms of being from political society in a manner similar to the way kinship rules for citizenship (including territorial birth criteria) render certain people aliens in a particular political society. By taxonomizing the orderly and disorderly forms of being of its population—through the reproduction of kinship rules on birth certificates, marriage licenses, passports, and so forth—the state's relation to normal and deviant forms of being is not stenographic, but pornographic. The state puts on display the sexual and other outlaws and aliens who exist as such only by virtue of that same state.[6]

The overarching task of this project, then, is to inquire into the political processes that produce the family as well as the equally discursive state of nature that is experienced as the pre-political origin of that family form. The result is an argument that connects the specific confusions associated with our perception of these affiliations with their underlying and superimposing forms, as our confusions are not mistakes or partial answers to conundrums of being, but themselves crucial evidence of who we are. The implications of this line of analysis render the strategies to dislodge these affiliations from their current oppressive structures both theoretically more obvious and politically more remote-seeming than discussions that are largely philosophical. Once it is understood that the most fundamental structures of the modern state—the rules regulating marriage and immigration—are what enable the state to reproduce itself and what make possible the power relations associated with nationality, ethnicity, race, and family roles, then it is clear that piecemeal approaches to eradicating certain inequalities will not work. As long as there are political societies based on kinship forms, there will be far-reaching practices of violence that follow from the corollary forms of nationality, ethnicity, race, and family roles.

[6] According to the *Oxford English Dictionary*, 2d ed., 'pornography' is first defined in the Dunglison Medical Dictionary (1857) to mean "a description of prostitutes or of prostitution, as a matter of public hygiene." Because it is political society that establishes the kinship regime that defines prostitution as such—by defining sex for money as (il)legal behavior—the law works in a manner consistent with the medical dictionary's definition of 'pornography', constituting what it claims merely to observe.

REPRODUCING THE STATE

Introduction _____

Majorities and Minorities in Political Theory: Who Are They?

Contemporary political theorists who address conundrums of group conflict, particularly those who write in the tradition of democratic, liberal, or communitarian theory in North America, have tended to be more concerned with elaborating rules to alleviate group conflict than with examining how these groups come to appear as such.[1] The Marxist tradition's debate as to what "class" means has no long-standing counterpart among political theorists who elaborate principles of distributive justice that would speak to concerns about gender or race inequalities, for instance. While feminist theorists and critical race theorists have as their major task a theoretical exposure of the meanings and even the origins of these affiliations, the implications of this research for a political theoretical understanding of the dynamics of inequality prompted by these forms of being within the state have not been fully explored.

---

[1] In a communitarian vein, Alasdair MacIntyre writes: "[We] all approach our own circumstances as bearers of a particular social identity. I am someone's son or daughter, someone else's cousin or uncle; I am a citizen of this or that city, a member of this or that guild or profession; I belong to this or that clan, that tribe, this nation ... As such I inherit from the past of my family, my city, my tribe, my nation, a variety of debts and inheritances, rightful expectations and obligations. These constitute the given of my life, my moral starting point" (*After Virtue*, 2d ed. [Notre Dame: University of Notre Dame Press, 1984], p. 220). Charles Taylor begins his essay "The Politics of Recognition" by writing of the "urgency" given by "minority or 'subaltern' groups, in some forms of feminism and in what is today called the politics of 'multiculturalism' ... by the supposed links between recognition and identity, where this latter term designates something like a person's understanding of who they are, of their fundamental defining characteristics as a human being" (in *Multiculturalism*, Charles Taylor, et al., eds. [Princeton: Princeton University Press, 1994], p. 25). Though approaching forms of being from very different assumptions, MacIntyre and Taylor both treat as axiomatic the existence of ancestral groups. Their texts discuss the particular political and psychological significations of the groups they consider, and not how these forms of being come into existence as such. Similarly, Will Kymlicka theorizes the grounds for preserving aboriginal Canadians' rights to "cultural survival," but without interrogating the form of being that makes such a project seem so pressing to him (*Liberalism, Community, and Culture* [Oxford: Clarendon Press, 1989]).

Of course there are numerous impressive histories, deconstructions, and critiques of the affiliations mentioned above. W.E.B. Du Bois is perhaps the first U.S. American scholar to undertake this critical work on forms of being, which has been continued by subsequent generations of Marxist, feminist, and Foucauldian scholars. However, those who work on

Political theorists who write about minorities and majorities tend not to inquire into the conditions that give rise to the groups whose antagonisms and deliberations are under consideration, but seek to elaborate rules that would ameliorate tensions among them. John Rawls, for instance, optimistically treats forms of being such as race and religion as apolitical attributes that would be unhinged from any power dynamics by the universal veil of ignorance in the original position:

> We can note whether applying these principles [of justice] would lead us to make the same judgments of the basic structure of society which we now make intuitively. . . . There are questions which we feel sure must be answered in a certain way. For example, we are confident that religious intolerance and racial discrimination are unjust.[2]

Knowing that some people may be worse off because of racial discrimination, he reasons, inoculates against individuals under the veil of ignorance deciding on rules that would discriminate based on race. This static understanding of race reveals no attempt to think through how the affiliations of race might be instantiations of injustice that follow from the form of political society itself. Further, as Susan Okin has pointed out, Rawls strangely treats as axiomatic inequalities within the family, refusing to subject family position to the criteria of the original position.[3] Rawls understands political society as the location that settles differences, rather than the form that gives rise to them.

The problem is not simply that Rawls imagines citizens as a collective *tabula rasa*. One may criticize Rawls for this and still not pursue the logic of these forms of being. Iris Marion Young, for instance, argues that Rawls underestimates the political and hence ethical importance of being able to develop and maintain an identity as a member of a group: "Justice should refer not only to distribution, but also to the institutional conditions necessary for the development and exercise of individual capacities and collective communication and cooperation."[4] Elaborating this goal, Young writes,

> My starting point is reflection on the conditions of the groups said by [new social movements] to be oppressed: among others, women, Blacks, Chicanos,

---

democratic, communitarian, and liberal political theory make little use of inquiries into the forms of group difference.

[2] *A Theory of Justice* (Cambridge: Harvard University Press, 1971), p. 19.

[3] *Justice, Gender, and the Family* (New York: Basic Books, 1989). Symptomatic of the gulf between liberal political theorists and political studies of affiliation is the fact that Okin limits her critique to noting the exclusion of the family from Rawls' analyses, without discussing the ways that political societies entail the the kinship rules that produce families. Although in his elaborations and defense of his theory of justice as fairness Rawls responds to many of his critics, Okin is not among them. *Political Liberalism*, (New York: Columbia University Press, 1993).

[4] *Justice and the Politics of Difference* (Princeton: Princeton University Press, 1990), p. 39.

Puerto Ricans and other Spanish-speaking Americans, American Indians, Jews, lesbians, gay men, Arabs, Asians, old people, working class people, and the physically and mentally disabled.[5]

But despite stating that she regards "oppression as a structural concept," Young does not describe how the groups she names (but not Whites? Anglos? Christians?) are themselves constituted, other than to say that a "social group" is a "collective of persons differentiated from at least one other group by cultural forms, practices, or way of life."[6] This seems far too inclusive for her purposes. Presumably Young is not interested in explaining how the initiation rites of one sorority differ from those of another, or how the way of life of organic farmers differs from that of Wall Street stockbrokers. All this is to say that in the literature on group conflict where one might expect inquiry into the conditions that yield the particular minorities and majorities subject to theoretical scrutiny, the conditions that make possible certain (familial) forms of inequalities receive little or no attention.

Political Theories of Membership

Michael Walzer is one of the rare thinkers in this milieu who, by pursuing the problem of membership in particular, raises questions about the relation between the form of political society and its principles of distributive justice. The objective of *Spheres of Justice* is to present principles for a "society where no social good serves or can serve as a means of domination."[7] The most obviously arbitrary and unfair decision rule he first discredits is "birthright" as a prerequisite for holding political office or property. This entails a standard liberal renunciation of an aristocratic order that "rests upon birth and blood, with which the individual has nothing to do, rather than upon wealth, power, or education, all of which—at least in principle—can be won."[8] Such rules seem to preclude membership in political society as an automatic prerogative of birth. And yet ultimately the rules Walzer proposes for membership in a political society depend

[5] Ibid., p. 40.

[6] Ibid. I consistently capitalize names of racial groups so as to undermine those representations of race as ontological and given, as similar to the way we experience the colors black and white, for instance. Whatever the grammatical and semantic conventions that prompt the capitalization of French, for instance, are the ones I want to rely on for capitalizing Black and White, to emphasize the ways that races are proper nouns that are particular constructions peculiar to specific societies, and not commonplace objects that one might expect to find anywhere at all.

[7] *Spheres of Justice: A Defense of Pluralism and Equality* (Oxford: Martin Robertson and Co., 1983), p. xiv.

[8] Ibid., p. 16.

primarily on our own modern conventions of birthright and kinship: "States are like families rather than clubs, for it is a feature of families that their members are morally connected to people they have not chosen."[9] Ultimately, Walzer's theory of membership is a recapitulation of citizenship policies in the United States and other apparently liberal societies. These countries have laws reinforcing the notion that economic mobility within a political society must be entirely unrestrained, while individuals' mobility among states can be circumscribed, legitimately and inevitably, by the un-"winnable good" of birthright.

Walzer recognizes the difficulties of this position, when he challenges the following sentiment of an Australian minister of immigration: " 'We seek to create a homogeneous nation. Can anyone reasonably object to that? Is not this the elementary right of every government, to decide the composition of the nation? It is just the same prerogative as the head of a family exercises as to who is to live in his house.' "[10] Walzer complains that the minister is being unreasonable. After all, Whites were there *after* the "aboriginals," and besides, Australia is big and can accommodate a larger citizenry.[11] Admitting that his criticisms are ad hoc and might create a slippery slope along which his own principles supporting the family model of the state might slide, he offers that "There is no easy way to avoid the country (and the proliferation of countries) as we currently know it."[12] Coming from a writer who claims to do no less than describe the possibility of a society in which "no social good serves or could serve as a means of domination" (less utopian than imagining different membership rules for countries?) and who recognizes the importance of membership rules, this seems an enormous concession.

The Political Family

What is it about membership rules among countries that render them more impervious to theoretical intervention than the distributive rules within countries? Walzer's answer echoes that of the Australian minister.

---

[9] Ibid., p. 41.

[10] Walzer, *Spheres of Justice*, p. 46, quoting H. I. London, *Non-White Immigration and the 'White Australian' Policy* (New York: New York University Press, 1970), p. 98. Ann Dummett offers an exceptionally thorough liberal critique of immigration restrictions ("The Transnational Migration of People Seen within a Natural Law Tradition," in *Free Movement: Ethical Issues in the Transnational Migration of People and Money*, Brian Barry and Robert Goodin, eds. [New York, London: Harvester Wheatsheaf, 1992]). A less radical critique of birthright, one that endorses the principle of territorial birth as the basis of citizenship, is Peter Schuck and Rogers Smith, *Citizenship without Consent: Illegal Aliens in the American Polity*, (New Haven and London: Yale University Press, 1985).

[11] Walzer, *Spheres of Justice*, p. 47.

[12] Ibid., p. 44.

Both treat the family as a primal force that mere governments ought not challenge. Walzer accepts that children of citizens should be citizens (on the grounds that doing otherwise would be too difficult) and also believes that marriage should be a basis for citizenship. Alternatives would "require very high and surely unacceptable levels of coercion: the dominance of political power over kinship and love."[13] But the coercion that results in people starving to death in Ethiopia, dying in cattle cars en route to the United States from Mexico, and losing their homes for want of the right ethnicity in Bosnia implicitly are found acceptable, since all of these necessarily follow from the prerogatives of political societies to regulate membership according to family ties. These events are not accidents in a world system of familial-based nation-states, but rather are their bases and outcome. The oppressed majorities and minorities in these examples follow directly from the birth rule for membership, the rule Walzer thinks an unfair principle by which to allocate resources within a political society. Walzer presumably would express impatience if a British aristocrat or Southern farmer were to become misty eyed recalling the glorious social order and harmony of the last century's political contrivances that sustained class and race inequalities. But Walzer's affection for the political institutions that sustain family and nation does not arouse his suspicion.

Kinship rules never have had an especially cozy relation with romantic love and other experiences of happiness and well-being. Walzer writes of the need to protect "kinship and love" in a country with a divorce rate hovering around 50 percent and on record as opposing same-sex marriages. This suggests that the official rules of marriage do not map neatly onto existing practices of intimacy.[14] Rather than facilitate safe relations of respect among people, the state's regulation of "private" relations historically has done the opposite. For example, it is not the state's absence in the family that makes possible certain kinds of domestic violence, but rather, the statutes that would prosecute for rape, *except* when husbands are the culprits. The state that bestows the status "husband and wife" only to heterosexual couples excludes same-sex couples from the full range of the prerogatives of citizenship. If political membership relies on invocations of birth and marriage, it is not that there is a consensus that these principles have fairness at their root or as a consequence. Of course one might counter that Walzer's proposals are practical and justified by a norm of

[13] Ibid., p.34.

[14] Drucilla Cornell ridicules marriage law for assuming that the qualities associated with good sexual relationships are the same as those for responsibly raising children. If these relations require different skills, then law ought to separate the two as well. Rather than directing kinship benefits to sexual couples, the state should allocate them to any group of people who commit to raising a child together ("Adoption and its Progeny: Rethinking Right, Sexual Difference, and Patriarchy" [CSST Workshop Working Paper, University of Michigan, March 13, 1997]).

efficiency rather than justice. Yet if the goal becomes utility, then all sorts of other criteria deserve consideration as well.[15]

Here is another paradox in Walzer's ideas about familial-based membership criteria, which also exhibits a tension between two widely held beliefs. This one has to do with family structures themselves. Echoing commonplace intuitions about families, Walzer holds both that family forms vary among political societies[16] and that the family sphere is intrinsically pre-political. Walzer acknowledges injustice associated with the family, just as he recognizes inequities that follow from political borders. And yet Walzer does not call for principles of distributive justice to be used in these relations. Of inheritance and bequests he writes: "Love and commitment, like enterprise, have their risks and (sometimes) their windfalls, which it is not a necessary part of a theory of distributive justice to deny or repress."[17] Legal contrivances of inheritance are represented as merely the "external enforcement of principles originally internal to a particular understanding of family ties."[18] But why protect this understanding of family ties and not also the aristocrat's understanding of the family? Despite recognizing the family's variations over time, this formulation continues to suggest that pre-existing family ties, independent of a particular political environment, have a special status vis-à-vis distributive justice. Walzer's family is like the *National Geographic* special that cheerfully anthropomorphizes the loving lioness and her cubs, played back to convince ourselves that we too are "naturally" affectionate to our children and mates—no glimpses of the preying mantis here, nor acknowledgments of the systemic failures of human families. In any case, if having four legal wives in Iran would be seen in the United States as illegal polygamy, then this seems to suggest that the family form is not only a site of affect.[19] The non-Muslim state which uses kinship rules to determine membership will prosecute the polygamist, not allow his four wives to apply for citizenship. This is no less "internal to a particular understanding of family ties" than Walzer's reiteration of inheritance practices.

---

[15] The argument that immigration controls protect labor markets are not utilitarian, since most people in the world do not benefit from these protections. A chief result of these restrictions is the creation of segmented labor markets of relatively cheap wages. Labor market protections are useful only for those paid relatively higher wages, and not for those who happen to be born in countries with smaller markets and less capital.

[16] Ibid., pp. 227–28.

[17] Ibid., p. 128.

[18] Ibid., p. 232.

[19] Walzer seems to believe that "the family" is essential and eternal, while its particular manifestations vary. But if this is true, then it is also irrelevant. It is the variations among political societies' kinship rules that are responsible for whether the family is experienced as a place of warmth and intimacy, of fear and authority, of chaos or order, and so forth. As Lawrence Stone shows, different epochs and classes associated the family with a wide

Concepts of Membership

The nexus of the state and kinship rules would not elude the attention of the two immigrants from Iraq, for instance, who were charged in the mid-1990s with statutory rape in Nebraska, when they consummated what they took to be their marriages to the teenage daughters of a family friend.[20] While in Iraq arranged marriages for thirteen year olds are legal, in this country the attempt to marry in this way leaves men subject to criminal prosecution. The non-marriage in Nebraska announces some of the more central aspects of how the state actually constitutes and then regulates what Walzer characterizes as a sphere of intimacy (marriage and sexual relations). Both in form and function, marriage rules are taxonomized and taxonomizing with respect to nationality, as well as religion. The mistake in Nebraska was not due to either idiosyncrasy or to willful defiance of the state. Instead, particular marriage rules are associated with specific nations, and those subject to Iraqi law follow rules different from the rules in the United States. Further, to be born from parents wed by the conventions of a particular nation makes one a member of that nation, which is not possible from merely existing in a fuzzy zone of intimacy that is pre-political. In short, the overlaying patterns of familial and political membership rules are the ones crucial to the reproductions of the nation, ethnicity, and race that in turn make possible these same intergenerational rules.

In brief, *political societies* constitute the intergenerational *family* form that provides the pre-political seeming semantics of *nation*. The familial nation reinforces the membership rules of political society, and, at certain junctures, yields taxonomies of *race*. The example of Jewish identity may be useful to explore here. To call someone "Jewish" might indicate her "nationality," as it does on current Russian identity cards.[21] Or it could indicate her "race," as it did to a variety of European and American anthropologists at the turn of the twentieth century. Another possibility is that "Jewish" describes an "ethnic" group, e.g., the Jews who live in "Jewish" enclaves of New York City, or who simply exhibit stereotypical "Jewish" attributes. And "Jewish" might mean one's religion. To distinguish among these is to refer to different, yet related, taxonomies of membership.

These practices yielding nationality as a form of being may draw on

---

range of practices and values (*The Family, Sex, and Marriage in England, 1500–1800* [New York: Harper and Row, 1979]).

[20] Don Terry, "Cultural Tradition and Law Collide in Middle America," *New York Times*, December 12, 1996, A6.

[21] In Russian the term is 'natsíonalnost', and it refers to what Anglophones call 'ethnicity'. Thanks to Artiom Magun for this information.

those of a religion (and vice-versa), even as the dialectical relation between the two forms depends on moments of their forms' particularity as oppositional to the other. Membership in a political society (constitutive of the forms of nation and race) depends on invocations of birth and kinship— and *religious* affiliation *per se* does not.[22] Also, narratives of nation and race appeal to birth and the past, while those of religion are oriented primarily toward death and the future. (A *state* is a particular form of political society, which this book discusses almost exclusively as a *membership organization* and not a Weberian subset of forms of obligation, one that has a monopoly on the legitimate use of force.)

What are some examples of a political society? Is the Republican Party one? The Rotary Club? ACT-UP? No, because one does not belong to these by virtue of birth. One is a member of a political society (and hence a state) either because one's parents are or because one is born there.[23] This is not an observation about how citizenship functions in this country, or even in modernity, nor should it imply that political societies are aggregated families. Rather, this is an heuristic point that is also an anthropological one. Political societies and families require each other. To be born into a family is always to be born into a larger group that made possible the family form as such.[24] Paradigmatically, to be a member of a political society is to exist as one who is such by birth.

The Grammar of Membership

Political society and nation are two sides of the same familial coin. Whenever there is a "political society" there is also a "nation," and vice-versa. This is not to say that the state (as one form of political society) and the

---

[22] Stated so bluntly the contrast can be read only as at best provocative and at worst contentious. It will be the work of the following chapters to make the above claim persuasive. It is only by representing both birth *and* death that each form can be primarily oriented to one and not the other (which is to say that orientation toward one goal requires the negation of at least one other end, experienced as its opposite). In addition, Jews and Hindus, for instance, are paradigmatically such through lineage, but only because these identities are national, as well as religious, ones, an observation that Chapter 6 pursues.

[23] The advent of transnational alliances such as the European Union (EU) do not undermine this claim. When the European Union is really a sovereign body—as is the United States national government vis-à-vis the states—then the EU will be a political society, as opposed to its current status as an alliance among autonomous political societies. The form of the European Union is such that states may withdraw at any point, with sanctions no more severe than market disadvantages currently in effect for non-member states. As long as membership in the EU is voluntary among the states, the EU's existence is contingent, and so is membership therein at the level of the individual.

[24] This is Durkheim's point in *Elementary Forms of Religious Life*, tr. Joseph Swain (New York, London: Free Press, 1915), which I pursue in Chapter 1.

nation are identical. Political society is to the nation as grammar is to a sentence. The latter is the effortless-seeming embodiment of the rules, most effective when these rules are least apparent. This is also not to say that the state (or any political society) causes a nation. We would not say that one side of a coin causes the other side, or that grammar causes a sentence. Just as we may comparison shop without knowing the precise status of the money supply, mostly we read and write with little grammatical self-consciousness, disinterested in the fact that we are using certain conventions that convey, constrain, and constitute our meanings. For most exchanges this works just fine. But once the grammar grabs our attention, we might also discover new meanings and new possibilities. We might learn that the mushy-seeming sentiments of "family life" follow from the rules of political society, much as the melodious sonnet depends on the rigid requirements of iambic pentameter. Chapters 1 and 2 analyze the theories and practices that rely on kinship rules for membership in political societies, as well as the ways that these rules are experienced as binding because they are thought natural.

Whereas nation is the other side of political society, "ethnicity" is that coin's impression(s) somewhere else. An ethnic group follows from a prior national form, not a diffuse sense of "culture," as is sometimes implied among students of immigrant communities and rhetorics. The following list illustrates this: **Korean**- (American/French/Japanese), **Palestinian**- (American/French/Japanese), **Mexican**- (American/French/Japanese), and **Yuppie**- (American/French/Japanese). While the identity of "**Korean**-American" differs from that of "**Palestinian**-French" these two share more in common as forms of ethnicity than either does with any form of a hyphenated "**Yuppie**." Yuppies, Valley Girls, or the Hells Angels do not count as "ethnicities," despite the fact that all of these groups are associated with certain styles of dress, habits of speech, and even regions. What makes us recognize certain affiliations as those of ethnicity is their implicit or explicit invocation of a past, present, or future *political society/nation*. These are the groups, unlike the others mentioned above, that depend on ancestry for membership. This argument is developed in Chapters 2 and 3.

Race is what occurs under circumstances in which at least one political society/nation coin (frequently several) is represented as a subpopulation of human beings with observed or imagined physical characteristics associated with a geographical territory of origins.[25] Chapter 4 shows how continents and other geographical underpinnings of racial taxonomies are at bottom an aggregation of adjacent political societies/nations. Further, the chapter explains how these political societies/nations play a chief role in

---

[25] See also Sally Haslanger, "Gender and Race: (What) Are They? (What) Do We Want Them to Be?" Paper presented at the Institute for Social Research, University of Michigan, Ann Arbor, September, 1997.

circulating racial taxonomies through internal rules regulating the constitution of families, through juridical devices of miscegenation laws and
birth certificates.

Clearly the family is a crucial form in the elaboration of all of these
affiliations. Recognition of the centrality of the family to group formation
has prompted Marxist and feminist critics, such as Frederick Engels and
Simone de Beauvoir (not to mention the entire canonical history of political
theoretical speculation about the origins of political societies) to view sex
differences as the chief cause in the development of political institutions.
Chapter 5 shows that sex differences are constituted through, rather than
constitutive of, political societies. Marriage and other kinship rules, instrumental to the reproduction of political societies in their particularity, which
is to say, as political societies, produce the sex/gender dichotomies of
femininity and masculinity through controlling not women per se, but the
processes of reproduction that interpellate the bearers of children and
those who cannot bear children into particular relations with each other.
The sex/gender system is the difference that results from the compensatory
rules that put those "females" who bear children into a particular relation
with the "males" who cannot give birth.

Finally, Chapter 6 expands on earlier assertions about the overlaps and
differences between the metonymies among political society, family, nation, race, and those of religion. Religious organizations at times also
provide rules for how to form and maintain families. The use of familial
rhetorics by religious groups differs from those of nation and race, in that
the membership rules for religious groups and those for political societies
are fundamentally at odds. Insofar as political societies are at the core of
affiliations of family, nation, and race, to show how political societies differ
from religious ones is to show how religious societies differ from affiliations
of family, nation, and race, as well. Political society is the linchpin of
family, nation, and race, and hence the important site to isolate for this
contrast is the political society and the ways that it contrasts with religious
ones, again, as membership organizations, and not as administrative ones.

This book does not engage with most aspects of political societies,
families, nations, races, and religions. There are large literatures that explore the specific power dynamics of these affiliations and their psychological causes and effects. The intention here simply is to reflect on the alchemy
by which these affiliations articulate and sustain each other: the birth form
that is the crucible for all of these. And yet simply knowing the details of
how this birth form shapes certain forms of being cannot tell us whether
the resulting identity will be hegemonic or marginal, the attachments
fostered strong or weak, its deployments kind or brutal. I hope that the
experts who reflect on these questions, and others located on the vast
terrain of cultural studies, will forgive me my trespasses, as well as relevant
forays overlooked.

The General Problem of Differences

Membership forms differ and yet some among them bear certain resemblances. As opposed to either assuming or asserting that affiliations of political society, nation, ethnicity, race, family, gender, and religion are ontologically grouped together, a few examples—based on some lessons from ordinary language philosophy—may illuminate the logic if not the ontology that demarcates the objects of this study from the universe of all possible associations, political and otherwise.

1. "Men and women of full age, without any limitation due to race, nationality, or religion, have the right to marry and to found a family."—Article 16, United Nations Declaration of Human Rights (1948).

Men and women of full age, without any limitation due to race, nationality, religion, or food allergies, have the right to marry and to found a family.

2. "All persons shall be entitled to full and equal enjoyment of the goods, services, facilities, privileges, advantages, and accommodations of any place of public accommodation . . . without discrimination or segregation on the ground of race, color, religion, or national origin."—Title VII, 1964 Civil Rights Act, Section 2000a.

All persons shall be entitled to full and equal enjoyment of the goods, services, facilities, privileges, advantages, and accommodations of any place of public accommodation . . . without discrimination or segregation on the ground of race, color, religion, national origin, or what side of the bed they prefer to sleep on.

3. "If one 'is' a woman, that is surely not all one is; the term fails to be exhaustive, not because a pregendered 'person' transcends the specific paraphernalia of its gender, but because gender is not always constituted coherently or consistently in different historical contexts, and because gender intersects with racial, class, ethnic, sexual, and regional modalities of discursively constituted identities"—Judith Butler, *Gender Trouble* (1991).

And, gender intersects with pepperoni and plain cheese modalities of discursively constituted food preferences. One might be a woman pepperoni-aficionado or a plain cheese-eating woman.

These simple juxtapositions perform the intuition that the concepts of family, nation, race, and religion are associated; they may imply each other and at the same time exclude the relevance of other concepts. To inquire into race will always make plausible, though of course not necessary, questions about family and nationality, for instance. It is not that one question always leads to another, but that certain semantic contexts imbricate these and make others irrelevant. That is, for purposes of discussing issues of power, it is colloquial to associate some identities (e.g., race and nation may be idiomatically associated), while to pair others is strange (e.g., race and membership in the group of those with food allergies).

Only certain affiliations are associated—implicitly and explicitly—for purposes of contrast and comparison in daily life, as well as by investigators across the political and methodological spectrum.[26] Numerous authors have worked on the specificities, and more recently, the "intersections," of these affiliations—along with those of class. One goal in addressing this string of forms of being has been to discourage efforts to consider any single one of these affiliations as paradigmatic for others. "The concept of political intersectionality highlights the fact that women of color are situated within at least two subordinated groups that frequently pursue conflicting political agendas,"[27] according to Kimberlé Crenshaw. Or consider Butler's admonition to "resist the model of power that would set up racism and homophobia and misogyny as parallel or analogical relations."[28] Butler emphasizes that the structures of racism and those of homophobia do not share the same features.

Deferred by such injunctions is attention to the metonymic associations[29] that partake of what Michael Warner has aptly labeled "repro culture."[30] Repro culture produces a narrative structure that offers an individual a past and future via intergenerational families. Nations, ethnicities, and races provide and depend on such an intergenerational form quite explicitly. Religions have a more ambiguous relation to this pattern, as their practices are often in tension with the political societies that make possible the familial forms of nation, ethnicity, and race. Some identities depend

[26] The list of these four affiliations is not exhaustive of relevant associated concepts, among which, as Butler's quotation indicates, are also those of "gender," "sexuality," and "ethnicity"—and this too is not all-inclusive. These last three concepts receive extensive attention in this book, but as derivative of the family form (for concepts of gender and sexuality) and the nation form (for the concept of ethnicity).

[27] Crenshaw writes: "This process of recognizing as social and systemic what was formerly perceived as isolated and individual has. . . . characterized the identity politics of [women], African-Americans, other people of color, and gays and lesbians, among others." However, this has meant that those whose identities fall among two or more of these groups may not have their interests fully represented ("Mapping the Margins: Intersectionality, Identity Politics, and Violence against Women of Color," in *Critical Race Theory*, Crenshaw et al., eds. [New York: New Press, 1995], pp. 357, 360).

[28] *Bodies that Matter: On the Discursive Limits of 'Sex'* (New York, London: Routledge, 1993), p. 18.

[29] In metonymy an entity is evoked by association, as the "White House" stands for "the Presidency." By extension, metonymy may also refer to the way words associatively imply each other. For instance, 'birth', 'family', and 'nation' often entail mutual associations.

[30] "Repro-culture" is the "set of institutions and narratives through which your life is understood to gain meaning by its insertion in generational transmission" ("Van Winkle Family Values" CSST Working Paper, University of Michigan, presented December 1, 1994, p. 3).

on ancestry, such as being White, Chinese, or Irish. "Are you sure you're French?" "Yes, both my parents are" is idiomatic, whereas, to the question, "Are you sure you're lesbian?" (or a "member of the American Civil Liberties Union [ACLU]" or a "member of the New Haven Bowling League") the dispositive answer would not be, "Yes, both my parents are."

What are the conditions that make it possible for scholars to string together affiliations of family, nation, race, and religion, for purposes of supposedly taking them apart? How is it that certain group affiliations are so easily strung together that one might insist on their disentanglement? The analysis of the overlapping sets of rules that constitute affiliations (of political society, family, nation, ethnicity and gender) shows that it is invocations of birth (and death, for religion) that separate the identities shaped by these group forms from the subject positions that follow from statuses of health (allergies), personal quirks (bed-side or pizza-topping preferences, for instance), as well as numerous other predilections and conditions.

The mutually reinforcing rhetorics of family, nation, race, and religion have been observed and theorized in studies of family policy and the state, especially those focused on natalist and immigration policies.[31] These generally masculinist efforts to control reproduction by controlling women's sexuality and maternity have been noted as misogynist, but the compensatory character of these interventions—the idea that men's appropriation of birth that their own discourse deems feminine is an act of ressentiment—is seldom discussed.[32] The feminist work that begins with questions about birth and reproduction tends not to discuss the

---

[31] Though many studies touch on some of the above, among those specifically concerned with the link between the state's reproductive policies and affiliations of nation and race are Ann McClintock, *Imperial Leather: Race, Gender and Sexuality in the Colonial Context* (New York and London: Routledge, 1995); George Mosse, *Nationalism and Sexuality: Respectability and Abnormal Sexuality in Modern Europe* (New York: H. Fertig, 1985); Maria Quine, *Population Politics in Twentieth Century Europe: Fascist Dictatorships and Liberal Democracies* (New York, London: Routledge, 1996); Ann Laura Stoler, *Race and the Education of Desire: Foucault's History of Sexuality and the Colonial Order of Things* (Durham: Duke University Press, 1995); for a collection of essays with excellent histories of the nexus of immigration, citizenship, and natality policies in Europe, Africa, the Middle East, and Australia, see *Woman-Nation-State*, Nira Yuval-Davis and Floya Anthias, eds. (London: MacMillan Press, 1989).

[32] Luce Irigaray's work makes this point most insistently and clearly. McClintock's *Imperial Leather* is one of the rare books that use psychoanalytic work to analyze the specifically compensatory character of masculinity in world politics, and the slightly defensive tone she assumes in asserting her approach is symptomatic of the mainstream trends in this field: "All too often, psychoanalysis has been relegated to the (conventionally universal) realm of private, domestic space, while politics and economics are relegated to the (conventionally historical) realm of the public market. . . . Instead of genuflecting to this separation and opting theoretically for one or the other, I call for a renewed and transformed investigation in to the disavowed relations between psychoanalysis and socio-economic history" (p. 8). McClintock is really demonstrating that the Oedipal drama's occupation of the unconscious is an

implications of such gendered practices for citizenship,[33] while texts on "ascriptive identities" or on eugenically oriented natalist politics do not explore the theoretical and historical relevance of the gendered meanings of "birth" criteria.[34] That birth is the criterion for membership is often represented as a concern about generic categories of purity, without attention to the ways that birth is deeply connected to a web of gendered associations. Nonetheless, birth is the paradigmatic decision rule for inclusion and exclusion into all political societies, including the modern state. Territorial and descent criteria for citizenship both depend on invocations of birth. The birth rule for membership in a political society also holds for affiliations of nation, ethnicity, and race.

Metonymic associations among certain affiliations such as family, nation, and race invite generalization about the human psyche. Each of the forms of association are often presented as merely exemplary of some primordial dark side of the human condition. One benefit of considering these concepts together is that one can attend to specificities sometimes overlooked in some brilliant and influential psychoanalytic and postcolonial studies that use words and phrases like "the Other," "subalternity," "fetish," or "law of the father." Homi Bhabha, Julia Kristeva, Gayatri Spivak, and Slavoj Žižek have published works that are extremely useful for theorizing what amounts to semiologies of abstract group membership: analyses of ways that apparently symbolic forms are, have, and constitute meaning and

---

assumption that has been utterly absorbed by historical discourses, and not that conventional histories are bereft of psychoanalytic categories. The family romance is the latent backdrop that is rarely noticed, in the works of conservatives and liberals, as well as studies by radical feminists. Tacit assumptions about a specifically masculine political-economy are taken for granted: gender in politics is thought the incarnation of the unconscious Oedipal drama, for better or worse, although this is usually not regarded as a psychoanalytic position. The assertion that the unconscious is engaged in a different scene of family entanglements, one in which masculinity develops as a struggle to accommodate the desire to reproduce the mother's ability to give birth (more outlandish than the desire of girls for the penis?) is one McClintock rightly realizes will be read as an observation invested in a psychoanalytic framework. Rather than distinguish McClintock's writings as psychoanalytically engaged, it might be more accurate to suggest that, as opposed to other writers, McClintock has made her more unusual psychoanalytic beliefs explicit qua psychoanalytic.

[33] Mary O'Brien, *The Politics of Reproduction* (Boston, London and Henley: Routledge and Kegan Paul, 1981); Adrienne Rich, *Of Woman Born: Motherhood as Experience and Institution* (New York: Norton, 1976); Joyce Trebilcot, ed., *Mothering: Essays in Feminist Theory* (Totowa: Rowman and Allanheld, 1983).

[34] When certain traits are regarded as natural, what one is born as, then they are often called 'ascriptive'. And yet the word is from the Latin *ascribere* and means "to write in, inscribe." Ascriptive identities in the fourteenth century, when the word was first written, referred to the status roles that were legally documented at one's birth. Robert K. Barnhart, ed., *The Barnhart Dictionary of Etymology* (New York: H. H. Wilson, 1988), p. 55. So in the fourteenth century it was understood that one's identity as a serf was a matter of a written record, but the 'ascriptive' identities of race or sex, for instance, are thought natural.

reality.[35] But such approaches do not help us to understand the particular semiotics of "nation," as opposed to "family" or "race." Insofar as each of these is taken as exemplary of underlying psychological or other structural (dis)orders, sometimes lost in such analyses of discourse is the particularity of each manifestation of difference.[36]

Implicit in Bhabha's and Kristeva's discussions of the nation, for instance, is something like the phrase "it just so happens that one place to study what Freud describes is the affinities of the nation." Kristeva writes: "Can the 'foreigner,' who was the 'enemy' in primitive societies, disappear from modern societies? . . . [S]hall we be, intimately and subjectively, able to live with the others, to live **as others**, without ostracism but also without leveling? . . . No 'Nationality Code' would be practicable without having that question slowly mature within each of us and for each of us."[37] The long reach of "the foreigner," a concept that is about the universally transhistorical other, prompts useful questions, but these are the sort that do not lead to a consideration of the relational contrasts among different kinds of interrelated others. While bearing in mind that these affiliations bear resemblances, the contrasts among them are also important to note, if family, nation, and race are to appear as more than abstract spaces occupied by similar manifestations of Hegel's lord and bondsman dialectic, Marx's and Freud's fetish, or Lacan's law of the father.

Family Resemblances

One reason that scholars may discuss "the other" as an apparently generic site of certain differences is that the concepts of family, nation, race, and religion bear a "family resemblance."[38] I borrow Wittgenstein's terminology here to recall the paradigm whereby things that differ among numerous details nonetheless answer to the same word:

[35] By calling attention to the language peculiar to post-structuralist and psychoanalytic theory I am by no means disparaging the use of these rhetorics, but simply pointing out that they are often used in ways that may overgeneralize the symptoms which they describe.

[36] Examples of these discussions of the other are: Bhaba, "DissemiNation," in *Nation and Narration*, Homi Bhabha, ed. (London, New York: Routledge, 1990), pp. 291–322; Spivak, "Subaltern Studies: Deconstructing Historiography," in *In Other Worlds* (New York and London: Methuen, 1987), pp. 197–221; and Žižek, *On the Sublime Object of Ideology* (New York, London: Verso, 1989).

[37] Tr. Leon Roudiez, *Strangers to Ourselves* (New York: Columbia University Press, 1991), pp. 1–2, emphasis in original.

[38] *Philosophical Investigations*, tr. G.E.M. Anscombe, 3d ed. (New York: MacMillan, 1968), remark 67. For a more general explanation of the relevance of ordinary language analysis to political theory, see Hanna Pitkin, *Wittgenstein and Justice* (Berkeley, Los Angeles, London: University of California Press, 1973).

Why do we call something a 'number'? Well, perhaps because it has a direct relationship with several things that have hitherto been called number; and this can be said to give it an indirect relationship to other things we call the same name.[39]

Like the various things that may or may not be associated with the same word, words themselves can be represented by relative discursive proximities. Perhaps one might employ Wittgenstein's metaphor of a rope here, only instead of the overlapping fibers being different twists on the uses of the same word, the intertwined 'race'—'family'—'nation' itself constitutes a rope, each word simultaneously stringing together a certain set of meanings that gain their particularities through their associations in this interweaving.[40]

Cognitive language psychologists represent a similar phenomenon in their study of idiomatic word associations, which include antonyms ('hot'-'cold'), functional relations ('hammer'-'nail'), phrasal relations ('private'-'property'), conceptual relations ('election'-'vote'), and category coordinates ('dog'-'cat'). This last type best characterizes the association of 'race' with 'nationality',[41] which is to say that we seem to speak of 'race' and 'nation' as being in a category that does not idiomatically accommodate 'food preferences'. For purposes of developing heuristics to think about institutionalized forms of affiliation constitutive of power relations, what matters as much as the fact that the subject position "teenage mother" is racially taxonomized and taxonomizing, is that "teenage mother" is not idiomatically taxonomized by pizza-topping preference. An idiomatic asso-

---

[39] Ibid.

[40] Potentially imputed to these notational conventions is the incorrect notion that race-without-quotation-marks, for instance, refers to race as it **really** is, that race has an ontology independent of its status as a concept or word. This is the case, for instance, in the notational conventions in the work of Anthony Appiah, discussed below. I do not believe that race refers to something especially real, while "race" makes it clear the entity is merely a concept, and so, not real. Race, "race," and 'race' are three signifiers. That is, all of these are notations on a piece of paper. Using "race" and 'race' draws attention to more nuanced facets of race. There are not separate substantive meanings for "race" or 'race' that are better or worse associations or labels for race. The word 'race' is part of what race is. 'Race' and race are not separate. At the same time, it is useful for theoretical purposes to be able to indicate the different levels of analysis of race. See Preface, note 1.

[41] Helen Moss et al. "Accessing Different Types of Lexical Semantic Information: Evidence from Priming," *Journal of Experimental Psychology* (1995), 21 (4), pp. 863, 864, 865. The studies show that associations may follow certain patterns, those I am calling 'idiomatic.' This does not mean that in any particular case an individual will indeed make one of these. What is crucial is not that people may play with language in ways that are unusual, but that our tendency to follow certain linguistic conventions makes it possible to recognize other utterances as strange.

ciation with the phrase 'teenage mother' is not 'pizza toppings' just as 'cat' idiomatically may prompt 'dog' or 'soft' but only esoterically 'toothpaste'. Instead, 'teenage mother' may lead to thoughts about race or legitimacy or poverty, even though particular teenage mothers of course have unique experiences and self-understandings. Not all differences are equally different: some differences have something in common.

Further, these particular family resemblances (of certain affiliational forms of being) follow from the very family form that makes possible Wittgenstein's metaphor, "for the various resemblances between members of a family: build, features, colour of eyes, gait, temperament, etc. overlap and criss-cross in the same way."[42] Wittgenstein is suggesting that there is something like an essential basis to the associations we notice, a grounding similar to that which allows us to recognize the commonalities of traits within families. At the same time that Wittgenstein challenges the possibility of any definitional certainty in the use of words for things—"Can you give the boundary? No."[43]—he reaffirms an ontological certainty about the family, a clarity without which his exercise is impossible. Wittgenstein's point about indeterminacy depends on a metaphor that invokes at least plausible certainty. We have to have some notion that 'family' means those who are naturally and visibly related in the ways Wittgenstein lists in order for the metaphor to work, in order to imagine that there is an underlying "belonging" or "togetherness" among some things. Of course Wittgenstein does not say we need to pick out exactly where the family ends. It may include third cousins or it may not, or some children may be difficult to recognize as such, since they may not resemble their parents. Still, the familial resemblance metaphor depends on the idea that families betray the kinds of "overlap and criss-cross" among relatives that appear among "related things." The expectation is that given a collection of photographs one could say who most likely was and was not related.

But could one? If one lacked an array of photographs already laid out according to principles of biblical genealogy, if all one had were video clips of every human being who ever walked on earth, could "family resemblances" alone be relied on to approximate a series of biblical families? Or, rather, might one come up with clusters that had features in common, even if they weren't *really* families? And might one come up with different kinds of clusters at different times or in different moods? And if this is true, if what counts as the possibility of family does not emerge from some pre-existing array of genetically related individuals whose obvious phenotypical differences correspond with innate genotypical ones, then

[42] Wittgenstein, *Philosophical Investigations*, remark 67.
[43] Ibid., remark 68.

the source of the concept of the family must lie elsewhere, must depend on a particular diachronic discourse about "intergenerationality," for instance, and on ideas about beginnings and endings.

Method and Knowledge

The approach I use to describe forms of being in this study has an affinity with some strains of both deconstruction and Foucauldian methods, which, broadly defined, refer to examinations of discourse in scientific fields, legal institutions, and philosophy, as well as in more popular texts. However, three infelicities in some of the more influential uses of this method bear explication prior to a fuller statement of the phenomenological approach embraced below. The first problem is that some critiques—of race and sex in particular—smuggle in a positivist framework that is ultimately damaging to the larger project of addressing the political inequalities that manifest in certain forms of being. Those who rigorously adhere to a strictly discursive framework manifest a second oversight, which is the failure to effectively explicate and address the naive intuition that discourse analysis is a matter of mere words. Finally, a third impediment to the persuasive use of a discursive framework has been the idiomatic, unexamined clustering of certain forms of being into objects of study, a technique that implicitly endorses the naive belief that such discursive clusters manifest in something that is objectively static and subject to easy apprehension.

Discursive Strategies for Positivist Obstacles

The problem of taxonomizing individuals according to their membership in certain families, nations, races, or sexes is one example of more general epistemological quandaries that arise whenever certain phenomena—considered discretely—manifest gradual differences even as they are associated with categories that are rigid and exclusive. Idiomatically, one either is or is not thought to be a member of a particular family, nation, race, and sex, even though it is quite easy to locate examples of people who do not fit into any of the available groups, as well as to note logical inconsistencies in prevailing definitions of each of them. Yet one of the most misleading assertions in the social sciences and humanities has been that the difference between the gradually changing appearances of empirical phenomena and the crudely obvious differences implied by their categories means that the categories we use are "non-existent" or "unfounded" or "mistakes."

The inconsistencies of the various taxonomies—are there three or three hundred races? two or five sexes?—are no more extreme than those of numerous other categories that we use idiomatically, such as those that characterize colors and sounds. Like "clinal" or gradual variations among human genes, the variation among shades approaches infinitesimally small differences, but philosophers who study color do not demand that we stop using the concept of "lavender" because it is not always clear where that ends and "purple" begins.[44]

The observation that certain forms of being manifest categories that pose extraordinary challenges either to epistemology or their plausibility yields an odd result. Despite explicit commitments to language as the site of meaning and knowledge, some ostensibly post-modern arguments point away from a critique of the paradoxical tensions among equally real different experiences of a thing, and back toward a model of right and wrong understandings of the truth. For instance, Barbara Fields writes:

> Anyone who continues to believe in race as a physical attribute of individuals, despite the now commonplace disclaimers of biologists and geneticists, might as well also believe that Santa Claus, the Easter Bunny and the tooth fairy are real, and that the earth stands still while the sun moves.[45]

The premise of Fields's argument is that "race" might refer to something out there and yet it does not. Hence race, like the Easter Bunny, is not real. Such an epistemology implies that there is an ontological thing (what the biologists study) separate from our concepts of it. There are two problems with this. First, the disjuncture does not necessarily lead to an

---

[44] A famous study of color perception notes that individuals show a high degree of consensus as to whether a particular point on the color spectrum is "blue" or "purple," while they are very bad at agreeing on the boundaries as to where particular colors begin and end: "Repeated mapping trials with the same informant and also across informants showed that category foci placements are highly reliable. It is rare that a category focus is displaced by more than two adjacent chips. Category boundaries, however, are not reliable, even for repeated trials with the same informant . . . In fact, in marked contrast to the foci, category boundaries proved to be so unreliable, even for an individual informant, that they have been accorded a relatively minor place in the analysis." The test used 329 color chips from Munsell Color Company, and asked participants to "indicate for each basic color term [one of 11] 1) all those chips which he would under any conditions call X; and 2) best, most typical examples of X" (Berlin and Kay, *Basic Color Terms* [Berkeley and Los Angeles: University of California Press, 1969], p. 13, cited in C. L. Hardin, *Color for Philosophers: Unweaving the Rainbow* [Indianapolis: Hackett, 1988], p. 120).

[45] "Slavery, Race and Ideology in the United States of America," *New Left Review*, no. 181, (May/June, 1990), p. 97. Barbara Fields concludes, "If race lives on today, it can do so only because we continue to create and re-create it in our social life, continue to verify it, and thus continue to need a social vocabulary that will allow us to make sense, not of what our ancestors did then, but of what we ourselves choose to do now" (118). But this "ideology" of race is no different than virtually any other power/knowledge nexus, and hence to show the historical contingency of this concept does not demonstrate something particularly suspect about "race"—Fields' thesis—but simply exemplifies how discourse functions.

outright rejection of the concept, even among geneticists. Scientists might reject racial classifications, or they might decide that what is needed are more nuanced, accurate representations of race that do not depend on ideology, for instance. The second problem is that Fields privileges the natural scientific approach to a field of study. She successfully uses positivist criteria[46] to challenge one local example of a bad fit between empirical phenomena and their concepts, but at the expense of reinforcing a naive understanding of reality that energizes the most reactionary uses of all forms of being constituted through invocations of birth.

That words sometimes are associated with things in ways that appear flawed according to positivist criteria about how to label certain objective facts seems a bad choice of premises from which to pursue phenomenological and deconstructive inquiries. To point to the contingency of categories to defeat the argument that 'race' is real, to point out that 'gender'-s are constructed, that 'nationality' is imagined—and therefore all of these forms of being are ideological—is to recede into the realm of the positivists that only a handful of people actually occupy, mostly social scientists. The problem with "race" is not that it is phantasmatic and our knowledge of it as otherwise is flawed. Rather, the problem is that its specific form of naturalization disadvantages African-Americans, for instance. To "naturalize" is to express the necessity of a form of being or practice, to make something seem impervious to human intention and immutable. Investigators call attention to the disjunction between the signifier and the signified because of political circumstances, not troubling metaphysics. Were absence of an easily discernible ontology the major defect of "race" and "sex," we would expect deconstructionists to carp about how progressive tax brackets invidiously divide people into groups that are experienced as real but are in fact artificial.

---

[46] My use of "positivism" is consistent with the description of twentieth century logical positivism offered by Herbert Fiegl:

> In contradistinction to the still largely prevailing speculative (e.g. Hegelian) tendencies in (transcendent) metaphysics, the Viennese and Berliners were convinced that most (if not all) allegedly unsolvable problems of philosophy . . . rest on conceptual confusions or on closely related misuses of language. . . . The sentences in a language (be it the language of common usage, of science, or of metaphysics) were said to make factual sense only if it was logically conceivable that they might be confirmed or disconfirmed (i.e., at least partially and/or directly verified or refuted) by empirical evidence . . . [According to Kant's *Critique of Pure Reason*] [A]nalytic propositions are true by virtue of presupposed meanings (which can be articulated by explicit definitions or meaning rules), whereas synthetic propositions are nonanalytic, and thus require grounds of validity outside of mere meaning assignments or definitions. The logical positivists— being staunch empiricists—recognized only the data of experience as the grounds of validity for synthetic knowledge-claims.

"Positivism in the Twentieth Century," in *Dictionary of the History of Ideas*, vol III (New York: Charles Scribner's Sons, 1973), p. 547.

The most obvious example of such an approach is the convention—begun by Kwame Anthony Appiah and imitated by others—of putting "race" in quotation marks. Appiah, after suggesting that geneticists' doubts about racial classifications mean that races do not exist, writes: "I have spent enough time arguing against the reality of 'races' to feel unhappy about using the term without scare quotes." He also notes that "every human identity is constructed."[47] Does this mean that every human identity should be in scare quotes? This is not the convention Appiah follows when he describes "gender, ethnicity, nation, 'race,' and sexuality" as "large categories."[48] Why bracket only "race" with quotation marks? Insofar as the positivist truth of race is so tenuous, its phenomenological status—how race is experienced at various levels of conceptual sophistication—is all that more important. The very denial of race stipulates something there to be negated. Hence complete transcendence of the concept—what Appiah desires—cannot be achieved this way. Finally, setting the concept of race off by putting it in quotation marks suggests that those other concepts Appiah lists alongside it must have a more certain ontological status, or they would incur similar notations.

A Phenomenology of Words and Things

Another response to the use of categories to characterize certain forms of being has been a truly consistent discursive understanding of forms of being, one that is not concerned with a bad match between a label and a thing. For instance, Butler rightly disparages certain readings of the tension between discourse analysis and positivism:

> The debate between constructivism and essentialism thus misses the point of deconstruction altogether, for the point has never been that 'everything is discursively constructed'; that point, when and where it is made, belongs to a kind of discursive monism or linguisticism that refuses the constitutive force of exclusion, erasure, violent foreclosure, abjection and its disruptive return within the very terms of discursive legitimacy.[49]

Butler argues for, as a way to displace this argument, analyses of what she refers to as "materialization," of the ways that Foucauldian regulatory powers produce, in this case, sex. Discourse is then the field where the regulatory norms of sex are observed.

[47] *In My Father's House: Africa in the Philosophy of Culture* (New York, Oxford: Oxford University Press, 1993), pp. 174–75.

[48] "Identity, Authenticity, Survival: Multicultural Societies and Social Reproduction," in Amy Gutmann, ed., *Multiculturalism* (Princeton: Princeton University Press, 1994), p. 149.

[49] *Bodies that Matter: On the Discursive Limits of 'Sex'* (New York, London: Routledge, 1993), p. 8.

To effectively challenge the reduction of deconstruction to "linguistic-ism" requires not simply impatience with the oafs who imply an equivalence between the two, but a deeper explication of how this mistake is made. The reason for the resistance to deconstruction is that its application often seems at odds with the everyday lives of most of those for whom forms of being are quite vivid and palpable. To hear a practice called discursive may prompt the inference that it follows from the merely whimsical, playful qualities of language, that who one is might be a matter of "mere words," and not the necessary pulls of life and death many find in their forms of being. How is it that language might ever seem to be a matter of mere words, that there is no parallel sensibility that would dismiss an experience as "merely material"?

The sense that some things are "linguistic" and others "material" is an idiomatic dichotomy that informs our daily patterns of thought. What is further important to recognize is that these patterns of knowledge privilege knowledge of what is thought to be material: "Are you just naming it a 'rose', or is it really a rose?" is a form of inquiry that reveals the centrality of nominalist thinking to consciousness. If one said, "It's not a rose, but nonetheless I'm going to use the word 'rose' to refer to it," that simple linguistic act would not persuade us that this is a rose. Although language is performative, we also know that in certain unusual circumstances it can be simply ostensive. We grasp that when language is used ostensively it is liable to be used arbitrarily and misleadingly. Another way to put this is that the possibility of nominalist mistakes per se occurs only through language, which is why the study of discourse arouses the kind of skepticism not directed to the study of things. Of course scientists are no more immune to mistakes than deconstructionists, but when this occurs there is the sense that language has failed us, not the things. When medieval astronomers misrepresented the sun as revolving around the earth, the error was regarded later as one of representation and not of the relation between the planets.[50] This nominalist aspect of language needs to be acknowledged in order to distinguish it from the ways that language is also productive of reality.

Metonymic Chains: The Prisoner's Dilemma

Finally, the very fact that certain dynamics are idiomatically strung together itself has the effect of overdetermining their apparent necessity. Butler's claim, for instance, about the differences among the concepts of family,

---

[50] A more thorough presentation of the relation between language and things would pursue the limits of language and the dialectical relationships between language and things, but the narrow purpose here is simply to demonstrate what it is about language that prompts certain resistances to discourse analysis.

nation, and race may encourage a belief in Quinean "natural kinds," a metaphysics that takes for granted a pre-discursive natural order in which the task of the philosopher is to explain the principles underlying the conventions of labeling them.[51]

Until a metonymic chain (such as the ones quoted at the beginning of this chapter) is represented against the possibility that it might exist otherwise (or not at all), and the phenomenal meanings of its (non)related concepts are pursued, the givenness and immutability of these concepts may be reinforced in ways similar to the effects of positivist dogma. When one carefully deconstructs, say, the family, or diligently shows how the operations of sex, race, and nation are not parallel, the long-standing resistances of certain affiliations to critical inquiry are also being performed. One effect is to make these and not other forms of being appear especially resilient. Discourses apparently critical of certain ways that desire is produced have the effect of inciting attachments: "Stop thinking about X in Y way!" is a utopian injunction that inevitably (re)constitutes X and Y in the very ways that are to be undone. This is not a claim about individual psychological resistances, but rather, about the discursive effects of prohibitions, of reminders that these ways of thinking are inherently desirable. Offering instructions to stop thinking in a manner to which we are accustomed suggests that but for the admonitions we would think this way, or reprimands would be unnecessary. The challenge for deconstructivists seeking knowledge of consciousness—in particular, in understanding subjectivity, subjection, objectification, and being—is to detail the complete set of intermediary steps that result in apprehension, to demonstrate rather than assume the full logic of the heterosexual regulatory system, for instance. The portrayal of group forms is as much a philosophical and linguistic project as it is a historical, legal, and political theoretical one: such a project will gather together the various levels of consciousness that simultaneously and paradoxically build on and negate previous understandings and not anoint as most accurate any particular approach.

The method of inquiry best suited for capturing the dialectical relations among various forms of consciousness, being, and things can be understood by considering the meanings of the German 'Wissenschaft' and 'Phenomenologie'. 'Wissenschaft', virtually always translated as 'science', refers to all sorts of intellectual endeavors, from studies of physics to those of philosophy. Hegel insists that his and all serious efforts at revealing reality require a systematic Wissenschaft, and not approaches that are merely argumentative or superficially empirical, which is why the use of 'science'

---

[51] Thomas Quine writes: "One part of the problem of induction, the part that asks why there should be regularities in nature at all, can, I think, be dismissed. *That* there are or have been regularities, for whatever reason, is an established fact of science." ("Natural Kinds," in *Ontological Relativity and Other Essays* [New York, London: Columbia University Press, 1969], p. 126, emphasis in original).

does such a disservice to Hegel's project. 'Science' connotes people in lab coats using the "scientific method," which is to say, testing falsifiable hypotheses by doing empirical research. Such a method seems to have little to do with philosophy, nor does it have much to do with Hegel's concerns. A more literal rendering of what Hegel has in mind (and what 'Wissenschaft' means) is not 'science' but "knowledge activity"[52]—a phrase that implies that knowledge is not passively learned but requires an engagement on the part of the investigator.

The knowledge activity developed here is that of phenomenology: showing how things (e.g., intuitions, the objects of sensory perception, concepts, our language, and especially laws) are experienced and produced through various levels of consciousness.[53] The nation, for example, is the vague assumption that the Irish, for instance, are a nation; the questions about what a nation is; a belief that the nation is a historical fact; a strategic myth; the word 'nation'; and so on. None of these characterizations provide the single privileged truth about the essence of the nation. Rather, the nation exists as the dialectical correspondences and negations among all of these and other concepts of the nation.

This description of phenomenology differs in significant ways from the phenomenological method of Edmund Husserl, especially in its emphasis on the centrality of language to knowledge and consciousness, a notion Hegel and Husserl reject. 'Phenomenology' is from the Greek *phainomenon*, "that which appears or is seen," from *phainein*, "to bring to light, show."[54] The study of how things make appearances must include the study of language that views words as things.[55]

In addition, the forms of being of nationality, ethnicity, race, and sex are considered by reducing them to their laws. The reason for stressing a

[52] 'Wissen' means "knowledge" and the verb 'wissen' means "to know," while '-schaft' is a suffix referring here to doing something.

[53] This list is based on Hegel's *Phenomenology of Spirit*, except for the mention of language.

[54] *The Barnhart Dictionary of Etymology.*

[55] Heidegger notes the difference between Hegelian and Husserlian uses of phenomenology. The latter takes the realm of human categories as the touchstone of knowledge. For Husserl the dichotomy between things in themselves and our intuitions is maintained; the task of phenomenology is simply to clarify our intuitions so that they most accurately state the conditions of human experiences. Husserl rejects the implications of Hegel's insight that consciousness and the things of experience are constantly in movement (Bewegung), that there is no static point from which one can name and organize conceptual work as such: "With the expression 'science of experience,' Hegel does not want to emphasize that this science should be confirmed and proved in the experience of either a sensible or an intelligible intuition. Therefore, it is quite misleading to try, from this point of view or in general, to establish a connection between contemporary phenomenology and that of Hegel ... as if Hegel were concerned with the analysis of the acts and experience of consciousness," and then Heidegger quotes Hegel: "Consciousness is 'comprehended in the experience itself.'" (*Hegel's Phenomenology of Spirit* [1980], tr. Parvis Emad and Kenneth Maly [Bloomington and Indianapolis: University of Indiana Press, 1988], p. 21, quoting the *Phenomenology*, II, 72).

phenomenology of laws for forms of being follows from a political theoretical understanding of two uses of 'law'. A law may refer to the irreducible forces that underlie certain patterns of behavior, among people or things. There are laws of gravity, for instance. This meaning of law is inseparable from a second sense of 'law' as that which follows from the authoritative edicts of a political sovereign. That we have laws of physics as well as laws of the United States constitutes and confirms the ways that the meaning of political laws and physical ones, or even logical ones, are mutually determining.

The double sense of a law as something that must exist and must be obeyed is revealed, peculiarly, in Kant's preface to the first edition of his *Critique of Pure Reason*, where he writes:

> Time was when metaphysics was entitled the Queen of all the sciences. . . . Her government, under the administration of the *dogmatists*, was at first *despotic*. But inasmuch as the legislation still bore traces of the ancient barbarism, her empire gradually through intestine wars gave way to complete anarchy.

Kant then briefly recounts the various attacks and counter-attacks that ensued, concluding that the current moment has issued a

> call to reason to undertake anew the most difficult of all its tasks, namely, that of self-knowledge, and to institute a tribunal which will assure to reason its lawful claims, and dismiss all groundless pretensions, not by despotic decrees, but in accordance with its own eternal and unalterable laws. This tribunal is no other than the *critique of pure reason*.[56]

The quintessential form of the law is simultaneously "eternal and unalterable" and passed on by a political institution.

For purposes of this project, laws are studied as ways that certain forms of being are regarded as necessary and irreducible, in a manner akin to the laws of gravity. Therefore the chief objects of analysis are the political laws that constitute these forms of being—the kinship laws that exist, with or without being written or enforced by a bureaucratic government—in every political society.

Classifying Class

Political society, family, nation, race, religion, "but-where's-'class'?" 'Class' is not on this list because those aspects of capitalist relations that lead to inequalities among individuals as a consequence of laws of intergenerationality are not accommodated by the Marxian definition of class. Hence the

---

[56] *Critique of Pure Reason* [1787], tr. Norman Smith (New York: St. Martin's Press, 1965), pp. 8–9, emphases in original. 'Gesetz' means "law" and has similar connotations.

economic dynamics that prompt the material differentiation over time among groups of people are best examined through an analysis of laws producing property rights (including inheritance laws) and political sovereignty. This study undertakes this, which, again differs from an analysis of the Marxian "class." Those aspects of capitalism that contribute to exploitation and surplus value in Marx's lexicon are separate from the forms of being of nationality, ethnicity, race, family, and religion.

Among Marxians, "class" usually refers to subpopulations constituted by the requirements of capitalism. The amount of labor necessary for capital reproduction requires large numbers of workers to sell their labor for wages at rates lower than the value they contribute to the commodity, and at a rate less than what is necessary for their own reproduction at a level historically appropriate to the epoch. Marx characterizes absolute surplus value as the amount gained by increasing the length of the working day, and relative surplus value as the gains associated with increasing productivity. Exploitation is not the difference between a set standard of need and what the worker is paid but is always relational to the capacity of production at any particular moment. The workers' surplus labor value accumulates as capital, and is controlled by a relatively small group of people.

This is the story Marx narrates in *Capital* [1867], and one of its hallmarks, which appears in other works as well, is his insistence on the subtlety of the forces that divide classes under capitalism. The commodity first appears as a simple object with a particular use. Under more careful inspection, it becomes clear that the commodity always entails capital and surplus labor— that it is the culmination of an exchange relation. The success of capitalist obfuscations result, as Marx and Engels explain in the *German Ideology* [1845–46], paradoxically, from the absence of obvious (i.e., state-implemented) impediments to egalitarian power relations:

> By the mere fact that it is a *class* and no longer an *estate*, the bourgeoisie is forced to organise itself no longer locally but nationally, and to give a general form to its average interests. Through the emancipation of private property from the community, the state has become a separate entity, alongside and outside civil society; but it is nothing more than the form of the organisation which the bourgeois are compelled to adopt, both for internal and external purposes, for the mutual guarantee of their property and interests.[57]

A briefer statement of this might be, The bourgeoisie need police, roads, and bridges to pursue their commercial needs, so they develop an organization that appears as though it is in the interests of everyone, in order to have at their disposal resources of coercion and infrastructure necessary

[57] Marx and Engels, *The German Ideology* (Moscow: Progress, 1976), p. 99.

for industrial capitalism. Marx writes that this formally separate entity, however, is "never independent."[58] "The most perfect example of the modern state," Marx explains, "is North America." He continues:

> The modern French, English and American writers all express the opinion that the state exists only for the sale of private property, so that this view has also been accepted by the average man . . . Hence the illusion that law is based on the will, and indeed on the will divorced from its real basis—on *free* will.[59]

On Marx's reading, at least here, the government is auxiliary to class divisions—class divisions he sees as produced by the dynamics of capital accumulation, and not by the obviously particularist rules associated with feudal estates.

Marx is astute as to how political societies shape conditions that result in uneven economic development—and hence in internationally segmented labor markets that he thought needed to be unified before a proletariat-led revolution would be feasible. He is, however, rather vague, uninterested really, in the sources and structures of these nations-states. While Marx offers an account of the **government**, i.e., the coercive and administrative aspects of the state in relation to capital, he is apparently at a loss when it comes to explaining the **nation**, i.e., the membership characteristics of a state. Indeed the *German Ideology* performs this lacuna. The section heading "Origin of the State and the Relation of the State to Civil Society" is followed by the editors' comment "[Blank page.]"[60]

Marx and Engels wrote the heading because, in the course of engaging with Feuerbach, they were responding point by point to Hegel's *Philosophy of Right*. In criticizing, i.e., reversing, Hegel's account of the dialectical development of the family, civil society and the state, Marx and Engels write that the family is the "natural" and initially the "only social relation."[61] Given such a belief, it would make sense for Marx and Engels to provide a more detailed description of how exactly the state follows from the family, if Hegel's account is mistaken. Marx and Engels reject Hegel's view but offer no substitute narrative, unlike other disagreements where they offer alternative stories at great length. In the case of the family, the alternative narrative does not appear until after Marx's death, when Engels writes the *Origin of the Family, Private Property, and the State*.[62]

---

[58] Ibid.

[59] Ibid., emphasis in original.

[60] Ibid., p. 58.

[61] Ibid., p. 48.

[62] Marx died on March 14, 1883. Engels wrote *The Origin* in 1884. In revising *Capital* after Marx's death, Engels, in Marx's name, directly contradicts Marx's naturalizing claims about the family. Marx's text states: "Within a family, and after further development within a tribe, there springs up naturally a division of labour, caused by differences of sex and age,

A chief sign of Marx's own understanding of his materialism and his empiricism was his reiteration of the location of certain "natural" feelings underlying certain groups, in particular, families and nations. Marx criticizes Hegel's *Philosophy of Right* for conceptualizing the family as the outcome of the state, whereas he sees the family as pre-political:

> The family and civil society are the preconditions of the state; they are the true agents; but in speculative philosophy it is the reverse. . . . [T]he family and civil society make *themselves* into the state. They are the driving force. According to Hegel, however, they are produced by the real idea. . . . In other words, the political state cannot exist without the natural basis of the family and the artificial basis of civil society. . . . [T]he fact is that the state evolves from the mass existing as members of families and of civil society.[63]

And later, in the introduction to the *Grundrisse*: "The more deeply we go back into history, the more does the individual and hence the producing individual, appear as dependent, as belonging to a greater whole in a still quite natural way in the family and in the family expanded into the clan [Stamm]. . . ."[64] Marx misreads Hegel's dialectical method, claiming here that the "whole point of the exercise is to create an *allegory*, to confer on some empirically existent thing or other the significance of the realized idea. . . . It is self-evident that the true way is turned upside down. The most simple thing becomes the most complicated and the most complicated becomes the most simple."[65] But Hegel's dialectic never conceives of empirical objects on the one hand and their conceptual form as utterly distinct on the other. Such a dichotomy is Kantian, and it was Hegel's ambition to erase the rigid barrier that divided objects into things-in-themselves and appearances.

Once Marx describes the family and the nation as natural, he is as likely as the bourgeois economists to overlook the role that state-sanctioned kinship rules play in the production of class divisions through family and nation. Marx's descriptions of trade barriers such as the Navigation Act

a division that is consequently based on a purely physiological foundation, which division enlarges its materials by the expansion of the community, by the increase of the population, and more especially, by the conflicts between different tribes, and the subjugation of one tribe by another" (*Capital*, vol. 1, tr. S. Moore and E. Aveling [London: Lawrence and Wishant, 1974], p. 351). In a "Note to the 3d ed." Engels writes: "Subsequent very searching study of the primitive condition of man led the author [the dead Marx] to the conclusion that it was not the family that originally developed into the tribe, but that, on the contrary, the tribe was the primitive and spontaneously developed form of human association, on the basis of blood relationship, and that out of the first incipient loosening of the tribal bonds, the many various forms of the family were developed" (Ibid).

[63] "Critique of Hegel's Doctrine of the State" (1843; rpt.), in *Early Writings* (New York and London: Penguin Books, 1975), pp. 62–63.

[64] *The Grundrisse*, tr. Martin Nicolaus (1857–58; rpt. New York: Vintage, 1976), p. 84.

[65] Ibid., pp. 99–100.

note the uneven international distribution of natural and other resources among nations, but Marx overlooks the underlying political, not natural, dynamics that yield the taxonomic unit of "nation" (or "tribe" or "clan" or "gens") on which he relies for his economic analyses.[66] If one does not accept these political groups as primordial, then their role in the reproduction of economic inequalities looks quite different from those proposed (though for the most part simply overlooked) by Marx.

Once the political rules productive of the intergenerational family and its associated discourses are represented as real, and not idealist epiphenomena, it becomes possible to sharpen the elusive image of the Marxian "class," the meaning of which has as much consensus as that of "state" among Marxologists. The quandary has been that Marx's crystal clear, detailed, relentlessly logical and historically rich account of capital accumulation is not matched by his choppy, vague, and most importantly, politically challenging, definitions of "class." According to Marx, capitalism entails three main classes: those who own the means of production, those who own only their labor power, and those who own land. The last group is less important in Marx's general theory of class antagonisms under capitalism and seems to receive attention for purposes of analytical thoroughness—as a relation that lies outside the central political-economic conflict between capital and wage labor, but one that is nonetheless necessary to characterize in order for Marx's theory to be complete. In any case, while this taxonomy of resources (capital, labor, and land) accounts for the process of capital accumulation and also for various organized interests and political parties, it has not provided a satisfactory theory of the psychological and political being that would entail the class-for-itself.[67] Right or wrong, Hegel offers an organic description of the dialectical growth of the individual person into a specific being who expresses the individuality of his state. Although Marx offers a theory of the individual worker's alienation, his portrait of the proletariat in relation to the development of class consciousness is arguably the weakest, most ill-defined aspect of his project.

While Marxists in the late twentieth century will concede the failure of Marx's revolutionary vision, supplemental explanations follow from analyses of civil society, and not a renewed discussion of Marx's theory of political

[66] For instance, Marx writes that free trade has destroyed the "natural exclusiveness of separate nations." *German Ideology*, p. 81.

[67] In the final paragraphs of the end of the third volume of *Capital*, under the heading of "Classes," Marx writes: "The first question to be answered is this: what constitutes a class?— and the reply to this follows naturally from the reply to another question, namely: what makes wage-labourers, capitalists, and landlords constitute the three great social classes?" Marx offers a few words on why these are the three classes, and then we see only, "(Here the manuscript breaks off.)" (*Capital*, vol. 3, Chapter LII [London: Lawrence and Wishart, 1974], pp. 885–86).

society. "Distractions" of either consumerism or new social movements are typical explanations for the current failure of Marxism. In particular, Marxists ranging from late nineteenth century revolutionary actors to late-twentieth-century progressive academics have criticized mobilizations around affiliations of sexuality, gender, nation, ethnicity, and race as bourgeois sidetracks that thwart challenges to the most central source of inequality, and that would be the divisions that follow from our relations to the means of production.[68]

Yet rather than attack progressive social actors who for the most part are questioning authority and conventional forms of hierarchy—as opposed to their academic critics, for whom the alternative is clearly not leafletting with the Trotskyites—it might make sense to question Marx on the topic of certain connections between the family, the state, and wealth—the dialectics among which his theory does not adequately recognize. If people are organizing and fighting over identities of ethnicity, nationality, gender, and sexuality, then perhaps it makes sense to ask how it is that people take these divisions as productive of power relations, rather than dismiss them because they do not follow a rather vaguely written Marxian script.

The fact is that juridical rules are not incidental but absolutely crucial to capital accumulation, not largely because of the coercive and administrative functions of government that Marx describes, but because laws and the state reproduce the intergenerational political societies that in turn produce the chief taxonomies for controlling and distributing wealth, and, of course, the inequalities therein.

In addition to being accumulated through corporations, capital is also accumulated through politically constituted familial groups. These familial alliances produce economic divisions in two ways, both of which have virtually nothing to do with Marx's definition of class relations under capitalism. The first form of systemic economic differences occur through conventions of inheritance. Inheritance rules make possible capital accumulation within families, and not only within the corporations that Marx describes. The second intergenerational form that constitutes economic status is that determined by the laws prohibiting mobility of individuals among political societies. Whether one is born in Tijuana or San Diego affects one's economic status for reasons that are strictly juridical. Rather than perpetuate a contemporary overstatement that civil society has superseded political society as the site from which power emanates, it is impor-

[68] Nancy Fraser, "From Redistribution to Recognition? Dilemmas of Justice in a 'Post-Socialist' Age," *New Left Review* no. 212 (July/August, 1995), pp. 68–93. In a subsequent debate of these matters, both Fraser and Judith Butler invoke Marxian categories of analysis to justify their respective positions (Judith Butler, "Merely Cultural," *Social Text*, nos. 52/53 [Fall/Winter, 1997], pp. 265–78; Nancy Fraser, "Heterosexism, Misrecognition and Capitalism: A Response to Judith Butler," *Social Text*, nos. 52/53 [Fall/Winter, 1997], pp. 279–89).

tant to stress the vivid economic effects of plain, old-fashioned juridical rules that control membership via the familial forms determining inheritance and immigration possibilities.

The reason that capitalism is characterized by dramatic inequalities among individuals is, in large part, that wealth is passed on through families, through political institutions like inheritance laws and property rights. John Kennedy, Jr. was born a millionaire via a trust fund, a possibility not available to most children in this country.[69] This Kennedy, though he lives off capital, falls into none of the major classes Marx describes. He is neither a capitalist, a worker, or a land owner—vis-à-vis his personal role in capital accumulation. According to Marx's description, a capitalist does not merely live off the interest or profits generated by his or her assets but actively participates in the decisions about how that capital is to be reinvested:

> So far, therefore, as his actions are a mere function of capital—endowed as capital is, in his person, with consciousness and a will—his own private consumption is a robbery perpetuated on accumulation, just as in book-keeping by double entry, the private expenditure of the capitalist is placed on the debtor side of his account against capital.[70]

Referring to the division of labor Malthus describes, Marx says that it

> assigns to the capitalist actually engaged in production, a business of accumulating, and to the other sharers in surplus-value, to the landlords, the place-men, the beneficed clergy, etc. the business of spending.

And Marx concludes by drawing his own contrast between the "industrial capitalist and the rich idler."[71] But if the rich idler is not a capitalist, then how is his wealth, and that portion of all wealth that is not earned by the individual's investment decisions but by interest and so forth, to be thought of vis-à-vis economic divisions among the population? What is the political significance of that portion of wealth that is earned through capitalism but not by capitalists?

To the point, Marx is uninterested in the dynamics of the intergenerational accumulation of wealth among families, and focusses exclusively on corporate structures of accumulation. To recognize the impact of intergenerationality on the accumulation of wealth and the overdetermination of poverty is not to challenge Marx's major observations about how capitalists are able to maintain and acquire surplus value through their exploitation

---

[69] For a fascinating account of the myriad of ways that inheritance practices "reproduce" familial identities, see Remi Clignet, *Death, Deeds, and Descendants: Inheritance in Modern America* (New York: Aldine de Gruyter, 1992).

[70] *Capital*, vol. 1, p. 593.

[71] Ibid., p. 595.

of labor, but it is to draw attention to the implications of this for political-economic analyses of power relations, and more specifically, for what Marx calls class divisions. In 1996 over half of those on the list of the Forbes 400—the wealthiest individuals in the United States—inherited their wealth. The only Jordan on the list is a family that inherited wealth made in media and retailing, not basketball. Other studies support this, finding that on average, among those families that have wealth, approximately one half of the wealth is inherited.[72]

At first it seems odd that Marx would explore only the ways that capital reproduces within the lifetime of a single entrepreneur or through the centralization of joint-stock corporations,[73] without recognizing that some people start out with capital and others do not. Marx is adamant about dismissing intergenerationality as a significant economic factor, stressing that capital accumulation is best viewed as a synchronic, not diachronic, process. The infusions of labor's surplus value create the circumstances that compel exploitation at every single point, in ways that do not change but simply repeat, immune to time and chronology: "However long a series of periodical reproductions and preceding accumulations the capital functioning today may have passed through, it always preserves its original virginity."[74] Important to the dominant pattern of capital accumulation is not the ways of "old" versus "new" money, but the fact that all of it tends to dynamics of centralization.

While the above is absolutely correct—profits do not lead to cheaper prices or higher wages but to more production—Marx uses this point to make another illogical one, that family wealth, diachronic by nature, bears no role in capital accumulation, the corollary of which is that class inequality is also synchronic. That is, if class position is determined strictly by one's relation to the means of production, then one focuses only on that immediate relation, and not the systematic dynamics that overdetermine

---

[72] *Forbes* 400, October 14, 1996, pp. 345–60. This figure has been declining. As recently as 1991 it was 59%. The reason seems to be that a growing number of the Forbes 400 are entrepreneurs in the quickly growing computer industry. See also Herbert Inhaber and Sidney Carroll, *How Rich is Too Rich? Income and Wealth in America* (New York, London: Praeger Press, 1992), p. 73. Studies of inheritance frequently are thought uncertain and unreliable, but if there is a consistent error it would be to underestimate the amounts of inheritance. Funds inherited through trusts are not tabulated by the IRS. Also, many lawyers refer to inheritance taxes as "voluntary," and presumably tax-cheaters will not report their indiscretions to social scientists. Finally, our culture honors the "self-made man," and it might strike some as unseemly to admit to having inherited their wealth.

[73] "As simple reproduction constantly reproduces the capital relation itself, i.e., the relation of capitalists on the one hand and wage-workers on the other, so reproduction on a progressive scale, i.e., accumulation, reproduces the capital-relation on a progressive scale, more capitalists or larger capitalists at this pole, more wage-workers at that" (*Capital*, I, p. 613; see also pp. 605–8, 627–28, and 630).

[74] Ibid., p. 587.

who will and will not be forced into the labor market, an analysis one would imagine would significantly clarify analyses of class consciousness.

The reason Marx avoids discussing the class implications of inheritance is hinted at in his marginal notes on Mikhail Bakunin's pamphlet "International Alliance of Social Democracy." Bakunin writes that the alliance "wants above all political, economic, and social equalization of classes and individuals of both sexes, commencing with abolition of the right of inheritance, so that in the future enjoyment be equal to each person's production." Marx's marginal response reads, "Hermaphrodite Man!/Just like the Russian Commune!/ The old St.-Simon panacea."[75] Marx's distaste for the anarchists' politicization of the family reappears in the same document, in his comment next to the names of the signatories: "Asinus Asinorum! And Madame Bakunin!" implying that M. Bakunin is an "ass of asses" because he either is influenced by, or is acting as, "Madame Bakunin." The family is natural, so that only a hermaphrodite would challenge it. Inheritance is juridical, so that solving inequality by fixing the family is only an illusory antidote.

Marx is responding, as well, to writers like F. M. Eden, who also explains inequality as a consequence of inherited wealth. Marx quotes Eden writing about those who, because of their inheritances, " 'owe their exemption from labour solely to civilization and order. . . . They are peculiarly the creatures of civil institutions.' " Eden is observing that class inequalities are caused by laws that give some people and not others wealth at birth. Marx replies in a fashion that, from anyone else, would be regarded as a crude caricature of Marx: "Eden should have asked, whose creatures, then, are 'the civil institutions'? From his standpoint of juridical illusion, he does not regard the law as a product of the material relations of production, but conversely the relations of production as products of law."[76] Marx seems to think it necessary to trivialize capital accumulation through families because this is a dynamic Marx had pigeon-holed as strictly "feudal." Feudal relations are those sustained in the political sphere, whereas Marx insists that capitalist inequalities are primarily a function of the "material relations of production" in civil society, and not state laws. Class relations are what follow from the relations to the means of production, unregulated by the state, so that at any point a certain portion of society needs to sell its labor at a rate below that which is socially necessary to reproduce itself at a historically appropriate level. Marx emphasizes the constant need of individuals to sell their labor and dismisses the importance of the structures that, as Eden notices, cycle wealth systematically to those individuals who

[75] "Marx's Remarks on the Programme and Rules of the International Alliance of Socialist Democracy" (pamphlet published December 15, 1868), in Marx-Engels, *Collected Works*, vol. 21 (New York: International Publishers, 1985), p. 208.
[76] Ibid., p. 209.

are members of certain families. While this last fact may be irrelevant to the general exploitation required by capitalism, inheritance patterns of accumulation are absolutely central to the experience of familial identities as important and productive of economic, i.e., class, inequalities.

To appreciate the extent to which inheritance leads to class difference, consider an alternative to the current form of wealth accumulated through families. Imagine that upon one's death one's wealth were to revert back to the companies or banks where one's assets were invested. This is different from a socialist intervention of, say, a 100 percent estate tax, since capital would continue to be concentrated among firms, as in Marx's story of capitalism. Still, the result would be far less extreme inequalities of wealth among individuals than that which obtains under current regimes promoting family inheritance. If shares or money reverted to banks, the stockholders or other investors would find the value of their assets increasing. So the concentration of wealth would vary with respect to the number of investors in each firm where that particular individual had her investments. In almost all cases, the wealth distributed among the stockholders would amount to a smaller fraction than that which would be awarded to the individuals who were members of the much smaller nucleus of one's immediate family. This thought experiment specifies that wealth go to firms and not the government in order to hold constant the form of capital accumulation Marx describes under capitalism. The extent to which current norms diverge so radically from this thought experiment, such that we can imagine implications as far-ranging as decreased levels of entrepreneurship—people crafting ways of sheltering wealth for their family before they die, or being less motivated to accumulate assets—reveals the centrality of the intergenerational family to our economy. This thought experiment shows that the concentration of capital in firms is not the single source of inequalities associated with class differences. The intergenerational pattern of wealth's distribution, regulated by the form of the juridical family, contributes substantially to class differences.

Inequality and Political Boundaries

Numerous other inequalities follow from the intergenerational family form, among political societies and not just within each one. Disparities of wealth and other resources among political societies, rather than among individuals within those societies, are not "class" differences, but evidence of uneven economic and power relations. The inequality in the distribution of wealth, average rates of infant mortality, as well as torture *among* political societies are at least as extreme as those *within* political societies: "Of 100 babies born in sub-Saharan Africa, nine will die before reaching the age of one. In the developed countries, it will take about 60 years for these nine deaths to occur."[77] The life expectancy in sub-Saharan Africa is 50 years, while in developed countries it is 74 years. At least as important as the differences between large regions—sub-Saharan Africa and Europe— is that neighboring countries also reveal differences in wealth, health, and political practices. Afghanistan, Cambodia, and Haiti have more than 100 infant deaths for every 1,000 live births, while the rates in the respectively proximate Russia, China, and the Dominican Republic are less than half of this.[78] Another example of life chances that vary by country is found in gendered rates of infant mortality. In Cambodia the infant mortality rate for boys is 116 per 1,000 and 100 per 1,000 for girls, while in mainland China, the rate is 32 per 1,000 for boys and 49 per 1,000 for girls; in Taiwan the rates are essentially the same. Per capita annual income statistics tell a similar story. In 1991 per capita income in Lebanon was $613, in Saudi Arabia $9,340, and in the United Arab Emirates $15,301.[79] Due to immigration restrictions, these averages reveal more than the fact that some regions have more oil than others. It is the artifice of colonialists, and before them tribes and clans, that constitute these borders, that make it possible for some and not for others to be included in the average GNP for Saudi Arabia.

That these statistics vary between countries that are in the same region, and may use the same language, and practice the same religion suggests that it is not "culture," but rather certain juridical rules, that yield disparities relative to units of geopolitical sovereignty. This is not to suggest that China has laws that require the death of a certain ratio of girls to boys, or even that one might not be able to control for less obvious extra-juridical practices between, say, Taiwan and China to explain the difference. Regardless of what may be learned from elaborate regressions, the simple fact is that the movements of people are restricted by nothing else but political borders. This means that while an equation might be able to shift around causal accounts, the people themselves must stay put, that they cannot move to another region that might have practices more consonant with a better quality of life, or more fairness and equality. Indeed that is why, in comparing human experiences, the state is the unit of analysis. From the point of view of the individual resident, the question

[77] United States Department of Commerce. Bureau of the Census. *World Population Profile* (Washington, D.C.: GPO, 1996), p. 38.

[78] Ibid., Table A-9, pp. 40–41.

[79] United Nations. *Statistical Yearbook*, no. 39 (New York: United Nations, 1993), Table 24 "Gross Domestic Product, Total and Per Capita," pp. 205-7. Such statistics are notoriously misleading, since they do not reflect the different levels at which wealth may be concentrated nor do they tell us much about relative standards of living. However, for the simple purpose of detecting differences among political societies, these statistics are adequate.

whether China's infant mortality rates are produced by laws or "culture" does not affect her chances of going somewhere else and leaving these lower rates behind. So we do not need to know the precise level at which some regression (never accurate in any case) would predict the contribution of X to Y to know it makes sense to conceptualize the disparities in that region as political ones.

If one is born in China, one may not freely travel within or among countries. No such restrictions exist in neighboring India. India's "Human Rights Rating" is 54 percent. China's is 21 percent, despite the two countrys' proximity of region and GNP.[80] Mobility from a country that tortures political dissidents to one that does not is restricted by political borders more than anything else, that rely on birth criteria for their inclusions and exclusions. Yet Marx and others put to one side these effects of juridical power: "The Roman slave was held by fetters: the wage-labourer is bound to his owner by invisible threads. The appearance of independence is kept up by means of a constant change of employers and by the fiction juris of a contract."[81] For the illegal immigrants tracked by the United States national guard, as well as for the members of Congress who seek to protect United States goods and labor, the problem and solution do not (dis)appear as "invisible threads." The obstacles are 12-foot-high barbed wire fences, 20-foot-deep barricades, and armed sentries at border-crossing checkpoints. The fence being built at the Mexican border is there because of the appropriations mandated by Rep. Duncan Hunter's "Immigration in the National Interest Act of 1996" and could not exist without the state forms of "Mexico" and the "United States of America."

The logic of immigration controls often is expressed as a worry about the disproportionate number of poor who will flock to the countries with wealth. This is not the full story. As Chapter 2 documents, even very poor countries may have very strict requirements for citizenship. When Botswanan administrators refuse to recognize the children of a U.S. citizen—with the various ties to resources this implies—it is clearly not economic rationality that motivates citizenship restrictions. All countries, not just relatively wealthy ones, have barriers to immigration. Further, worries about the economic consequences of mobility do not affect rules internal to this country. People in Mississippi earn less money than do people in California. Not surprisingly, from 1985 to 1990, Mississippians settled in California at a rate 25 percent higher than Californians moving to Mississippi. Overall, Mississippi experienced a slight decline in its population, while California's population increased by over three million, from

---

[80] The GNP per capita (US$) in China is $330; in India it is $340. The above data are all from Charles Humana, *World Human Rights Guide* (New York, Oxford: Oxford University Press, 1992), pp. 72–73; 137–39.

[81] *Capital*, I, p. 574.

people moving there from other states within this country alone.[82] No one in California has complained that the state is being invaded by Mississippians. Attracting other United States residents is perceived as good for business, even if these citizens are associated with a poor state that has a low-ranked education system. New residents from Mexico are seen as a social problem.

Marx and liberal analysts are not alone in de-emphasizing the role of the state in enacting divisions among people. Wendy Brown has astutely observed that a "noteworthy lost object of critique among those on the Left and among Foucauldians as well" is the "domination entailed in domestic state power."[83] Brown shows the adverse consequences of the state's domestic regulatory and coercive practices—pertaining to identities of gender and sexuality in particular—but internal class inequalities have sources in international borders as well. Harvard economist and former Secretary of Labor Robert Reich correctly observes that capital's mobility (and hence the difficulty of taxing corporate wealth) can only increase domestic disparities in the distribution of wealth.[84] One reason for this is that corporations play off the tax and other incentives of one country against those of another. If Honda's capital were stuck in Japan, it could not win certain concessions from the state of Tennessee and simultaneously deprive Japan of its revenues. If capital could not move, the citizens of Tennessee would be better positioned to enforce their overall tax policies.[85] Reich also might have pointed out that the geopolitical segmentation of labor further exacerbates inequities of capital mobility. While General Motors can move production to Mexico, Mexicans cannot move to Detroit. This structures the possibilities for transnational unionization in a way that is deleterious for workers in both countries. As long as Mexicans perceive their jobs as tied to relatively cheaper labor costs and U.S. workers see their higher wages as dependent on the exclusions of Mexicans, for instance, transnational organizing and alliances are extraordinarily difficult.

Reich's solution of "positive economic nationalism," which would restrict capital's mobility, can at best aid citizens of the countries where multinational corporations are based. It does not help the citizens of Ethiopia, for instance, since there is little capital there to retain. Reich's plan

---

[82] United States Department of Commerce, Bureau of the Census, 1990 Census of Population and Housing, *Geographic Mobility*, CD-Rom (SSTF) 15.

[83] *Wounded Attachments: Power and Freedom in Late Modernity* (Princeton: Princeton University Press, 1995), pp. 14–15.

[84] Reich, *Work of Nations: Preparing Ourselves for the 21st Century*, "Who Is 'Us'?" (New York: Knopf, 1991), pp. 301-15.

[85] A more banal advantage that the mobility of capital yields corporate owners comes from the ease with which companies can simply hide their assets from regulatory authorities in particular countries by shuffling figures in their ledger books, making it increasingly difficult to enforce the tax liabilities incurred by international companies.

does not ultimately ameliorate inequality within the United States, either. If labor markets were free (i.e., no immigration restrictions), then corporations would have no incentive to lay off American workers to hire people in Singapore, since unions would be transnational and labor would be almost as likely to move as capital. From the point of view of justice (for those in poorer countries), as well as pragmatism (for workers in the more wealthy nations) Reich's proposals fail.

This provisional sketch of some of the consequences of political borders for class inequalities suggests that those interested in cultivating the consequences of a class in itself need to foreground the political mechanisms that reproduce the international conditions of capital accumulation, conditions that restrict labor mobility through citizenship requirements based on the most restrictive and arbitrary rules of birth and kinship. The demands of immigration rules rooted in laws pertaining to birth and family allow people born in Alaska, but not those born in Nova Scotia, to live and work in Manhattan; allow firms to pay low wages in South Korea courtesy of a repressive state that beats union organizers who cannot work across state borders; make it impossible for someone who falls in love with someone of the same sex from another country to live with that person.

Against the above claims about the importance of political boundaries, numerous scholars mark the decline of the state's sovereignty, and therefore its centrality to daily practices. Introducing *Culture/Power/History*, the editors describe their authors'

> radically deinstitutionalized understanding of the political process, in which questions of conformity and opposition, of the potentials for stability and cohesion in the social order, and of the strength or fragility of the dominant value system, are all displaced from the conventional institutional arena for studying them (that is, the state and public organizations in the narrower sense) onto a variety of settings previously regarded as 'nonpolitical' . . . above all, the family and the home.[86]

Similarly, Betty Reardon's interest in transnational organizations and treaties seems an example of the Foucauldian post-modern post-mortem of the king, the sovereign state that political thought ought to behead.[87] In a preface to essays discussing how economic, environmental, and strategic changes have undermined state autonomy Reardon writes:

> During the latter half of the twentieth century, the first half of the global age, human society has outgrown most of its political institutions. The scope and

---

[86] Nicholas Dirks, Geoffry Eley, and Sherry Ortner, eds., *Culture/Power/History: A Reader in Contemporary Social Theory*, introduction (Princeton: Princeton University Press, 1994), p. 4.

[87] *History of Sexuality*, tr. Robert Hurley, vol. 1 (New York: Vintage, 1980), pp. 88–89.

severity of the problems of this age has brought the world political system to a point of crisis. There are few who would continue to defend the total inviolability of national sovereignty, and most recognize that international interdependence requires significant adjustment in the nation-state system.[88]

Regardless of the specific iteration of concern—ranging from the Foucauldian attention to power manifest at the margins, to Reardon's hopes for justice, to Samuel Huntington's Schadenfreude over allegedly anti-cosmopolitan tendencies in the "Middle East" and elsewhere[89]— shared among these writers is the belief that the state is far less a formidable actor than it has shown itself to be in the past.

Marxists have always been skeptical of efforts to equate domination with juridical institutions. They criticize the illusory freedom of citizenship, because it is only formal, though more recently some have sought to have its promises materialized.[90] Rather than accept the dismissal of the state as a site of power, I want to return to the concerns of late-nineteenth and early-twentieth-century anarchists, as well as those indictments of the state from among internationally minded Communists preceding and during World War One—all of whom proceeded on the assumption that the state was a crucial source of oppression and hardship in itself. They understood that the facade of "citizenship" which follows from the state obliterated the rights of human beings around the world. In the early twentieth century Rosa Luxemburg criticized various Social Democrats and communists who sought to broaden the support of the Left by appealing to national sentiments:

[88] From the preface, Richard Falk, Robert Johansen, Samuel Kim, eds., *Constitutional Foundations of World Peace* (Albany: State University of New York Press, 1993), p. xi.

[89] Gramsci astutely points out the politics of the mapping itself: "Obviously East and West are arbitrary and conventional, that is, historical constructions, since outside of real history every point on the earth is East and West at the same time. This can be seen more clearly from the fact that these terms have crystallized not from the point of view of the hypothetical melancholic man in general but from the point of view of the European cultured classes who, as a result of their world-wide hegemony, have caused them to be accepted everywhere. Japan is the Far East not only for Europe, but also perhaps for the American in California and even for the Japanese himself, who through English political culture, may then call Egypt the Near East" ("Problems of Marxism," in *Selections from the Prison Notebooks*, tr. Quentin Hoare and Geoffrey Smith [New York: International Publishers, 1971], p. 447; Richard Falk, *On Humane Governance: Toward a Global Politics* [University Park: Pennsylvania State University Press, 1995]; Samuel Huntington, "The Clash of Civilizations?" *Foreign Affairs* 72 [Summer, 1993], pp. 22–49).

[90] Ernesto Laclau and Chantal Mouffe conclude *Hegemony and Democratic Socialism* by affirming the notion of separate democratic regimes, offering a socialist understanding of rights indistinguishable from that produced several decades before by T. H. Marshall. Citizenship, according to Laclau and Mouffe, is not to be overcome, but rather, its idea of right is to be expanded "from the classic 'political' domain to that of the economy" (*Hegemony and Socialist Strategy: Towards a Radical Democratic Politics* [London: Verso, 1985], p. 185).

The duty of the class party of the proletariat to protest and resist national oppression arises not from any special 'right of nations,' just as, for example, its striving for the social and political equality of sexes does not at all result from any special 'rights of women' which the movement of bourgeois emancipationists refers to . . . A 'right of nations' which is valid for all countries and all times is nothing more than a metaphysical cliché of the type of the 'rights of man.'[91]

Of course Luxemburg was assassinated. The ideology responsive to the genocide of the Second World War was a cosmopolitanism shrouded in flags. The United Nations Declaration of Human Rights protects one's "right to a nationality."[92] Such a right depends on nation-states, and is antithetical to diminishing the national group form that depends on (and annihilates) the gens, that is, the politically constituted notion of intergenerational group identities.[93]

The references to impediments to freedom wrought by kinship rules and political borders are the crude and obvious examples of state interference in ostensibly private relations. The power of the political birth form of the state, however, also asserts itself in places so delicate and remote from

[91] "The National Question and Autonomy" [1908–9], in *The National Question*, Horace Davis (ed.), (New York: Monthly review, 1976), p. 185. After World War One Luxemburg writes: "In the present imperialistic milieu there can be no wars of national self-defense. Every Socialist policy that depends upon this determining historical milieu, that is willing to fix its policies in the world whirlpool from the point of view of a single nation is built upon a foundation of sand" (*Crisis of the German Social Democracy* [1915] [New York: Socialist Publication Society, 1919], p. 95).

[92] Article 15, from United Nations Department of Public Information, *These Rights and Freedoms* [1st ed.] (New York: United Nations Department of Public Information, 1950), p. 173.

[93] While I take the lack of interest in the state form to be a strong tendency in the academy, there are important studies that carefully attend to the ways that the state constitutes identities of nation, race, and sexuality. Among those not previously mentioned are Hannah Arendt, *The Origins of Totalitarianism* (New York: Harcourt, Brace, Jovanovich, 1951); Etienne Balibar and Immanuel Wallerstein, *Race, Nation, Class: Ambiguous Identities* (London: Verso, 1991); Partha Chatterjee, *The Nation and Its Fragments: Colonial and Postcolonial Histories* (Princeton: Princeton University Press, 1993); Oliver Cox, *Caste, Class, and Race: A Study in Social Dynamics* (Garden City: Doubleday, 1948); W.E.B. DuBois, *Dusk of Dawn: An Essay Toward an Autobiography of a Race Concept* (New Brunswick: Transaction Books, 1992); Virginia Domínguez, *White By Definition: Social Classification in Creole Louisiana* (New Brunswick: Rutgers, 1986); David Evans, *Sexual Citizenship: The Material Construction of Sexualities* (London, New York: Routledge, 1993); Ian Haney-López, *White By Law: The Legal Construction of Race* (New York: New York University Press, 1996); G.W.F. Hegel, *Philosophy of Right*, tr. T. M. Knox (London, New York: Oxford University Press, 1967); James Scott, *Seeing Like a State: How Certain Schemes to Improve the Human Condition Have Failed* (New Haven, London: Yale University Press, 1998); Anna Marie Smith, *New Right Discourse on Race and Sexuality: Britain, 1968–1990* (Cambridge and New York: Cambridge University Press, 1994); Roger Smith, *Conflicting Visions of Citizenship in U.S. History* (New Haven: Yale University Press, 1997).

government offices as to confuse some critics into thinking these expressions "cultural," by which they often mean apolitical practices that distinguish one people from another. An exemplary list of these includes accent, habits of dress, food preferences, and artistic creations that are perceived as condensations of the particularity of local, regional, and national differences. To label these cultural is implicitly to endorse the legitimacy of the political borders that separate "us" from "them."[94] The argument is something like this: groups have intrinsic differences that political borders respect. The requirement of distributive justice among individuals is a fine one, this line of thought continues, but so too is that of difference, of cultural autonomy.[95] And if there really are groups with fundamental differences of language and origin, as well as other practices, like music or dance, then it makes sense to set these groups off from each other so that they might establish laws particular to their unique preferences. And yet closer inspection reveals that here too the state form is crucial to such reproductions.

Reproducing the State: Semiotics, Family, and Law

Seagram's Canadian Whiskey

One way that the state as a membership organization reproduces itself is through the frequent invocation of a state's proper name adjacent to things with which the state has no necessary, ontological tie. Often this takes the form of an adjective for goods or practices the state form apparently qualifies, e.g., "Canadian whisky," "Canadian bacon," or the "Canadian soccer team"—Canada, whisky, bacon, and soccer having as much in common as the random objects arrayed in Magritte's "L'Alphabet revelations" (1935).[96] But somehow these things do not appear unrelated, but tied to a common source: Canada, a nation-state, or more precisely, a state-nation.[97] This occurs because the naming process itself produces a distinctive "state"-ness associated with such objects, to yield effects somewhat similar to the way that "leaf" may evoke "green," even when the actual association of states with particular things or practices is far more arbitrary.

[94] This is the approach advocated by Charles Montesquieu, *The Spirit of the Laws*, tr. Anne Cohler, et al. (New York, Cambridge: Cambridge University Press, 1989).

[95] See Charles Taylor, *Multi-Culturalism and the Politics of Recognition: An Essay* (Princeton: Princeton University Press, 1992).

[96] Reproduced in Foucault, *This Is Not a Pipe* (London and Berkeley: University of California Press, 1983). The painting shows various various words alongside objects that have no idiomatic semiotic relation to them.

[97] I reverse the more idiomatic phrase "nation-state" in order to challenge the view that accepts the priority of the nation and sees the state as its merely legal superstructure.

Peter Bronfman, whose cousin Edgar Bronfman Jr. controls the Seagram beverage company, stated that if Quebec seceded from Canada, Seagram's would be forced to relocate its Montreal headquarters: "Seagram's produces 'Canadian' whiskey," he explained.[98] Clearly it is the political, not the physical, location of Seagram's that defines whether the product is "Canadian."

Consider the following sentences: "When I tasted the whiskey, I thought it was from Canada, but it turned out to be really from Quebec." And: "When I saw the leaf, I thought it was green, but it turned out to be really brown." The whiskey tastes the same if it is distilled in either "Canada" or "Quebec." But the phenomenology of the first (mistaken) leaf color differs from the second: the leaf before the discovery appears different from the leaf after the mistake is corrected. This is not to say that the best way to judge what something "really is" is whether one confirms its supposed ontological features. Our experience of a thing is often imbricated in the discourse of that thing. Still, the possibility of distinguishing ostensive from ontological-seeming impacts on our experiences is part of consciousness. We are aware that some characteristics—what we believe we know because of advertisements—seem arbitrary and some seem essential to the condition of a thing—what we believe we know directly through our five senses.

In the above example, Canadianness is being constituted, in part, through its association with a thing that "Canada" has itself supposedly created. "Canadian whiskey," as opposed to, say, "smooth whiskey," reproduces the notion of Canadianness. What is especially important in the case of Canadian whiskey is that the association is not experienced as symbolic, but as ontological. The effects of "Canadian whiskey" differ from those of, say, the "Canadian flag" by virtue of the contingency of "Canada" and "whiskey" being partially submerged by the concrete phenomenology of whiskey. A flag is experienced as "symbolic" and if all a country had to claim for its distinction were that, it would be laughed out of the United Nations. But subsets of things like whiskey, wool, fish, wines, and, especially, families, are phenomenologically concrete—marks of what seem to be real differences.

The Birth(s) of the State

In addition to reproducing itself by virtue of the semiotics of things and practices associated with the state form, the state reproduces itself through highly elaborated practices of familial reproduction. The state appropriates

[98] CBC television broadcast, "In Depth Magazine," January 3, 1997.

the script of matrilineality, attempting to match the certainty of identity that follows from maternal knowledge (by the mother of her child). Kathleen Jones writes:

> The history of the Western cooptation of feminine powers of generativity in representations of the 'birth of the state' as an essentially masculine act of political natality both suppresses and ironically preserves the connections between charismatic rule and female symbology.[99]

The consequences of birth practices appropriated by the state vary tremendously. Sometimes state-led eugenics lead to widespread, murderous assaults, as in Nazi Germany and Serbian-dominated Bosnia. At other times, eugenics takes the form of fertility campaigns. In Israel the "Fund of Encouraging Birth" was established in 1968 to "subsidize housing loans for families with more than three children." This happened because the "pro-natal lobby in Israel" was intent on "reproducing and enlarging the Jewish people which has dwindled, first through the Nazi Holocaust (caused by anti-Semitism) and then through the 'Demographic Holocaust' (caused by assimilation and intermarriage)."[100] Not just militarist, nationalist states, such as Israel, but ostensibly liberal ones as well employ these rhetorics and policies. The state as a membership organization (as a political society) constitutes a familial rhetoric that naturalizes that state's particularity by creating a naturalized touchstone of families.

The Narrative State

One tactic among contemporary commentators on the state-nation has been to challenge the stories of the 'birth of a nation' by calling attention to the narrative form itself, as it has appeared especially amenable to such fictions. To dislodge the truth of certain exclusionary myths of a people's origins has seemed recently to require the rejection as well of histories that take the form of tracing the present moment of a practice from its origins. This same set of concerns has also prompted many to follow a certain iconographic Foucauldian reluctance to study historical continu-

---

[99] *Compassionate Authority: Democracy and the Representation of Women* (New York: Routledge, 1993), p. 113. The editors of *Woman-Nation-State* refer to "women" as reproducing the state in five ways, though it is largely women as "mothers" who do this: "a) as biological reproducers of members of ethnic collectivities; b) as reproducers of the boundaries of ethnic/national groups; c) as participating centrally in the ideological reproduction of the collectivity and as transmitters of its culture; d) as signifiers of ethnic/national differences. . . ; e) as participants in national, economic, political and military struggles" (Yuval-Davis and Anthias, *Women-Nation-State*, p. 7).

[100] Nira Yuval-Davis, "National Reproduction and 'the Demographic Race' in Israel," in *Woman-Nation-State*, pp. 96, 98.

ity,[101] in favor of "genealogies" of the present. The studies of various affiliations in this book are not part of this trend. Instead, these chapters endorse Hegel's insistence on the centrality of political society to history, and they also reflect Heidegger's insights on the connection between an origin and the present. Both of these positions require some elaboration.

Hayden White believes that "Hegel was right when he opined that a genuinely historical account had to display not only a certain form, namely the narrative, but also a certain content, namely a politico-social order."[102] And then White quotes from Hegel who writes: "It is only the state which first presents subject-matter that is not only adapted to the prose of history, but involves the production of such history in the very progress of its own being."[103] To the objection that certain influential histories have never done this, that Ferdinand Braudel, for instance, struggled to describe demographic patterns independent of administrative rules, the response is that even Braudel's history of the material facts of every day life provides a history of states and other political societies. The chronologies, civilizations, and nations he describes in movement, war, and famine reinscribe the unit of political societies.[104] Even when the focus is not on state policies, history is always a story of a political group and its time.

Taking the state as the object of inquiry, especially given the Hegelian connotations of its form and content, seemingly overdetermines a mistake that post-structuralist scholars have diligently pointed out and attempted

---

[101] Here I take issue with a certain strain in Foucault's writings that is reiterated in much research presented in his name. I am not concerned with whether all of Foucault's work manifests this. I think Foucault was more aware of, and also more frustrated by, the inevitability of the narrative form than some of his followers. This "iconographic Foucault" may not be the one most true to Foucault's intentions, but it exerts a tremendous intellectual influence nonetheless.

[102] *The Content of the Form: Narrative Discourse and Historical Representation* (Baltimore and London: Johns Hopkins University Press, 1987), p. 11.

[103] Ibid., p. 13, quoting from *Philosophy of History* [1830-31], tr. J. Sibree (New York: Dover, 1956). Michel de Certeau seems to follow this Hegelian approach as well: " 'The making of history' is buttressed by a political power which creates a space proper (a walled city, a nation, etc.) where a will can and must write (construct) a system (a reason articulating practices)," *Writing History*, tr. Tom Conley (New York: Columbia University Press, 1988), p. 7. This is precisely what Foucault rejects, when he refers to a "certain image of power-law, of power-sovereignty . . . that we must break free of, that is, of the theoretical privilege of law and sovereignty, if we wish to analyze power within the concrete historical framework of its operation" (*History of Sexuality*, p. 90).

[104] Braudel emphasizes the limits of "material life" on the various possibilities for "what was possible in the pre-industrial world," but Braudel's analyses remain imbricated in the Hegelian categories of family, nationality, and political society. The scope shifts, from the population of "Mexico" to that of "Mexico City," from the "Amerindian" to the "European," but the details of this or that population can always be understood as those constituted through some permutation of a dialectics of political society and nation, mediated through the concept of family or kinship (*The Structures of Everyday Life* [New York: Harper and Row, 1981], pp. 25, 36–37).

to pre-empt. Attention to the state risks simply mimicking its own conventions of telling continual narratives, of looking to the past to legitimate the present, considering the origins of a practice to be connected to its present manifestations. If we are persuaded that there is no rational kernel in Hegel's mystical shell, then the elucidation of earlier practices may hold the attention of the intellectually curious, but knowledge of these will be irrelevant to analyses of power dynamics among contemporary membership practices. "What do etymologies of words, or references to past activities tell us about contemporary practices?" ask the Foucauldian-influenced readers, who know that history is not continuous but replete with epistemological breaks, and who seek to "define the *objects* without reference to the *ground*, the *foundation of things*," who study these objects "by relating them to the body of rules that enable them to form as objects of discourse and thus constitute the conditions of their historical appearance," who aim "[t]o write a history of discursive objects that does not plunge them into the common depth of a primal soil, but deploys the nexus of their regularities that govern their dispersion."[105] The affiliations studied here all depend on ideas of origin and birth, treating the form of the past as the primal soil Foucault ridicules.

To note that the present exists in relation to the past in the following chapters means attending to the ways that certain concepts develop as they articulate epochal differences that congeal and are themselves implied each time the "present" or "past" as such are mentioned. Part of what "Christianity" means since Nietzsche is that it might be all wrong—since "God is dead"—*and* still be persuasive because many of those aware of Nietzsche's announcement disagree with it. This is the continuity in apparent discontinuities, the phenomenology of the present in its (non)relations with the past, the impossibility of discontinuity.[106] When the meaning of any particular moment is rendered as distinct from prior ones, these differences are aspects of, and at times even the essence of, a practice's

---

[105] *The Archaeology of Knowledge*, tr. M. Sheridan Smith (New York: Pantheon, 1972), pp. 47–48. Compare the above phrases with Certeau, who appreciates the phenomenological necessity of origins: "In historical discourse, investigation of the real therefore comes back, not only with the necessary connections between conditions of possibility and their limitations, or between the universals of discourse and the particularity attached to facts (whatever their delimitation may be), but in the form of an *origin postulated* by the development of a mode of 'the thinkable' " (*Writing History*, p. 44).

[106] Stoler offers a different reading of Foucault's method, pointing out that "he identifies not the end of one discourse and the emergence of another, but rather the refolded surfaces that join the two" such that "new elements (new planes) in a prior discourse may surface and take on altered significance as they are repositioned in relation to a new discourse with which they mesh" (*Race and the Education of Desire*, p. 72, and note 19). Stoler's analysis of race as functioning in these ways is absolutely correct, but this approach is not the one Foucault emphasizes. What Stoler has in mind is really no different than a good history of ideas—an approach to which Foucault objected.

phenomenology. The accounts of the state, marriage, nations, and so forth in this study look to the effects of their "origins" on their current forms, since these are concepts that contain the effects of being in time. To capture these relational changes in the meaning of a concept requires recognizing that a certain narrative form carries them along. The practice of marriage, for instance, is not identical in all eras or places, nor is it necessary, much less blessed or superior at one point compared to another. Still, each episode of its practice frames prior and subsequent meanings, simply because consciousness experiences marriage that way, as "traditional," as rooted in a society's deepest sources of its particularity.

The truism most directly challenged by these arguments about historical continuities is that the nation is a creature of modernity. Initiating this periodization, Ernst Renan wrote: "Nations . . . are something new in history. Antiquity was unfamiliar with them."[107] Liah Greenfield writes: "The original modern idea of the nation emerged in sixteenth century England, which was the first nation in the world (and the only one, with the possible exception of Holland, for about 20 years)."[108] Ernest Gellner locates nationalism as coterminous with requirements of "literacy and technical competence" for mass citizenship, needs that can "only be provided by something resembling a 'national' educational system" such as that characterized by Weber's description of late-nineteenth-century bureaucratic rationality.[109] Benedict Anderson writes that in "Western Europe the eighteenth century marks . . . the dawn of the age of nationalism."[110]

These theorists, and numerous others, take this position in part as an effort to question popular beliefs that the nation is based in "blood," that it is pre- or ahistorical, in short, that it is natural. Because advocates of the nation invoke ancestry to justify their image of the nation, part of the project among those bent on demystifying these primordial views of the nation has been to note the ways that these stories depend for their effectiveness on other (modern) technologies and cultural accoutrements. The anti-nationalist scholars want to demonstrate that ideas about blood depend on other forms of political capital for their circulation.[111] And yet the

---

[107] "What Is a Nation?" in *Nation and Narration*, p. 9.

[108] *Nationalism: Five Roads to Modernity* (London, Cambridge: Harvard University Press, 1992), p. 14. Note how Greenfield's initial tautology (the "original *modern* idea of the nation . . . is modern") elides into the claim that this establishes the criteria for the "first nation in the world. . ."—which raises questions about earlier "original" ideas of the nation.

[109] Ernest Gellner, *Nations and Nationalism* (Oxford: Blackwell, 1983), pp. 5, 34.

[110] Benedict Anderson, *Imagined Communities: Reflections on the Origin and Spread of Nationalism* (London: Verso, 1983), p. 11.

[111] For Anderson, this would be the printing press; for Gellner, a modern bureaucracy; and for Charles Tilly, capital intensive weaponry and warfare ("War Making and State Making as Organized Crime," in *Bringing the State Back In*, ed. Evans, Peter, Dietrich Rueschemeyer, and Theda Skocpol [Cambridge: Cambridge University Press, 1985], pp. 169–91).

nation is and always has been a concept tied to ideas about birth and ancestry. To observe this does not require or imply genetic evidence per se. Awareness of the past emerges through a discursive analysis of how the concept of birth has played a role in stories of a political community's origins in places and times ranging from those of ancient Athens to Polynesian tribes to the contemporary United States. Were this not the case, autochthony (self from the earth) myths from ancient Greece would be irrelevant to the current form of the nation. And yet these autochthony myths tell us a great deal about the nation, about and through the form of political society—the quintessential form that interpellates the past.

One _____

The State of Membership

The state . . . is a compulsory organization with
a territorial basis. [T]he differentiation between
the political community on the one hand, and,
on the other, the groups enumerated above
[i.e., kinship groups and religious organizations],
becomes less clearly perceptible the further we
go back in history.[1]

Every human society has some sort of territorial
structure. . . . To try to distinguish, as Maine and
Morgan did, between societies based on kinship
(or, more strictly, on lineage) and societies based
on occupation of a common territory or locality,
and to regard the former as more 'primitive'
than the latter, leads only to confusion.[2]

A good anthropological monograph looks as
though it might have been produced without
great difficulty, for it has already reduced to
order the complications and problems presented
by the mass of material collected piecemeal in
day-to-day inquiries. Once the lineage principle
in political structure has been elucidated, for
example, it seems obviously possible as a basis
for *political relations*. . . . [I]n fact the nature and
importance of lineage segmentation were for too
long obscure to knowledgeable students of
politics, whose only model of political structure
was that of the state.[3]

[1] Max Weber, tr. Ephraim Fischoff, et al., *Economy and Society: An Outline of Interpretive Sociology*, vol. I (Berkeley, Los Angeles, London: University of California Press, 1978), p. 56; ibid., vol. II, p. 903.

[2] Mayer Fortes and E. E. Evans-Pritchard, *African Political Systems*, introduction, p. xiv.

[3] Ronald Lienhardt, *Social Anthropology* (London: Oxford University Press, 1964), quoted in Joan Vincent, *Anthropology and Politics: Visions, Traditions, and Trends* (Tucson: University of Arizona Press, 1990), p. 265, emphasis in original.

Disciplining the (Familial) State

To study the state has, for the most part, entailed examining structures of coercion within a specific territory, and not evaluating kinship practices. The political scientist assumes that it is in primitive societies, and not states, that political communities and kinship structures overlap. But maybe the contrast is overstated, replies the anthropologist: to study a society anthropologically is to elucidate the lineage principle. State and kinship society, the modern and the primitive, Europe and Africa, and political science and anthropology: each of these pairings is a metonym of the others. The University of Michigan's Department of Political Science, with a faculty of approximately 45, has **one** professor who writes on Africa. The Department of Anthropology, with a faculty of approximately the same size, has **seven** faculty who specialize in the study of Africa.

Kinship and political society are attended to simultaneously in discussions of "primitive" or "tribal" societies of Africa (and those "pre-modern" societies in Asia and the Americas that resemble them), while a private/public heuristic is frequently relied on by political scientists to render invisible the familial aspects of the (European) state. To contrast the social contract theories of the origin of political societies with the actual practices of every political society, including the modern state, challenges this orientalist division of labor. The fact is that the paradigmatic membership structure for all political societies derives from invocations of birth and ancestry.

The modern notion that political authority and familial authority might be separate begins with seventeenth-century social contract theorists,[4] who put forth the idea that there is neither biblical nor logical force to the contention that monarchical rule should follow from principles of paternal rule within the family. If the Stuarts wanted to base their monarchical legitimacy on the idea of the family, then one possible response for their opponents was to claim that whatever works for the family is simply inapplicable to political society, that the two are entirely different realms. For example, after describing the authority of the father, John Locke writes: "But how a *Family*, or any other Society of Men, differ from that, which is properly *Political Society*, we shall best see, by considering wherein *Political Society* itself consists."[5] Then Locke tells a fib, which is that political

---

[4] Aristotle had argued earlier against using authoritarian family patterns as a model of political life, but he still maintained an organic view of the necessary ties between the patriarchal household and the political equality among its masters in public, thereby advocating a broader political order that was inherently hierarchical, and justified as such by gendered arguments about natural aptitudes among its members (*Politics*).

[5] Locke, *Two Treatises of Government*, ed. Peter Laslett (Cambridge: Cambridge University Press, 1960), II. §86.

societies consist of people who somehow have offered their consent to a particular government.[6] The remarkable aspect of this claim is Locke's stunning rhetorical victory, embellished by Marxists and liberals alike: Locke's strategic argument—that membership in political societies requires consent—seems to have stuck. Henceforth to study the state was, for Anglo political theorists, to defer from inquiry into the family—thought to be something else entirely.

It is the marked "feminist" political scientist, i.e., the professional other, who is the one taking up serious work on dynamics of the family, while the unmarked political scientist writes about the state. This is despite the fact that membership in political society is based on birth, and membership in a family is—always implicitly and often explicitly—based on law. Still, at times even this feminist work disappoints, when it accepts too much of the conventional wisdom on the division between private and public. "The personal is the political" has often been invoked to suggest that what happens in "private" is important, that a private realm contains power relations, and so therefore it is "political." This formulation, however, is not dialectical and therefore leaves intact the notion that there are essentially distinct spheres, with men legislating in public and women being abused in private. But the very iteration of different spheres is discursively given from the form and laws of political society. There is no "personal" absent the (discursive) forms of this constituted through political society.

Anthropology is a discipline that studies kinship—the principles and meanings associated with rendering some insiders and others outsiders.[7] Political scientists study the state, which is taken to be a structure of hierarchical power relations that regulate domestic affairs and protect citizens from other governments. In the realm of international relations, where we might expect to find some serious interest in the practices that render some populations "us" and others "them," the most influential practitioners display hostility to such concerns. Kenneth Waltz writes that "states" are "domestic political structure[s]" defined "first by the principle according to which they are organized or ordered, second by the differentiation of units and the specification of their functions, and third by the distribution of capabilities across units."[8] This is a bare-boned description of government functions, and nothing more. Waltz stresses that "Everything else is omitted," including "concern for tradition and culture."[9] He

---

[6] Locke, II.§89.

[7] The modern classic work on the relation between kinship and social structures is Claude Lévi-Strauss, *The Elementary Structures of Kinship*, tr. James Bell et al. (1949; rpt. Boston: Beacon Press, 1969).

[8] "Anarchic Orders and Balances of Power," in *International Politics: Anarchy, Force, Political Economy, and Decision-Making*, Robert Art and Robert Jervis, eds., 2d ed. (Boston, Toronto: Little, Brown, 1984), p. 10.

[9] Ibid.

also asserts that the state, again as a synonym for government, is the exclusive unit of analysis for the field of international relations: "States are the units whose interactions form the structure of the international-political system. They will long remain so."[10] Waltz's states do not contain families, just men who will calculate efficiently on behalf of their units.

And yet, the same computer-ready actor of rational choice political economic models; that diminutive, polite liberal celebrated by millenarians who have found the "end of history"; the monster of bureaucratic anonymity—all of these caricatures of members, or citizens, or subjects of the state fare no differently than "tribes" when it comes to membership principles. They all rely on either territorial or ancestral ties of birth for membership. This book might have been titled "Reproducing Political Society," since the arguments show a general pattern of rules governing affect and belonging in numerous contexts. But lost would be the specificity of the gap between the ideology of the (liberal) state and its actual dynamics vis-à-vis membership. At the bottom of every conflict between nation-states—ranging from those pertaining to NATO to immigration quotas to environmental treaties—are taxonomies of national difference that follow from invocations of family and birth.

Recent Work on the State[11]

Since the late nineteenth century, theorists of the modern state have been largely interested in its tendency to reflect the dynamics of a "civil society"

---

[10] Ibid., p. 15. Waltz's formulations do not go unchallenged. As noted in the previous chapter, others insist that transnational alliances and social movements also constitute units of international relations. Also, numerous feminist interventions in the field of international relations theory criticize many of its foundational assumptions and provide alternative accounts of what counts as an international relations problem, as well as new ways to think about them. See Cynthia Enloe, *Bananas, Beaches, and Bases: Making Feminist Sense of International Politics* (Berkeley: University of California Press, 1990); Rebecca Grant and Kathleen Newman, eds., *Gender and International Relations* (Bloomington: Indiana University Press, 1991); V. Spike Peterson, ed., *Gendered States: (Re)visions of International Relations Theory* (Boulder: Lynne Rienner, 1992); and Ann Tickner, *Gender in International Relations* (New York: Columbia University Press, 1992).

[11] What follows resembles some synopses offered by Theda Skocpol, though what she characterizes as "state autonomy" could also be called "government autonomy." Skocpol's effort to "bring the state back in" differs from my study of political society as a membership organization. Skocpol says she has in mind "more than government," but this "more" ends up entailing little more than the observation that the state influences "many crucial relations within civil society." Her working definition of the state as an "organization claiming control over territories or people" also holds for a definition of "government," but one may also define the state as a membership organization, which is what this chapter pursues below ("Bringing the State Back In: Strategies of Analysis in Current Research" in *Bringing the*

defined primarily as a sphere of economic interests.[12] One reason for the interest in civil society was the failure of nominally democratic institutions to redistribute wealth. Under capitalism, wealth is allocated hierarchically. In the late nineteenth century, attention turned to economic and social patterns that prevented the majority from achieving a more egalitarian distribution of wealth and power.[13] The belief of those across the political spectrum—and this dates from the time of ancient Athens—had been that manhood suffrage coupled with democracy would allow "the people" to control the institutions of property rights and hence enable them to redistribute wealth. This idea held for both those who supported and those who opposed such redistribution. During the Putney Debates (1647), for instance, officers worried that a broad franchise would give those five-sixths of Englishmen with "no permanent interest" the right to appropriate the wealth of the remaining sixth. Rainborough then admonishes Rich, who had made this point, that the alternative would be that "the one part shall make hewers of wood and drawers of the water of the other five, and so the greatest part of the nation be enslaved."[14] Once universal manhood suffrage was implemented and this class revolt by the ballot box failed to occur, theorists turned to closer analyses of civil society to account for political-economic complacency.

Theorists of gender and race, in their writings on the state, have borrowed from the Marxist literature, assigning class positions to men and

---

State Back In, ed. Peter Evans, Dietrich Rueschneyer, Theda Skocpol [Cambridge: Cambridge University Press, 1985], pp. 7, 9).

[12] Martin Carnoy writes: "The liberal vision of the bourgeois state . . . was a representative democracy, with power residing in a small group of the citizenry, largely because of a past pre-capitalist distribution of property," *The State and Political Theory* (Princeton: Princeton University Press, 1984). For surveys of the Marxist literature on the state, see the introductory chapters of Bob Jessop, *State Theory: Putting Capitalist States in Their Place* (University Park: Pennsylvania State University Press, 1990); Jean Cohen and Andrew Arato, *Civil Society and Political Theory* (London, Cambridge: MIT Press, 1992).

[13] See Paul Baran and Paul Sweezy, *Monopoly Capital* (New York: Modern Reader Paperbacks, 1968); Harry Braverman, *Labor and Monopoly Capital: The Degradation of Work in the 20th Century* (Monthly Review Press, 1974); Philip Green, *Retrieving Democracy: In Search of Civic Equality* (Totowa: Rowman and Allanheld, 1985); Ralph Miliband, *The State in Capitalist Society* (London: Wiedenfeld and Nicolson, 1968); C. Wright Mills, *The Power Elite* (New York: Oxford University Press, 1959).

[14] A.S.P. Woodhouse, *Puritanism and Liberty: Being the Army Debates (1647-1649) from the Clarke Manuscripts with Supplementary Documents* (Chicago: University of Chicago Press, 1951), pp. 63, 67. Marx, in his early writings, also believed in the redistributive promise of a broad franchise: "Only when civil society has achieved unrestricted active and passive suffrage has it really raised itself to the point of abstraction from itself, to the political existence which constitutes its true, universal, essential existence," which will lead to the supersession of civil society altogether ("Critique of Hegel's Doctrine of the State," in *Early Writings* [1843; rpt. London: Penguin Books, 1975], p. 99).

women, Whites and Blacks.[15] Often these accounts refer to groups in relation to a political regime that, having consolidated property rights for White men, is otherwise irrelevant to their daily lives. For those on the Left since the 1960s, interest in the state was in part an interest in its lacunae. Discussion abounded as to where the state did not, could not, go because of the dominant interests of capital. The contention was that labor force segmentation and capitalist friendly views of what was private maintained hierarchies of sex and race.

The starting propositions among liberal, or "pluralist," theorists resembled in many respects those of the Marxists. They too began with a question about the prevalence of governmental policies that apparently served the interests of a minority. The pluralists, however, challenged the instrumental schemas of the Marxists with laissez-faire models of competing interest groups and hypotheses about voter apathy, both of which emphasized the democratic nature of representative government in the United States.[16] Public policy was depicted as a reflection of underlying group formations and agendas that appear first in civil society.[17] In the era of formal political equality—after women have the right to vote, and after the 1964 Voting Rights Act assures racial minorities representation—the autonomous, instrumental state recedes as an object of serious analysis.

Alongside, indeed sustaining, the view that hierarchies of sex, ethnicity, and race are not caused by governmental rules is the belief that these

[15] W.E.B. Du Bois, "The Conservation of Races" [1897], in *W.E.B. Du Bois: A Reader* (New York: MacMillan Press, 1971); Richard Edwards, David Gordon, Michael Reich, *Segmented Work, Divided Workers: The Historical Transformations of Labor in the United States* (Cambridge, New York: Cambridge University Press, 1982); Zillah Eisenstein, *Capitalist Patriarchy and the Case for Socialist Feminism* (New York: Monthly Review Press, 1979); Frederick Engels, *The Origin of the Family, Private Property, and the State* (1884; rpt. New York: Pathfinder, 1972); Heidi Hartmann, "Capitalism, Patriarchy, and Job Segregation by Sex," in *The Signs Reader: Women, Gender, and Scholarship*, ed. Elizabeth Abel and Emily Abel (Chicago, London: University of Chicago Press, 1983), pp. 193-226; Catharine MacKinnon, *Toward a Feminist Theory of the State* (Cambridge: Harvard University Press, 1989); Manning Marable, *How Capitalism Underdeveloped Black America: Problems in Race, Political Economy, and Society* (Boston: South End Press, 1983); and Sheila Rowbotham, *Beyond the Fragments: Feminism and the Making of Socialism* (Boston: Alyson Press, 1981).

[16] David Truman's book was written at an early point in this debate, its prominence closely tied to Cold War accounts of the wonders of America's open government (*The Governmental Process: Political Interests and Public Opinion* [New York: Knopf, 1951]).

[17] One of the most important studies to advance this view in the United States is Robert Dahl, *Who Governs: Democracy and Power in an American City* (New Haven: Yale University Press, 1961). Criticisms of his argument, on theoretical and empirical grounds, suggested that what appeared as popular assent is the apathy of alienation, and that what appeared as representative government are the manipulations by elites. See Peter Bachrach, *The Theory of Democratic Elitism: A Critique* (Boston: Little, Brown, 1967); William Domhoff, *Who Really Rules?: New Haven and Community Power Re-examined* (New Brunswick: Transaction Books, 1970).

affiliations are largely natural, pre-political ones. Political scientists tend to view affiliations of family, nationality, and race as pre-constituted groups that then come into the public spheres (or are blocked from these arenas) to fight for their particular interests:

> The point about ethnic minority status leads to the next key variable that influences political behavior at the mass level: ethnic and racial identity. We now know that people everywhere take group identities seriously. The rule is simple: *people identify with people like themselves.* 'Human nature' is another of those weasley phrases that can be used to explain anything you want to believe, but in this case we may be close to something of an iron rule.[18]

Such assumptions by behavioralist political scientists studying U.S. politics treat identities of gender, race, and ethnicity as already coherent independent variables that have this or that effect on public policy or attitudes about public policies.

Studies of citizenship that interrogate problems of fairness or justice among individuals emphasize the rights and privileges that follow from membership, not the conditions that give rise to the possibility of membership.[19] T. H. Marshall, for instance, claims that citizenship means "full membership of a community." All citizens are due certain economic benefits based on rights that are "civil, political, and social." Marshall's narrative recounts the development of these rights, historically. He shows how class and gender have impinged on this definition of citizenship, but he does not interrogate the criterion of nationality that underlies his argument. He does not explain why poor British women have the right to claims on the British state that poor French women lack. Marshall sees citizenship in relation to an already-constituted political society and government that may or may not alleviate problems in civil society. He does not bother to justify the political society's decision rules for including some as citizens with claims on the government and excluding others from such prerogatives.

Defining the State

The use of the word 'state' in this study is not as a close synonym of 'government'. Rather, here the 'state' refers to one form of a political society. A state as a membership organization has rules for individuals' inclusions and exclusions. Thinking about the state as a membership orga-

---

[18] Oliver Woshinsky, *Culture and Politics: An Introduction to Mass and Elite Political Behavior* (Englewood Cliffs, NJ: Prentice-Hall, 1995), p. 146, emphasis in original.
[19] *Citizenship and Social Class* (London, Concord: Pluto Press, 1992), pp. 6, 7, 8, 13.

nization helps clarify how kinship[20] rules arise and are used for reproducing members in putatively "modern" political societies. It is precisely those political societies known as states that are oblivious to the sources and effects of kinship anxieties on laws regulating citizenship.

Just what the concept of the state refers to is often ambiguous. Weber's 'Staat' could easily be interchanged with 'Regierung' (government or state). In *Economy and Society* Weber writes that the state reaches its "full development" in modernity, suggesting that its "primary formal characteristics" are its administrative organization guided by a legislature. This "system of order" is sovereign over all of its citizens ("most of whom have obtained membership by birth") *and* over "all action" within its jurisdiction. He continues with these no doubt familiar phrases:

> It [der Staat] is thus a compulsory organization with a territorial basis. Further-more, today, the use of force is regarded as legitimate only so far as it is permitted by the state or prescribed by it . . . The claim of the modern state to monopolize the use of force is as essential to it as the character of compulsory jurisdiction and of continuous operation.[21]

The definition in this passage is attentive to the issues of membership ("by birth") but the focus, here and elsewhere, is on the means of regulating what happens to a particular population. Weber's discussions of the state do not have much to say about how this particular group is constituted as such.

Weber is more interested in the abilities of regulatory and punitive bodies to control populations and markets than in the membership provisions that set off the individuals in one political society from those in another. He writes that "the notion of 'ethnically' determined social action subsumes phenomena that a rigorous sociological analysis—as we do not attempt here—would have to distinguish carefully." He goes on to list a variety of factors, including heredity, tradition, language and religion, "and especially the belief in affinity or disaffinity of blood" as explanatory of "ethnicity."[22] These are all considered as phenomena separate from the imperatives of the state's sovereignty and legitimacy. When Weber focuses

---

[20] 'Kinship' is used more frequently than 'family' in Chapters 1 and 2 because this anthropological jargon makes strange the apparently natural nuclear family. Having shown that relations thought of as natural ('family') are artificial ('kinship'), 'family' is used to discuss the phenomenology of the artificial-as-natural, in Chapter 3. To state it slightly differently, to use 'family' in these opening sections might leave the wrong (i.e., naturalized) impression of what I am discussing, but after this family is shown to be constructed in particular ways, then I want to use the word 'family' to convey just that—the naturalized patina over the structure of group rules for membership.

[21] *Economy and Society*, vol. I, p. 56.

[22] Ibid., pp. 394–95.

on membership, it is in relation to a concept of "political community" (politischen Gemeinschaft), not the state (Staat)[23]: "The belief in group affinity, regardless of whether it has any objective foundation, can have important consequences, especially for the formation of a political community."[24] So *Economy and Society* is largely about "government," with references to the "state" appearing largely as near synonyms for "government." That means that when scholars refer to the Weberian concept of the state, they have in mind institutions of coercion, not rules for membership.

There is another use of 'state' which does refer to membership, and for which 'government' is not a near synonym. In some contexts it is idiomatic to refer to a 'state' as a certain type of membership organization.[25] The origins of 'state' in its current sense of a political organization are widely attributed to Ulpian, who writes: "Publicum ius est quod ad statum rei Romanae spectat."[26] But H. C. Dowdall points out that the Latin *'status'* "implies a condition of stability" only in a very general sense, and that Latin political tracts lack a "single instance from Cicero to Grotius in which *status*, standing alone, is used for State."[27] This suggests that Ulpian is referring only to something like a Roman "condition," and not providing a meaningful forerunner to, say, 'Staat' as it appears in Weber's definitions.

Perhaps the most compelling and interesting evidence to support the claim that the Latin 'status' meant "condition" is that the sixteenth century Latin translations of *The Prince* render Machiavelli's Italian " *'stato'* . . . by *imperium, principatus, ditio*, and the like, or avoid it by a paraphrase."[28] The sixteenth century translations of 'stato' are words with roots associated with forms of ruling, and not words for the etymological cognates of 'state'. These conventions seem evidence that the contemporary semantics of 'state' are relatively recent. The likely origin of 'state', according to Dow-

---

[23] See *Economy and Society*, vol. 2, chapter 9.

[24] Ibid., vol. 1, p. 389.

[25] An apparent difficulty applying the approach of ordinary language analysis to texts in translation is that Weber, for instance, is actually using different (i.e., German) words from those (predominantly English ones) considered here. Although the German etymologies are also included, more relevant to the concern is that regardless of Weber's personal intentions and language use, there is a lengthy two-volume English text that has proved influential among social scientists who research the state. That it appears as a translation may pose difficulties for those interested in matters of authorial intention or in comparative linguistics. These are not insignificant questions, but there are many important ones addressed by simply analyzing the English translation of this book.

[26] "Public law is that concerned with the Roman state" *Digest* [c. 530], 1.1.4.

[27] "The word 'state'," *Law Quarterly Review*, 39 (1923), p. 101. Dowdall's capitalized 'State' is his convention for referring to 'state' as the word is used in 1922.

[28] Ibid. Also, in 1355 *"status* is rendered in German as *Macht"* and there is no evidence of the word 'Staat' (ibid., p. 104).

dall, is from derivations of the use of 'status' to refer to "magnates or governing classes."[29] Dowdall's research underscores the frequent conflation of 'state' with 'government' by noting that unlike '*polis*' and '*politeia*' or '*civitas*' and '*cives*', State "derives from the permanent character of . . . a governing body . . ." He points out that "there can hardly be a single case in which *stato*, as used in '*The Prince*,' could not be translated by the word 'government' . . ."[30] Hence the word 'stato' begins to be thought of as one that evokes the concept of government.

Still, as early as 1620 Hobbes' "A Discourse upon the Beginning of Tacitus" contains the following: "The first form of government in any State is accidental" and "The next government of this State was Consulary."[31] The uses of the 'government' and 'State' here suggest that the former refers to a particular ruling body and the latter a political society. Clearly the two are not near synonyms, as is the case for Machiavelli. Similarly, Hobbes translates *civilibus* as 'State'.[32] Dowdall also notes that State has been used in subsequent English texts to suggest a concept of membership. Matthew Arnold refers to it as the " 'nation in its collective and corporate capacity' "; Blackstone writes " 'The state is a collective body' "; and Bentham uses 'state' interchangeably with 'political society'.[33]

'Government' is from the Latin *governare*, which means "to steer (a vessel), hence to direct, rule, govern," from the ancient Greek "*kubernan*, to steer." The *Oxford English Dictionary* defines 'govern' in two ways. The first is "the action of ruling, continuous exercise of authority over the action of subjects or inferiors; authoritative direction or regulation; control, rule." The second is "to rule with authority, especially with the authority of a sovereign; to direct and control the actions and affairs of (a people,

[29] Ibid., p. 105. Dowdall and the *Oxford English Dictionary* present fourteenth-century uses of 'estate' that refer to those with the status of landholders, authorized as such by the king on behalf of the kingdom. The *OED* states that the derivation of this as the "body politic" first appeared in the sixteenth century.

[30] Dowdall, "The Word 'State'," p. 109.

[31] In *Three Discourses: A Critical Modern Edition of Newly Identified Work of the Young Hobbes*, ed. Noel Reynolds and Arlene Saxonhouse (Chicago and London: University of Chicago Press, 1996), pp. 31, 32 and *passim*. In *Leviathan*, Hobbes writes: "For by Art is created that great Leviathan called a Common-wealth, or State, (*in latine Civitas*) which is but an Artificial Man" (New York, London: Penguin Classics, 1985), p. 81.

[32] Hobbes, *Three Discourses*, p. 37.

[33] "The Word 'State'," p. 122, citing Bentham, *Fragment on Government* [c. 1770]. Dowdall traces the early French 'l'état' back to Bodin, observing that Bodin uses 'republique' as a near synonym for 'l'état,' although Skinner points out that Bodin uses *l'état en soi* to refer to a site of "indivisible and incommunicable sovereignty" ("The State" in *Political Innovation and Conceptual Change*, ed. Terrence Ball, James Farr, Russell Hanson [New York, Cambridge: Cambridge University Press, 1989], p. 120), quoting from *Les Six Livres de la Republique* (Paris, 1576), pp. 282–83.

a state or its members)"—the first use for which is quoted from 1297.[34] The etymologies and definitions noted above suggest that 'state' has possible connotations for membership, as well as for ruling, while 'government' refers to the exercise of authority.

The word 'state' can almost always idiomatically be used as a near synonym for 'government', but the opposite is not true. For instance, "She depends on the government for her income" has a meaning virtually identical to "She depends on the state for her income." However, when 'state' is used to suggest a membership organization, the two words are no longer near synonyms. "The members of that state salute the flag" might refer to those belonging to one of the fifty states or of a country, but neither means the same thing as "The members of that government salute the flag." 'Government' in the last sentence refers only to specific officials ruling a political society, and not all of the members of a political society, as implied in the sentence using 'state'.

So, although one could idiomatically discuss the state as an administrative organization, I focus on the state as a certain kind of membership organization, namely, as a form of political society. The state varies from other types of political societies as a membership organization only vis-à-vis the methods by which membership rules are implemented, not by their content. Of interest then are not the prerogatives of participation but the parsing of units of political membership in the first place. My reasons for considering the state as a membership organization resemble those put forth by Pierre Clastre, when discussing the parallels between "primitive" and "European" forms of political authority. Protesting against the ethnocentrism that had prompted anthropologists to treat non-coercive forms of power as a- or pre-political, Clastre writes that anthropologists had to abandon their "*exotic* conception of the archaic world, a conception which, in the last analysis, overwhelmingly characterizes allegedly scientific discourse regarding that world."[35] Clastre's concern is to establish a "*continuity* between these various forms of [coercive and non-coercive] power."[36] Likewise, it is possible to show the similarities between kinship rules for membership in the political societies of "tribes" and "states."

Political Membership

Historian Rogers Brubaker, also describing the state as a membership organization, points out that, liberal intuitions notwithstanding, the main decision rules follow from birth:

[34] *Oxford English Dictionary*, 2d ed.
[35] *Society Against the State: Essays in Political Anthropology*, tr. R. Hurley (New York: Urizen, 1977; rpt. New York: Zone Books, 1989), p. 20, emphasis in original.
[36] Ibid., p. 17.

> Every state ascribes its citizenship to certain persons at birth. The vast majority
> of persons acquire their citizenship in this way. . .Despite the concern of liberal
> political theory to found political obligation on the voluntary consent of individu-
> als the state is not and cannot be a voluntary association. For the great majority
> of persons citizenship cannot but be an imposed, ascribed status.[37]

Brubaker reviews the differences between "political" and "ethnocultural" forms of citizenship by contrasting France and Germany. On his account, France produces citizens in relation to republican beliefs about member-ship, while for Germany, citizenship is tied to ideas about history and blood. Brubaker emphasizes the differences between what he terms "political" and "ethnocultural" practices, but he also notes that they have been "fluid, plastic and internally contested," to wit, he notes, the Dreyfus Affair and the ethnocultural movement of Jean-Marie Le Pen, which both took place in France. Given Brubaker's typology, these episodes appear largely as unexplained aberrations.

The reason Brubaker is unable to account for racially informed discrimi-nations in France and other "liberal" societies, including the United States, is that his dichotomous conventional wisdom about supposed differences between affiliations based on territory and those based on blood obfuscates the underlying connections between these two (often overlapping) mem-bership rules. The superficial distinction between territorial and ancestral routes to membership that Brubaker and others identify actually belies a more general unity between the principles, empirically as well as theoreti-cally. Ancestry is used to provide for citizenship. Children born abroad in Germany *and* in France to citizen parents are German and French citizens, respectively. The supposedly liberal criteria of territorial birth and educa-tion are used to establish French as well as German citizenship.[38] Ancestry and territory are not antagonistic membership principles in practice or even logically. Territory as the criterion for membership only defers the site of birth invocations from the politically constituted family to the politically constituted territory. The effect of the citizenship criterion of birth in a territory is to sacralize the political borders, not to defetishize birth as a membership criterion.

A membership criterion of birth by territory is not *ipso facto* "assimilation-ist" and it is intrinsically anti-liberal. According to territorial rules, one's nationality status is determined by where one was or was not born, and not the possession of certain republican competencies or individual consent. It is ironic that modern commentators so often represent birth by territory

---

[37] *Citizenship and Nationhood in France and Germany* (Cambridge, London: Harvard Univer-sity Press, 1992), pp. 31–32.

[38] For instance, the children of non-German guest workers who are raised in Germany have different prerogatives vis-à-vis citizenship than the children of non-German guest workers who are raised elsewhere, while children of French parents who are born abroad

as a decision rule for citizenship that is more inclusive than lineage criteria. In England from the early fourteenth century until 1699, the practice was thought to have the opposite effect, when "ligeance" followed from one's place of birth, a policy that effectively colonized Scottish and Irish "subjects" when those territories were under British rule.[39] The right of British subjects to have British children abroad (*jus sanguinis*) was perceived as an *enlargement* of subjects' prerogatives, since it allowed these children to inherit their fathers' estates and not to be treated at law as aliens.[40] From the point of view of an individual born to particular parents or on a particular territory, the birth principles of land and lineage are equally restrictive of that person's options for political membership.

Birth is the means by which one becomes a *member* of the state of France or Germany, regardless of the form of political *participation*. It is with respect to the form of participation that a state is generally characterized as "democratic," "liberal," "monarchical," "totalitarian" and so forth. As even this abbreviated list suggests, the forms of participation are numerous. Perhaps due to this variation, rules of political participation have received a great deal of attention in canonical and secondary political theoretical literatures, while rules for membership are accepted as natural and lack the same scrutiny. This is not to say that canonical theorists never mention membership rules, and it is a simple matter to review them.

A Short History of Political Theories of Membership: Plato through Machiavelli

Until the sixteenth century the question of political membership (as opposed to that of obligation) was not a seriously contested concept in what became canonical thought. Plato's *Republic* describes the class divisions that follow from autochthony, but autochthony is not invoked to explain the initial qualifications for membership in a particular *politeia*.[41] The Noble Lie is used to assign membership in a particular class. Training preparatory to one's duties occurred when *politeia* members were "down within the earth. . . . And when they were quite finished the earth as being their mother delivered them." Plato continues the autochthony story in relation

---

are eligible to be citizens. Hence a territorial principle is at play in German citizenship rules and an ancestral one in France.

[39] Chapter 2 discusses this in more detail.

[40] James Kettner, *The Development of American Citizenship, 1608-1870* (Chapel Hill: University of North Carolina Press, 1978), pp. 17-22.

[41] *The Republic* [*Politeia*], tr. Paul Shorey (New York: Bollingen, 1961). This work is translated as *Der Staat* in German, and earlier English editions also translated the title as *The State*.

to kinship ideas, with Socrates saying that they will "regard the other citizens as their brothers and children of the self-same earth."[42] Autochthony is used to justify strictly distinctions and cohesion within a *politeia*, but Plato does not invoke autochthony to explain why guardians are members of one *politeia* and not another.[43]

In a later, supposedly more realistic dialogue, Plato does discuss membership rules. In the *Laws*, the initial citizenry will flow from various sources, "to unite in one lake" and be unified.[44] Thereafter the *politeia* provides marriage rules that will be used to determine citizenship. Families and political societies reproduce together: "Each man who receives a portion of land should regard it as the common possession of the entire state. The land is his ancestral home and he must cherish it even more than children cherish their mother." By designating the familial land as simultaneously belonging to the state and the citizen-son and citizen-father, Plato politicizes the family (its objectification—its land—is an aspect of the *politeia*) and sacralizes the land. The land is not a circumference of dirt, but a very special objectification of the state. Plato then explains the laws for primogeniture, necessary to join in eternity the tie of the Athenian people with its territory, by overlaying the concepts of property, family membership, and political society (the grouping of certain members, associated with a fixed territory in this case).[45] The Athenian says that the first topic of discussion "will be the very first step that leads to the birth of children in the state. . . . So the correct policy for every state will probably be to pass marriage laws first."[46] Officials will record each birth on the wall of the home. (An early enthusiast of bureaucratic rationality, Plato also suggested this inscription on the wall include the "sequence numbers of the officials who facilitate the numbering of the years," so that subsequent officials might verify that the information provided was accurate.)[47]

Plato reiterates the Athenian rules of his period that overdetermined the conjuncture of nationality and wealth. According to the *Laws*, for children born out of a sexual relation between a slave and a free man or woman, "female officials are to send the free woman's child along with its father to another country, and the Guardians of the Laws must similarly send away the free man's child with its mother."[48] Plato seems to accept the notion of an initial citizenry that somehow flows into one place from

[42] *The Republic*, III. 414d-e and 415b.

[43] Logically, Plato's *Republic* requires at least one other *politeia*; otherwise the guardian class, lacking an enemy, is superfluous.

[44] *Laws*, tr. J. Saunders (Middlesex: Penguin, 1970), V. 736a–b.

[45] Ibid., V. 740.

[46] Ibid., IV. 721.

[47] Ibid., VI. 785.

[48] Ibid., XI. 930.

elsewhere, but subsequent membership derives from a sacred relation to the property of that political society, a relation controlled by birth and marriage.

Unlike Plato, Aristotle calls critical attention to the contrivances of membership. He notes that "in practice a citizen is defined to be one of whom both the parents are citizens (and not just one, i.e., father or mother)" and then poses the problem of the initial citizen-parents. He addresses this with a quotation from Gorgias of Leontini: " 'Mortars are what is made by the mortar-makers, and the citizens of Larissa are those who are made by the magistrates; for it is their trade to 'make Larissaens'."[49] Aristotle also muses over whether a *politeia* means a place or a people, and observes that "the word 'state' [*politeia*] is ambiguous."[50] Aristotle concludes that the identity of a *politeia* over time depends on the preservation of its constitution, not the imagined underlying "race [*ethnos*] of its inhabitants." If a new constitution were imposed, he implies, Athens would no longer be the same Athens.[51] To support his point he analogizes a *politeia* to a chorus that has the same membership but changes its identity when it reads tragedy and then comedy.[52] One might interpret the analogy in the opposite fashion; Athens could remain Athens, even with a different government. For instance, after its Communist Revolution, Cuba is still Cuba.

Augustine lacks Aristotle's curiosity about how people come to be citizens in this or that political society. Augustine's concern is exclusively with the membership criteria for the city of God: having faith and following Christian practices. He holds stridently anti-hereditary beliefs about the source of these abilities. Esau and Jacob, he points out, come from the same parents; their differences in virtue indicate that differences of circumstance and motive trump birth in determining whether one will join the city of God,[53] a point that continues some of the anti-family themes found in the New Testament and followed by early Christian communities. Coming from a North African colony, Augustine certainly held no nationalist views on the criteria for belonging to a church based in Rome. He does not confront directly the question of membership in political society, and rules for political membership cannot be inferred from his contrast between membership in the city of God—which is potentially universal, i.e., "catholic"—and the conditions of membership in the earthly city, which are instrumental and parochial. It seems clear that everyone is eligible to join the city of God. Those who have the right degree of faith

---

[49] *Politics*, tr. B. Jowett, Bk. III. 2. 1276a (p. 2025).

[50] Ibid.

[51] Whether Athens would be Athens at all, if it is not the same Athens, is not explored.

[52] *Politics*, Bk. III.3.1276a.

[53] *Concerning the City of God against the Pagans*, tr. Henry Betteson (Middlesex, New York: Penguin, 1972), Bk. V. 4.

and commitment to the Bible and the Church are Christians. No one is precluded by birth from this, but nothing about political membership follows. Objecting to a notion of government as signified uniquely by force, Augustine writes: "Remove justice, and what are kingdoms but gangs of criminals on a large scale? What are criminal gangs but petty kingdoms?"[54] Augustine does not explore how one finds oneself attached to one gang (of Romans) and not another (of Persians, for instance).

Among the authors reviewed here, Cicero is the first to offer a narrative that does not propose ancestry as either the dominant or the preferred story of the origins of his republic's citizenry. Cicero takes his origins story of Roman membership from Cato, recounting the myth of Romulus. According to Cicero, Romulus selected the territory because he found the land and climate favorable. This differs from the autochthony principle of Plato, which is echoed in the different account of Romulus given by Livy, who writes: "[I]f any nation deserves the privilege of claiming a divine ancestry, that nation is our own; and so great is the glory won by the Roman people in their wars that, when they declare that Mars himself was their first parent and father of the man who founded their city, all the nations of the world might well allow the claim." As Livy describes it, the connection between Romulus and Rome is that Romulus and Remus were "seized by an urge to found a new settlement on the spot where they had been left to drown." This fatalistic narrative is not the same as Cicero's economic fable, in which Mars had surveyed the countryside for an area that might bode well for good living.[55]

Cicero decides to characterize Rome's founding as one of Romulus's choice, and not (as in Livy) as a matter pre-destined by Mars raping a Vestal Virgin in a certain place. This is a much more cosmopolitan view than those advanced previously. Unlike Aristotle, Cicero is not granting hegemonic status to an account he finds implausible. Cicero instead constructs a counter-narrative that is anti-hereditary:

> [E]ven at that period the new nation [*populus*] perceived a fact that had escaped the Spartan Lycurgus; for it was his thought that the king should be, not one freely chosen. . . but one retained in power, whatever sort of man he might chance to be, if he were but the offspring of Hercules. Yet our ancestors, rustics though they even then were, saw that kingly virtue and wisdom, not royal ancestry [*progeniem*], were the qualities to be sought.[56]

Cicero emphasizes that the first post-Romulus king (Numa Pompilius) is "foreign" [*alienigenam*] and "chosen."[57] The fact that "foreign"ness is a

[54] Ibid., Bk. IV.4.
[55] *The Early History of Rome (Ab urbe condita)* I, prologue and I.vi.
[56] *The Republic*, tr. Clinton Keyes, Book II. xii.
[57] Ibid., II.xiii.

category and that Cicero refers to "citizenship" [*civitatem*] being granted to Lucius Tarquinius, who had been Greek and was elected king,[58] means that there are rules of subsequent inclusion and exclusion that Cicero's treatise does not discuss. Presumably he has in mind the citizenship rules of his time, which followed from marriage rules (explored in Chapter 2). While various commentators, including Herodotus and Aristotle, had critically explored the ideas and implications of autochthony, Cicero is perhaps the first official whose writings offer these anti-natalist assumptions as politically dominant.

Finally, at the cusp of what would be known as modernity, Machiavelli considers in some depth the distinction between a state and a nation. Drawing on his observations of the Roman Empire, Machiavelli recognizes that a government might be run by a group of people who differ from those they administer. After a conquest, new states "may or may not be of the same nationality and language."[59] He observes it is more difficult to conquer a people whose laws and culture differ from that of the imperialist state. On the "origin" of cities, he writes that they are all "founded either by natives of the country or by strangers."[60] He does not explain, much less attempt to justify, a principle that would force an individual to belong to one city or state and not another. Presumably he simply accepts the prevailing ancestral practices of his period. Indeed, while most of the writers considered so far have radical notions about how to arrange their governments vis-à-vis obligation and participation, they offer few theoretical analyses of the terms of membership, preferring instead to reiterate membership conventions of their times.

Social Contract Theories of Political Membership

Sixteenth- and seventeenth-century social contract theorists are the first to discuss terms of membership as pre-requisites to legitimate sovereignty. Until this point, political theorists had suggested that citizens owed allegiance based on birth, the goodness of the government, or coercion. While Aristotle had advocated some measure of equality in the polis, the criteria of eligibility excluded most residents (but did not preclude their obligation to the rules the assembly passed). Still, the protests against exclusions from participation in antiquity did not refer to the "contract" as a metaphor for suggesting individuals' political prerogatives to a partnership with a sovereign for the purpose of personal security.

[58] Ibid., II.xx.
[59] "The Prince," in *The Prince and the Discourses*, tr. L. Ricci (New York: Random House, 1950), p. 7.
[60] "The Discourses" (ibid.), p. 105.

Paradoxically, the earliest use of social contract discourse expressed the absolute authority of the monarch and was not used to dislodge conventional notions of obligation. In the writings of sixteenth- and early-seventeenth-century theorists Theodore de Béza and Hugo Grotius, social contract rhetoric legitimated monarchies. Instead of a private business contract, these writers took the marriage contract as paradigmatic for political relations. The analogy of the marriage contract was used by the royalists to distinguish their power over subjects from the illegitimate coercion of slave owners. Taking up the analogy of the social and marital contracts for purposes of challenging the monarchy, Béza justifies some instances of resistance to the government by equating subjects with wives: "But if not even the Canons of the Church consider that a wife who cannot safely live with her husband, should be compelled to live with him, why shall a subordinate magistrate not be allowed to take precautions on behalf of himself and his people?"[61] Béza questions the monarchists, but reiterates their view of the monarch as the political power that holds a dominant position over his subjects—as does the husband vis-à-vis the wife.

Despite its appropriation by critics such as Béza, the marriage contract model of the relation between a king and his subjects continued to be used by those who favored the monarchy. Just as the marriage contract was for the good of both husband and wife, Grotius argued, so too the social contract was for the good of both monarch and subject: "There are also some Governments that are for the mutual benefits of both parties, as that of an Husband over his Wife,"[62] notwithstanding that the relationship in both cases is not an egalitarian one, as the "Wife is put as part of the Husband's Family: and therefore it is the Husband's Right to appoint Laws in his own House."[63] The king and his subjects have a relation of formal mutual benefit, even as the king has the sole prerogative to make all the laws. Similarly, J. W. Gough, explaining the social contract views of John Winthrop, writes, "The liberty of the subject is like that of the Wife: 'The woman's own choice makes such a man her husband: yet being so chosen, he is her lord, and she is subject to him, yet in a way of liberty, not of bondage.' "[64] The mutuality of the marriage contract language does not evoke ideas about equality, but of a legitimate hierarchy.

---

[61] *Concerning the Rights of Rulers over Their Subjects and the Duty of Subjects towards their Rulers* tr. Henri-Louis Gonin (1574; rpt. Capetown: NV Drukkerij v.h. C. de Baer Jr., 1956). p. 70.

[62] *The Most Excellent Hugo Grotius: His Three Books Treating of the Rights of War*, Book I (1622; rpt. London: Basset, 1682), microfilm, p. 40.

[63] Ibid., p. 104.

[64] *Social Contract: A Critical Study of Its Development* (Oxford: Clarendon Press, 1957), p. 88, quoting *Winthrop's Journal: History of New England, 1630-1649*, ed. James Kendall Hosmer (New York: C. Scribner's Sons, 1908), vol. 2, pp. 238–39.

This analogy between marriage and the social contract prompts the question Carole Pateman has asked of the marriage contract: Why bother with even the form of the contract, when it diverges from every other contract in such crucial ways?[65] Unlike any other contract, the sixteenth-century marriage contract established a relation of virtually inescapable inequality. And unlike any other relation of inequality, marital relations required consent. Serfs never achieved their status by consent but by required oaths.[66] Presumably this is because everyone assumed that no men would freely consent to conditions of servitude or disenfranchisement. Marriage rituals disregarded this norm. The mutuality associated with the initial requirement of consent implied by contract was undermined by the character of the actual contract: "When a woman married, she retained certain rights over her real property, but her personal property she surrendered completely to her husband; in giving up her personalty, she gave up her personality, the two words which originally meant the same thing."[67] Further, any other contract can be renegotiated and changed by the parties who initiated it. A marriage contract, however, is and was a contract between the husband, the wife, and the state (or politically recognized religious body), and its terms could be changed only with the assent of this third party as well.

To put this in the language of Rawls, in the original social contract theory hierarchy was preferred over equality among individuals. In the marriage contract, it was understood that women were subordinate and would consent to being in a dependent relation to their husbands. Similarly, early social contract theorists, far from rejecting such hierarchical assumptions—on the grounds that one might find oneself subordinated—yielded to relations of subordination thought best for all. One might argue that the men writing these treatises never imagined themselves in the position of the "wife." But within their own terms, this position of subjugation was contemplated, rendered satisfactory, and even admired. Only within an individualist framework is it possible to imagine consensus on the rejection of status relations. With roots in the initial analogy to marriage, the social contract tradition has its origins in ideas about kinship and obligation.

In the seventeenth century the historical puzzle of the consenting subject is not only that of the contractually subordinated wife, but also, moving

[65] Carole Pateman, "Feminism and the Marriage Contract," in *The Sexual Contract* (Stanford: Stanford University Press, 1988), p. 158.

[66] Edward Coke, *First Part of the Institutes of the Laws of England: Or a Commentary Upon Littleton, Not the Name of the Author Only, But of the Law Itself,* 16th ed.; rev. and cor. ed. London: L. Hansard and Sons, 1809, sec. 86.

[67] David Ogg, *England in the Reigns of James II and William III* (Oxford: Oxford University Press, 1955), p. 71.

to the terrain of property, the "happy slave."[68] To ask the question Pitkin asks of social contract theory in general: why bother with making consent a prerequisite for obligation?[69] The writings of Béza and Grotius demonstrate that the similar paradoxes of the marriage contract and social contract theory alike stem from a common source—an acceptance of hierarchical status relations. No doubt absolutism was doomed for reasons of industrialization and market expansion, but the spectacle of the effeminate royalty was no less attractive than that of the feminized public, consigned as wives to a virtual harem apart from the political and military arenas of the Crown, gendered as masculine. That is, men during this period would not accept that their role was to be that of the submissive wife. Rather than challenge the inequality of the marriage contract, the seventeenth-century social contract theorists simply rejected the analogy. By severing the private sphere of obligation that follows from the marriage contract, from the public sphere of obligation that follows from an egalitarian social contact (albeit among men only), the contract language could be used in a manner quite different from its original purposes. The analogy of wives with subjects broke down in the work of Locke in particular. Wives and children were dependent, but that was no reason to think that freemen, who were not so dependent, should be subordinate to the monarch. The family was one thing, politics another. These are the views that framed the social contract beliefs about membership as well. Although the history of political societies has been that membership is determined by birth and kinship, in his effort to separate the logic of the family from the practices of political society, Locke formulates a different strategy altogether.[70]

Lockean Social Contract Theories of Membership

Locke's work contains many of the intuitions evoked in contemporary discussions of political membership. In most cases it is difficult to separate the source of any parallels between what an author writes and the broader Weltanschauung. In the case of Locke's social contract, though, it is much

---

[68] Don Herzog, *Happy Slaves: A Critique of Consent Theory* (Chicago and London: University of Chicago Press, 1989), pp. 59–63.

[69] "Obligation and Consent—I," *American Political Science Review*, 59 (December, 1966), p. 997.

[70] Still, even here the primary discussions among social contract theorists regard sovereignty in relation to obligation and participation, not membership. Hobbes and Locke, similar to Béza and Grotius, inquire into when a particular sovereign has legitimate authority over particular individuals. Their stories of the origins and reproduction of political societies are largely guided with these problems of obligation in mind, and not questions of exclusions and inclusions that yield consequences in themselves.

easier. Were it not for the wide circulation of Locke's *Second Treatise*, few would think that political membership followed strictly from individual consent, since this has never been the case, anywhere. Because Locke is a widely cited source on this point, it makes sense to turn to his influential claims.

On the one hand, like Hobbes, Locke asserts the artificiality of any particular government. Locke infers from the plurality of existing governments that people must have strayed from their allegiances of birth. Otherwise, he reasons, we would all still live in the same kingdoms from the Hebrew Bible. Since this is not the case, some people must have split off and established new political regimes. Locke then infers that the prerogative to do this is a natural right: "[I]f anyone, born under the domain of another, may be so free as to have a right to command others in a new and distinct empire, everyone that is born under the dominion of another may be so free."[71] Likewise, if anyone can start a kingdom, this "plainly prove[s] that it was not the natural right of the father, descending to his heirs, but made governments in the beginning."[72] Still, though political authority might not be a prerogative based in natural right, Locke also saw that some political societies are patriarchal, and reproduced through kinship principles.[73] Locke, then, is writing two contradictory histories of political development: one is about consent and the other is about kinship. The patriarchal kinship model is utterly persuasive, consistent with the lineage principle at the root of the reproduction of all political societies. There is no confusion as to why Locke would take note of this. What requires close attention is Locke's insistence as well that the **consent** of individuals was an historical device used to establish political societies. Locke offers an account of what one might see in a political society that truly was separate from familial patterns of authority and membership. It is as logically coherent as it is untrue to the actual dynamics of political societies.

Since a state[74] is something people join, he argues, whereas a family is something into which they are born, we ought to have different principles for obligation associated with each of these.

> For if an *English-man's* Son, born in *France*, be at liberty, and may [unite himself to France], 'tis evident there is no Tye upon him by his Father being a Subject of this Kingdom; nor is he bound by any *Compact of his ancestors.*[75]

---

[71] Locke, II, §113.

[72] Ibid., II, §115.

[73] Jeremy Waldron reconciles these two accounts by emphasizing the importance of Locke's characterization of even patriarchal arrangements as ultimately subject to consent, which is to say, the tacit consent of children to their parents ("John Locke: Social Contract Versus Political Anthropology" *Review of Politics* [Winter 1989] 51, pp. 3–28).

[74] Locke does use the word 'state' II, §45, §66, §218.

[75] II, §118. I want to defer until Chapter 3 discussion of the empirically misleading aspects of Locke's claim, rightly mentioned by Laslett's footnote: "In Locke's day as in our own, a

The French-born son of an English-man is not obligated to be English or to follow any other compacts made by his ancestors, on the one hand. But on the other hand, perhaps anticipating Leslie Stephen's worry that "this paragraph leads straight to anarchy,"[76] Locke goes on to offer a substantial caveat: "[S]ufficient Declaration of a Man's consent" is the only mechanism that can make him "*subject* to the Laws of any Government," but being a "subject" is not a prerequisite for being obligated to follow the laws. Consent for purposes of legitimate authority can be inferred from a non-member's "Possession or Enjoyment, of any part of the Dominions of any Government." The French-born son may not be English, but as long as he is hanging out in England, he needs to obey English rules. This obligation is a result of what Locke calls "tacit consent." Tacit consent is expressed by activities ranging from possession of land to "Lodging only for a Week" to "travelling freely on the Highway."[77]

Rightly focused on Locke's also salient question about legitimacy within the "Dominions of any Government," critics of tacit consent have not explored in depth the implications of the disjunction Locke proposes between individual obligation and membership.[78] Not only is it the case that tacit consent obligates, but interestingly, it obligates without making one a member. The focus of inquiry into tacit consent has been on the legitimacy of the government that commands without one's explicit consent, and not on the legitimacy of its exclusions despite the offer of explicit consent. In addition to asking why Locke bothers with consent, the reciprocal question is why Locke thinks membership important. If everyone is obligated, then why does it matter that some are members by explicit consent and others are not? Tacit consent averts anarchy—by compelling obedience—but it "*makes not a Man a member of that Society.*"[79] Locke continues:

> Nothing can make any Man so, but his actual entering into it by positive Engagement, and Express Promise and Compact. This is that, which I think, concerning the beginning of Political Societies, and that Consent which makes any one a Member of any Commonwealth.[80]

---

child of British subjects born in France was a British citizen, under the statute *De natis ultra mare* of 25 Edward III, and it was decided by a case of 1627 that either the father or mother would suffice." Laslett also writes of Locke's claim about the lack of an English King's sovereignty over a child born in France: "This does not seem to have been a general rule" (p. 347).

[76] Ibid., p. 346.

[77] Ibid., II, §119.

[78] Waldron emphasizes the prerogatives of the sovereign that follow from tacit consent. I am interested in the significance of membership principles that provide for emigration but not for disobedience or immigration.

[79] Ibid., II, §122.

[80] Ibid.

This is a most peculiar claim, which Locke fails to support with any examples or serious argument.[81]

Locke, who generally shows facility with historical, contemporary, and biblical evidence, falls short here, and one imagines it is not by lack of effort. Against Filmer's interpretation of God's grant of patriarchal authority to Adam when Adam and Eve are being escorted from paradise, Locke drily counters, "This was not a time, when *Adam* could expect any Favors, any grant of Priviledges, from his offended Maker."[82] Nor was it a time when God was all that interested in the consent of either Adam or Eve. While Locke makes a theoretically convincing case against Filmer, that God granted the earth in common to all men, not Adam and his patriarchal successors,[83] it does not necessarily follow that the kingdoms and commonwealths that emerge do so, as Locke insists they do, by compact among individuals.[84]

Locke recognizes the objection that there are *"no Instances to be found in Story of a Company of Men independent and equal one amongst another, that met together, and in this way began and set up a Government."*[85] He responds that this is a flaw in recorded history: "For 'tis with *Commonwealths* as with particular Persons, they are commonly *ignorant of their own Births* and *Infancies.*" His own efforts to provide examples, drawn from "accidental Records" are Rome, Venice, Indians in America, Sparta, and ad hoc selections from the Bible.[86] But even these do not support Locke's claim; indeed, accidental records suggest the opposite. Rome has a famous autochthony story taken from the Greeks.[87] Venice was notorious for its exclusivity, allowing citizenship in its republic only to those whose family names were maintained in a city register.[88] Locke's example from America refers to "no Government at all" but provisional military leaders. How these "Troops" maintain themselves over time as the political society of "Cheriquanas" is not explained. Not once does Locke document individual consent as the mechanism by which individuals affiliate with one or another nation. "Recorded history" suggests that it is kinship rules of exogamy and endogamy that determine membership in what Peter Laslett refers to as " 'a wild

[81] Hume took issue with Locke on the grounds that political societies are founded by conquest and perpetuated through the threat of violence, but Hume is really describing governments. "Of the Original Contract," in *Essays: Moral, Political and Literary* (Indianapolis: Liberty Press, 1987), pp. 465–87.

[82] Locke, I, §45.

[83] Ibid., II, §29.

[84] Ibid., II, §115.

[85] Ibid., II, §100.

[86] Ibid., II, §100–103; II, §109.

[87] Livy, *Early History of Rome* (*Ab urbe condita*).

[88] Eco O. G. Haitsma Mulier, *The Myth of Venice and Dutch Republican Thought in the Seventeenth Century*, tr. Gerald Mora (Assen: Van Gorcum, 1980), p. 11.

tribe in forests to the east of the Andes'."[89] The establishment of a city, Tarentum, by Palantus in the eighth century B.C. may well be a founding moment of the sort Locke describes, but only because subsequent generations maintained the institutions and sovereignty "Tarentum." Without later "Tarentums" Palantus would have established only a temporary military campsite, not a political territory. And finally, the Bible is not the place to find stories of freely given consent, but rather, tribes and nations that follow from patrilineal descent. Apparently Locke is not explaining the form of political *membership* or political society, but the founding of this or that *government*—in the Weberian sense of the institutions with a monopoly on the legitimate use of force. Hence his efforts to infer subsequent rules for membership from the founding rules for establishing government fall short.

Especially after Locke himself has noted that the Israelites did not depend on consent for membership, to write that the establishment of political society by consent "has been the practice of the World from its first beginning to this day" [90] seems somewhat disingenuous. Eco Mulier's point about Venice historiography during the period in which Locke writes is instructive:

> Without the conviction that Venice had always lived in freedom, able to defend its existence and actively create its own institutions, the later idealization of the perfection of those institutions would have been impossible.[91]

Inventing a history of people who became members out of choice was a strategy for justifying that practice in the present. Hume says as much as well, when he observes that monarchs believe their subjects are their property, and that, but for exposure to the inventions of social contract thought, the subjects would believe this as well.[92]

Locke's origin stories are those of a strategic consensualism, no more historically accurate and no less politically embedded than contemporary origin stories associated with what Gayatri Spivak calls "strategic essentialism."[93] Covenant in the Hebrew Bible works in a manner opposite from

---

[89] Locke, II, §102; Laslett, II, §102, note 3.

[90] Locke, II, §116.

[91] Mulier, *Myth of Venice*, p. 6.

[92] Hume, "Contract," p. 446.

[93] *The Post-Colonial Critic: Interviews, Strategies, Dialogues* (New York: Routledge, 1990), p. 11. Waldron also notes the inventiveness of Locke's account of consent but attributes this to Locke's reading of paternalism as a practice of "tacit consent." Characterizing Locke as an author of moral history, Waldron describes tacit consent as what legitimates children's obedience to the parents. This is a genuine moral principle, and not a contrivance to ensure everyone's obedience. The notion that Locke might render certain events through a post-hoc moral lens is methodologically intriguing, but because of the patriarchal context of this particular example, I am not convinced that this is what Locke is up to here. Waldron does

that described by Locke's consent model, a fact he himself acknowledges, although it would seem to greatly undermine his case. Locke uses Genesis and Exodus against Filmer, so it seems a rather shaky proposition to add an "excepting the Jews" proviso for his own account of political foundings.[94]

Regardless of historical infelicities, Locke's conceptual point is that without conventions of consent for membership, monarchies are either illegitimate political societies or not political societies at all.[95] Consent underlies a truly political society, whereas one cannot choose one's family. Hence the family/state analogy of Filmer and other theorists is unpersuasive and should be abandoned. For instance, the "power of life and death" afforded the sovereign is denied the father.[96] Although such a dichotomy might be expected to result in an argument for women's political equality, a central lacuna of Locke's challenge to patriarchy is the absence of any serious discussion of women's exclusion from political society.[97] Pateman has pointed out that if only men consent to political rule then it should follow that women are not obligated to obey the laws. Her broader narrative suggests the exclusion is not incidental to social contract theory, but a central component in a plot of fraternal regicide. While such an account of the actual bourgeois revolutions in England and France is persuasive,

---

not explain how we are to reconcile this notion of tacit consent with Locke's explicit exclusion of children from the prerogative of consent. Also, there is the difficulty of collapsing the *fact* of a practice (that children do oblige) with their *consent*. The reading highlights the difficulties with Locke's concept of tacit consent, making it virtually impossible to distinguish a practice that survives because of consent from those that endure through necessity or coercion. And what about birth? It is precisely because birth cannot be a decision rule for consent that Locke excludes it from being a basis of membership. Hence it is unclear why a familial role, also determined by birth to this or that parent, could be a matter of consent. Finally, what about daughters, whose obligation to obey does not approach the threshold of even tacit consent? They are unable to participate in the intergenerational exchange of tacit consent and obligation, which is the moral basis of this practice, according to Waldron.

[94] Locke, II, §102.

[95] In one place Locke says an absolutist monarchy is "inconsistent with civil society, and so can be no form of civil government at all" because it leaves one person unconstrained by the majority (II, §90, §91). Elsewhere Locke recognizes earlier absolutist regimes, in which sovereignty lay with the father founded on their children's trust, writing that "in the beginning [men] generally pitched upon this form" (II, §106). Locke refers to these kingdoms as "commonwealths" and "governments," although his earlier definitions require a prior moment of consent to establish a civil (i.e., political) society and would thus imply these regimes are not those of civil societies, but are still in the state of nature.

[96] Locke, II, §86.

[97] At the same time Hobbes and Locke do go out of their way to challenge prevailing ideas about gender. Hobbes weighs in against naturalist justifications of patriarchy—based on inferences of men's superior strength—by pointing out that the Amazons posed a force with which men had to reckon (*Leviathan* [London: Penguin, 1985], p. 254). And Locke offers perhaps the first serious intellectual blow to Pythagorean and other ancient justifications of patrilineal descent when he writes that children owe a greater debt to their mothers than their fathers because all fathers do is provide a little sperm (I, §54, §55).

Locke's political theory is not an obvious site for reading such an event. Unlike Aristotle, Locke does not set out consent, either in practice or metaphorically, as an exclusively masculine or patriarchal convention. While there are references to "freemen" and "liberty," it is too far a stretch to see these as symptoms of a specifically masculine craving for autonomy or a rejection of social conventions. Indeed one might easily read his justifications, muted as they are, of the patriarchal family as a means of insulating the political sphere from metaphors of sexual domination. Locke's point is that one can concede sexual inequality in the family, in private, and this bears no implications for inequality in political society. Though women are not given the franchise in the seventeenth century, nothing in Locke's writings precludes such a possibility. Locke's dichotomization of the family and political society challenges the Aristotelian synecdochal organicism of sixteenth-century social contract theorists. Inequality in the family does not mean or require inequality in political society.[98]

The more serious difficulty in Locke's and other consent theories of membership is their silence as to what this consent might look like for a "second generation"-s obligation, or for anyone else who may want to join a political society subsequent to its founding. Locke requires unanimous consent for the establishment of a political society that will be governed "by the will and determination of the majority."[99] This proposition thus seems to speak to the principle that would explain obligation for subsequent members, who will likewise be governed. Locke's theory of consent as requisite to obligation, even a theory of tacit consent, can be rendered coherent.[100] Thus I want to leave aside this line of criticism. The problem

---

[98] Locke writes: "But the Husband and Wife, though they have but one common Concern, yet having different understandings, will unavoidably sometimes have different wills too; it therefore being necessary, that the last determination, i.e., the Rule, should be placed somewhere, it naturally falls to the Man's share, as the abler and stronger. But this, reaching but to the things of their common Interest and Property, leaves the Wife in the full and free possession of what by Contract is her peculiar Right, and gives the Husband no more power over her Life, than she has over his," II, §82.

For competing interpretations, see Lorenne M. G. Clark, "Who Owns the Apples in the Garden of Eden?" in *The Sexism of Social and Political Theory: Women and Reproduction from Plato to Nietzsche*, Lorenne M. G. Clark and Lynda Lange, eds. (Toronto, Buffalo: University of Toronto Press, 1979), pp. 16–40; Alison Jagger, *Feminist Politics and Human Nature* (Sussex: Harvester Press, 1983), pp. 28–30; Linda Nicholson, *Gender and History: The Limits of Social Theory in the Age of the Family* (New York: Columbia University Press, 1986).

[99] Locke, II, §96. Hobbes writes: "A *Common-wealth* is said to be *Instituted*, when a *Multitude* of men do Agree, and *Covenant, every one, with every one*, that to whatsoever *Man*, or *Assembly of Men*, shall be given by the major part, the *Right* to *Present* the Person of them all. . ." *Leviathan*, p. 228.

[100] For a reading of tacit consent's meaning in the context of seventeenth century politics, see my "The Reasonableness of John Locke's Majority," *Political Theory*, 24 (August, 1996), pp. 423–63.

with the "next generation"-s tacit consent is not that it mystifies an otherwise straightforward requirement that members obey the reigning sovereign. The problem is that Locke divorces conditions of political membership from terms of political obligation. It is clear in his argument that
everyone who simply lives in England must obey the English sovereign;
but it is unclear how one person and not another becomes English, and
what this Englishness implies (if anything) about one's political status.

Locke describes a market mechanism for the establishment and continuity of government. According to the rules Locke sets forth, a common-
wealth that people did not like would be diminished along the lines of
generational replacement. As males coming of age moved to the jurisdictions they thought better, they would abandon the government that did
not satisfy them.

> *The Obligation* any one is under, by Virtue of such Enjoyment, *to submit to the*
> *Government, begins and ends with the Enjoyment*; so that whenever the Owner,
> who has given by such a *tacit Consent* to the Government, will, by Donation,
> sale or otherwise, quit the said Possession, he is at liberty to go and incorporate
> himself into any other Commonwealth, or to agree with others to begin a new
> one, in *vacuis locis*, in any part of the world, they can find free and unpossessed.[101]

The displacement here is generational because once the individuals have
expressly consented to join a political society, they cannot withdraw their
consent at a later date.[102] An oath binds for life, and all of those born in
"the realme" were required to swear allegiance to the king when they
turned 21.[103] The exception is if the government fails to live up to its end
of the bargain, an event that renders all deals null and void, returning
society to the state of nature.[104]

At this point these unencumbered individuals would make a pact amongst
themselves to establish a new political society. They would move to another
part of the world, one without an existing sovereign. Or perhaps they would
simply secede peacefully—whether the political society Locke envisions is
based on territory or simple allegiance to a sovereign is unclear.[105] Or they

---

[101] Ibid., II, §114.

[102] Ibid., II, §121.

[103] Kettner, *Development of American Citizenship*, p. 18.

[104] Locke, II, §90. Locke's opening history of groups of people withdrawing from one
kingdom to establish another would not conform with the lifetime oath requirement, unless
a number of people prior to the age of consent, in the same or in different political societies,
signaled ahead their intention not to expressly consent to the society of their current residence.
They would need to defer giving their consent until a number of similarly minded individuals,
sufficient for the establishment of a new political society, had come of age.

[105] Locke says governments have jurisdiction over territory, including over those not members of the territory (II, §121). But he does not specify, in his section on the beginnings of
political societies, that by definition political societies are territorial (II, §95). This seemingly

would affiliate themselves en masse or as individuals with other commonwealths. While Locke is clear about the possibilities for individuals to
withdraw from the political society of their residence and offer their
consent elsewhere, none of these principles establish the conditions under
which existing sovereigns are to accept new members. Locke's membership
principle of explicit consent is only a condition for **exit**. It provides a way
out of being a subject, but not a way out of being obligated to obey rules
in the country in which one resides. Further, Locke does not provide a
rule for deciding who should belong, and hence be able to possess land
and political rights in a particular society. By formulating consent as a
membership rule that allows for exit, Locke entirely ignores problems
of exclusion.

An individual may withhold consent, but what of a sovereign? Locke
says that people are at "liberty to go and incorporate . . . into any other
Commonwealth," but must a sovereign allow membership to all those who
offer their consent? Perhaps not, but the conditions of the sovereign's
refusal, or the requirements to accept all comers, are not laid out. This is
a strange omission. During the period in which Locke wrote, the problem
of entrance into another community or parish was more pressing than
that of exit, which receives no political notice whatsoever.

A. C. Beier notes the relevance of vagabondage to sixteenth and seventeenth century British political thought,[106] but Locke was apparently immune to this particular context. Similar to contemporary international
immigration restrictions, the laws that prohibited movement from one
parish or borough to another prompted careful scrutiny of the juridical
status of newcomers upon entry to a new place, not exit from one's previous
place of residence:

> A statute of 1388 required passports, or 'letters of testimonials,' of servants
> leaving masters, able-bodied pilgrims, wandering beggars, university students
> and persons returning from abroad . . . Tudor and Stuart governments kept the
> requirement . . . because of their pre-occupation with public order.[107]

"Vagabounds" were to be restricted to their parishes of birth:

> to the end that they should not scatter abroad [to other parts of England] and,
> by begging here and there, annoy both town and country. . . . [I]f they refuse

---

would allow a band of 18-year-old men residing in England to form a nomadic political
society that would impose a variety of rules on its members, even as they would be compelled
to obey the property rules of the English, or any other sovereign in whose territory they
were to live.

[106] *Masterless Men: The Vagrancy Problem in England, 1560-1640* (London and New York:
Methuen, 1985), p. xx.

[107] Ibid., p. 154.

to be supported by this benefit of law and will rather endeavor, by going to afro, to maintain their idle trades, then are they . . . instead of courteous refreshing at home . . . often convicted with sharp execution and whip of justice abroad.[108]

The standard punishment, "if he happen to be convicted for vagabound" is that he is "immediately adjudged to be grievously whipped and burned through the gristle of the right ear with an hot iron of the compass of an inch about, as a manifestation of his wicked life."[109] The third time one is convicted of this crime, the penalty is death. These Poor Laws stay in place through the seventeenth century. Christopher Hill explains that the "effect must have been widely felt in Claywroth, Nottinghamshire," where "over sixty percent of the population disappeared between 1676 and 1688."[110] Hill continues: "These villages may not have been typical, but it was a pretty foot-loose society so far as the unpropertied were concerned. No wonder Francis Quarles tells us that the poor feared to have children."[111]

In a similar vein, Marx writes:

> Simultaneously with the beginning of manufactures there was a period of vaga- bondage . . . connected with the disintegration of the feudal system . . . These vagabonds were so numerous that, for instance, Henry VIII of England had 72,000 of them hanged. . . .[112]

Locke was clearly aware of all this. The problem of the vagrant poor had not diminished, and in 1697 as a Trade and Plantations Commissioner, Locke endorsed a plan first broached under Elizabeth. He recommended "for the more effectual restraining of idle vagabonds" that "all men sound of limb and mind, above fourteen and under fifty years of age, begging in maritime counties out of their own parish without a pass . . . be sent to

---

[108] William Harrison, *The Description of England* (1587; rpt. Ithaca: Cornell University Press, 1968), p. 181. Clearly the worry about vagabonds is about internal migration, about how English communities were to respond to those arriving from other parishes: "The worthy ones forsake the realme for altogether and seek to live in other countries, as France, Germany, Barbary, India, Moscovia, and very Calicut, complaining of no room to be left for them at home" (ibid., p. 182).

[109] Christopher Hill, *Reformation to Industrial Revolution* (Middlesex: Penguin, 1969), p. 185.

[110] Ibid., p. 41.

[111] Ibid., p. 60. Ogg supports this account as well: ". . . there is no large section of English society nowadays which can reasonably assume that most of its members are likely to die on the scaffold; whereas in the past this was considered, for some classes, not an assumption, but almost a certainty" (*England in the Reigns of James II and William III*, pp. 101–2).

[112] *German Ideology* (Moscow: Progress Publishers, 1976), p. 77. The editor's note indicates Marx's source as Harrison, *Description of England*. Harrison cites Girolama Cardano (1501–76) as his source. Cardano, in a horoscope of Edward VI, cites the Bishop of Lisieux as his authority. The editor of a modern edition of Harrison's *Description of England* writes, "The figure is clearly inflated" (Harrison, p. 193, note 8). And yet the vagabond penalties in the late sixteenth century were severe enough for Harrison to find Cardono believable.

the next seaport town, there to be kept at hard labour, till some of his majesty's ships, coming in or near there, give an opportunity of putting them on board, where they shall serve three years, under strict discipline...and be punished as deserters if they go on shore without leave." The importance of these passes is further emphasized when Locke advises that "whoever shall counterfeit a pass shall lose his ears for the forgery the first time . . . and the second time . . . shall be transported to the plantations."[113] On the one hand, Locke acknowledges the problem of migration is so bad that the only way to staunch movement is to put people out to sea. On the other hand, his political theory of membership is entirely oblivious to the real problem of immigration. The theory of membership instrumental to Locke's account of obligation does justice to neither the historical nor contemporaneous problems posed by mobility in England.

Hegel's Theory of Political Membership

Brubaker is right to note that liberal political theory does not adequately engage in the problem of membership,[114] but not all modern political theory is "liberal." Hegel, in particular, is a philosopher with a great deal to say about birth in relation to citizenship, as well as about the function of citizenship in relation to the reproduction of the state.[115] Against social contract thought, which advocates "private judgment, private willing, and private conscience" as the conditions of membership and obligation,[116] Hegel writes:

> What is of the utmost importance is that the law of reason should be shot through and through by the law of particular freedom, and that my particular end should become identified with the universal end, or otherwise the state is left in the air. The state is actual only when its members have a feeling of their own self-hood and it is stable only when public and private ends are identical.[117]

According to Hegel, the state's actualization occurs only when the interests of people in civil society—as family members, workers, church-goers, and

---

[113] ("Board of Trade Papers, 1697" quoted in Henry Fox Bourne, *The Life of John Locke*, [1876] vol. 2. [Darmstadt: Scientia Verlag Aalen, 1969], pp. 379, 380).

[114] Brubaker, *Citizenship and Nationhood*, p. 32.

[115] The implicit characterization of Hegel as a conservative nationalist has its skeptics. For a discussion of this, see: Shlomo Avineri, *Hegel's Theory of the Modern State* (London, Cambridge: Cambridge University Press, 1972) and Walter Kaufmann, ed., *Hegel's Political Philosophy* (New York: Atherton, 1970), especially the essays by Karl Popper and Avineri.

[116] *Philosophy of Right*, tr. T. M. Knox, (1821; rpt. London and New York: Oxford University Press, 1967), §280.

[117] Ibid., §268 addition.

so forth—come to be identified with those of the state. Unlike Locke, Hegel does not begin by conceptualizing the formation of political societies in relation to individuals' aggregated consent, or by theorizing the movement of individuals among already existing states. Hegel sees the problem of political membership as intrinsically connected to the underlying logic that makes possible distinct states. He believes that this very plurality of political societies is itself conceptually linked to the ways that individuals become members of them.[118]

Hegel insists that his concept of the state refers to membership, not participation. He writes that the "recent" use of the idea of the " 'sovereignty of the people' is that it is opposed to the sovereignty existent in a monarch."[119] Hegel rejects this portrayal of the problem of representation—a crucial aspect of theories of participation. It misleads, he writes, because a "people" depends on the existence of the state as a membership organization:

> [As] opposed to the sovereignty of the monarch, the sovereignty of the people is one of the confused notions based on the wild idea of the 'people' [Volk]. Taken without its monarch and the articulation of the whole which is the indispensable and direct concomitant of monarchy, the people is a formless mass and no longer a state.[120]

This is no chicken-egg disagreement over whether first there is a monarch and then a people or vice-versa. Hegel's point is that social contract thought focuses on individual participation, and that this neglects problems of membership, which is what makes possible the participation of individuals in a particular society in the first place. To secure people in their identity Hegel sets out a monarch as necessary for an actual state. If "the 'people' is represented . . . as an inwardly developed, genuinely organic, totality, then sovereignty is there as the personality of the whole, and this personality, is there, in the real existence, adequate to its concept, as the person of the monarch."[121] The Hobbesian Leviathan is an "artificial," metaphorical personality, but the Hegelian sovereign has a "real existence." This formulation eliminates the paradoxes of, say, compulsory military service that requires individuals to forsake the very preservation of their lives which prompted consent to the sovereign in the first instance. The state is a personality. As a part of that personality one would vanish—like the arm

---

[118] Hobbes and Locke address the problem of the relation between the individual and a particular political society. Relations among political societies remain, for both, in the state of nature, and hence, given their frameworks, unresolved (Hobbes, *Leviathan*, p. 187; Locke, II, §145).

[119] Hegel, *Philosophy of Right*, §279.

[120] Ibid.

[121] Ibid.

on the dead Aristotelian corpse—if that body, that personality is annihilated in war. Military service, according to Hegel, is necessary to preserve one's identity because each individual is organically connected to the individuality of the state.[122]

To the question of how a particular person attains the determinate affiliation with the state, becomes the hand sustained in relation to the body, Hegel provides a more convincing account than that offered by Locke. Birth, not consent, according to Hegel, joins one to a political organization. Marriage is a key component of the connection: "Marriage, and especially monogamy, is one of the absolute principles on which the ethical life of a community depends. Hence marriage comes to be recorded as one of the moments in the founding of states by gods or heroes."[123] In a telling presentation of parallels and differences among the forms of being wrought by birth, state affiliation, marriage, and contract, Hegel places certain moments of marriage and contract under the rubric of choice and contingency, while birth, marriage as an ethical-legal relation, and state membership are moments of necessity and determinacy. Contractual relations, Hegel tells us, occur among equals, an "origin which marriage too has in common with contract." He continues:

> But the case is quite different with the state; it does not lie with an individual's arbitrary will to separate himself from the state because we are already citizens of the state by birth . . . Permission to enter a state or leave it must be given by the state; this then is not a matter which depends on an individual's arbitrary will and therefore the state does not rest on contract, for contract presupposes arbitrariness.[124]

[122] 'Individuality', 'personality', and 'identity' in English translations of Hegel's work are connected in ways that may seem unidiomatic. Hegel's 'Individualität' and 'Einzelheit' have meanings similar to that of 'identity' as used by students of "identity politics." All have uses that suggest a group designation for an individual or a collectivity (e.g., §7, §126, §259 addition, §271, §280). This use of 'individuality' or, better, 'oneness', for Einzelheit, suggests none of the connotations of 'individualism', which implies a complete disregard for the existence of others, and does not speak to the position of a state. For this reason, Hegel's use of 'Individualität' resonates in contemporary Anglo problems of identity. One can substitute 'identity' for 'Individualität' in the above sentence and the meaning would be idiomatic and consistent with Hegel's framework, although 'Individualität' has a better etymological claim to use here than 'identity' or 'Identität'. 'Individualität' is from the Latin *indiuiduus*, which is *in-*, "not," + *diuiduus*, "divisible from," which connotes a relational framework. 'Identity' is from the Latin *idem*, which means simply "the same," which is how Hegel uses Identität (Partridge, *Origins: A Short Etymological Dictionary of Modern English*, 4th ed. [New York: MacMillan, 1966]. pp. 160, 304).

[123] *Philosophy of Right*, §167 remark.

[124] Ibid.

One may decide to enter this or that contract on a whim. But this is not how one joins a state (by birth) or enters into a real marriage, according to Hegel. Marriage as well as citizenship overcome the contingencies of contract by virtue of their association with the state: "Marriage . . . is an ethico-legal (*rechtliche-sittliche*) love, and this eliminates marriage from the transient, fickle, and purely subjective aspects of love."[125] Likewise, the sheer fact of a monarch's status as hereditary (and not elected) provides the form of a state's determinacy. The people can never second-guess what they themselves did not choose.[126]

While Hegel astutely represents some of the chief features of the state's official ideology, the account taken as a whole is incoherent. It is one matter to present antinomies in mutually constituting discursive relations, but quite another to claim that two mutually exclusive positions are both simultaneously true. Hegel is not content to allow marriage to gain meaning strictly from its recognition by the state; he also claims a biological basis for marriage's objectification, the same biological dynamic that elsewhere Hegel says has nothing to do with politics. But this biological relation is no different from what binds mating animals. Hegel disparages feelings that follow from embodied impulses as merely reflexes, as unselfconscious, vulgar, and, in keeping with his gendered metonymies elsewhere, as feminine.[127] By laying equal stress on the natural, blood ties through which marriage is objectified and the ethical character that distinguishes marriage from sex, Hegel accurately portrays the ideological temper of his (and our) time. But there is a difference between a very good description of prevailing fetishes, and a thoroughgoing account that attends to the underlying dynamics constitutive of these competing meanings.

Hegel does not reconcile the ways that marriage is determinate by virtue of biology with the political and ethical dimensions of the relation. As other critics have noted, women remain the unresolved term in his dialectic,[128] perennially outside his state by virtue of the very blood ties that supposedly render marriage determinate. Kelly Oliver observes: "The family, then, is in the paradoxical position of both challenging rational moral judgements and giving birth to rational moral judgment, challenging the nation and

---

[125] Ibid., §161 addition.

[126] Ibid., §280.

[127] Ibid., §166 addition.

[128] Benjamin Barber, "History's Owl, Spirit's Phoenix and the Incoherence of Dialectics in Hegel's Account of Women," *Political Theory* 16 (February, 1988), pp. 5–28; Kelly Oliver, "Antigone's Ghost: Undoing Hegel's *Phenomenology of Spirit*, *Hypatia* 11 (1), (Winter, 1996), pp. 67–90. Luce Irigaray writes: "The weakest link in [Hegel's] system seems to be the level of his interpretation of spirit and right within the family. Hegel, who always tries to break down every non-differentiated unity, does not succeed in thinking the family other than as *one* substance in which individuals lose their rights as particulars" (The Necessity for Sexuate Rights," in *The Irigaray Reader*, ed. Margaret Whitford (Oxford, Cambridge: Blackwell, 1991), p. 198.

giving birth to the nation."[129] The easy route of resolution, available in other Hegelian antinomies, is denied because Hegel is so adamant about the mutually exclusive aspects of family ties by blood and political ties fostered by ethical commitment. The contradiction is between the two forms—both of which Hegel claims to be ultimate and foundational—as well as between Hegel's simultaneous contempt for and celebration of the blood ties of family.

Hegel recognizes three forms of heterosexual relations. Either sex is purely a matter of physical desire or love—both of which are contingent and therefore unsuitable for the state—or it exists in a marriage relation.[130] The marriage relation is determinate and objective, he explains here, not because it is a contract made under the supervision of the state, and not because of a couple's love, "because even if their feeling is their substantial unity, still this unity has no objectivity." He says here that children are what make a marriage: "Such an objectivity parents first acquire in their children, in whom they can see objectified the entirety of their union."[131] In the *Phenomenology* Hegel had written something similar: "This relationship has its actual existence not in itself but in the child—an 'other', whose coming into existence is the relationship, and is also that in which the relationship itself gradually passes away; and this alternation of successive generations has its enduring basis in the nation."[132] Hence, the bond between a married couple—the founding bond of the state—is made real by birth and its role in the nation, a nation which seems here to be a big family. The proof and embodiment of the ethical marriage tie on this account is not the state's recognition, but the brute fact of birth. Birth constitutes a relationship by the very ties of blood that Hegel elsewhere says need to be renounced in order to achieve full citizenship—a lesson Antigone's feminine nature leaves her unable to grasp.[133]

Hegel's "history" of the family's development into civil society,[134] told just at the transition to the section "Civil Society," has much in common with the accounts offered by Locke, Hume, and Rousseau.[135] The difference

---

[129] Oliver, "Antigone's Ghost," p. 70.

[130] *Philosophy*, §167, §168.

[131] Ibid., §168 addition.

[132] *Phenomenology*, p. 273. Hegel makes a similar claim in the *Philosophy of Right*: "The expansion of the family, as its transition into a new principle, is in the external world sometimes its peaceful expansion until it becomes a people, i.e., a nation, which thus has a common natural origin, or sometimes the federation of scattered groups of families under the influence of an overlord's power or as a result of a voluntary association produced by the tie of needs and the reciprocity of their satisfaction" (§181 remark).

[133] *Phenomenology*, pp. 274–75.

[134] Hegel's "civil society" (bürgerliche Gesselschaft) includes government institutions.

[135] Locke writes, "The first society was between man and wife. . ." and then shows how this leads to "political society." Hume writes: "Most fortunately, therefore, there is conjoined to those necessities, whose remedies are remote and obscure, another necessity, which having

is that Hegel's dialectic explicitly acknowledges the juridical aspect to the family. Hegelian marriage overcomes an ontologically natural relation. And yet at the same time, the family is natural, mere existence, in contradiction with the ethical community: "Being natural self-knowledge, knowledge of self on the basis of nature and not on that of ethical life [the husband and wife relation] merely represents and typifies in a figure the life of spirit, and not spirit itself actually realized."[136] Man and woman, copulating and reproducing, are swept away by natural relations they do not control. By posing a contrast between sex as natural and sex as political, Hegel reinstantiates the view that heterosexual monogamy is natural and marriage its political effect. Judith Butler rightly criticizes such dichotomies for producing the very effects they portend to discover. "[S]ex-as-matter, sex-as-instrument-of-cultural-signification . . . is a discursive formation that acts as a naturalized foundation for the nature/culture distinction and the strategies of domination that the distinction supports."[137] (Of course in the case of Hegel, the accusation that his categories serve as discursive strategies of domination, not simple observations, might be the highest compliment one could give him.)

Ultimately, and incoherently, man and woman are the only subject positions in Hegel's philosophy that can be reduced to the same nature that the rest of his philosophical edifice utterly undermines and overcomes. When it comes to the family, the systematic privileging of ethical relations over natural ones in Hegel's oeuvre as a whole turns into an ad hoc misogynist set of justifications for keeping women out of politics. On the whole one learns that membership in political society has something to do with birth and marriage, but Hegel's quick resort to nature as the basis of these obscures a more careful understanding of these arrangements. By viewing the role of "nature" in the reproduction of political societies as universal, necessary, and ahistorical, Hegel is unable to account for the difference between species reproduction and the intergenerationality of a particular political society.

---

a present and more obvious remedy, may justly be regarded as the first and original principle of human society. This necessity is none other than that natural appetite betwixt the sexes." And Rousseau states, "The oldest of all societies, and the only natural one, is that of the family. . . . The family may therefore perhaps be seen as the first model of political societies." In his "Origins of Inequality" Rousseau's story line comes closest to that of Hegel, but while Rousseau's family is there by artifice—in contrast with the biological reproduction among savages who anonymously procreate in a state of nature—the constitution of the family is explained by vague gestures toward culture and morality, not laws (Locke, *Treatise*, II, §77; Hume, *A Treatise of Human Nature* [New York: Dolphin Press, 1961], p. 438; Rousseau, *The Social Contract* [New York: Penguin Books, 1968], p. 50).

[136] *Phenomenology*, p. 474.

[137] *Gender Trouble: Feminism and the Subversion of Identity* (New York: Routledge, 1993), p. 37.

Hegel's and Durkheim's Model of "Religious" Membership

Although specifically religious institutions have played a large role in the ideologies and practices of marriage, this topic has been left aside until now for two reasons. First, unlike affiliations of family role, nationality, ethnicity, or race, those of religious identity develop in a very different way, out of a dialectical tension with (rather than direct reproduction of) the birth invocations associated with membership in political societies. It seemed best to begin to explain the dynamics of membership in political societies before proceeding to an account of religious membership. Second, Hegel and Durkheim offer very different understandings of what counts as a religion, and it seemed sensible to commence inquiry into religion, albeit briefly at this point, by comparing Durkheim's and Hegel's views on the relation between religions and membership rules for political society.[138]

Hegel's work implicitly gives rise to questions about the dynamic between political society and religion that are presented in a more explicit, though still unresolved, context in Emile Durkheim's *Elementary Forms of Religious Life* [1912]. Hegel believes that religions contain doctrines of morality and truth, but these remain abstract. Only when the state institutionalizes these ideas do they become worldly and actual. The oaths of the church,

> like the marriage bond, entail that inner permeation and elevation of *sentiment* which acquires its deepest confirmation through religion. But since ethical ties are in essence ties within the actual rational order, the first thing is to affirm within that order the rights which it involves. Confirmation of these rights by the church is secondary and is only the inward, comparatively abstract, side of the matter.[139]

Religion is the discourse of churches, and the ethical ties religion produces will be concrete only through their recognition by the state, according to Hegel. Hegel's religion is abstract as well as transcendent. Religion is to the membership rules for a particular state—including those that follow from marriage—as the idea of music is to an orchestra. Music requires the presence of notes, as well as musicians to play them, just as religion requires doctrine and worshipers. The organizational rules and conductor that make an orchestra out of an otherwise random group of musicians are like the state that makes coherent a disparate group for spiritual fulfillment.

---

[138] Chapter 6 contains an extended discussion of religion.
[139] *Philosophy of Right*, §270 remarks.

Durkheim: Political Society as a "Religion"

Whereas Hegel's notion of religion is that it is motivated by a truth that is remote, ethereal—a divine spirit that is everywhere and nowhere—Durkheim describes religion as always already identical with the concrete practices of a society that is expressing its particularity as such. That is, Hegel's religion exists as a dialectical inspiration and grounding of a political society, while Durkheim's religion is that political society itself, not because all political societies have separate organized religions associated with them, but because the very form of inclusions and exclusions that political societies take, for their reproduction, requires what Durkheim refers to as a dichotomy between the sacred and the profane. So, whereas Hegel sees religion as something separate from political society, Durkheim defines religion as the sacred/profane distinctions that constitute a (political) society in its particularity. But this is not the whole story.

The *Elementary Forms of Religious Life* advocates the view that religion is also an intergenerational form of being. Durkheim opens *Elementary Forms* by describing "religious" life as consisting of rules for sacred/profane distinctions. After testing out competing definitions of religion—ruling out "magic," "superstition," and "bad science," among others—Durkheim initially settles on the following:

> All known religious beliefs, whether simple or complex, present one common characteristic: they presuppose a classification of all the things, real and ideal, of which men think, into two classes or opposed groups, generally designated by two distinct terms which are translated well enough by the words *profane* and *sacred* (*profane, sacre*).[140]

He later defines these terms:

> Sacred things are those which the interdictions protect and isolate; profane things, those to which these interdictions are applied and which must remain at a distance from the first. Religious beliefs are the representations which express the nature of sacred things and the relations which they sustain, either with each other or with profane things.[141]

These definitions would seem to make a "religion" of a variety of practices, ranging from high school football in Texas to an IBM business meeting, since both combine practices that are crudely instrumental with those that are ritualistic displays of toughness and power. However, when studying "primitive," "totemic" religion, Durkheim refines his definition so that

---

[140] Durkheim, *Elementary Forms of Religious Life*, tr. Joseph Swain (New York and London: Free Press, 1965), p. 52.

[141] Ibid., p. 56.

religion exists only and definitively in relation to the constitution and perpetuation of a certain kind of group, or society: "If religion has given birth to all that is essential in society, it is because the idea of society is the soul of religion."[142] As we shall see, Durkheim's definition of religion slips into a more general characterization of intergenerationality. When Durkheim looks for sacred/profane practices and group life, he finds intergenerationality (i.e., society) as the key feature characteristic of a religious society. Durkheim highlights details of the socially produced ideas about intergenerationality—a "religion"-s rules about membership. The rules for inclusion and exclusion, viewed as the chief objective of sacred/profane distinctions, are what Durkheim problematizes, as he questions the form of the intergenerational principles that reproduce societies.

Society establishes ideas about ancestry; that we even have ancestors as such depends on societies. Durkheim invites us to reflect on the various ways in which societies produce concepts of intergenerationality that then are reproduced in micro-practices of membership, in a particular "family" or "clan." This religion is the "most primitive one that is now observable and even, in all probably [*sic*], that has ever existed. In fact, it is inseparable from a social organization on a clan basis."[143] By writing that religion is a "social organization on a clan basis," Durkheim is not analogizing religions with societies, but effectively defining a religion as a political society. That is, many societies that are associated with wielding secular, profane power and authority—ranging from tribes to monarchies to republics—produce their memberships based on clan, or kinship, rules. Another way to put this is that modern France as well as the Arunta both fit Durkheim's definition of a religion.

Rather than distinguish religious from political relations, Durkheim collapses the two group forms. Durkheim's decision to classify tribes as "religious" groups and his reluctance to call them political societies is exemplary of the heuristic orientalism Clastre sees in works that treat "primitive" tribes as apolitical in juxtaposition to states as sites where power is institutionalized. Durkheim sees patterns in "primitive societies" that resemble those in "modern" France. "Primitive" societies cannot be truly "political" ones, such as France, on this rendering. The exoticized mystique of their "religious" practices attracts Durkheim's interest. But still the parallels to his own society are overwhelming. The effect of the constant analogizing is such that Durkheim seems to be equating "religious" with "political" relations. The parallel jars, because it suggests that the Arunta as a religious group must resemble the Catholics. Insofar as Durkheim has described membership rules for the Arunta that are the same as those

---

[142] Ibid., p. 466.
[143] Ibid., p. 194.

for France, the further unsettling inference is that the membership form
of France, for the metonymy to continue, is a version of the membership
form of the Catholic Church, an observation that is perhaps superficially
provocative but deeply unpersuasive. A better interpretation of Durkheim's
odd definition of secular political societies such as France as "religious" is
that he is noticing that political societies, like religions, invoke sacred/
profane distinctions in their membership rules. More particularly, Durkheim's work provokes thought on the ways that intergenerational patterns
of political societies' reproduction sacralize, in particular, sexuality and
birth. Durkheim shows how political societies constitute and are constituted by kinship relations, not individual consent, nature, or Geist.

Finding the idea of society as that which is at the heart of religion leads
Durkheim to examine the phenomena by which what he calls the "totemic
society" (which turns out to be all societies) is reproduced.[144] Chief among
these dynamics is not individual consent, aggregated individual beliefs, or
even physical proximity. Rather, invocations of birth are the terms of
membership and hence group continuity. Discussing initiation rites, Durkheim observes:

> It is said that at this moment the young man dies, that the person that he was
> ceases to exist, and that another is instantly substituted for it. He is re-born
> under a new form. Appropriate ceremonies are felt to bring about this death
> and re-birth, which are not understood in a merely symbolic sense, but are
> taken literally.[145]

Birth is linked to membership in totemic societies by virtue of a totem
thought to be shared among common ancestors: "The collective totem is
part of the civil status of each individual: it is generally hereditary; in any
case, it is birth which designates it, and the wish of men counts for nothing."[146] The "tribes" Durkheim studies "believe that the mythical heroes,
the founders of the clan reincarnate themselves periodically; *but this is in
human bodies only*; each birth, as we shall see, is the product of one of these
reincarnations."[147]

A skeptical, "scientific" response to this scenario might be that Durkheim
has made a methodological misstep in treating religious beliefs as real in
themselves. Perhaps recent studies in genetics might affirm the intuition
that there is an actual, i.e., biological, connection among members of
intergenerational families. One might hypothesize that beliefs about ancestral relations, expressed in a rather superstitious or naive manner among

[144] Ibid., p. 107.
[145] Ibid., p. 54.
[146] Ibid., p. 188.
[147] Ibid., p. 197.

the societies Durkheim studies, simply affirm an underlying biological truth. Rather than overlook this possibility, Durkheim confronts the scientistic, genetic view as itself a particular representation that is dependent on prior religious ones of the sort he describes. Beliefs about ancestral ties constitute ideas associated with what we might call "blood relations," not vice-versa:

> [T]he totems [of the Arunta] are attached neither to persons nor to determined groups of persons [like one's biological grandparents], but to localities. In fact, each totem has at its centre at some definite spot...The child has neither the totem of his father nor that of his mother, but the one whose centre is at the spot where the mother believes that she felt the first symptoms of approaching maternity.[148]

The totemic affiliations centered on kinship do not depend on biology. It is what Durkheim calls the religious (or perhaps better, the sacral) character of the group that promotes ideas about what counts as kinship, or family: "the primitive family organization cannot be understood before the primitive religious beliefs are known; for the latter serve as the basis of the former. This is why it is necessary to study totem as a religion before studying the totemic clan as a family group."[149] This order is required because what counts as a "totemic clan" is constituted by the society in which it is situated. The intergenerational family is a product of certain ideas generated by society, rather than the material basis of that society. And yet, the fact that the family is based on certain beliefs does not mean that families are pseudo-groups.

Just as scientists may not legitimately view their empirical paradigms as productive of irrefutable facts (and yet still take them to be real), there is every reason to take as real those experiences obtained through thought or ideas. Religion has been a concept that has invited a misguided distinction between "thought" and what is "real." Durkheim points out that the two cannot be so easily separated.[150] If people experience their beliefs as real, then they are real:

> The only question is to learn from what part of nature these realities come and what has been able to make men represent them under this singular form which is peculiar to religious thought. But if this question is to be raised, it is necessary to commence by admitting that they are real things which are thus represented.[151]

Of those who in the name of science treat religion as a series of "errors," Durkheim asks, "What sort of science is it whose principal discovery is

[148] Ibid., p. 209.
[149] Ibid., p. 126, note 24.
[150] Ibid., p. 234.
[151] Ibid., p. 87.

that the subject of which it treats does not exist?"[152] Durkheim's phenomenological premise is that "religious forces are real," *because* and not despite the fact that they are representations. He writes that all "consciousnesses ... express one and the same object, the world" and continues: "[A]s the world itself is only a system of representations, each particular consciousness is really only a reflection of the universal consciousness."[153] The categories of understanding themselves yield the world, not God, as Kant believes, and not Geist, as Hegel would have it: "[R]eligious forces are real, howsoever imperfect the symbols may be, *by the aid of which they are thought of.*"[154] These methodological commitments mark Durkheim's presentation of religion as one of a thoroughgoing phenomenology; he does not give us a history of religion as a series of mistakes, nor as a superstructure arising from other exigencies.

Durkheim inverts Hegel's reasoning from nature to political societies, by pointing out the extensive variation among political societies, in contrast to the repetitive, universal practice of sexual intercourse and birth. Rather than asserting that the universality of intercourse leading to children illustrates the objectification of a family (Hegel's argument), Durkheim takes the basic, underlying identity of biological reproduction as refutation of the argument that mating is the source of distinctively political societies' reproduction. It is not procreation per se that reproduces a political society as such, but the rules specific to the kinship form that makes possible a group's particularity.

Precisely because Durkheim observes tremendous variation in the ways that birth prompts totemic membership, he argues against the belief that political associations follow from the putatively natural site of parentage per se: "As Spence and Gillen declare for the Arunta, commerce of the sexes is in no way the determining condition of generation. ... Birth is due to the reincarnation of ancestral personage. ..."[155] This ancestral parentage is not a matter of nature.[156] The particularity of a group-specific totem enables an intergenerational association that creates and binds mem-

---

[152] Ibid., p. 88.

[153] Ibid., p. 306.

[154] Ibid., p. 234, emphasis added.

[155] Ibid., p. 287. Durkheim explains that "not the whole soul ... fertilize[s] the mother, but only an emanation from this soul" (p. 287, note 70).

[156] Of the Alcheringa, Durkheim continues: "In other words, the personality of the ancestor, his curinga and his nanja tree, are sacred things. . .So they transmute themselves into one another: in the spot where an ancestor lost his churinga, a sacred tree or rock has come out of the soil, just the same as in those places where he entered the ground himself. So there is a mythological equivalence of a person of the Alcheringa and his churinga; consequently, when the former throws a namatuna into the body of a woman, it is as if he entered into it himself" (ibid). The form of these sacred connections is what renders a child a member, and not the biological ties of the parents.

bers as ancestors and descendants. This does not mean that the totem is the exclusive source of group identity, while kinship rules and marriage are irrelevant. The point is simply that ancestry is not based in biological ties.

Durkheim documents a variety of practices by which ancestral souls or totemic beings enter into the unborn fetus or recently born child through the body of its mother. This entrance may depend on where the mother is when she conceives, what the mother recognizes as a totem when she realizes she is pregnant, or where the placenta has been buried. In addition to these possibilities, Durkheim notes that

> among the Gnanji, it is not necessarily near the oknanikilla that the conception takes place. But they believe that each couple is accompanied in its wanderings over the continent by a swarm of souls of the husband's totem. When the time comes, one of these souls enters the body of the wife and fertilizes it, wherever she may be.[157]

Practices of spiritual, ancestral fertilization serve to connect the children with the society into which they were born.

As Durkheim sees it, the intergenerational totem effects the continuity of the group in the face of the mortality and natality of its individuals. The group does not die when its members pass away, but rather reproduces itself via practices of intergenerationality mapped onto kinship relations:

> We have seen that the souls of new-born children are either emanations of the ancestral souls, or these souls reincarnated. But in order that they may either reincarnate themselves, or periodically give off new emanations, they must have survived their first holders. So it seems as though they admitted the survival of the dead in order to explain the birth of the living . . . Individuals die, but the clan survives. . . . there is something like a germinative plasm, of mystic order, which is transmitted from generation to generation and which makes or at least is believed to make, the spiritual unity of the clan through all time.[158]

These observations about the function of intergenerationally maintained totems apply, as Durkheim has begun to hint much earlier in the book, to a variety of societies. Modern political societies are also in fact totemic ones: "The soldier who dies for his flag, dies for his country; but as a matter of fact, in his own consciousness, it is the flag that has the first place. It sometimes happens that this even directly determines action."[159] The function of the national flag serves the same purpose for France as that of the animal or plant totems among Australian tribes. The totem is the

---

[157] Ibid., p. 281, note 49.
[158] Ibid., pp. 304–5.
[158] Ibid., p. 251.

symbol of a determined society called the clan. It is its flag; it is the sign by which each clan distinguishes itself from the others, the visible mark of its personality, a mark borne by everything which is a part of the clan under any title whatsoever . . . So if it is at once the symbol of the god and of the society, is that not because the god and the society are only one?[160]

The sentiment produced by the association of the individual with the totem "explains the Crusades, for example, or many of the scenes, either sublime or savage, of the French Revolution."[161] Continuing the comparison, Durkheim suggests further:

> This aptitude of society for setting itself up as a god or for creating gods was never more apparent than during the first years of the French Revolution. At this time, in fact, under the influence of the general enthusiasm, things purely laical by nature were transformed by public opinion into sacred things: these were the Fatherland, Liberty, and Reason.[162]

That these totemic alliances are of an intergenerational form among European nations, as well as among the nations he studies, is suggested when Durkheim writes that the "objective" basis of the sense of valor is thought to be peculiarly ancestral, "in the Roman *genius*, the individual totem, or the Alcheringa ancestor; and this is why they have survived, in various forms, up to the present day."[163] The analogy is as striking for what Durkheim captures as for what he overlooks. Whereas religions may be acquired through habits of devotion, and pursued, indeed intensified by vows of celibacy and renunciation of family ties, the Roman citizen or the French republican—as members of political societies—are such through their own births and through ensuring more progeny for the "Father-" or "Motherland."

Such analogies between rules described for the Alcheringa and those for France may trouble some, on the grounds that they reek of cultural imperialism. On this view Durkheim's accounts misconstrue the actual practices he undertakes to narrate, because he interprets them through those of his own, Western, taxonomies. Durkheim may share with other anthropologists culpability for representing the other in a manner that is

---

[160] Ibid., p. 236.

[161] Ibid., p. 241, and see 242.

[162] Ibid., pp. 244–45.

[163] Ibid., p. 317. Durkheim also writes: "Today we are beginning to realize that law, morals and even scientific thought itself were born of religion, were for a long time confounded with it, and have remained penetrated with its spirit" (87). And: "Students of American totemism had already known for a long time that this form of religion was most intimately united to a determined social organization, that its basis is the division of the social group into clans" (108), and that totemism has been usefully studied "both as a religion and as a legal institution" (108).

not true to their own self-understandings. However, it is quite easy, in reading Durkheim, to follow anthropologist Marilyn Strathern's instruction to make use of the ways that studies of the other convey the social structures and categories of the European investigator.[164] Durkheim's constant movement between Australian tribes and French politics—similar to the studies of Marcel Mauss and Claude Lévi-Strauss—makes it sensible to view his observations about the Alerchinga, for instance, as symptomatic of the anxieties of French intellectuals—about religion, society, the state, and the family. At this level of interpretation, it is not crucial to know whether the studies Durkheim relies on accurately portray the Alcheringa. Even if his accounts are questionable, they provide insights on practices of the French state. The murky boundary between anthropology as a way to learn about the other and anthropology as symptomatic—as a way of gaining insight into the practices of one's own context—is revealed in the translation of the original French title from *Les Formes Elémentaires de la vie religieuse: Le Système totémique en Australie* [1912] to simply *The Elementary Forms of Religious Life* [1915]. The English publisher infers and then implies that whatever is important about specifically Australian totemic practices can be universalized to speak to "religious life" *in toto*.

The ability to extrapolate from the categories of analysis for one group to the prevailing practices of the investigator's own group does not mean the societies are ontologically identical in form. But it would also be a mistake to imagine that membership practices differ so widely that Durkheim's concepts are too esoteric (or idiosyncratic) to use for purposes of generalization, for reasons that have more to do with the production of consciousness than the independent existence of empirical similarities. The kinship patterns of the Alcheringa, for instance, are inextricably imbricated in the taxonomies of modern Europe, even as this "modernity" is shaped by the formal distance between its own and other "primitive" practices.

Political and Religious Organizations: Some Differences

Durkheim conflates the concept of "religion" with "civil society,"[165] but this is misleading. There are very different rules for inclusion and exclusion associated with these two forms. When a group regulates membership by controlling kinship, then that group is a *political* one. Kinship rules have long been closely associated with political societies, ranging from the

---

[164] *The Gender of the Gift: Problems with Women and Problems with Society in Melanesia* (Berkeley, London: University of California Press, 1988), especially chapters 1, 11, and 12).

[165] Durkheim follows Hobbes, Locke, and compatriot Rousseau, who use "political society" (*société politique*) and "civil society" (*état civil*) interchangeably. Both stand in contrast with the state of nature (*état natural*).

ancient Greek *politeia* through the modern state. These kinship practices are challenged by *religious* communities that rely on sacred/profane taxonomies that differ from those of political societies—particularly those of the individual's faith, relation to God, spirituality, and relations with other members of that community. It is precisely because of different membership forms that political and religious societies overlap and can also come into conflict. A description of a religion vis-à-vis its membership rules may seem to violate a competing, Lockean view of religion as a matter of individual conscience. On this view, explored more fully in Chapter 6, individuals choose of their own free will whether or not to have faith in a certain mix of metaphysical and moral principles. And yet to view religion simply as a matter for the individual to decide, independent of a larger group, does not account for how Locke, for instance, knows how to classify some matters as "religious" and others as located in "political society." The notion that religion is strictly a matter of individual beliefs overlooks the fact that a religious belief requires a religious organization, with membership rules of inclusion and exclusion. The possibility of an individual choosing among religions (or choosing to have none at all) no more means that the individual conscience is the source of religious faith than the fact that one may choose to buy chocolate or vanilla ice cream means that the individual conscience is the source of ice cream. The existence of a religion requires a community of believers (and non-believers) and rules for what counts as such that are not determined by the individual per se. A private religion is as untenable as a private language.

In drawing parallels between religions and political societies, Durkheim obscures the specific relevance of sacred/profane birth practices to group continuity. His opening taxonomic comparative exercise of ascertaining the meaning of religion by running through various possibilities in the form of "religion versus X" fails to pursue the difference between all sacred/profane distinctions and those associated with the maintenance of a group's intergenerationality. Durkheim distinguishes religion from magic, for instance, on the grounds that magic per se does not set out a structure of sacred/profane distinctions for a group as a whole: "Wherever we observe the religious life, we find that it has a definite group as its formation," which is not the case for magic, since this "does not result in binding together those who adhere to it, nor in uniting them into a group leading a common life. *There is no Church of magic.*"[166] Implicit in the contrast is the notion that some set of rules associated with a "religion" provides for the group's reproduction as that group, even as its individual members are born and die. Durkheim conflates the sacred/profane distinctions of a society's intergenerationality with those of "religion" but does not discuss how sacred/profane distinctions that do not take on the kinship form may

---

[166] Ibid., pp. 59–60, emphasis in original.

still contribute to a group's continuity. That is, some sacred rituals preserve group continuity and have nothing to do with birth or intergenerationality.

The Masons and sororities, as well as religions, use rituals that depend on sacred/profane distinctions that do not invoke kinship principles and that preserve that group's particularity over time, nonetheless. A special handshake, an initiation rite, have no meaning outside the significance ascribed them by the group. Everyone knows that it is not hand movement *per se* that makes one a Mason. Rather, what makes the hand movements sacred and not spastic is that they ritually distinguish outsiders from insiders. One meaning of "sacred" is that it marks a group's particularity, independent of daily, instrumental (profane) activities of the group. What distinguishes long-standing fraternities and sororities, social clubs, and religions from political societies is that the sacred/profane mappings of the former do not control membership in relation to birth. A Rotary Club father may prefer that his daughter marry the child of another Rotary Club member, or a Protestant may prefer to marry another Protestant, but neither organization uses kinship rules as the basis for membership. Certainly churches take an interest in marriage and sexuality, but this is different from a membership provision that paradigmatically requires entry at birth.

In some societies religious practices of membership are completely interwoven into practices of the political society. This is the case for countries with official state religions, for instance, and may prompt the belief that one is also born into a religion, that religions and political societies do not differ in the ways suggested above. Therefore, it is important to call attention to extra-political religions and their ability to thrive regardless of the support from political authorities—e.g., Christian communities in Turkey, Muslim communities in Germany, Jewish communities in India— and to reflect on how the possibility of religious diversity means that political and religious spaces are not coterminous. Anthropologist Jack Goody challenges Durkheim's views about tribal religion on precisely this point, observing that in African languages there is "no equivalent for the Western word 'religion' (or indeed 'ritual')," and that it is not "until the competition from Islam or Christianity that the idea of Asante religion, as distinct from the more inclusive concept of an Asante way of life, began to take shape, first in the mind of the observer, then in the mind of the actor."[167] One is Asante by birth, and whatever counts as "Asante"ness for particular practices follows from the fact that it is Asantes performing them.[168] Only after rituals become disassociated from a society are these

[167] *The Logic of Writing and the Organization of Society* (Cambridge: Cambridge University Press, 1986), p. 4.

[168] Goody argues that literacy is required for societies to constitute specifically religious forms of membership distinct from birth because of the need for a text to insure continuity: "You can spread them [written doctrines] like jam. And you can persuade or force people

rituals experienced as religious and not practices intrinsic to political societies' intergenerational group(s).

For non-ancestral spiritual communities the idea of the totem or god
comes first, not that of reproducing the society per se. An example of the
difference between ancestral and non-ancestral membership rules is that
between the group form described in the Hebrew Bible and that portrayed
in the New Testament. Whereas the Israelites are such by virtue of their
ancestral patrilineage, to join Christ is to break from the family and not
to participate in its reproduction:

> Think not that I am come to send peace on earth: I came not to send peace
> but a sword. For I am come to set a man at variance against his father, and the
> daughter against her mother, and the daughter in law against her mother in
> law. And a man's foes shall be they of his own household.[169]

Durkheim does not reflect on this anti-familial aspect of Christianity or
Buddhism, even though both religions are mentioned. Buddhism, in Durkheim's discussion, is about the perpetuation of certain rituals and attitudes,
not the preservation of a clan. For the Buddhist, salvation requires "only
that one know the good doctrine and practice it,"[170] and not the reincarnation of an ancestral totem. Hence, although Durkheim's work recognizes
religions that are not based on intergenerationality, he does not explore the
implications of this particular aspect of sacred/profane Buddhist practices.

To name apparent exceptions to the above anti-ancestral characterizations of "Christian" or "Buddhist" groups is easy, since today many groups
perpetuated in their names are tied to family forms of being, so that one
is indeed Buddhist because one's parents are. Since the rule of Emperor
Constantine in the West, the family has been a focus of intense interest
for a variety of Christian sects, for instance, and not just pagan cults and
Jews. Buddhism in Tibet is closely tied to national identity, which takes
an intergenerational form: one is distinctively Tibetan and not Chinese
by virtue of one's ancestors. (The Dalai Lama is a member of a formerly
dynastic land-owning family that controlled the majority of Tibetan territory, rendering serfs of most of the pre-Communist population in that
area.) However, this does not mean that the concept of religion is necessarily tied to intergenerational identities. Rather, the frequent coincidence
of a religious and familial or political identity means simply that particular
religious identities may have become absorbed by political societies. To
be Croatian is to be Roman Catholic; to be Serbian is to be associated

---

to give up one set of beliefs and practices and take up another set" whereas in oral cultures,
"conversions are impossible" (ibid., pp. 65–66).

[169] Matthew 10:35–36.

[170] Durkheim, *Elementary Forms*, p. 47.

with the Serbian Orthodox Church, and so on.[171] The fact that children often have the same political party affiliation as their parents, however, does not mean that one becomes interpellated into a political party in the same way one becomes interpellated into an intergenerational political society. Hence the heuristic that allows us to distinguish different norms for membership—those that are political and based on invocations of intergenerationality, from those that are religious and based on individuals repeating certain rituals (at times out of their own "free will" and at other times because they are coerced, or because they are socialized by their childhood environments)—remains an important one, especially when we turn to the role of political societies in the perpetuation of national and racial forms of being. Regardless of the superficial resemblances in their effects, the formal difference in these rules for membership yields the distinctive meanings of these affiliations.

The above distinction between political (intergenerational) and religious (volitional) societies may be still overly broad. That is, it may still result in the over-inclusivity similar to that observed when Durkheim calls both kinship and non-kinship groups "religious." To distinguish the exclusions wrought by kinship rules from other sacred/profane taxonomies does not mean that these others require no further heuristic interventions. To say that high school football is the "state religion" of Texas makes sense only in association with the notion of a more official, institutionalized form of religious worship. This does not mean the two practices are identical. Rather, they differ in ways that instruct our thinking about high school football in Texas.[172] Political societies are different from religious ones. But this does not mean that all political societies, or all religious societies, are identical.

Revisiting Civil Society

The view that claims political societies provide the rules for what counts as the families that comprise that political society, it could be objected, might hold true for certain clans, monarchies, and dictatorships, but not the modern democratic state. In a democracy the political society's membership practices do not stand against "the people" but passively reflect their aspirations. "The state" is no more than the formal embodiment of

---

[171] The apparent counter-examples, of "Orthodox Serbians" who are Croatian citizens, only proves the point, since it is their Orthodox Serbian status that marks these Croatians as having a specifically Serbian ancestry. At this point, the only possibility for a person to be Orthodox Croatian would be if one were the offspring of a "mixed" marriage.

[172] Anticipating Derrida, Durkheim writes: "Every time that we unite heterogeneous terms by an internal bond, we forcibly identify contraries" (271).

"the people." If kinship norms prevail in the reproduction of the democratic state, that is just a reflection of what most people prefer. These norms indicate something about "the people," and nothing structural about the state. The democratic follower of Rousseau, to follow perhaps the strongest proponent of this kind of argument, would suggest that one study "the people," which is to say, their pre-political habits, customs, and traditions— not abstractions of "the state"—to grasp the appropriate causes for a country's rules, about kinship or anything else. According to this line of reasoning, a true democracy's laws do not emerge from an autonomous government but rather are the institutionalization of the ways of life of that people. However, in the matter of membership rules, laws are inevitably more than a passive reflection of the aggregated beliefs of individuals. Consider that each law does at least one of the following: 1) controls the behavior of all individuals in a group so as to **prevent harm to individuals**; 2) controls the behavior of all individuals to **prevent offense to majority group sensibilities**; and 3) establishes rules to **determine who can and cannot belong** to that country.[173]

Distinctive about the third purpose is that in principle it cannot be achieved by collective action absent the political societies' interventions, whereas it is possible that the objectives of protection against harm and moral offense could be met by an aggregation of individual practices, without any laws at all. Laws against speeding, murder, sodomy, and pornography, and laws requiring, say, taxes for public services, serve coordinating functions. They do not eliminate entirely individual malfeasance, but provide a form of central coordination, through force and the threat of force, so that the preferences of the majority can be successfully implemented. Otherwise, a majority of individuals who do not drive quickly and dangerously still will be in danger from the minority who do, and so forth. But again, it is possible to imagine a condition in which everyone in a particular society behaves in a similar fashion, desired by everyone, such that these laws would be redundant. Law intervenes in a majoritarian context when the aggregated efforts of a majority of individuals are neither sufficient nor secure enough (collective action problems occur) for the preferences of the majority qua "the people" to be implemented.

Laws that establish state sovereignty and membership in majoritarian contexts serve functions different from those that prohibit, regulate, and

---

[173] I am assuming strict majority rule as the basis for these laws, because a constitutional system protecting minority rights violates the strong version of the state as a passive medium of "the people." I am also assuming an already-constituted political society, since the point of the exercise is to show how the form of membership decisions differ from others, to challenge intuitions that simply assume the prior existence of a group. For a review of competing criteria for representation, see Hanna Pitkin, *The Concept of Representation* (Berkeley, London, Los Angeles: University of California Press, 1967).

coordinate aggregate individuals. Whereas law **restrains** already possible (and avoidable) activities of harm and offense, law **constitutes** conditions of membership. If everyone drove 55 MPH, speed limit laws would be unnecessary. Safe driving is logically possible without the law. However, if the people of the Pacific Northwest regarded themselves as part of a political society "Oceana" that comprises a certain sovereign territory, this aggregate of individual imaginations would not result in the existence of Oceana. That everyone in Quebec might imagine themselves at some point as a sovereign country with identifiable members does not make a legislative action—popular or representative—logically redundant. In the case of rules for membership and, relatedly, sovereignty, the state cannot passively reflect the people's preferences. "The people" alone do not a state (or any political society) make, as Hegel persuasively argues. A state requires recognized rules of inclusion and exclusion, something entirely different from aggregated behaviors.

Another difference between policies against harm or offense and those concerning membership is that the former occur in degrees and the latter are absolute. A majority defeat of pornography restrictions would not require that Quebec be plastered with pornography. The number of stores selling pornography would depend on market demand. However, a majority defeat of Quebec's sovereignty referendum means that no one is part of a sovereign Quebec. Hence the very nature of a state as a membership organization means that it must actively create laws for exclusions and inclusions; these cannot, by definition, emanate "from below," so to speak.

When Is a State Not a State?

An entirely different type of objection to the idea that the state, again, as one form of a political society, creates membership rules might be that the state in its current incarnation is not a true state. Regimes that might claim to be states rely on kinship principles, but, the objection might run, a real state has separated the logic of kinship from citizenship. A real state uses consent or other more universal criteria to determine membership.

Marx's reply to Hegel's *Philosophy of Right* contains this kind of objection to Hegel's view of the state.[174] In his fullest defense of democracy, Marx says Hegel is wrong because the Hegelian state is not a real state, which would be democratic:

> Democracy is the generic constitution. Monarchy is only a variant and a bad variant at that. Democracy is both form and content . . . Democracy is the

---

[174] This early view is at odds with Marx's later writings. I rely on it here only because it crystallizes a certain kind of objection to my analysis with which I think it useful to engage.

solution to the riddle of every constitution. In it we find the constitution founded on its true ground: real human beings and the real people; not merely implicitly and in essence, but in existence and in reality. The constitution is thus posited as the people's own creation. The constitution is in appearance what it is in reality: the free creation of man. . .Hegel proceeds from the state and conceives of man as the subjectivized state; democracy proceeds from man and conceives of the state as objectified man.[175]

Marx's particular concern is with the need for a state to be democratic, but a similar claim could be advanced about membership within the state. The crux of the disagreement lies in Marx's Platonic critique of Hegel's Aristotelianism. Marx challenges the equation of the actual with the rational, on the grounds that the good is the true.[176] Marx is implying that since the modern European state is not a good state, it cannot be a true state, either: "Hegel has analyzed the fundamental idea of these presuppositions" of the state, which "does not mean that he has demonstrated their validity."[177] Marx is accusing Hegel of simply describing the principles of the existing state, without showing whether they are good or bad. These principles may be in effect, but also illegitimate, and therefore, wrong. In the same vein, Marx says that Hegel's

> speculations necessarily appear at their most profound when the most abstract, socially wholly unrealized determinations, the natural bases of the state, like birth (in the case of the ruler) or private property (in the case of primogeniture) appear as the highest Ideas, the direct human incarnations of the Idea. It is self-evident that the true way is turned upside-down.[178]

Marx believes that Hegel foolishly reiterates the naturalizing rhetorics of birth and property. What he ought to do, Marx suggests, is criticize the underlying dynamics that give rise to such oppressive relations, which are ideological and not philosophical, much less the true form of social life. Against the observation that birth is the basis of political society, Marx might echo Locke's insistence that only procedures of consent can truly establish such a community.[179]

Marx's approach here reveals a fundamental divergence from Hegel's method, as well as from Marx's own later method. Althusser draws attention to this when he contrasts Marx's critique that "stands Hegel on his feet"—

---

[175] Marx, p. 87.

[176] John McMurtry, *The Structure of Marx's World-view* (Princeton: Princeton University Press, 1978).

[177] Marx, "Hegel," p. 97.

[178] Ibid., p. 99.

[179] Locke seems to believe that the existence of a practice validates it. He presents a pseudo-history of consent that Marx's method does not entail.

simplistically inverting Hegel's beliefs—with the Marxian analysis that finds the "rational kernel in the mystical shell."[180] The former critique, which is present in Marx's early essays, including the one discussed here, does not attempt to understand the relation between Hegel's "mistaken" concept of the state and the actual state (as opposed to the existing state). The premise of Marx's critique is that there is the **concept of the state** on one hand (Hegel's incorrect one and Marx's correct one), and the **existing state** on the other hand (which is bad and inauthentic if it coincides with Hegel's definition and good and authentic if it coincides with Marx's definition). The distinction Marx draws between their visions of the state requires a complete rejection of the Hegelian method, and not simply Hegel's beliefs about the state. By failing to connect Hegel's concepts to specific institutions of political society, Marx's critique of the state is far weaker than his discussion of capital.

Georgy Lukács understood this, and so was able to use Hegelian dialectics against Hegel, by showing that the dominant ideology's version of the state was connected in particular ways to the actual state.[181] In Lukács' account, then, Hegel's arguments are not mistakes, but another moment in the unfolding of history. On this reading, the state to be overcome is organically connected with the form into which it will develop. That form is not a state with membership rules based on either birth or individual consent, but rather, one that has refused the birth principle for membership and has fully institutionalized the possibility for genuine consent as the basis for its sovereignty. These two possibilities are explored in the Conclusion.

[180] "Ideology and Ideological State Apparatuses," in *Lenin and Philosophy* tr. Ben Brewster (New York: Monthly Review Press, 1971), pp. 127–88.

[181] *History and Class Consciousness*, tr. Rodney Livingston (Cambridge,: MIT Press, 1983), p. xlvii, and "What Is Orthodox Marxism?" p. 8.

Two

The Nation and the Tragedy of Birth

[Mayor] Akayusa said go kill the Tutsi men,
because they are the ones who make children,
and if you come across a woman who is
pregnant, rip the baby from her belly.[1]

In France we risk being overwhelmed by an
Islamic invasion from North Africa. In France,
bigamy is against the law. Yet we are importing
bigamous, or even polygamous, unemployed
foreigners and their children. The risk is that
our country—a product of its heritage and its
combined genes—will be transformed.
  (*Mayor Le Cevallier*[2])

The State of the Nation

Chapter 1 argued that the state, as one form of political society, is a
membership organization with inclusions and exclusions based on birth.
Some might argue that while such membership criteria do exist, they are
the consequence of pre-existing "nations," and not manifestations of states
or other political societies. 'Nation' is from the Latin root *nasci* (to be
born). So perhaps "nation," and not "state," is the concept best suited for
characterizing the daily affinities of political membership rooted in one's
birth. If the "state" is a Leviathan, the outward display of unity among
individual members, then "nation" evokes its blood and guts. One might
change one's appearance, but one cannot change what one **is**. Perhaps this
is what Michael Walzer is suggesting when he writes: "The national clan
or family is different from the state. . . . Hence it is possible, say, for
an Algerian immigrant to France to become a French citizen (a French

---

[1] Benadette Ntakurtinka, Hutu tortured for hiding Tutsis, quoted in James McKinley Jr.
"Ex–Mayor on Trial, a Rwanda Town Remembers," *New York Times*, September 27, 1996, A3.

[2] Quoted in Roger Cohen, "French Book Fair Writhes, Poisoned by Politics," *New York
Times*, November 22, 1996, A4.

'national') without becoming a Frenchman."[3] This distinction between a national status and a juridical one also appears in the dictionary definition of the word. The noun 'national' means "one that owes allegiance to or is under the protection of a nation, without regard to the more formal status of citizen or subject."[4] To be a national seems prior to and separate from the legal technicality that confers the political status of "subject" or "citizen."

The difference between the concepts of "nation" and "state" is also apparent in the ordinary uses of these words and their cognates. Among cognates of 'nation' are words that denote one's 'nation'-ality, while no similar form of being is derived from any cognate of 'state'. One may have an American 'nationality' or be a French 'national', but no cognates of 'state' associate a particular individual with a specific country.[5] The English words that are used to suggest a political association between an individual and a juridical body derive, instead, from 'citizen', though United States passports refer to 'national' and 'citizen' almost interchangeably. The passport states: "The Secretary of State of the United States of America hereby requests all whom it may concern to permit the citizen/national of the United States named herein to pass without delay or hindrance and in the case of need to give all lawful aid and protection."[6] 'Citizen' derives ultimately from the Latin *civis* or "city" and means "an inhabitant of a city or (often) of a town; especially one possessing civic rights and privileges, a burgess or freeman of a city," and is first used in 1605. In this use, 'city' resembles the meaning of 'state', referring to its membership aspects as a political society, and not to the coercive functions of government.

Some idiomatic uses of the words 'national' and 'citizen' differ in ways suggested by their dictionary definitions. For instance, the question, 'What are the standards for good citizenship?' is idiomatic. 'What are the standards for good nationality?' is not. 'She is a good citizen' is a phrase used, for example, to describe someone who assists her community, even if that community is not a specifically political one. The phrase may be used to

---

[3] Michael Walzer, *Spheres of Justice: A Defense of Pluralism and Equality* (Oxford: Martin Robertson, 1983), p. 52.

[4] *Merriam-Webster's Collegiate Dictionary*, 10th ed.

[5] The *Oxford English Dictionary*, 2d ed. provides a contemporary definition only for 'nationals' (in the plural), claiming that the meanings of the noun 'national' in the singular are obsolete and rare. 'Nationals' means "persons belonging to the same nation, one's fellow country-men." Both the Merriam-Webster and the Oxford dictionaries date the origins of this meaning to 1887.

[6] U.S. Passport, 1995. Interestingly, all sections from the preceding passports of the 1980s referring to 'nationals' now refer to 'citizens': "LOSS OF NATIONALITY" has become "LOSS OF CITIZENSHIP," and "DUAL NATIONALS" has been replaced by the heading "DUAL CITIZENSHIP."

describe a faculty member's service to her department. This sense is not idiomatic for the phrase 'She is a good national' because that phrase itself is not idiomatic. The concepts of participation that 'citizen' connotes are not those of 'national'. 'Citizen' may refer to a popular form of government while 'national' does not: 'It is a citizen-led government' is idiomatic and 'It is a national-led government' is not idiomatic. 'National' may refer to an all-encompassing governmental realm, as opposed to a local one, so that 'national' refers to the relative scope or inclusivity of an administrative unit—the boundaries of jurisdiction—and not the rules for participation. Finally, 'national' entails connotations of particularity that 'citizen' may not. 'Citizen of the world' is an idiomatic phrase that cannot be rendered 'National of the world'. Indeed, the *Oxford English Dictionary* uses "citizen of the world" as a phrase definitive of the meaning of 'citizen'. In sum, while 'nation' has a cognate that may be used to identify an individual in relation to a particular group ('national'), 'state' does not. The word that is used to make this association ('citizen') has possible connotations of procedural rules and universality that are not idiomatic for 'national'.

The Nation as Primordial

According to Harold Isaacs, certain "ties and connections" are "primordial" in the "human experience," a "basic group identity [that] consists of the ready-made set of endowments and identifications that every individual shares with others from the moment of birth by the chance of the family into which he is born at that given time in that given place." One's "nationality" is one of these characteristics, Isaacs claims.[7] Clifford Geertz offers a similar definition: "By a primordial attachment is meant one that stems from the 'givens'—of social existence. . . ." The tribal affiliation that follows from a "kin connection" is among these.[8] But the attachments with which Isaacs and Geertz concern themselves cannot be powerful solely because they are "given." No less given is that some people are double-jointed and others not. Double-jointedness does not appear on Isaac's list of primordial affiliations, even though that is arguably determined at birth, too.

Although the view of the nation as "given" endures, there has been a longstanding countermovement to these beliefs.[9] The challenge to the idea

[7] *Idols of the Tribe: Group Identity and Political Change* (New York, San Francisco: Harper and Row, 1975), pp. 16, 36, 38–39.

[8] *The Interpretation of Cultures* (New York: Basic Books, 1973), p. 259.

[9] For a discussion of the nineteenth-century counter-narrative of race, see Ann Stoler, "Racial Histories and Their Regimes of Truth," *Political Power and Social Theory*, 11 (1997), pp. 183–206.

that nations are primordial appeared a couple of thousand years before contemporary treatises on "constructed identities." Throughout the *Histories* Herodotus grapples with the problem of classifying a group as one people [*ethnoi*] when its members may speak different languages and have disparate geographical origins. (Or they may speak the same language, and still have different origins.) Herodotus does not assume any one identity as "given," but is interested in learning how various forms of being are appropriated and cast off. Despite the existence of a tradition of thought that questions the bases of primordial ties, the challenge recurrently takes the form of a counter-method, a counter-intuition, as when Weber writes:

> It goes without saying that 'national' affiliations need not be based upon common blood. Indeed, especially radical 'nationalists' are often of foreign descent. . . . Nevertheless the idea of the 'nation' is apt to include notions of common descent and of an essential, though frequently indefinite, homogeneity.[10]

The nation as a concept that has warranted theoretical scrutiny is not based on blood, but on the belief that this is so. Authors as chronologically distant as Aristotle and Weber see other political elites and the masses as foolishly mistaken when they take their national affiliations as "given."

Specific counter-arguments to the belief that ontological or evolutionary properties of ancestry produce strong attachments within kinship groups take several forms. Some feminists and psychoanalytically oriented scholars point out the often gendered pathologies that the national community betrays. References to a nation as the "Fatherland" or "Motherland," for instance, may mean that the nation is a stage on which the worst family traumas are reenacted. On this account, familial-like national attachments are not necessary characteristics of human society, but maladaptive neuroses.[11] Others explain attachments as fostered by specific technological

---

[10] Weber, *Economy and Society*, tr. Ephraim Fischoff, vol. 2. (Berkeley, Los Angeles, London: University of California Press, 1978) p. 923.

[11] Among the relevant texts not already cited are: Sander Gilman, *Difference and Pathology: The Stereotype of Sexuality, Race, and Madness* (Ithaca: Cornell University Press, 1985); Susan Jeffords, *The Remasculinization of America: Gender and the Vietnam War* (Bloomington: University of Indiana Press, 1989); George Mosse, *Nationalism and Sexuality: Respectability and Abnormal Sexuality in Modern Europe* (New York: H. Fertig, 1985); Klaus Theweleit, *Men's Fantasies*, tr. Stephen Conway (Minneapolis: University of Minnesota, 1987).

There is an underappreciated psychoanalytic literature on "pregnancy envy," a phenomenon Freud explored in his early writings where he pointed out that boys and girls have no understanding of the role of penises in reproduction but early on grasp that babies come from inside mothers and not from fathers. Freud and others describe young boys insisting, when they see pregnant women, that they too will have a baby, only to be rudely confronted by a parent, usually a mother, explaining that they are boys and so they will not be able to enact the omnipotent-seeming role of life-giver they behold in their mothers. To observe that boys may have compensatory fantasies associated with a desire to give birth and that these may lead to adult practices whereby they act on these fantasies by interpellating

developments: the nation is understood, for instance, as the "imagined community" peculiar to modernity's "print-capitalism."[12] Finally, an increasing number of scholars advocate "bringing the state back in." They focus on changes in government rules and practices as constitutive of the nation. Charles Tilly, for instance, suggests that nation-states create beliefs in external threats to extract income and maintain sovereignty.[13] Here the sense of community that to some seems rooted in the intimacy and connectedness imputed to certain family arrangements is actually a consequence of instrumental incentives that induce particular behaviors. All of these accounts are energized by the mystery of the space between the recognition that familiarity among those of the same nationality is manufactured and that it has a force of something seemingly deeper, more foundational than what would follow from contrived rules.

But perhaps 'space' is not the right word to refer to the apparent difference between deep-rooted feelings of attachment and the various forms of artifice that nurture such affiliations. "Space" evokes a gulf, an *aporia* where sentiment and rules do not mesh. Yet it is precisely the repeated conjuncture of emotion with politics that has defined family and nation in terms of each other. The goal of this chapter is to be as specific as possible in laying out the grammar of the nation, to discover how intergenerational semiotics entail certain affective possibilities and preclude others. To study emotion in politics is generally work for political psychologists, but the contours of nation are not simply psychological. Studies that use a largely

---

themselves as political associates with the mother, through marriage rules, is not to claim that giving birth is the irreducibly most powerful activity in social relations. That infant boys may have fantasies and that these are acted out in their adult activities only underscores Freud's point that when we behave in accord with such phantasmatic beliefs, that is irrational; that is neurotic. One might say that stipulating birth as a membership rule is just one such effort to replicate the phantasmatic role of the mother. The best essays on pregnancy envy are the "Translator's Introduction" and "Translators' Analysis of Case," by Ida Macalpine and Richard Hunter in their edition of Daniel Paul Schreber, *Memoirs of My Nervous Illness* (London: W. W. Dawson and Sons, 1955), pp. 1–28 and 369–412. See also Eva Feder Kittay, "Womb Envy: An Explanatory Concept," in Joyce Trebilcott, ed., *Mothering: Essays in Feminist Theory* (Totowa: Rowman and Allanheld, 1983), pp. 94–128; Sigmund Freud, "Analysis of a Phobia in a Five-Year-Old Boy", in *The Standard Edition*, tr. James Strachey, Vol. 10 (1909; rpt. London: Hogarth Press, 1955), pp. 5–147. Madelon Sprengnether also notes the maternal themes in the Schreber text, in *The Spectral Mother: Freud, Feminism, and Psychoanalysis* (Ithaca: Cornell University Press, 1990).

[12] Benedict Anderson, *Imagined Communities: Reflections on the Origin and Spread of Nationalism* (London: Verso, 1983). A more state-centered view of the role of written language in the consolidation of a nation appears in Robert Wuthnow, *Communities of Discourse: Ideology and Social Structure in the Reformation, Enlightenment, and European Socialism* (Cambridge: Harvard University Press, 1989).

[13] "War Making and State Making as Organized Crime," in *Bringing the State Back In*, ed. Peter Evans, Dietrich Rueschemeyer, Theda Skocpol (Cambridge and New York: Cambridge University Press, 1985), pp. 169–91.

psychological idiom are not specific enough for the task of articulating the nation against and in association with families, ethnic groups, races, and religions. To grasp only what these forms share is to miss the metonymic subtleties of their interconstitutive patterns. And yet to point out the specificity of the nation does not require that it be utterly *sui generis*, for instance, a form isolated to modern Europe. The nation is not the new vessel that contains our innate preferences to be with our kin. Rather, the nation entails specific political conventions that produce affective, familial-like attachments. Every political society does this, which is to say that every political society exists in tandem with a familial nation.

Of course this goes against the conventional wisdom that has located the nation as an affiliation peculiar to European modernity. Nonetheless, although the experience of what it means to be "germanische" might be expressed differently under Frederick the Great than in the roaming bands of eighth-century tribes, the simple fact of that difference does not mean that the 'germanische Staat' and the 'germanische Stamm' (tribe) are refer-ring to completely different collective groups, that in both periods the concept of "germanische" cannot be seen as referring to a nation. There are always features that may distinguish one particular thing from another. What determines whether we call these two different objects by the same name is not their identity, but their resemblance, as no object is ever truly identical with anything save itself (and even then certain conditions may preclude self-identity). What determines whether things resemble each other sufficiently for the use of the same word are neither the things nor the words alone. For purposes of knowledge, the thing and the word are inseparable. That is, the **uses of the sign**, the word-thing together determine whether certain word-thing clusters are sensible. If the point is to understand the patterns of articulation among political societies and families, then it is useful to call all of these forms those of a 'nation'. A 'Louis XIV' piece of furniture for sitting differs from a 'Danish contempo-rary' piece of furniture for sitting, but just as we call both of these 'chairs', it seems sensible to call the group that is produced in part by ancient oral myths and the group that is realized in part through print-capitalism both 'nations'.

Metaphors of family connections have been too frequently pushed aside in recent studies of the nation, largely because of a belief that, even if nations are not genetically homogeneous, families are. The idea among sophisticated scholars is that nations are not based on "blood ties" (whereas families are), and therefore it makes no sense to turn to the family for ontological or historical (as opposed to psychoanalytical) understandings of the nation. The tendency to look toward forms of "culture," or other technologies of group consolidation ignores the effects of the blatant famil-ial imagery of the nation, as well as invocations of family ties, and erroneously takes the family and its rhetoric as natural. The next section documents how political societies constitute the rules that determine the family form that, in turn, gives rise to inclusions and exclusions of the nation. The kinship ties used for this purpose are a matter of artifice, but often, though not always, experienced as natural. Despite the apparent tension between the experience of law (artifice) versus nature as the underlying bond of the political community, the state (or political society) are not concepts at odds with the logic of the nation.

Rather, the "state" and "nation" are two sides of the same familial coin. Instead of Gellner's or Tilly's positivist assertions that governmental institutions create conditions that give rise to the nation, the Sausserian metaphor suggests a non-causal relation whereby neither "state" or "nation" has currency without the other. The family rhetoric of the state-nation is not obscure, metaphysical, or difficult to locate. The familial nation exists through practices and often legal documents that set out the kinship rules for particular political societies. These political rules constitute both the legitimate family and, more specifically, the legitimate children by announcements of the methods of endogyny, exogamy, inheritance, and family roles on which all political societies rely for their continuity and reproduction.

The history of these kinship rules in Europe is one of dramatic conceptual reversals that nevertheless reveal certain constancies of relational terms. Nothing about the practices in ancient Greece is unfathomable to a twentieth century audience. This is not a claim about ontological essences of repetition, but, to return to Heidegger, a statement about ourselves as creatures of history. We are the past, a phenomenon that requires neither Hegelian complacency nor Nietzschean apoplexy. To observe that "we are the past" is not to say we are produced by a past that is an ontologically separate set of events. And yet this is also not to say that the familial discourses among various political societies are synonymous, or even largely in agreement. Today's public would not endorse the marriage rules of ancient Athens. To say "we are the past" is to acknowledge that we cannot help but (mis)understand such rules. Whether we would endorse or reject rules from the past is irrelevant to the heuristic goals of turning to the past. Our own contemporary marriage laws frequently are disobeyed, but that is not evidence that they are incoherent to us. Similarly, one might infer that the prevalence of divorce shows a certain lack of clarity about the purpose of the institution in our own time. Nonetheless, marriage laws exert a regulatory force. Implicitly that force is through the institution's authority as that which is traditional or simply ancient. But the sheer existence of the laws also shapes our forms of being. Perhaps the most interesting difference between contemporaries and Athenians is that the latter, 2,500 years ago were, it seems, more aware of the effects of these laws than today's Christians.

In describing Roman marriage practices Susan Treggiari writes: "Because all Latin literature, but especially philosophical writings, was inescapably influenced by Greek tradition, it will be necessary to go back to classical Athens to disentangle some of the main themes and place Roman conventional theories in cultural context."[14] The relevance of that ancient Greek context did not stop with the Romans, and its continued relevance is not limited to the United States. Due to colonization, this rhetoric of the ancient Greeks has approached something of a universal touchstone for thinking about politics.[15] When the Botswanan Supreme Court was deciding, in 1990, whether the children of a Botswanan woman married to a foreigner were citizens, that Court used Athens to guide their views: "[The] development of the concept of citizenship, like most other political concepts, dates as far back as from ancient Greece," wrote Judge President Amissah. The opinion then quotes at length from a text describing laws for Athenian citizenship.[16] To understand the connection among kinship rules, political societies, and nations is to understand their and our histories, and that leads, again, to Athens.[17]

The following accounts of marriage policies show that political societies relied on marriage for consolidating the kind of legal family that could serve to distinguish citizens from foreigners. The familial unit was not regarded primarily as an outcome of biology or nature, which is instructive on two points relevant to this chapter. First, it indicates that the family model relied on for images of national affiliation based on long-standing roots had initially juridical, formal connotations, as opposed to the concept of the family's contemporary resonances as apolitical and traditional. The rules for intergenerationality and membership were simply much more apparent then than they are today. The impulse for believing the intergenerational practices of the nation to be natural has a very specific

---

[14] *Roman Marriage: Iusti Coniuges from the Time of Cicero to the Time of Ulpian* (Oxford: Oxford University Press, 1991), p. 181.

[15] This is not to say that these ideas were indeed original with the ancient Greeks. But even if every word of Martin Bernal's argument is true—and much of it is quite persuasive—the more accurate intellectual history has not manifest in major political institutions referring to Egypt as the source of their great ideas. (*Black Athena: The Afroasiatic Roots of Civilization*, vols. 1 and 2 [New Brunswick: Rutgers University, 1987]).

[16] From *Attorney General of the Republic of Botswana v. Unity Dow* (1990), in Unity Dow, *The Citizenship Case* (Gaborone, Botswana: Lentswe La Lesedi, 1995), p. 136.

[17] Again, why Athens? What about Egypt? one might counter. Even if Bernal is correct in observing the influence of Egyptian religions and philosophies on those of Greece, the evidence does not mean that history must be revised to place "our" origins in another time and place. To accede to that implication of his work is not merely to acknowledge "origins," but to fetishize them in precisely the ways that have rendered Athens and "the West's" origin stories so damaging. To provisionally recognize the Atheninan experience as the phenomenological fount of others does not mean this was either good or necessary.

origin. Ideas about forms of being based on intergenerationality were not and need not be regarded as requiring faith in a pre-political family. Also, the actual rules for constituting membership in the ancient Greek polis and the contemporary state are both dependent on practices related to birth and intergenerationality, and hence to the rules that constitute families. To see the artifice of the family (and its appearance as natural) is to see the artifice of political society (and its appearance as a nation).

Political Histories of Marriage and Membership

Aeschylus's Orestes would have been somewhat confused if confronted with presidential candidate Pat Buchanan ridiculing those who see the law as shaping what counts as a family.[18] According to Orestes, blood ties run through the maternal line, under the auspices of the female Furies. It is the work of Apollo and political society to replace this natural tie with the juridical marriage relation. On Apollo's rendering, invoked by Orestes, the blood vengeance exacted by Clytemnestra against her husband (for killing their daughter Iphigeneia) is unjust because it sunders the juridical marriage union of husband and wife. On the cycle of retribution occasioned by "blood vengeance" the Chorus says: "Bloodshed bringing in its train/ Kindred blood that flows again,/Anger still unreconciled/Poisoning a house's life/With darkness, treachery and strife/Wreaking vengeance for a murdered child."[19] This was the way of the Furies, the vengeful feminized system of retributive justice that law and order would replace.

Orestes' murder of Clytemnestra is not that of an arbitrary figure vindicating marriage, but of a son who privileges the father (king)/child relation over that of mother/child and brother/sister relations.[20] The Chorus instructs Orestes, "And when she whimpers, 'Child, Orestes!'/Answer, 'I am—my father's!'"[21] Clytemnestra has committed three crimes against the

---

[18] Buchanan's 1992 Republican Convention nominating speech calls Hillary Clinton a "radical feminist" because of her work on behalf of children suing to leave abusive households ("Pat Buchanan for President in 2000" [database online, EXCITE http://www.excite.com], April, 1996).

[19] *Agamemnon*, lines 145–62, in *The Oresteian Trilogy* [458 B.C.], tr. Philip Vellacott (London: Penguin, 1959), p. 47.

[20] I refer to the primary parental dyad as that of father/child and not just father/son because the daughter Electra also endorses her brother's matricide. Adhering to a similar message in the Oedipus trilogy, the polis is placed above the blood ties among siblings. That Orestes' father killed Orestes' sister does not prompt concern about that tie, even though Sophocles' Antigone has said that the only irreplaceable blood relation is the sibling, and therefore one might expect both Orestes and Electra to be angry at their father for murdering their sister. Orestes weighs only his mother's murder of his father (Sophocles, *The Three Theban Plays*, tr. Robert Fagles [New York, Middlesex: Penguin, 1984]).

[21] *Choephori*, lines 812–37.

emergent Athens: first, she has murdered her son's father; second, she has murdered her husband; and finally, she has killed the king.[22] The roles of father, husband, and monarch are represented as what is revered. Maternal duties, on the contrary, are, according to Apollo, mundane. The mother is merely a "nurse who tends the growth/Of young seed planted by its true parent, the male."[23]

Of special interest is that the positions on marriage and the *politeia* are legitimated as "new" and not traditional.[24] The Chorus initially protests that Orestes' crime was worse than Clytemnestra's. Clytemnestra and Agamemnon, though married, are "not kin; therefore such blood is not self-spilt."[25] But Apollo tells them that marriage "stands more sacred than an oath." The husband/wife relation, once updated, is presented as what is sacred, while the old-fashioned mother/child relation is not.[26] One oft repeated lesson of the play—the chorus' line "The old is trampled by the new!"[27]—suggests that it is the maternal tie and blood lines that are old. Hence, the new status of the polis—the citizens sit as jurors in Orestes' trial—is overtly radical, anti-traditional.[28] It is the mother/child tie, precisely because it is based merely on biology, that is undermined by the more judicious interventions of political society.

This theme seems evident in Sophocles' Theban trilogy as well. Incest, blood vengeance and infidelity are not unnatural. They are inevitable moments that reproduce the kingdoms of Laius and Oedipus. Without vigilant awareness of political roles (of "husband" and "wife" with a legitimate child), such reproduction takes accidental and tragic forms, far from the orderly patrilineal societies some nineteenth-century anthropologists naturalized. Absent articulated rules one might sleep with one's mother and not know it, or so the anxiety goes. In fact, a deeper worry is that absent myths, like that of Oedipus, one might sleep with one's mother and not even care about it. Only the presence of kinship rules makes it possible to notice that one has violated them, that one has broken a taboo by having sex with one's mother. That it is impossible to decide whether Oedipus and Jocasta's shame is in the realm of nature and instincts or politics is also suggestive of the thoroughgoing imbrication of these two realms when it comes to kinship.

In *Oedipus* the discourse of desire and fate is not imputed to the marital, i.e., political, roles of husband and wife, but to the very transgressions that

[22] Ibid., lines 477–502.
[23] *Eumenides*, lines 632–61.
[24] Ibid., lines 478–511.
[25] Ibid., lines 199–223.
[26] Ibid.
[27] Ibid., lines 752–81.
[28] Sophocles' Athens hasn't completely escaped traditional practices of justice (*dikē*). The jury is evenly divided and Athena casts the deciding vote on Orestes' behalf.

make this family impossible. The transgressions, once recognized as such, have the self-consuming effect of reinforcing a sense of order, on the one hand, while literally destroying that order that makes transgression possible. Fate does not require a legitimate marriage but destroys it. The "deviance" of the desire underlying incest annihilates the very order that makes deviance possible. Oedipus's son Eteocles, for instance, cannot have an "oedipal complex" because his mother, Jocasta, is already his half-sister and his Aunt Jocasta. Hence, subsequent to Oedipus's tragic mistake the order that underlies possible anxieties about incest is undermined and superseded.

The truth is that the idea that the incest taboo is based on some kind of **instinctual** aversion to sexual intimacy within a kinship group is a relatively recent one.[29] Hugo Grotius, as late as 1622, writes in a tradition that sees obedience to kinship rules largely as a matter of authority and morality, not innate repulsion:

> [F]rom this general rule [that people may choose whom to marry], we must except the Marriages of Parents with their Children in what degree so ever, the reason of which is sufficiently evident. For neither can the Husband, who by the law of Matrimony, is the head of the Wife, pay that respect and reverence, that Nature binds him to give his Mother, nor the Daughter to her Father: For though she be subordinate to her Husband by Matrimonial Right, yet doth her Marriage allow her so great a Familiarity with her husband, as is altogether inconsistent with the duty of a Child.[30]

Nothing here indicates that the thought of incest sickens Grotius. His tone seems closer to aggravation over gridlock—also disorderly—than to a stomach curdling disgust. According to Grotius, the natural (incestuous) mother-son relation is one that affords women the kind of authority that men (as husbands) can gain only from the artifice of the "law of matrimony." Because the matrimonial power men are granted as husbands is so apparently fragile, it may not overcome the natural power of maternal rule. Stated slightly differently, the (natural) subordination of the son to his mother overwhelms the (political) subordination of the wife to the husband.

---

[29] Lévi-Strauss writes that the instinctual "justification for the prohibition of incest is of recent origin, appearing nowhere in our society before the sixteenth century" (*Elementary Structures of Kinship*, tr. James Bell et al. [Boston: Beacon Press, 1969], p. 13).

[30] Grotius, *The Most Excellent Hugo Grotius: His Three Books Treating of the Rights of War*, Bk. I (London: Basset, 1682), microfiche, p. 107. Kingsley Davis also takes exception to the "instinctual repulsion" school of thought, suggesting that a "confusion of generations would be contrary to the authoritarian relations so essential to the fulfillment of parental duties," though his functionalist justification is at odds with Grotius' moral one (*Human Society* [New York: MacMillan, 1949], p. 403).

Hence the husband's familial authority requires the supplement of incest prohibitions. Otherwise weak sons might turn into weak husbands and be under the sway of the stronger mothers/wives.[31]

Citizenship in Ancient Greece

That Sophocles and his near contemporaries undertook repeated inquiries into their *politeia*'s marriage practices is not at all surprising, given that marriage law was ultimately constitutive of the ancient Athenian polis as such.[32] (Indeed, what is rather interesting is the relative lack of concern over the relation between marriage and its relation to citizenship among modern public figures.) In brief, the only way to be an Athenian citizen was to be the legitimate child of a citizen father and generally a citizen mother;[33] the only way to be legitimate was to be born to parents who were married;[34] and after Pericles, for the most part, only Athenian citizens could marry.[35] The marriage ceremony was the performance of a contract between the father of the bride and her husband-to-be, both of whom were related to her as a *kyrios* (master). The *kyrios* giving the woman said,

[31] For a view of ancient Greek men's anxieties about punishing mothers, see Philip Slater, *The Glory of Hera: Greek Mythology and the Greek Family* (Boston: Beacon Press, 1968).

[32] Nicole Loraux, *The Children of Athena: Athenian Ideas about Citizenship and the Division Between the Sexes*, tr. Caroline Levine (Princeton: Princeton University Press, 1993).

[33] The first law requiring maternal citizenship was passed, on Pericles' recommendation, in 451–50 B.C. Ralph Sealey believes that prior to this citizenship required only that the father be Athenian. During times of war the requirement of women's citizenship was some-times relaxed (*Women and the Law in Classical Greece* [Chapel Hill and London: University of North Carolina Press, 1990], pp. 12–13). Illegitimate children could be rendered citizens if the fathers subsequently adopted them. See Demosthenes, "Against Boeotus," line 31, and "Against Boeotus, II," line 41.

[34] Sealey, *Women and the Law*, pp. 15–16.

[35] Ibid., p. 31 and A.R.W. Harrison, *The Law of Athens: The Family and Property* (Oxford: Clarendon Press, 1968), pp. 24–25. The modern association of political membership with political prerogatives of participation has led to a collapse of the concept of "citizenship" with norms of participation. But political membership in Athens was important for women. During most periods women's citizenship was tracked to determine the legitimacy of their children. No political rights for women followed from this, save the ability to marry someone with real property. It should be pointed out that Charles Hignett challenges the dominant interpretations of the citizenship requirements. Hignett claims that the rule requires only that "both parents be citizens" and **not** that they "should have been united in marriage before the applicant's birth"—referring to eighteen-year-old men requesting membership in their father's deme (*A History of the Athenian Constitution* [London, Oxford: Oxford University Press, 1952], pp. 343–44). For a discussion of "active" and "passive" citizenship practices in the early twentieth century United States, see Caroline Danielson, *Citizen Acts: Citizenship and Political Agency in the Works of Jane Addams, Charlotte Perkins Gilman, and Emma Goldman*, dissertation (Ann Arbor: University of Michigan, 1996).

" 'I pledge (*engyo*) [X] for the purpose of producing legitimate (*gnēsioi*) children."[36] Slaves and metics might be in lifelong unions and have children, but they could not perform the above vow. Violations of marriage rules incurred penalties that seem to have been enforced.[37] The prerogatives of citizenship for men were two-fold: first, they were eligible to participate in the *ekklēsiai* (political assembly); and second, they could hold real property. Holding real property was tightly connected to being Athenian, since the land itself was regarded as sacred. Therefore it was important to link ownership of land to the lineage principles denoting citizenship: "[T]he institution of marriage was brilliantly contrived by Greek cities as a way of reproducing the citizen estate. . . . Refusal of marriage jeopardized not just the reproduction of the human species but the continuity of the civic community."[38]

In ancient Athens what we might think of as class seems largely to have been absorbed into distinctions between citizens and aliens. To put this in the Marxist idiom, it was fundamentally one's ancestry that determined one's relations to the means of production. Slaves were, for the most part, non-Athenians captured in war. The legal status of a *metic* referred to resident aliens who had freely immigrated, were former slaves, or the children of slaves. Metics might accumulate personal wealth as merchants, but the inability to own land was a serious obstacle to the accumulation of serious assets. Because one chief end of marriage was to determine the control of real property, it is unsurprising that legal marriages were not performed for those unable to own land, a practice echoed in the Middle Ages, where extra obstacles in canon law and the parishes themselves limited the prerogative of serfs to marry.[39]

The widely known Athenian narrative that anticipates and reinforces the exclusionary practices of Athenian citizenship is the myth of Erichthonios.[40] In this origins story, Athena is chased by Hephaistos, who attempts to rape her. The effort goes unconsummated. As she runs away Athena wipes the sperm off her leg with a piece of wool, which she

---

[36] Sealey, *Women and the Law*, p. 25.

[37] Harrison, *The Law of Athens*, pp. 26–28. Like many laws in ancient Athens, punishment was pursued through a bounty system. If a citizen successfully testified against a fraudulently married couple, he would receive one-third of their property and the *politeia* the rest. Of course this gave rise to false accusations, or "sycophancy."

[38] Louis Zaidman and Pauline Schmitt Pantel, *Religion in the Ancient Greek City*, tr. Paul Cartledge (Cambridge: Cambridge University Press, 1992), p. 71; and pp. 71–72, citing Ephoros, in Jacoby, *Fragmente der griechischen Historiker* (Berlin, 1923–) 70 F 149 (Strabo, *Historical Sketches* x.4.20, C482).

[39] Boswell, *Same-Sex Unions in Premodern Europe* (New York: Villard Books, 1994), p. 35; Harrison, *The Law of Athens*, p. 177; Jenny Teichman, *Illegitimacy: A Philosophical Examination* (Oxford: Blackwell, 1982), p. 58.

[40] See Loraux, *Children of Athena*.

tosses on the ground. The earth—Ge or Chthon—then gives birth to Erichthonios, who is raised by Athena. In honor of his foster mother, Athena, the spot of his birth becomes her namesake, one that remains over generations as Erichthonios himself reproduces others that—if the marriage rules are held to—would have a seemingly organic connection to Athens.[41]

This account appears to suggest that Athenians felt they had a natural (earth-based) prerogative to their political society and hence their land. Controlling kinship would enforce "their" rights. But individual Athenians may not have believed this story, any more than atheists who marry in the Church believe in God, or adults who give Christmas presents to their children believe in Santa Claus. Instead, Cleisthenes' interventions into the allocations of *demes* and *phratries*; the plays of Aristophanes; Plato's "noble lie"; and Aristotle's radical critique of citizenship by ancestry[42] all reveal the artifice of these conventions repeatedly pointed to as such and often mocked, as well as argued for and enforced.

If ideas about blood ties were the basis of the Athenian polis, then in 507 B.C., the leader (*arkhōn*) Cleisthenes would not have succeeded in regrouping the Athenian demes from ostensibly ancestral tribes into phratries divided by completely new geographical boundaries. Old phratries faded and new ones emerged.[43] Weber writes of this, "It is true that the original division may have been induced by political or actual ethnic differences, but the effect was the same when such a division was made quite rationally and schematically."[44] Sometimes new political geographies

[41] Although Genesis yields problems of first and second generation incest, at least in Genesis Adam has a woman to help him reproduce, while the method of Erichthonios's reproduction remains mysterious. Another story holds that Erechtheus, son of Erichthonios, is the founder. His daughter Creusa was raped by Apollo. Creusa abandons her son Ion out of fear that people will think him the offspring of an illicit union between her and a slave. Apollo later arranges things so that Creusa's husband Xuthus (an Achaian) will think Ion his and raise him (Euripides, *Ion*, in *The Bacchae and Other Plays* tr. Philip Vallacott [London: Penguin, 1973]).

[42] See above, Chapter 1.

[43] Prior to the reforms representation in the assembly was based on ancestral political groups called phratries. Membership was not based on residency, only patrilineage. Afterwards, a phratry was one of 50 geographical districts, although for subsequent generations membership again depended on patrilineage. Hence the new phratries were still ancestral. Cleisthenes' reforms might be likened, in the context of the United States representative system, to a simultaneous redrawing of Congressional districts and the requirement that one's current residence determines membership in a particular district, while one's sons, regardless of where they would reside, would vote in the district of their father's birth.

[44] Weber, *Economy and Society*, vol. I, p. 389. Weber's reference to "actual ethnic differences" is perplexing. The point of the paragraph is to demonstrate the "artificial origin of the belief in common ethnicity" in all contexts (ibid.). If ethnicity is always artificial, then it makes little sense to distinguish "actual" from "artificial" ethnicity.

result in new ancestral associations, which is what happened subsequent to these reforms in ancient Athens. Sometimes they do not, as in Yugoslavia, where Tito imposed new political associations to cross-cut older ones. The ancestral bases of political society are amenable to a variety of manipulations by political elites, but for purposes of membership, it is always lineage and birth that are the objects of interventions,[45] the ultimate linchpin of membership.

In the *Ecclesiazusae* (392 B.C.) Aristophanes dramatized the legal contingencies of Athenian marriage. Women disguised as men pack the assembly and vote new laws. Among other things, the laws require men to have sex with "ugly" women before they may have sex with women they desire, and they must have sex with their wives.[46] When Epigenes tells the "hag" he does not want to have sex with her, she says: "It's not me, it's the law." And, reporting on the new law, Chremes says: "We'll have to fornicate to earn our breakfast." Blepyros insists: "But forced! . . . I wouldn't" and Chremes replies: "No we must obey. If it's concluded for the public good that we should do it, do it like a man."[47] The preceding exchange over these "innovations" may also be read as a critique of the prevailing Athenian laws, which required men to have intercourse with their wives at least three times monthly,[48] and precluded them from marrying non-Athenians. Charles Hignett observes that this made "obvious gainers" of the "unmarried women of Athens, since it improved their chances of obtaining husbands."[49] Apparently citizens were having too much extra-marital sex and not reproducing Athenians at a sufficient rate. Aristophanes' play, making fun of women's "new" conventions, may also be read, then, as mocking the current *politeia*'s state interventions into sexuality and reproduction.

Though Athenians may not have taken their marriage laws to be natural, these laws were quite important to the regulation of sexuality. Foucault writes that in ancient Athens there were "few interdictions" regarding sexuality and that sexual austerity was not a result of "essential prohibitions," but an "elaboration and stylization of an activity in the exercise of its power and the practice of its liberty."[50] Yet if one considers the elaborate marital rules in Plato's *Laws*, the actual laws of ancient Athens, and Aris-

---

[45] Language, art, and education are all instrumental to preserving a certain intergenerational group.

[46] *Ecclesiazusae*, in *Complete Plays of Aristophanes*, ed. Moses Hadas (New York: Bantam, 1962), lines 1050–55, p. 458. For an alternative reading of this play, see Arlene Saxonhouse, *Fear of Diversity: The Birth of Political Science in Ancient Greek Thought* (Chicago: University of Chicago Press, 1992), chapter 1.

[47] Ibid., lines 469–78.

[48] Sealey, *Women and the Law*, p. 156.

[49] *A History of the Athenian Constitution*, p. 345.

[50] *The Use of Pleasure*, tr. Robert Hurley (New York: Vintage, 1990), p. 23.

tophanes' protests against them as symptomatic of how Athenians experienced sexuality and prohibitions, it appears that law was an extremely prominent force in the articulation of their sexual practices. Foucault, in his effort to mark breaks in epistemic regimes of sexuality, seems to underestimate the extent to which juridical rhetorics underlay the discourses of reproduction, and, in turn, of sexuality—even if people did not take these laws to reflect a higher, ethical truth. When the behaviors the laws condoned were affirmed, marriage was glorified as a specifically political act. Those challenging heterosexual conventions of reproduction then took to decrying the ethos of marriage as merely political. Same-sex sex, indeed all extra-marital sex among Athenians in general, was a problem because it tended to deplete the potential number of legitimate Athenian children. The military implications of this decrease in the ranks of the Athenian citizen-soldiers seem to have been the object of political concern, rather than the immorality of same-sex sex.[51] Another way the Athenian state controlled the family was its law that required citizens to continue their family line, even if this required adoption:

> [E]ven if [men] die without natural issue, they at any rate adopt so as to leave children behind. Nor is this simply a matter of personal sentiment; the state also has taken public measures to see that adoption is practised, since it trusts the (eponymous) Arkhon by law with the duty of preventing family lines from dying out.[52]

The *politeia* uses a rhetoric of sentiment, associated with "natural" longings for heirs, in order to reproduce those family lines and hence political communities by the artifice of law.

Citizenship in Rome

Membership in the Roman republic also followed from its marriage policies, although these were less restrictive than those of Athens. Livy opens his account of Rome's origins with a story about divine birth. The story

---

[51] Plato advocates sexual restraint in a context remote from worries about law or reproduction. But this is the discourse of philosophers. The sexuality of the rowdy, farting husbands of Aristophanes' *Ecclesiazusae* and the knowledge-seeking youth in Plato's *Phaedrus* have as much in common as the British comedian Benny Hill, known for his scatological humor, and Virginia Woolf's *Orlando*. It is impossible to generalize about sexuality based on the practices represented by either Plato or Aristophanes. The two pairs seem to reside in entirely separate worlds, despite a general correspondence of chronology. We may lack certainty about the details of Athenian sexual practices and mores. But marriage law indisputably had resonance in other discourses and shaped Athenian rules for membership.

[52] Zaidman and Pantel, *Religion*, p. 75, quoting Isaios VII, "On the Estate of Apollordoroso." On the requirement of hereditary citizenship in Athens, see Joint Association of Classical

of birth on a sacral spot, among the numerous narratives appropriated from
ancient Greece, this time yields results of inclusivity. The autochthonous
Romans must intermarry with their enemy Sabines early in the establishment of the political society because of a shortage of women. Livy recasts
the Greek origin story from one of primal belonging to one of instrumentality: "In antiquity the founder of a new settlement, in order to increase
its population, would as a matter of course shark up a lot of homeless and
destitute folk and pretend that they were 'born of earth' to be his progeny;
Romulus now followed a similar course."[53] Though challenging the strict
autochthony rules of Athenian antiquity, the kinship model remains the
basis for the production of new citizens. Not coincidentally, just as the
citizenship criteria were less rigid, marriage laws in Rome were also less
patriarchal than those of Athens. Rather than one master contracting with
another one, Roman marriage required at least the nominal consent of
the wife and the husband.

Still, citizenship and kinship rules remained linked. According to the
Justinian *Institutes* [533] citizenship practices in Rome were as follows:

> The off-spring of slave women are born slaves. . . . He is free-born if his mother
> is free and his father a slave. The same is true if his mother is free and his father
> unknown because he was conceived casually. It is enough for the mother to be
> free at the time of conception. Even the other way around, with the mother
> free at conception but a slave by the birth, it is accepted that the child is
> born free.[54]

Although Rome provided for different kinds of life-long unions, which
varied primarily with respect to inheritance rules and the reach of the
patriarch's dominion,[55] as in Athens, citizenship and inheritance rights
were intertwined. To be a citizen one had to be the son of a citizen father,
by a "regular marriage." While freed slaves could have the right of property
ownership, they could not legally marry or hold political office unless they

---

Teachers, *The World of Athens* (London, Cambridge: Cambridge University Press, 1984),
pp. 153–63 and "Citizenship, Greek" in the *Oxford Classical Dictionary*, 2d ed.

[53] Livy, *The Early History of Rome* (*Ab urbe condita*) I.1, 8. For a discussion of the relative
exclusivity of Greek and Roman citizenship, see Timothy Cornell, "Rome: History of an
Anachronism," in Anthony Molho, Kurt Raaflaub, Julia Erden, eds., *City-States in Classical
Antiquity and Medieval Italy* (Ann Arbor: University of Michigan, 1991), pp. 62–65.

[54] *Justinian's Institutes*, 1.3 and 1.4. The *Institutes* characterizes "slaves" and "marriage" as
follows: "Slaves, in Latin 'servi', are so called because it is the practice of army commanders
to order captives to be sold and thus saved—'save' in Latin is 'servare'—instead of killed. . . .
A Roman law marriage is a marriage between Roman citizens who meet the law's requirements" (1.3:3; 1.10.).

[55] Treggiari, *Roman Marriage*.

became citizens.[56] According to Paulus, "Marriage cannot be contracted, but cohabitation can exist between slaves and persons who are free." To further protect the sanctity of estates—and presumably to prevent the hired hands from getting the wrong ideas, "It has been decided that a freedman who aspires to marry his patroness, or the daughter of the wife of his patron, shall be sentenced to the mines or to labour on the public works, depending on the dignity of the person in question."[57] Former slaves could marry—but not the patroness or her daughter. As slaves their rights were limited, including the right to inherit from mothers, since "neither slaves nor freedmen are understood to have mothers under civil law."[58] To be a full citizen required "inscription in a Tribe"—modeled on the Athenian demes as territorial units that generated membership based on heredity, not domicile,[59] although Rome offered more possibilities for resident aliens and even freed slaves to obtain these prerogatives than did Athens.

The convention of adoption was used to pass wealth on to friends in the same generation. The device was necessary because landed property could be passed on only within a family. Adoption turned one's friend into the child eligible to inherit.[60] Both the fact of adoption and its uses in this context suggest that the autochthony metaphors were paradoxical. If adoption renders the alien a citizen, then kinship can be copied, and hence possibly regarded as less rigid than when kinship forms cannot be mimicked. Yet the blatantly manipulative reproductive discourse did not undermine the sanctity of the kinship system, or its ability to make "a people." The same is true of making one's friend one's "child." Although the practice suggests the possibility of evading the kinship system, it also underscores the power of that system. As Judith Butler suggests in her discussion of the "original"/"copy" relation between heterosexuality and homosexuality, the very fact that the adoption is indeed a "copy" performs the "originality" of legitimate birth.[61] That one relation is authentic and

[56] Ibid., pp. 52–54.
[57] *Opinions* 2.1–9; 2.20.1; 3.10.1–2, quoted in Mary Lefkowitz and Maureen Faust, comps., *Women's Life in Greece and Rome*, rev. ed. (Baltimore: John Hopkins University Press, 1982), p. 196.
[58] Paulus at 2.22.1, quoted in Lefkowitz, p. 196.
[59] Leon Homo, *Roman Political Institutions: From City to State* (London: Routledge, 1962), pp. 74–75.
[60] Treggiari, *Roman Marriage*, p. 380.
[61] "Imitation and Gender Insubordination," in *Inside/Out: Lesbian and Gay Theories*, Diana Fuss, ed. (New York: Routledge, 1991), pp. 13–31. Butler concedes too much to conventional notions of ontology—simple empiricist approaches—when she writes that the effects of gender binaries are "disingenuously renamed as causes, origins, disingenuously lined up within a causal or expressive sequence that the heterosexual norm produces to legitimate itself as the origin of all sex" (p. 29). The notion of "disingenuity" suggests a manipulative

another a copy means simply that, and not that a biological child and an adopted one need to be indistinguishable for kinship rules to retain legitimacy. The contingency of adoption does not disrupt the stability of the Roman kinship system. The obvious legal character of the "outsiders" and "insiders" does not upset the land-holding system. Again, the political society is the arbiter of these rules, affirming at each step Durkheim's insight that society provides the rules for what counts as kinship, rather than simply existing as a function of private relations of ancestry. In ancient Greece and Rome, kinship rules simultaneously constituted families and a familial-based political society. In the consolidation of political society and lineage, through invocations of autochthony stories, this kinship system bears all the marks of a nation, a people made such by birth.

In 312 Emperor Constantine converted to Christianity, and then systematically began to absorb his religion into the government in very pronounced institutional ways. This included his consultation with various Church priests over whether Jesus was produced by God or was God, which resulted in the Nicean Creed in 325, as well as his (and subsequent emperors') prerogative to confirm all heads of the Church. The state's appropriation of Christianity changed both the history and the historiography of marriage, insofar as the conjuncture deflected attention from the brute legal facts of the institution, in contrast with their prominence in histories of Athens and Rome. Marriage in antiquity, as we have seen, had a range of juridical effects. Modern Anglo legal histories of classical Athens and Rome, describing their marriage practices, pay little attention to the invocation of "pagan" gods at these ceremonies. The sacral ritual activities surrounding marriage had either been absorbed by the state (if previously non-Christian) or constituted through public offices, or identified as "foreign" and therefore illegitimate by dint of their association with other political communities (Persia, Egypt, and so forth). Practitioners of foreign rites were threatening to a unified national community. They are depicted in modern heuristics as the equivalent of Christianity's "heathens," for having alien political ties and connotations. Similar to the modern legal histories of Athenian marriage that minimize religious meanings, histories of the Christian era frequently elide the political content and effects of marriage. Marriage is represented as Christian, and hence as specifically "religious."[62] Here the approach tends toward careful demographic reports and analyses of various sexual mores and practices, but still away from the

---

schema whereby names are ostensively attached to a pre-semiotic population and its behaviors—"renamed." A more apt representation might show how the effects of the dichotomous "original" and "copy" define the limits of the investigation, so that there is no pre-discursive object to be obscured, hidden, or renamed.

[62] An important exception to this, offering an instrumental assessment of Church policies regulating sex, marriage, and inheritance, is Jack Goody, *The Development of Family and Marriage in Europe* (Cambridge: Cambridge University Press, 1983).

economic and legal dynamics of marriage. One possible explanation of this emphasis on law in studies of marriage in pagan communities and on culture or religion in examinations of Christian periods is that Christians were more observant, more invested in the sacred aspects of marriage, than pre-Christians. Therefore, to consider marriage was to look into specifically religious rituals and their violations. But it is hard to see evidence for heightened religious overtones among Christians compared to pagans (as well as difficult to know what would count as evidence of this).[63] Marriage was not treated as a sacrament, according to canon law, until the thirteenth century.[64] Until then it seems that the primary effects of the institution in Christian countries are the same political and economic ones as in ancient Greece and Rome.[65]

Early Christians tended to manifest Augustine's skepticism of the city of man by challenging its intergenerational rhetorics of nation and family. Not birth or marriage, but spiritual commitment, would be the sine qua non of the Christian community. That is, the family and its materialist values (of wealth and the mute givenness of particularity rooted in the biological child) were seen by the Essenes, for instance, as creatures of the state. To effect a Christian identity and spirituality depended on breaking from this materialist institution, through which economic and political power flowed. This new kind of vow—to God and not a spouse or one's military leader—might incite conflict, which, again, is why Jesus is said to have announced, "For I have come to set a man against his father, and a daughter against her mother."[66] This is not an arbitrary loyalty test, but an instance of early Christianity's thoroughgoing opposition to the worldly pre-occupations expressed in patrilineal and other inheritance rules imposed by the Roman state.

As Peter Brown puts it, for some Christians in the second century "Married intercourse was treated as the linchpin of the towering structure of the 'present age'," a practice that reproduced their corrupt society instead of prompting people to turn to their spiritual salvation.[67] A belief that the end of this world was imminent further deterred Christians from investing too heavily in it. Brown explains: "By refusing to act upon the youthful stirrings of desire, Christians could bring marriage and childbirth

---

[63] There are too many "exceptions" to the above dichotomy of studies on marriage to list. Inheritance practices were as closely tied to marriage in modern Europe as in ancient Athens, but the political-economic aspects of marriage are often neglected in studies of marriage in the Christian era while attention to religion virtually never overshadows political implications in studies of ancient Athenian marriage practices.

[64] Boswell, *Same-Sex Unions*, p. 178.

[65] Goody, *Development of Family*, pp. 103–55.

[66] Matthew 10:34–36.

[67] *The Body and Society: Men, Women and Sexual Renunciation in Early Christianity* (New York: Columbia University Press, 1988), pp. 98, 99.

to an end. With marriage at an end, the huge fabric of organized society would crumble like a sand castle."[68] To reject the political order was to reject the marriage practices that sustained it. Crucially, for the Christians to resist marriage was for them to reject political society, and not natural law, suggesting an association of marriage with the state, not pre-political culture or values.

A similar theme emerges in the story of Thecla, an actual or fictional contemporary of Paul. On learning of Paul's arrest, she breaks off her wedding engagement to join him. Thecla's mother's response, represented in a play from this period, is "Burn the lawless one!" but Thecla escapes, disguising herself as a man to prevent being raped during her travels, and eventually receiving Paul's blessing to pursue a vocation as a religious teacher.[69] Refusing marriage, Thecla is shown to be renouncing its metonyms of law and family, and embracing religion.

By the time Augustine writes with great enthusiasm about marriage, the Roman empire has become a mainstay of the Roman Catholic Church, and so marriage rules become absorbed into the core of "Christian" practices auxiliary to the reproduction of political society. This must have seemed almost blasphemous to the Christian Marcionites, who advocated celibacy, denounced marriage, and "deliberately wrenched the individual out of the familiar structures of society." This was not some vague splinter group. In many areas outside of Rome the Marcionites "monopolized the term Christianity **until the sixth century**."[70] And yet, in the seventh or eighth century, a Roman wedding blessing would state: "May thy providence, Lord, and thine ineffable grace dispense to each of them in different ways that what creation accomplished for the peopling of the world, reproduction may achieve in the enhancement of the church."[71]

One puzzle that an understanding of early Christianity's skeptical relation to the family clarifies is the discovery of Catholic same-sex unions. If Christian weddings are seen as reproducing the logic of pagan ones, then these unions are quite striking, and clear evidence of tolerance (if not endorsement) of homosexuality, for they suggest that the political conventions of Roman pagan marriages are being copied by Christian-era same-sex unions. However, once we appreciate the extent to which certain factions of Christianity viewed the family and religious devotion as two separate enterprises, the practice of same-sex unions that John Boswell has documented from the fourth through the twelfth centuries begins to make sense.

[68] Ibid., p. 32.

[69] Elaine Pagels, *Adam, Eve, and the Serpent* (New York: Random House, 1988), pp. 19–29.

[70] Brown, *The Body and Society*, p. 90, emphasis added.

[71] "Incipit Actio Nuptialis," from H. A. Wilson, *Liber sacramentorum Romanae Ecclesiae* (Oxford, 1894), pp. 265–268; tr. and quoted by Boswell, *Same-Sex Unions*, p. 289.

Boswell infers from documents in which priests bless different-sex and same-sex unions on the same occasion that the early Catholic Church, at least in particular places and times, not only tolerated homosexuality but blessed lifelong commitments between men.[72] Although Boswell's evidence of these church vows is quite impressive, another interpretation of them seems at least as plausible. During this period churches were also performing what were known as "chaste" marriages.[73] One possibility is that churches blessing same-sex unions were *not recognizing a sexual union* of same-sex couples, but rather the priests were *recognizing the mutual vows of chastity and spirituality* between same-sex couples. The similarity of same-sex and different-sex vows, then, could be viewed as the Church endorsing those same-sex couples who, like different-sex couples, rejected the rhetorics of family and intergenerationality located in political society:

> Influenced by . . . the belief that sexual abstinence was the highest Christian calling, many Christians in many times and places forswore sexual relations altogether, even with their spouses. These are called 'spiritual' marriages. . . . Several Christian splinter groups made asexual marriage a requirement.[74]

If the goal is to challenge the intergenerational logic of political society, then the anti-familial vows of the same-sex couple may form an even more perfect union than the anti-familial aspiration of the different-sex couple.[75]

Canon Marriage Law and the State

There is further evidence that the Church's views on marriage played second fiddle to the juridical discourse dominating the institution for political purposes in the practices regulating marriage for serfs and servants. Although nothing in the New Testament deters the recognition of vows between servants on religious grounds, the clergy did not perform such weddings, absent the consent of the servants' and serfs' lords, until the twelfth and thirteenth centuries. The Church was not interested in challenging the various governments that continued strict regulation of the marriage of servants, and hence that controlled the economic and political

---

[72] Boswell, *Same-Sex Unions*, pp. 186–87.

[73] Brown, Pagels, and Boswell discuss this at some length.

[74] Boswell, *Same-Sex Unions*, pp. 119–21.

[75] Boswell does not see it this way. He writes that the union ideally joined man and woman as brother and sister and could "imply an absence of sexuality," but adds, "It is doubtful that the average Christian felt this way" (p. 24). But again, it is hard to know exactly what the "average Christian" felt about this, or even if such a creature existed. What counts as today's "average Christian"? Average for where? Ann Arbor? Michigan? The United States? The world? The last decade? The last year?

privileges of its members in a manner quite similar to the regimes in the pre-Christian era.

The eighth-century canonists handled the conflict between Christian and secular requirements over the status necessary for marriage (none in the New Testament and many in secular law) by reading secular definitions back into Christian ones. All adults should be able to make marital vows, but only if they are free agents, the canonists held. Lacking that status, slaves could not require the Church to recognize their vows as legitimate.[76] One source of the ambiguity lay in the canon law's different definitions of marriage. The Italian commentator Gratian later includes texts and commentary in which the Church acknowledged unions between those who could not legally marry, even if they were of different classes or violated other juridical codes. The Church viewed these as "second class marriages."[77] The Church's validation of unions among the poor and peasants as "marriages" protected these individuals from punishment for those sins associated with "fornication."[78] As long as the Church vaguely legitimated its members' sexual relations, absence of state recognition was not a significant problem, from the point of view of the Church. Despite the Church's evolving views on marriage, and their control of the ecclesiastical courts from the thirteenth century in England, the standard for what counted as a legal marriage continued to be whatever the state said it was. However, after the sacralization of marriage vows throughout Europe, the state began to enforce the views of the Church.[79]

Hence, against the view of marriage as a spiritual relation practiced by Christians, for the purpose of achieving the grace of God, the extensive compromises manifest in in the Church's recognition of marriage—and the state's reliance on the institution to control property and other feudal privileges—suggest that marriage continues to have economic effects remarkably similar to those of the pagan epochs. As was the case for collapsed

---

[76] Michael Sheehan, *Marriage, Family, and Law in Medieval Europe: Collected Studies* (Toronto, Buffalo: University of Toronto Press, 1996), pp. 224, 226, 230. Sheehan adds that this distinction continued in Roman canon law until 1983.

[77] James Brundage, "Concubinage and Marriage in Medieval Canon Law," in *Medieval Canon Law* (New York: Longman, 1995), p. 119. Brundage believes that Gratian came up with this two-tiered system based on a misreading of previous rules and practices: "Gratian's misunderstanding of his texts may have been colossal, but it guided subsequent generations of canonists in formulating a new law of concubinage for the western Church" (ibid., p. 122). Less important than Gratian's accuracy is his presentation of his convictions as legitimated by what has been done in the past, even as he is in fact offering rather substantial innovations. Whereas some practices, e.g., changes in laws regulating trade, might be justified in terms of the future, marriage laws are legitimated by virtue of what (is said) occurred in the past.

[78] Sheehan, *Marriage, Family, and Law*, pp. 216–17.

[79] Frederick Pollock and Frederic Maitland, *The History of English Law Before the Time of Edward I*, vol. 2, 2d ed. (Cambridge: Cambridge University Press, 1911), p. 367.

economic and political privileges in Athens and Rome, medieval parishes also based their memberships (and their prerogatives of guild and parish benefits) on principles of birth and kinship. If the ethos from the New Testament were followed, then any man could marry any woman and live anywhere, regardless of their ancestry or place of birth. That this was not the case shows the dominance of the intergenerational political society's views on marriage, and the substantive irrelevance of Church doctrine. In short, marriage practices in the medieval era do not follow from religious tenets, and they continue to reproduce the economic and political alliances of what Marx refers to as Stände (usually translated as 'estates'). Membership in parishes throughout Europe required legitimate birth in a particular parish. The use of wealth as a criterion for marriage ensured that offspring would be arranged for, and hence not burden the manor or the parish.[80] When poor people, denied the right to marry, had children, these children were illegitimate. Therefore not only were the parents prohibited from receiving support by the parish, but in the thirteenth through fifteenth centuries in England, they were also fined: "On many medieval manors single women and widows of unfree status who fornicated had to pay a fine called 'larwyte'. . . . On some manors one finds another fine called 'childwyte' which servile women had to pay for bearing children out of wed-lock."[81] As in ancient Athens, the poor could not have legitimate children—since they could not marry—and therefore their (illegitimate) offspring would not be the legal responsibility of the village.[82]

Marriage Discourse: The Shift from Positive to Natural Law

During the medieval period in England, civil courts were in charge of property rights and inheritance, while ecclesiastical courts controlled marriage. Obviously cases would arise where the two jurisdictions overlapped and disagreements arose. One chief difference, alluded to above, was the matter of marriages among servants. Canon law did not proscribe marriage among servants and hence might be viewed as more open than, say, Athenian and even Roman law. But in practice norms circumscribed this prerogative. The ecclesiastical courts would bow to the conventions of the feudal lord's absolute authority, as when one court annulled a marriage with the

[80] The class character of marriage was such that the word 'husband' meant what it does now, as well as a man who "held a substantial tenement." Similarly 'Anilepi' meant both "only" and referred to an unmarried man as well as a landless man (George Caspar Homans, *English Villagers of the Thirteenth Century* [New York: Russell and Russell, 1960], pp. 136–37).

[81] Zvi Razi, *Life, Marriage and Death in a Medieval Parish: Economy, Society and Demography in Halesowen, 1270–1400* (Cambridge: Cambridge University Press, 1980), p. 64.

[82] Ibid.

justification that the status of the "husband of servile condition was a fact at issue."[83] In nullifying a marriage on these grounds, the Church court accepted the status distinction imposed by positive law, not God.

At the same time, the authors of various decretals and treatises began to develop a competing view of marriage, that marriage was natural. The argument that privileged the Church's view of marriage over that of the state asserted that the relation of the serf to the lord was merely one of "positive law," and that this tie was superseded by natural law, which was represented as the basis of species reproduction. When in conflict—when a lord would not give a serf permission to marry—natural law ought to prevail: "Towards the middle of the thirteenth century, theologians such as Albert the Great and Thomas Aquinas would lift the discussion to a new level with the doctrine that the exercise of the appetite which continues the human species by generation pertains to natural law. Since servitude is of positive law, it must yield to the former."[84]

Jack Goody points out certain financial consequences of (incentives for) the Church's new views. At the same time that the Church was expanding marriage rights for the poor, Pope Gregory restricted marriage for the wealthy. In ancient Athens and Rome men would marry the widows of their deceased brothers, to preserve wealth in the patrilineal family. The marriage of first cousins was common for similar reasons of estate continuity. The Roman Church, with little or no scriptural basis, banned both practices, as well as adoptions and concubinage relations among the degrees of family. One consequence was an increase in lands and wealth donated to the Church, through one of two routes. Either the families would obey the rules and lack suitable heirs, or they would bribe the Church to grant them special exemptions. Had the Church not placed so many restrictions on marriage, property would have remained in various families rather than being under the control of the Church.[85]

Even in Lutheran-dominated areas during the Reformation, where one might expect a more individualistic, decentralized pattern of marriage—commitments subject to the wishes of the potential husband and wife rather than either the state or religious officials—the restrictions on marriage were, ironically, even more severe. Until the nineteenth century "most [German] states had long-standing laws forbidding marriage to those unable to demonstrate steady work and some savings."[86] Isabel Hull shows that throughout the early modern period "marriage was a colossally over-determined institution," as "[w]ealth, social standing, adulthood, independence, livelihood, communal responsibility, (for males) political represen-

---

[83] Everard f 55Bv, cited in Michael Sheehan, *Marriage, Family, and Law*, p. 44.
[84] Ibid., p. 235.
[85] Goody, *The Development of the Family*, pp. 46, 72, 74, 95.
[86] Ibid., pp. 142–43.

tation and sexual expression were all joined symbolically in this one estate."[87] For purposes of internal movement and employment, birth and lineage reproduced class privileges. To be a guild member, one had to be a legitimate son, but that required that one's father have a certain amount of wealth to have qualified for marriage: "The main principle driving guild morality was exclusion," and the criteria used for this were birth and marriage. Hull notes that the guild's insistence on legitimacy was an "obsession."[88]

The elimination of these laws in the nineteenth century in Germany had as much to do with capitalism as with the success of Christian ideology: "[W]hereas before productive work was supposed to be guaranteed before marriage and acceptance as a citizen of a village, now marriage came to be seen as almost a panacea guaranteeing the will to work and order society from inside, so to speak, from the volition and self-interest of the individual."[89] But what Hull describes as the motivation to work seems not to be "self-interest," since that would presumably motivate a man to work for himself, and deter him from being encumbered with a family. Instead, the shift in the rules expresses the view that families provide motives for one to work on behalf of others. The idea is that there is something special about being in a family that will foster the work ethic, not because one is an individual, but because one is a husband and a father.

The New Familial State and the State of Nature

The most significant change during the thirteenth through fifteenth centuries in the practices and rhetoric of the family and political society entail a reversal within the metonymic relationship ordering the two. In ancient Athens and Rome, to repeat Peter Brown's observation, the family was a "microcosm of the social order."[90] The family was a set of relations that clearly followed from the requirements of the state. By the late middle ages, the relation had reversed, with the king widely recognized as the father and the embodiment of an ostensibly pre-political family, one given by natural law. Through discourses of Christianity and other rhetorics that invoked nature, the family came to be represented as the primary building block of political society, and the state as the macro-cosm of the family. In both periods the state, and, intermittently, later the Church, are responsible for producing these discourses. The difference is that in

[87] *Sexuality, State, and Civil Society in Germany, 1700–1815* (Ithaca: Cornell University Press, 1996), p. 31.

[88] Ibid, pp. 42–43.

[89] Ibid., p. 144.

[90] Brown, *The Body and Society*, p. 17.

the earlier period, the state's interventions were fairly obvious. From the plays of Sophocles and Aristophanes to the political treatises of Plato, the juridical character of marriage is palpable. Whereas the elected Cleisthenes assigned deme membership based on his sovereignty, England's King Edward would assign himself sovereignty based on his birth, and that of his subjects, claiming his authority as a consequence and not a cause of the family and of political membership.

The British monarchy claimed its prerogatives from God and natural law, not political norms. One underlying difference in regime form that may help to explain why ancient Athens and Rome did not base the legitimacy of their rules on nature is that the democracies did not have hereditary kings but elected leaders. Hence there were no instrumental reasons for the leaders to insist on accounts of their authority that would depend on a naturalized model of a hierarchical family as the basis for political rule. In ancient Athens and Rome, marriage and citizenship rules were decided by the same leaders and the same *politeia* that passed all other laws. Hereditary monarchs, however, in medieval and early modern Europe had good reasons to obscure the political character of the family form, and to claim the family both natural and divine.

From the twelfth century onward, rather than the family reproducing the order of political society, the metonymy's dominant causal arrow points in the opposite direction. Familial images associated with the prerogative of fathers are thought to be reflections of what is natural and original, while political society is represented, ideally, as reproducing these arrangements. Of course the family before and after the twelfth century is always a political, as opposed to a natural, imperative, but its phenomenology changes markedly. The juridical rules after the twelfth century constitute a so-called natural family, the idea of which the monarchy depends on for its legitimacy. The king, as father, creates subjects. For instance, James's sovereignty over Scotland is enough to make Scotland one with England and, by extension, to make the "Scottish" people "English." After the conquest the two people had become a "natural family where a common paternity made sons and daughters into brothers and sisters."[91]

Modern Citizenship Rules

Although in the eighth through twelfth centuries the discourse linking family with nature was used by the Church to challenge the exclusionary marriage rules enforced by the king's courts, the natural family as the basis of political legitimacy was a model later successfully used by the monarchies

---

[91] Kettner, *The Development of American Citizenship 1608–1870* (Chapel Hill: University of North Carolina Press, 1978), p. 22.

throughout Europe, as a justification for their prerogatives to both subjugate populations and to regulate marriages within their particular kingdoms. Once the view that marriage and families are natural was in place, the monarchs could use this rhetoric as a means to legitimate the authority of the king qua father, the figure with a natural right to absolute power. This is not a fancy retrospective view, but the very history of the knowledge of political power that royalist Robert Filmer offers in 1680, in the opening lines of his "Patriarcha: Or the Natural Power of Kings":[92]

Chapter 1
That the First Kings Were Fathers of Families

I. Since the time that school divinity began to flourish there hath been a common opinion maintained, as well by divines as by divers other learned men, which affirms:

'Mankind is naturally endowed and born with freedom from all subjection, and at liberty to choose what form of government it please, and that the power which any one man hath over others was at first bestowed according to the discretion of the multitude.'

This tenet was first hatched in the schools, and hath been fostered by all succeeding Papists for good divinity.[93]

According to Filmer, Catholics, i.e., foreigners (in this case, Francisco Suarez), were responsible for the English Puritan and other seventeenth-century democrats who were falsely claiming that people had natural rights that the kings could not abrogate. Filmer does not see the view justifying patriarchy as an ancient one. Rather, Filmer's arguments are contemporary corrections of mistaken egalitarian, Christian histories of the canonists (who were untrustworthy for, among other failings, being Catholic, although their Puritan counterparts are Filmer's direct targets).[94] Filmer thus positions his argument against a "recent" interpretation of older texts, so that his views and those of his sympathizers may be seen as a challenge

---

[92] Gordon Schochet offers an extended compelling argument for viewing Filmer's understanding of the familial metaphor for the king as one that "differed from previous ones" (*The Authoritarian Family and Political Attitudes in 17th-Century England: Patriarchalism in Political Thought* [New Brunswick and London: Transaction Books, 1988], p. 139).

[93] From *Locke, Two Treatises of Government, with Filmer's Patriarcha* (New York: Hafner, 1947), p. 251. Filmer is paraphrasing Deuteronomy 17:15.

[94] In his 1644 "Presbyterian Principles of Resistance" Samuel Rutherford writes: "And if all men be born equally free (as I hope to prove), there is no reason in nature why one man should be king and lord over another; therefore. . .I conceive all jurisdiction of man over man to be, as it were, artificial and positive, and that it interfereth some servitude whereof nature from the womb hath freed us, if you except that subjection of children to parents, and the wife to the husband." in A.S.P. Woodhouse, *Puritanism and Liberty: Being the Army Debates (1647–1649) from the Clarke Manuscripts with Supplementary Documents* (Chicago: University of Chicago Press, 1951), p. 201, and see pp. 206–7.

to the current intellectual climate, and not its hegemonic reiteration.[95] Filmer's seventeenth century monarchists represent a tradition that had been broken by the schoolmen and the social contract thinkers, and then, in Filmer's work, resumed: "Late writers have taken up too much upon trust from the subtle schoolmen, who, to be sure to thrust down the king below the pope, thought it the safest course to advance the people above the king, that so the papal power might take place of the regal."[96] By locating the king's authority neither in "the people" nor in the Church, but in "natural law," Filmer uses his alternative reading of the Bible (at odds with its invocation by franchise-seeking "freemen") to legitimate the monarchy. Rather than revert to the Augustinean and sixteenth century contract belief that political societies are conventional (and perhaps even contractual), Filmer accepts the natural law doctrine of the Church, but then uses it to argue that, like families, political societies are naturally patriarchal.

Filmer does not argue that monarchies are legitimate because they are themselves natural families, since this is not the case: "It is true, all kings be not natural parents of their subjects, yet they all either are, or are to be reputed, the next heirs to those first progenitors who were at first the natural parents of the whole people."[97] Patriarchal authority is legitimate because it **resembles** families. The "fatherly right of sovereign authority" is "**substituted** properly by God, from whom he receives his royal charter of an universal father."[98] The law of nature that leads to families is presented by Filmer as the metonymic path that leads toward the legitimacy of monarchical authority, which is not a claim that kings are ontological fathers. Patriarchy's legitimacy, on Filmer's account, lies not in people believing themselves the direct descendants of any particular king. Patriarchal monarchies are thought legitimate because nature makes families: Kingdoms began as families, and therefore whatever holds for families holds for kingdoms as well, even if they are not really families. The natural law model of legitimacy is not at odds with the positive law of kings, but rather, is its basis. Instead of emphasizing how families are miniature political societies, Filmer says that monarchies are big families: "as the father over one family, so the king, as father over many families, extends

---

[95] It is possible that Filmer was paranoid, and that "common opinion" was on his side all along. He would not be the first political writer to have a false sense of marginality. Regardless of the actual character of public opinion, Filmer makes a plausible argument locating the sources of patriarchal authoritarianism as recent, which is especially interesting in light of his so-called traditionalism and conservatism. For an argument advancing the thesis that Filmer was an iconoclast, see James Daly, *Sir Robert Filmer and English Political Thought* (Toronto, London: University of Toronto Press, 1979).

[96] Filmer, "Patriarcha," p. 253.

[97] Ibid., p. 258.

[98] Ibid., p. 259, emphasis added.

his care to preserve, feed, clothe, instruct, and defend the whole common-
wealth."[99] Whereas in antiquity, the authority associated with governmental hierarchies is used to legitimate the power relations of the family, in
early modern England the power relations of the family are the bedrock
for those in political society.

Modern Nations

Filmer's work is of the sort that presents justifications for a particular form
of government. He is not interested in rules pertaining to the inclusions
and exclusions of members. Yet the implications of the natural family view
of the commonwealth are not confined to theories of participation and
obligation but extend to contemporary rules governing the nexus of citizenship, property rights, and eminent domain. After Filmer's side loses, after
kings are overthrown, the patriarchal logic of familial belonging—rejected
for its rules of **governmental** legitimacy—is nonetheless appropriated by
"the people" to define new, republican **policies of membership**. The
citizenship criteria of lineage and birth that were regarded as political in
antiquity are revived, but now as natural. This is the point at which most
recent histories of the nation and nationalism begin, but as we have seen,
the origins of nation, meaning a political community defining its members
through birth, are much earlier. If we consider the specific rules of inclusion
and exclusion that dominate citizenship policies throughout the world, the
resonance and continuation of the past can be seen in the present.

Selected Modern Citizenship Policies

The following cases show that modern and contemporary citizenship rules
are largely similar across political societies, despite the very different locations and longevity of these political societies. Paradigmatically, citizenship
requires that one either be born in a particular territory or have at least
one parent as a citizen of that political society, though whether that parent
be a mother or a father varies, along with the requirement of the potential
citizen's legitimacy, i.e., that one's parents be married. These variations
among modern societies are the same ones that existed in ancient Athens,
over the course of approximately three hundred years, and are what make
it plausible to locate a continual grammar of political society and nation,
rather than date the concept of the nation as peculiarly modern, or
uniquely Western.[100]

[99] Ibid., p. 260.
[100] The following cases were selected because they reflect a diversity of region, religion, and
age of political society. I have come across no cases of political societies whose paradigmatic

BOTSWANA

According to the Citizenship Act of 1984: 4. 1) a person born in Botswana shall be a citizen of Botswana by birth and descent if, at the time of his birth: a) his father was a citizen of Botswana; or, in the case of a person born out of wedlock, his mother was a citizen of Botswana. 5. 1) A person born outside Botswana shall be a citizen of Botswana by descent if, at the time of his birth:—a) his father was a citizen of Botswana; b) in the case of a person born out of wedlock, his mother was a citizen of Botswana. **NB:** This restriction to patrilineal citizenship was ruled unconstitutional in 1990; the citizenship of the wife is now sufficient for rendering her children citizens.[101]

GREAT BRITAIN

One is a citizen if either parent is a citizen, or if one parent is a settled resident. One may also become a citizen if one was a commonwealth citizen and had a parent or grandparent born in the United Kingdom. Children born in Great Britain to parents who have restrictions on their residency are not automatically granted citizenship. Children of non-settled residents may acquire citizenship if: 1) either parent becomes a citizen or settled before the child is 18; or 2) the child remains in the United Kingdom for ten years after his birth. If a child is found abandoned in the territory of Great Britain the assumption will be that the parent is a citizen. One may also become a citizen by marrying a citizen. If a child is born abroad to unmarried parents then the mother must be a citizen.[102]

ESTONIA

"In March 1993, the Estonian Parliament approved amendments expanding the eligibility for citizenship through one's ancestors. Thus citizens are those . . . persons who are regarded as citizens by international treaties;

---

membership rules did not rely on invocations of birth. For a more thorough rendering of modern citizenship rules in Europe, see *Citizenship and Nationality in the New Europe*, Síofra O'Leary and Tija Tiilikainen, eds. (London: Sweet and Maxwell, 1998).

[101] Citizenship Act of 1984, from *The Citizenship Case: The Attorney General of the Republic of Botswana vs. Unity Dow*, compiled and edited by Unity Dow (Gaborone, Botswana: Lentswe La Lesedi: 1995). This case was brought when Unity Dow's son, who was born in Botswana, was not allowed to become a citizen. Unity Dow, who is a Botswanan citizen, had married an American citizen. She eventually won her lawsuit and her children were given Botswanan citizenship.

[102] British Nationality Act of 1981, in Ivor Stanbrook, *British Nationality* (London and Brussels: Clement, 1982), and Anna Marie Smith, *New Right Discourse on Race and Sexuality: Britain, 1968–1990* (Cambridge: Cambridge University Press, 1994), pp. 180–81.

persons born to at least one parent who was a citizen at the time of birth; and children residing in Estonia whose citizenship in another country cannot be established."[103]

INDIA

Indian citizenship is regulated by the Citizenship Act, 1955. This provides for citizenship by being born in India "on or after 26th day of January, 1950"; or, if one is born elsewhere, "if his father is a citizen at the time of his birth . . . and his birth is registered at an Indian Consulate within one year of its occurrence . . ."; or they may obtain citizenship "by naturalisation," which would require that the applicant render "distinguished service to the cause of science, philosophy, art, literature, world peace or human progress generally"; finally, people may be made citizens "if any territory becomes a part of India . . . the Central Government may by order notified in the Official Gazette specify the persons who shall be citizens of India by reasons of their connection with that territory and those persons shall be citizens of India as from the date to be specified in the order."[104]

JORDAN

According to the 1986 laws, one is a citizen if one: 1) acquired citizenship from the laws of 1928; 2) had Palestinian citizenship before May 15, 1948 and lived in Jordan from December 20, 1939 to February 16, 1954; 3) one's father is a Jordanian citizen; or 4) one's mother is a Jordanian citizen and one was born in the Hashemite kingdom, and one's father is of unknown citizenship or stateless.[105]

LITHUANIA

"The Lithuanian Citizenship Law [1991] extends citizenship to persons who were born in the territory of the Republic of Lithuania, who were citizens prior to 1940 (as well as their children and grandchildren), or who became citizens under the legislation in effect prior to 11 December 1991. . . . In order to qualify for naturalization, an applicant must pass a

---

[103] *Israel Yearbook on Human Rights*, vol. 23 (Tel Aviv: Tel Aviv Faculty of Law, 1993), p. 255. This includes an excellent compendium of citizenship rules for countries of the former Soviet Union.

[104] Justice E. S. Venkataramiah, "Who are Indian Citizens?" in *Citizenship: Rights and Duties* (Naga: Proprietrix, 1988).

[105] Uri Davis, "Jinsiyya vs. Muwatana: The Question of Citizenship and the State in the Middle East," *Arab Studies Quarterly*, vol. 17 (1/2) (Winter/Spring, 1995), pp. 31–36.

Lithuanian language examination; must have been resident in Lithuania for the past ten years; must have a permanent job or source of income; and must renounce his current citizenship."[106]

Despite some differences that vary along lines of matrilineal or patrilineal descent and requirements for language proficiency, the pattern is fairly clear. Citizenship depends first on ideas about ancestral lineage, and then on conventions of marriage, territory, and possibly language. Although the lineage principle in many countries operates independently of juridical rules for legitimacy, in other contexts marriage and the nationality of a legal relation are extremely important. For instance, the child of the unknown father in Jordan and the abandoned child in Great Britain may be citizens, while the child of a Jordanian woman and a German man may not be a citizen of these respective countries, even if born in either Jordan or Great Britain. Less important than inconsistencies in the details of these kinship schemes is the fact that these state-nations use some nexus of ancestry and land for purposes of citizenship. Overall, there is nothing random about these rules, and little aspirational to norms of merit.

Membership Certified by Birth Not Choice

The logic of familial membership for one's status as a citizen restricts individuals' choices by criteria other than those of achievement and certainly prevents residence based on whimsy. When the state wants to call on its marriage rules to determine membership and then inflict punishments, simple self-identification is irrelevant. Consider the following event in Rwanda: "A child of a mixed Hutu and Tutsi marriage, [Godence M.] walked for days, passing herself off as a Hutu, until a militia man demanded her identity card at a roadblock and discovered that in the eyes of the law she was Tutsi. He offered her a choice; she could die at once or agree to be his sexual slave." Godence became pregnant and delivered the child: "It's a big problem for me . . . because everyone knows I had a child from the interhamwe. They say I'm a wife of the interhamwe."[107] In this case her Hutu mother's marriage puts Godence into a legal relation with her Tutsi father. There is no "Tutsi" gene that trumps the mother's "Hutu" gene. It is the laws of paternity that render Godence Tutsi, and it is the logic of political societies that they select a line of maternity or paternity to guarantee that a child is only one ethnicity or another. That in Rwanda

---

[106] *Israel Yearbook*, pp. 253–54.
[107] James McKinley Jr., "Legacy of Rwanda Violence: The Thousands Born of Rape," *New York Times*, September 23, 1996, A9.

and elsewhere one may often pass under an identity of one's choosing should not distract from the fact that it is the form of political society itself that constitutes the range of possible identities, and that a political society's regulatory authority over this is supreme.

Birth, Marriage, and Citizenship in the United States

Even the United States, with no patina of autochthony myths or patriarchal legacy of former monarchies, invokes principles of birth in the territory and descent to determine citizenship. Anyone born in United States territory is considered a citizen. For those born abroad to U.S. citizens, marriage continues to affect the citizenship of husbands and wives, as well as their children. The specific background to kinship rules used for citizenship in modern political societies begins in France, in 1803, when Napoleon passed a law expatriating French women who married aliens. To avoid a scenario of stateless wives, France pressed other countries to pass reciprocal laws, so that simultaneous with the loss of French citizenship upon marriage to a U.S. man would be the assignment of, say, United States citizenship.[108] After years of such reciprocity in practice, and following England's passage of a similar law in 1844, in 1855 the United States Congress passed a law allowing naturalization for alien women who married U.S. citizens: "Any woman who might lawfully be naturalized under the existing laws, married, or who shall be married to a citizen of the United States shall be deemed and taken to be a citizen."[109] From 1855 to 1907 this law was used to deprive women in the United States of their citizenship. The reasoning was that if alien women gain their husbands' nationalities, then United States women must also take their husbands' nationalities. The law's most significant impact was on the status of children born to a United States woman and an alien man. The question was confined to children born abroad, after the civil rights amendments of the 1860s stipulated that birth in the territory of the United States conferred citizenship (except on Indians). In 1802 *jus sanguinis* rule in the United States applied only to citizens who were fathers, and not to mothers.[110] The culmination of these practices gendering citizenship was a 1907 law that explicitly expatriated women who married aliens. It required "merging . . . the nationality of an American woman in that of her alien husband." This law consolidated the previous court rulings that adopted similar positions. The law was modified

---

[108] Waldo Emerson Waltz, *The Nationality of Married Women: A Study of Domestic Policies and International Legislation* (Urbana: University of Illinois Press, 1937), p. 59.

[109] Ibid., p. 23.

[110] *Davis v. Hall* House Doc. 326, *Barzias v. Hopkins* (1824), cited in Waltz, *Nationality of Married Women*, p. 32.

in 1922 so that only women marrying men "not eligible for citizenship" were expatriated,[111] and in 1931 the law finally held that women "shall not be expatriated because of marriage."[112]

Currently, the citizenship requirements in the United States are: 1) one is born in the sovereign territory of the United States; or 2) one's mother is a United States citizen; or 3) one's father is a U.S. citizen and married to one's mother.[113] Citizenship by marriage occurs when an alien is married to a citizen in a ceremony deemed consistent with United States marriage laws. The U.S. Defense of Marriage Act (1996) therefore affects citizenship. If a United States male citizen marries three wives in Iran, that marriage will not be recognized in the United States and none of the wives will receive citizenship. Similarly, if a same-sex couple is legally wed in Denmark, the fact that one partner is a United States citizen will not render his or her non-American spouse a citizen. The federal Defense of Marriage Act codifies what had been Immigration and Naturalization Service (INS) and other federal agency practices that had been upheld by the courts:

> In determining the meaning of any Act of Congress, or any ruling, regulation, or interpretation of the various administrative bureaus of the United States, the word 'marriage' means only a legal union between one man and one woman as husband and wife, and the word 'spouse' refers only to a person of the opposite sex who is a husband or a wife.[114]

So it is not marriage *per se* but a marriage that fits the definition of United States law that may constitute United States citizens. There is nothing natural about this definition of marriage. If this union were natural, it would not require a law. And yet though marriage is not natural, this particular version of marriage has been naturalized and is the basis for citizenship. Hence the juridical family form that determines immigration policy also regulates a naturalized discourse of nationality, one that renders this form of being to be inherited from one's parents: " '[N]obody is quite so apt to be of the same national origins of our present citizens as are the

---

[111] For a survey of 72 countries' rules on marriage and nationality, through 1928, see U.S. House Hearings Before the Committee on Immigration and Naturalization, 70th Congress, 1st session, *Effect of Marriage Upon Nationality*, statement by Emma Wold, May 19, 1928 (Washington, D.C.: GPO, 1928). See also E. P. Hutchison, *Legislative History of American Immigration Policy, 1798–1965* (Philadelphia: University of Pennsylvania Press, 1985).

[112] Waltz, *Nationality of Married Women*, pp. 51–52.

[113] *Fiallo v. Bell*, 430 U.S. 787 (1977). A June, 1995 report from a governmental commission on immigration policy recommends reducing the number of spaces available for immigration based on work skills and extended family relations and suggests the state "emphasize the importance of the nuclear family as the basic unit of immigration" on grounds that it is "not in the national interest" for nuclear families to be apart. Robert Pear, "Change in Policy for Immigration Is Urged by Panel," *New York Times*, June 5, 1995, A1, A7.

[114] Public Law 104–199.

members of their immediate families.' "[115] This widely held intuition does not follow from something intrinsic to groups or biological reproduction of the species, but from specific conventions that regulate membership in a political society, and hence one's identity vis-à-vis the familial rules that produce these forms of being.

The Family Estate and the Nation

Among the purposes of the patrilineage, marriage, and membership rules discussed above, a major objective appears to be ensuring that wealth shall be passed on through families. With this observation in mind, inheritance practices that articulate with marriage rules may seem to be instrumental to consolidating strictly private wealth and have little to do with the articulation of a particular political membership. Yet the exclusions of certain residents from the prerogative to own or inherit land do more than establish the rules for broad economic alliances and antagonisms of class. In addition, the exclusion of aliens from the right to own land and the invocation of territorial sovereignty for purposes of legitimating monarchical sovereignty over "subjects"—and other kinds of governments' sovereignty over "citizens"—has the effect of sacralizing the land, and rendering control of it a symptom of the particularity of membership. When one must be a member (subject or citizen) to own certain kinds of property; when birth in the land bestows citizenship; and of course, when the government can assert the prerogative to control what happens on any property in its territory, then land is not private property, but the sovereign's eminent domain. It is this notion of the sovereign's co-extension with his realm, the metonymies of the king's body, the political body, and the actual territory of the realm that defined the European state-nations. The details of how birth in a realm constitutes one's membership in it suggests that the territorial principle is complementary to membership by lineage, not in tension with it.[116]

A territorial birth criterion for membership does not allow for consent, since a fetus does not decide where it will be born. Further, contrary to the view held by some contemporary historians and others, laws assigning

[115] David Riemers, *Still the Golden Door: The Third World Comes to America* (New York: Columbia University Press, 1992), p. 72, quoted in Carla McKenzie, "Assessing the Similarities Between Quotas and Family Reunification: Membership Rules in the 1924 National Origin Quota Act, the 1952 McCarran Walter act, and the 1965 Immigration and Nationality," unpublished typescript, University of Michigan, Ann Arbor. McKenzie provides an excellent analysis and documentation of the racial effects of the family reunification immigration policies.

[116] Ernst Kantorowicz, *The King's Two Bodies: A Study in Medieval Political Theology* (Princeton: Princeton University Press, 1957).

membership by birth in a territory are neither empirically or logically more inclusive than those assigning membership by birth to parents who are members. The relative inclusivity of each rule depends entirely on specific patterns of migration, and the existence and enforcement of laws regulating transnational movement. In the case of political membership, the relevant bounded territory is always more than a geological mass. That it is sometimes land and not ancestry that confers membership entails a politically determined geographical space as another metonym of kinship. The fetish of birth in the modern state-nation is Durkheim's totemic spot, invoked as sacred and constitutive of membership. That is why Mrs. Ching, despite being born in Mainland China, may be able to gain legal residency in Hong Kong. One of her six children was born in Hong Kong and was therefore considered a legal resident. His status as legal resident, then, "entitles Mrs. Ching and the rest of the family to Hong Kong residency as well."[117] Despite being the son of a Chinese citizen, birth in the territory gives the son citizenship in Hong Kong, and then, by extension, his mother also. Birth in the territory and kinship are complementary principles, with the territory itself serving as a metonymic parent—conveying the prerogative of membership in a political family.

In British common law—the basis of the contemporary practices of countries that grant citizenship by birth in a territory and still the center-piece of the English judiciary—the sacred area is the territory associated with the divine prerogative of the king. Edward Coke, an English jurist (1552-1634) whose writings developed into crucial resources for British common law, writes, "All the lands within this realme were originally derived from the crown, and therefore the king is sovereign lord, or lord paramount, either mediate or immediate of all and every parcell of land within the realme."[118] This sovereignty takes its form through the ligeance that binds those born within "the realme" to the king. That the lands of the realme "originally derived from the Crown" means that the king **is** and therefore **has** the realm, embodying it as much as owning it, and this includes the inhabitants as well. Coke describes "*legeantia naturalis*" as the "true and faithful obedience of the subject due to his sovereign. For as soon as he is born, he oweth by birth-right allegiance and obedience to his sovereign."[119] Contrariwise, an "alien" is one "borne in a strange country . . . out of the ligeance of the king."[120] The logic of membership initially denoted the obligations, not the rights, that "aliens" have toward the

---

[117] Edward Gargan, "Illegal Chinese Race to Get Toehold in Hong Kong," *New York Times*, May 23, 1997, A3.

[118] *The First Part of the Institutes of the Laws of England*, 16th ed. (London: L. Hansard and Sons, 1809), section 85.

[119] Kettner, *Development of American Citizenship*, p. 7, quoting Coke.

[120] *First Institutes*, section 198.

Crown. Full political membership, including the right to own land and pass it on as an inheritance to one's children, was reserved for those with British parents. This right applied only intermittently to the children of English subjects born abroad, leading Pollock and Maitland to write that "every Child born elsewhere is an alien, no matter the nationality of their parents."[121] The principle for membership at first seems quite straightforward: "The place of birth is all-important."[122] But the exception to this rule is so large that one wonders whether birthplace is in fact the main rule.

If children born to English parents out of the king's ligeance (England and those lands conquered and occupied by England) were not subjects, as Maitland and Pollock maintain, then one would infer that ancestry was not an important criterion for membership in the English nation. But it was also the case that prior to 1699 birth within the realm did not grant "alien" children the rights of freemen. By excluding alien children born in England from the prerogatives of the English, England was relying on ancestry as a prerequisite for the claim to be an Englishman. As early as the thirteenth century, "there is the cry of 'England for the English.'"[123] Birthplace therefore was a condition that was necessary but not sufficient for English nationality.

That numerous individuals were affected by rules of alien status can be inferred from the many alien communities that could pay a "fine" and buy out of British politics and the legal system entirely.[124] Aliens might also request mixed juries to decide criminal as well as civil matters. A mixed jury required that equal numbers of resident aliens and English sit for a trial of a resident alien. Marianne Constable sees this requirement as indicative of a communitarian sensibility, also implied in the practice of what is called "personal law." This practice required that "judgment of a person must be according to the law or customs of that person's community."[125] The fact that such specifications existed is parasitic on the

---

[121] Pollock and Maitland, *The History of English Law: Before the Time of Edward I*, vol. I, 2d ed. (Cambridge: Cambridge University Press, 1968), p. 458.

[122] Ibid.

[123] Ibid. p. 463.

[124] William Cunningham, *Alien Immigrants to England* (London and New York: MacMillan, 1897), p. 38. These communities were still ultimately in the King's ligeance, which is why they had to negotiate the conditions of their temporary sovereignty over particular matters. Of the 'alien' Coke writes: ". . . the etymologie of the word signifieth one borne in a strange country, under the obedience of a strange prince or country . . . out of the ligeance of the king." But these 'aliens' have children born within the realm, who still are not regarded as English. *First Institutes*, sec. 198.

[125] *The Law of the Other: The Mixed Jury and Changing Conceptions of Citizenship, Law, and Knowledge* (Chicago: University of Chicago Press, 1994), p. 25. A slightly more cynical understanding of this practice may be gleaned from the fact that mixed juries were also used to verify economic information recorded in the Domesday Book. The purpose here was clearly not to

possibility of recognizably alien communities within the realm, and contradicts the membership principle Coke emphasizes, of ligeance obtained simply by birth within the realm.

Just as those who were borne in the realm (of either Scottish or English parents) had a natural tie to the king, those who were born elsewhere lacked this tie and therefore could not pass on land to their heirs. According to Coke, "If an alien Christian or infidel purchase houses, lands, tenements, or heritaments to him and his heirs, albeit he can have no heire, yet he is of capacity to take a fee simple, but not to hold." This means that upon his death, the estate of the alien goes to the king.[126] The common law reason for this was that men were "presumed to bear Faith and Love to that Prince and Country where first he received Protection during his Infancy,"[127] a familial image suggesting that the king's territory is metonymic of his body. But why assume that the place where one "first received protection during Infancy" is the place to which one would be loyal? Why not the country where one was raised after infancy, when one is, by definition, linguistically and culturally competent? Why not the country where one is able to work? Why not the country where others speak the language one speaks? To reduce the principle of foreignness to simply birth in a territory requires that a political society be regarded as a family, which one also joins at birth. In sum, the details of how territory is combined and separated from lineage are less important than the familial form of being that results from all of these permutations.

In medieval and late-medieval England there is a conflation of nationality with land ownership, similar to the overlap in ancient Athens and Rome. Under the ancient feudal practices of war captured enemies are enslaved. Coke writes that the villeanage system "begins in war, when men [were] captured but not allowed to be killed."[128] For this reason, medieval historian Susan Reynolds refers to the period from 900 to 1300 as "military" and not "feudal."[129] The military paradigm is one that suggests antagonistic communities, while "feudal" relations might be associated with a single

---

represent culturally specific interpretations of how to answer questions about one's occupation, but rather, to demonstrate that one side was not cheating or being cheated. As J. H. Round puts it, " 'Conquerors and conquered were alike bound by their common sworn verdicts," *Feudal England* (London, 1895), p. 120, quoted in H. C. Darnby, *Domesday England*, p. 5.

[126] Coke, *First Part of the Institutes*, chapter 1, section 2a-b.

[127] Kettner, *Development of American Citizenship*, p. 31, quoting Matthew Bacon, *A New Abridgement of the Law* in 3d ed. Corr., I (London, 1768), p. 76. The observation makes no sense of the fact that this principle would have rendered aliens subjects and potential property owners, and this was not the case. For instance, in 1324 Edward II confiscated the land held by those descending from "any born beyond the seas whose ancestors were [from the time of John] under the allegiance of the king of France" (Kettner, p. 5).

[128] Coke, *First Part of the Institutes*, section 172.

[129] *Kingdoms and Communities in Western Europe, 900–1300* (Oxford: Clarendon Press, 1984), p. 6.

unified hierarchialized community: "Medieval people thought of themselves as divided into distinct and aboriginal peoples. . . . [M]edieval ideas about kingdoms and peoples were very like modern ideas about nations."[130] As in ancient times, the victor, by withholding death, won the services of the opponent. By stressing that the fighting was between communities, Reynolds points out that villeanage is intrinsically political, a practice concerned with borders and alliances, and not with economic class differences internal to a homogeneous group. Reynolds's framework is consistent, as well, with the treatment of Jews as an alien community, one that was "brought hither from Normandy, brought hither as the King's dependents and (the word will hardly be too strong) the King's serfs."[131] Rather than make too much of the usefulness of Reynolds's "military" appellation for this period, it seems instructive to note the ways that political and economic relations were coterminous.

Marc Bloch's definition of "feudal" as "the vengeance of a kinsman"[132] is the definition Reynolds claims to be criticizing. But Bloch's vengeance of kinsmen is no different than the type of violence Reynolds describes. Implicit in the contrast Reynolds advances is that Bloch has ignored the juridical character of the local communities who are in warfare; these ruling and ruled, conquerors and subjects, are members of different political societies, Reynolds believes. The serfs are not abject members of a homogeneous society, but others in a heterogeneous one. But Bloch need not be read as asserting that these kinship cleavages are apolitical. The problem is that Reynolds does not see the political character of Bloch's kinsmen. The work of Bloch as well as Reynolds captures the experiences of politically reproduced kinship alliances. According to Reynolds: "A kingdom was never thought of merely as the territory which happened to be ruled by a King. It comprised and corresponded to a 'people' (*gens, natio, populus*), which was assumed to be a natural inherited community of tradition, custom, law, and descent."[133] So these "feudal" territories are particular political communities that constitute membership by invocations of birth.

Land, Family, and Nation

The ancestral communities of England and elsewhere in Europe seem to be at odds with the principle of ligeance by birth in the realm supposedly in effect in England. It seems contradictory that ligeance could be wrought from birth in the realm on the one hand (the right to pass on land to the

[130] Ibid., pp. 8–9.
[131] Pollock and Maitland, *History of English Law*, p. 468.
[132] Bloch, *Feudal Society*, tr. L. A. Manyon (Chicago: University of Chicago Press, 1961), p. 126.
[133] Reynolds, *Kingdom and Communities*, p. 250.

next generation), while children of aliens whose fathers had not bought the right of naturalization were born aliens themselves. Yet this was how England legitimated its sovereignty over the political societies it had colonized: the territorial criterion of birth in English territory as the mark of a British subject—first used in Scotland and later Ireland—would be invoked to claim jurisdiction over British subjects across the globe. By claiming jurisdiction over a territory and arguing that ligeance follows from birth in a territory, King James (for whose Court Coke wrote) could argue that those born in Scotland were not "aliens" and were obligated to follow his rules (and pay him taxes). Hence the territorial notions of membership were offered to extend the king's sovereignty and were not intended for (nor did they have the effect of) increasing the possibilities of land ownership or political rights for the children of those individuals who emigrated outside the realm.

What seems an outright contradiction (between exclusionary and inclusionary functions of territorial and ancestral principles) begins to make sense once the English system of colonization is contrasted with that of the Greeks and the Romans. All three relied on lineage for membership, and captured foes were assigned a political status resulting in economic hardships that would be reproduced for their heirs. The different forms of government, however, produced a tension in English laws on nationality absent in Greece and Rome. When democratic Athens colonized a people, it enslaved them. When Rome's republic or empire colonized people, they became Romans. But England was a monarchy, which meant that it was more difficult to at once preserve one group as distinctly English *and* to dominate another people in a way that was different from the authoritarian relation between the government and its own people. The theory of monarchical legitimacy incorporates a whole people into a kingdom. That is what England wanted, for the Irish and the Scots to be in their ligeance once James I ascended. But the monarchs were not confident enough to think that birth in the realm would be enough to overcome feelings of affinity that the children of aliens might experience for their parents' homeland. If these children were nominally English, they might own English land. By virtue of their ownership—if indeed they considered themselves French, for instance, and not English—a portion of the kingdom would also be "French." That is, if land is equated with political prerogative, then by assigning land rights to "aliens," the Crown risked losing that land permanently to another kingdom. This was not a worry in Athens because birth in the territory was never sufficient to make one a citizen, so metics were never allowed to own land. And Rome's conquered people were also subjects from other lands that Rome had colonized, while England had not conquered France. Furthermore, Roman citizens, under the Roman empire, were procedurally absorbed into the government in a way that even English subjects were not, in any period. And these citizens were most likely to be affiliated with areas over which Rome had political control, so they were not all that "alien" in the first place. If England had colonized France, then perhaps French "aliens" would have been able to own land. However, the fact that the sovereign France was an autonomous country frequently hostile to England meant that those who were "French English" were treated with suspicion. Hence the connection between birth and territory effects an ancestral tie between the individual and the nation akin to that produced by rules of membership by descent. In the latter the body politic is mediated through kinship rules of descent; in the former the body politic absorbs as its own all those who are born within its borders.

Ethnicity

The fact that birth in a particular place renders one a member affirms the tie between a political authority and the land; it particularizes sovereignty and makes it concrete. That one might have a form of being based on one's place of birth that is different than the form of being that results from one's ancestry is often represented through the concept of "ethnicity" among Anglophones, which is similar to the concept associated with derivations of *ethno-* or *nasci-* in other languages. In Germany one might be a German citizen (Staatsbürger) with a Turkish nationality (Nationalität). So one criticism of the foregoing might be that it explains the consolidation of the politically constituted familial nation but ignores a prior, truly primordial grouping of ethnicity. Yet contrary to the widely held intuition voiced by Walzer and others, a potential difference between citizenship and ethnicity does not mean that one's ethnic form of being is historical and based on the past while one's formal political identity is created in the immediate present. Rather, there is a dialectical tension at any given point in time between these two processes of reproducing a state-nation and its people, one that yields the form of ethnicity as well.

The **diachronic** national family form—which exists through time— may compete with the **synchronic** political territorial family form—which reproduces each instant—for the prerogative to control entry of new members. Neither the diachronic nor synchronic national family are original or authentic but depend on the form of the other. Were it not for synchronic membership, a political society could neither originate nor absorb "new" members at any particular point. Were it not for the diachronic national family form, a political society could not reproduce itself over time. Ethnicity, which is diachronic, triumphs over the synchronic form of ligeance because ethnicity expresses the sense of time and history that is always implied in the concept of the nation. The moment there is a nationality there is a potential ethnicity. Evidence of the dialectical relationship between diachronic and synchronic processes of membership is that one may have an "ethnicity" of, say, Canadian, if one is a Canadian national and moves to South Korea, even if one's Canadian nationality was achieved only by being born in Canada, that is, even if one's parents were born in Ireland, for instance. (Of course, this same person might claim additionally to have an Irish ethnicity, even though one's French great-grandparents had moved to Ireland to make that possible, and so on.)

To acknowledge one's affiliation as a national one is to join that nation's history, to become one with it. This happens by birth in a particular lineage as well as by birth in a territory. Henry David Thoreau, for example, whose paternal grandfather was born in France, did not resist the United States government on the grounds that he was French, and therefore the state had no claim over him.[134] His resistance took another form. Thoreau never asserted an identity other than the U.S.-American one conferred by birth in America. As soon as the territorial principle works, it melts into that of ancestral nationality or ethnicity. The same principle of birth in the ligeance that gave the English monarchs jurisdiction over the Scottish gave the United States jurisdiction over Thoreau. Simply by being born in the United States territory, he had become subject to it, as had his personal property.

When a church had tithed Thoreau without his consent, he resisted payment, answering in writing, " 'Know all me by these presents that I, Henry Thoreau, do not wish to be regarded as a member of any incorporated society which I have not joined."[135] Likewise Thoreau has the same feeling about his membership in the state: "I simply wish to refuse allegiance to the State, to withdraw and stand aloof from it effectively."[136] But he cannot do so. Thoreau's claim took the form of the individual standing against the government, but Thoreau also recognized that it was more than this. The state Thoreau described differed from that associated with Augustine's robber, and not because the nineteenth-century United States government was just. A robber does not claim that one owes him taxes because one has given one's ligeance but simply takes what he wants against one's will. Thoreau did not see himself as immune from taxes because the government was unjust, but because political society falsely claimed Thoreau as a member. Simply because he was born there, the government asserted he was an American, even if he did not see it this way.

Not all acts of affiliation based on territory culminate in an experience of nationality in that territory. One might not have abandoned one's ancestral ties to another nation. Thoreau might have said: "I am really an

[134] When Henry Thoreau's paternal grandfather, Jean Thoreau, immigrated to the United States he changed his name to John. Henry's father, also named John, was born in Boston (*Henry D. Thoreau* [Boston: Houghton, Mifflin and Co., 1892], chapter 1).

[135] From "Civil Disobedience," [1849], in *Walden and Civil Disobedience* (New York: Penguin, 1983), p. 402.

[136] Ibid., p. 407.

alien. Therefore 'your' laws do not pertain to me." The possibility of a disjuncture between citizenship by birth in the territory in one country and ethnicity associated with another place seems to bolster the intuition that membership in a state is accidental, transitory, not all that revelatory of one's identity, while one's nationality or ethnicity is essential, given, and permanent. Consider a French émigré now a citizen in the United States—an American citizen whose tastes and friends remain French. Marie's friends are French; they speak French, smoke Gitane cigarettes, wear clothes from Paris, and drink vast amounts of French wine. If these American citizens seem really to be French, absent laws requiring these "French" behaviors, then ethnicity seems to lack juridical dimensions.

If one can be ethnically French and an American citizen, and if ethnicity is an aspect of the nation, then nationality need not be rendered as a matter of political membership, this line of thinking might continue. Perhaps membership in a political society is actually associated with speaking a language, betraying a cultural sensibility, or showing familiarity with long-standing practices, and hence political membership is not primarily rooted in practices associated with birth, as birth determines only one's ethnicity and this is a separate matter altogether. In fact, however, the territorial principle that frequently dissolves into the diachronic one of ancestral determinacy—as when people at one point take on the ethnicity of the nation into which they were born and not the one from which their ancestors came—is not the only way that the state form (the sheer fact of birth in a sovereign political society making one a subject or national) determines ethnicity. It is precisely the link of ethnicity to nationality that renders both products of political society. Every ethnicity is such by reference to a specifically political society. Weber writes: "The concept of the 'ethnic' (*ethnische*) group, which dissolves if we define our terms exactly, corresponds in this regard to one of the most vexing, since emotionally charged concepts: the *nation* (*nation*), as soon as we attempt a sociological definition."[137] Weber then explains the **political** character of the **nation**. For example, Walzer's reference to the "Algerian" with "French citizenship" first evokes semantic associations (of primordial-ness) with Algeria, which is a state, a political society. Only by virtue of the specifically political societies of Algeria and France can there be a rupture between Algerian-ness and French-ness. Similarly, the Irish-American, French-American, Japanese-American, Korean-American, Honduran-American, Nigerian-American, Tibetan-American, and so forth, only exist by virtue of an Ireland, France, Japan, Korea, Honduras, Nigeria, and Tibet. Ethnicity is the embodiment of one political society's nationality in another political society. Ethnicity does not sever the conceptual tie of political society and nation, but is an example of it. The fact that cigarettes, clothes, food, and

[137] Weber, *Economy and Society*, vol. 1., p. 395.

wine are all "French" (not strong, stylish, rich, and full-bodied, respectively) reinvigorates the category of French-ness without describing any special ontological fact about these items or practices.

Ethnic affiliations that do not correspond with existing political societies still may be regarded as parasitic on the concept of nationality. "Palestinians," "Armenians," and "Kurds" name prospective or retrospective states that are associated with affiliations of nation.[138] To announce that one is a Palestinian is to proclaim either a nationality or ethnicity, depending on one's vision of personal possibilities for joining nationality and political membership. This is the principle that distinguishes a specifically ethnic group from other types of groups. To announce that one belongs to the American Political Science Association (APSA) does not signify membership in either a national or an ethnic group. Hell's Angels may share a worldview, styles of dress, idioms of speech, and even face expulsion for breaking the organization's rules, but Hell's Angels are not an ethnic or national group. Hell's Angels do not base membership on lineage or territorial birth in relation to an (aspirational) political community. A similar principle explains the ethnic status of Gypsies, or the Roma. Often regarded as a disparate group of beggars who wandered through eastern Europe, the Roma claim an origin in the political society referred to by the Greeks as Atsingoanoi. They began to "migrate from India in the early Middle Ages and reached Persia sometime in the ninth century."[139] The Roma are regarded as a distinct ethnicity throughout Eastern Europe. As a result of the new states and their requirements of ancestry for citizenship, many Roma are now stateless, not because of class or vague cultural differences, but due to political obstacles created by notions of intergenerational criteria of political membership.[140] Though one does not have to be Pales-

---

[138] The Kurds offer an excellent example of how a political territory constitutes a people. Kurds speak two languages that grammatically "differ from each other as English and German, although vocabulary differences are probably of the same order as those between Dutch and German." There is no notion of any physical difference between Kurds and those in adjacent non-Kurdish territories. What makes the Kurds Kurdish is a relatively recent set of boundaries that resulted in the oppression of various, much smaller nomadic groups in the areas occupied by modern Iran, Iraq, and Turkey: "[B]y the time of the Islamic conquest . . . the term 'Kurd' had a socio-economic rather than ethnic meaning. It was used for the nomads on the Western edge of the Iranian plateau and probably also of the tribes that acknowledged the Sassanians in Mesopotamia, many of which must have been Semitic in origin." By excluding nomads from the polities of Turkey, Iran, and Iraq these countries catalyzed the invention of Kurds, as an aspirational nationality by default (David McDowall, *A Modern History of the Kurds* [London, New York: I. B. Tauris, 1996], p. 9).

[139] David Crowe, *A History of the Gypsies of Eastern Europe and Russia* (New York: St. Martin's Press, 1994), p. 1.

[140] In most communist countries there was tremendous pressure for the Gypsies to assimilate, by changing their names and registering as one of the already recognized ethnicities, though some countries formally recognized the Roma (ibid).

tinian to support the cause of Palestinian statehood, one does have to have a parent who is Palestinian to **be** Palestinian. Conversely, one may exhibit no indications of especially liking France or its Gitanes, for instance, but it would still be idiomatic for others to regard one as "being French," if one's parents were. At bottom, then, there are Armenians, for example, because at some point there was Armenia, a political society that reproduced by invocations of birth and family ties.

Not all forms of citizenship require that one actually be born to certain parents, or in a particular territory, or married to a citizen in order to become a member. Still, non-kinship membership practices are parasitic on the family model: the Salvadoran political refugee or the Japanese business executive who become American citizens do so by copying (and hence reinforcing) the "true" form of citizenship, one that is based on birth. Birth is experienced as the real way of becoming a citizen. No one says of citizenship by birthright in the United States: "It's as good as a green card," but the opposite is true. This is apparent in the very designation 'naturalization' that characterizes the granting of citizenship.

Some have argued that the United States is not really a nation, precisely because it lacks a long-standing story explaining how its people are bound by culture, blood, and land.[141] The nation of immigrants is perhaps not really a nation, but a state with members who have ethnic ties elsewhere, it has been suggested. Such an analysis is relevant to consider here because it seemingly disrupts the argument that a political society and a nation always entail the other. Perhaps, in places of the "New World," this is not true, and political society may exist entirely separate from the concept of nation. Yet the fact is that regardless of the liberal ideology—borrowed from the equally contradictory France—the United States legal institutions have always advanced and supported some notion of an ancestral "us" based on the ideas of membership that motivated Rep. Duncan Hunter to press for the elaborate fences along the United States-Mexican border, to protect us from becoming what Forbes magazine editor Peter Brimelow refers to as an "alien nation."

Brimelow believes that the United States is not essentially a racially diverse political society, but one based on exclusions of race and nationality, a condition that he wants to celebrate. In his opening sentence, Brimelow breezily associates his views with those of Adolf Hitler, remarking, "There is a sense in which current immigration policy is Adolf Hitler's posthumous revenge on America,"[142] suggesting that Hitler was enough "right" about nationalism that he is entitled to laugh at the clumsy U.S. Americans who

[141] Samuel Huntington, *American Politics: The Promise of Disharmony* (Cambridge: Belknap Press, 1981), pp. 23–30.
[142] *Alien Nation: Common Sense about America's Immigration Disaster* (New York: Random House, 1995), p. xv.

challenged Nazism's ideology of eugenics. Not surprisingly, Brimelow, defending racism as part of this country's history, ridicules the notion that American nationality is "independent of race and blood," and he points out that the "first naturalization law, in 1790, stipulated that an applicant must be a free white person," a fact that, not surprisingly, is frequently mentioned by critics of racism. Brimelow remarks: "Maybe America should not have been like this. *But it was*."[143] For Brimelow "we" have been forged in Abraham Lincoln's references to the "mystic chords of memory, stretching from every battle field and patriot grave, to every living heart and hearth stone, all over this broad land."[144] The death of "our" soldiers in the past makes us a country, he contends. Unfortunately for Brimelow's thesis, this principle would limit true membership to people whose ancestors may have died as United States soldiers before the Civil War, and that is not what has happened.

Instead, the United States has provided a form of ancestral association by proxy. Later immigrants such as Brimelow (who was born Canadian) are not lesser citizens, but afforded a tie with the ancestors of their new compatriots. New immigrants have a nominal and hence actual familial relation to others simply by virtue of their citizenship. This is the case for every nation. The difference between the United States and elsewhere is simply that here the conventions are more recent, from the point of view of contemporary histories. That not everyone assimilates simply means that the state-nation association of an earlier country is more powerful for that immigrant than that tie in the United States. Again, this is not unique to the United States. While there are plenty of U.S. American citizens who self-identify primarily as "Irish" or "Catholic" or "Black," there are also those who identify exclusively as "American."

The features of the political family form whereby kinship rules are in fact juridical but appear "natural" suggest that Weber's and other efforts to challenge the familial determinacy of a nation are left with the difficult task of claiming as "false" that knowledge which may be logically unfounded, and yet has vivid historical effects. That "genetic change" might not *really* (positively—as in "viewed empirically") cause one nation to develop out of an older one has prompted some analysts to regard as mistaken those who think that the concepts of "ancestry," "family ties," and "kinship" are explanatory of the nation. Yet the notion of a familial nation is not a conceptual error, but a reiteration of the political semiotics of the nature/artifice form manifest in the dialectical relations among the concepts of political society (state), family, and nation.

---

[143] Ibid., pp. 14–15, emphasis in original.
[144] Ibid, p. xix.

Three ───────────────────────────

The Semiotics of Nationality

NAMING NAMES

THE PHENOMENOLOGY of national membership suggests that political societies create rules for intergenerational families. These families are experienced as the historically and substantively prior condition of that nation, providing the sense of the nation as an association that is 'given'. One *Oxford English Dictionary* example of the use of 'given' states: " 'The past cannot be seen as a fixed 'given'. . . ." Lévi-Strauss is translated as claiming that the "English language . . . from the point of view of any individual speaker . . . is a 'given'."[1] This notion of given-ness is rather paradoxical. On the one hand, the cognate 'give' suggests a transaction between two parties, and hence 'given' implies a prior condition, a moment *before* a particular identity is handed over. One must lack an identity in order for it to be given, or so it would seem. This is also the sense of the phrase "given name," which refers to the "name given at baptism," which the *Oxford English Dictionary* records as first used in 1827. *Bartlett's American Dictionary* (1859) explains that the Christian name is "*given* to a person, to distinguish it from the surname, which is not given, but inherited," a formulation that juxtaposes, rather than superimposes, the senses of given-ness and heritability. (Whereas previous uses align heredity and given-ness, this definition differentiates between the two forms of identity.)

However, a separate sense of 'given' as meaning "granted as a basis of calculation, reasoning, etc. definitely stated, fixed, specified" emerges earlier as a term used in explaining geometric principles. In the 1570 translation of Euclid, Henry Billingsley refers to a "right line geuen. . . ." This seems to be the sense of 'given' that underlies its use in contexts suggesting lineage. And yet while one paradox dissolves, another emerges, since the sense of a nationality as a 'given' is that it is something historically vibrant, dependent on the practices of its members to survive, and not merely a logical a priori rule. This tension among the meanings of given-ness—between that which is safely assumed and that which must be imputed and elaborated so as to be experienced as consolidated—is the background to

---

[1] *Oxford English Dictionary*, 2d ed. Note that in both instances, and in others quoted in this book, 'given' is rarely used absent quotation marks, implying that there is something consistently peculiar about its use.

the specific conundrums evoked in the semiotics of the nation. It is this space—between the strong sentiment evoked by family and national ties and the arbitrary-seeming form of their artifice, between the full-blooded feeling of belonging and the threadlike thinness of the ties themselves, between the narratives of a common existence and attention to the ways this is "only" narrative—that has prompted so many inquiries into affiliations of family and nation. As Anna Marie Smith asks, "How can the familial white Christian nation be simultaneously represented as a precarious space which urgently requires refortification and as an a-historical essence to which 'we' can always return?"[2] What are the specific devices that make the mantle of national identity such a seamless fit?

Naming Names

One site of national affiliations that is infrequently attended to by scholarly literatures on the nation, but widely relied on for idiomatic taxonomies of nationality, is the personal name.[3] First and last names connote national-ity or ethnicity; they are handed down by and through families, and appear to express natural familial continuities. Summarizing naming practices in 62 societies, one author writes: "Perhaps more than anything else, personal names emphasize family unity and continuity."[4] This may be one reason that nationality is thought of as an apolitical given. A name signifies a certain kind of particularity, not a random identity.[5] It is the specific imprint of individual identity that, when aggregated through a collection of ancestral lineages, seems to comprise a nation. Therefore a name is a semiotic cornerstone in the foundational effects of a nation. France is a nation of the French, so known and constituted, in part, by their French names. For instance, in responding to a questionnaire asking, "Can you name any New Orleans families you think are Creole? or Cajun? Or French?" one respondent writes "Creole names: . . . ." "Cajun names: . . . ." "French names: . . . ."[6] The family is the name of the family, and these are "national" and "ethnic" names. Pointing out the effects of names on the semiotics of "nation" does not preclude the possibility that other practices also manifest as "national." These include languages, food preferences,

---

[2] Anna Marie Smith, *New Right Discourse on Race and Sexuality: Britain, 1968–1990* (Cambridge: Cambridge University Press, 1994), p. 70.

[3] James Scott explores this topic in *Seeing Like a State: How Certain Schemes to Improve the Human Condition Have Failed* (New Haven: Yale University Press, 1998), pp. 64–71.

[4] Richard Alford, *Naming and Identity: A Cross-Cultural Study of Personal Naming Practices* (New Haven: HRAF, 1987), p. 55.

[5] Ibid., p. 1.

[6] Virginia Domínguez, *White By Definition: Social Classification in Creole Louisiana* (New Brunswick: Rutgers University, 1986), p. 178.

sporting teams in international competitions, and armies—to name just a few. However, the performance and construction of nationality through personal names explains one semiotic link between the affinity of family or kin and that of the nation. These names are heuristically and historically best understood as the effects of laws, of a political society's imprint on its members. This type of law is not produced by the instrumental practices of government, but emerges consistently through the simple form of a political society. To study the rules that produce names is to observe one more crucial law that produces the affinities of nation.

Mantitheus v. "Mantitheus"

One of the earliest recorded examples of the interacting effects of marriage law, family name, and nationality appears in a lawsuit argued by the Athenian Demosthenes. In this case, apparent half-brothers with the same name used the courts to argue for their legitimate birth, and provided evidence of clan origins—tied to the names of these clans (and their broader *ethnea*—also distinguished by names)—to make their respective claims to their own personal names. The sons were arguing over the right to use the name Mantitheus, for purposes of their legitimacy and, relatedly, their political membership.

In Athens, around 348 B.C., a certain Mantitheus, son of Mantias of Thoricus, brought suit against someone also registered in the deme as Mantitheus son of Mantias of Thoricus.[7] Both of these men claimed to be sons of Mantias of Thoricus and both claimed to have been named Mantitheus before the other. In addition, Mantitheus was the name of Mantias's father, and the likely inspiration of the name for his sons. For purposes of clarity—since they are two separate people with identical names—let us refer to the recognized legitimate son as Mantitheus and the adopted son as "Mantitheus," since the former is the one calling the name of the latter into question.

According to the legitimate son, another "Mantitheus" had declared himself the son of Mantias, by the daughter of Pamphilus. This "Mantitheus" had previously claimed that "he was being robbed of his civil rights" and hence sought to have his paternity affirmed by having his name officially recognized as "Mantitheus." When first called to court on this question, Mantias could have denied paternity of "Mantitheus" but Mantias did not do this. The legitimate Mantitheus explains to the jury, in a

---

[7] Demosthenes, "Mantitheus against Boeotus in Regard to the Name," 39, I; and "Mantitheus against Boeotus Regarding his Mother's Marriage Portion," 40, II, notes in *Private Orations*, tr. A.T. Murray, vol. 4 (Cambridge and London: Harvard University Press, 1936), pp. 444–46; and 452–53.

second trial, that the absence of any renunciation of "Mantitheus" occurred because Mantias did not trust the jury system and preferred to attempt to bribe his mistress (explained below), and not because Mantias really believed "Mantitheus" was his son and wanted to make a public record of this fact.

The only reason Mathias ends up in the position of acknowledging "Mantitheus," according to Mantitheus, is that Mathias was duped by a sneaky ex-mistress:

> My father (for the whole truth shall be told you, men of the jury) feared to come into court lest someone, on the ground of having elsewhere received some injury from him in his public life, should confront him here; and at the same time he was deceived by this man's mother. For she had sworn that if he should tender her an oath in this matter, she would refuse it, and that, when this had been done, all relations between them would be at an end; and she had also money deposited in the hands of a third party on her behalf [to be paid when she refused the oath] . . . On these conditions, then my father tendered her the oath. But she accepted it, and swore that not only the defendant, but his brother too, her other son, was my father's child.[8]

Thinking that his mistress would accept his bribe, Mantias had proffered the oath. (The reason to have the oath publically rebuffed was to insure against future blackmail on the same point.) When the mistress (whose name does not appear in this record but is referred to as the "daughter of Pamphilus") failed to reject Mantias's oath, Mantitheus continues to explain, Mantias was obligated to "abide by the arbiter's award . . . [but] did not even so consent to admit these men [the sons] into his house."[9] According to the arbiter, Mantias had to adopt the sons and enter them "on the list of clansmen." Mantias did so, using the names Boeotus and Pamphilus (the latter being the name of the maternal grandfather). Then Mantias died.

When it was time for the defendant "Mantitheus" to register in the **deme**, at the age of 18, the elder grandson of Pamphilus "enrolled himself in the register as Mantitheus, instead of Boeotus."[10] Ruling against Mantitheus, the Athenian juries decided this was the name "Mantitheus" could use. But the matter did not end there. In a second suit Mantitheus explains how the courts did not force Boeotus to abide by a ruling resulting from an intervening suit. In response to a suit Mantitheus had filed to have "Mantitheus" deprived of political prerogatives of the **deme** (and not just removed from its list as "Mantitheus"), "Mantitheus" seemingly heightened the confusion by, on the one hand having "his name inscribed on the list

---

[8] Demosthenes, "Mantitheus against Boeotus in Regard to the Name," lines 2–4.
[9] "Against Boeotus, II," lines 11–12.
[10] Ibid, line 5.

of the demesmen as Mantitheus." But on the other hand, Mantitheus continues, "when judgment had been given against him in an ejectment suit [a different case], he declared that it was not against him but against me that the judgment had been given."[11] "Mantitheus" had achieved legal recognition as such, and then, having been ruled against as "Mantitheus" apparently said the judgment was against Mantitheus, or at least that was what Mantitheus claimed.

More illuminating of naming conventions than the specific twists and turns in this case is that the evidence Mantitheus uses to challenge "Mantitheus" is rooted in ideas about political societies and ancestry. Mantitheus claims the right to the signifier 'Mantitheus' because his paternal grandfather was also Mantitheus. And further, this ancestry is associated with larger groups beyond the immediate family. 'Boeotus' is the name of a rival group, the Boeotians, which Mantitheus points out as a way of supporting his claim that "Mantitheus" was a nominalist deception, and that really the man calling himself "Mantitheus" was Boeotus and Boeotian. At the same time, the legal character of membership in the family, the phylos, or the clan, and in the Athenian polis is always prominent. The very fact that these questions are adjudicated by a jury of Athenians indicates that these ties are not regarded simply as those of nature.

The first argument against "Mantitheus" is that he "used to go to the tribe Hippothontis to dance in the chorus of boys." That was his mother's tribe. Mantias's tribe was the Acamantis. Had "Mantitheus" really been the son of Mantias, Mantitheus tells him, "it would have been just as much your right to go to school to the tribe Acamantis, and then the tribe would have been in manifest agreement with the giving of the name."[12] Because Mantitheus was the name of the father of Mantias, being named "Mantitheus" performs a false familial association. This is betrayed by the participation of "Mantitheus" in a tribe other than that to which Mantias belonged.

Names do not simply indicate family ancestry but are also associated with particular tribes. Mantitheus protests that "Boeotus" was not given as a name of "derision or insult,"[13] even though at the time the Boeotians "were looked down upon by the Athenians."[14] Had Mantias been so motivated, to taint his son by giving him a name that would embarrass him, then that would be viewed as an act of bad faith, of not living up to the terms of the arbiter's award. Mantitheus says that the real reason Mantias

---

[11] "Against Boeotus, II" line 34. The passage just quoted explains the translator's reference to this second suit "against Boeotus (to whom after his apparent victory in the preceding suit we should properly give the name Mantitheus)," p. 480.

[12] "Against Boeotus, I" lines 23–24.

[13] Ibid., line 32.

[14] Murray, *Demosthenes*, vol. 4, p. 447.

named this son Boeotus was that "Boeotus is the name of his mother's brother" (and the mother's father).[15] By naming him Boeotus, Mantias was simply recirculating a family name from the mother's side. Hence the inferences prompted by these names alone are that people will think Mantitheus and "Mantitheus" the same person; that the name 'Mantitheus' means "Mantitheus" was in the tribe of the Acamantis; that the name 'Mantitheus' means that he was the grandson of the father of Mantias; that the name 'Boeotus' is used for foreigners, and that one's name reflects a familial association with others of that name. The cases illustrate how the legal framework around political membership, ancestry, law and names were constitutive of identity and not simply reflective of a pre-political status.

One response to the above might be to claim that names and identities are completely independent, and that the anxiety over getting the name 'Mantitheus' right is a simple matter of nominalist order. Just as we cannot label every vegetable in the market 'cucumber', it would be silly to have everyone who felt the urge (or could blackmail Mantias) to be called 'Mantitheus'. The mix-up in names, this objection might continue, is a general problem in labeling and the mistakes and mishaps associated with personal naming gone wrong are no more significant than defects in other naming practices.

Yet personal names generate unique infelicities, including potential mistakes that themselves illustrate the specific connotations of personal names. If upon being introduced to people a short woman says, 'I am extremely tall.' they will think her confused or lying. She has said something about herself that can be detected immediately as mistaken. Simply telling people one is tall, if one is short, performs not height but wishful thinking. If upon being introduced to people one who is not Jane Mantias says, 'I am Jane Mantias.' those first meeting Jane will not know this is wrong, and may instead believe Jane is Greek or is married to someone who is Greek. The announcement of this name does not make this person Jane Mantias, but it does perform a Greek identity, even if it does so deceptively— and only ephemerally, as the deception may be quickly uncovered. That nationality and name may be briefly objects of misperception reveals some of the discursive laws of nationality and names that operate differently from those of other activities of sensory perception.[16] The reason that personal names reveal (mis)information, and the announcement of height does not, is not simply that one's height is visible, as opposed to one's nationality (and numerous other attributes), but relates to attributes pecu-

---

[15] "Against Boeotus, I," line 32.

[16] That height is a relative concept (someone who appears "short" in one group may seem "tall" in another) is irrelevant to the point of the example, which is that consciousness regards height as a physical quality, and hence one that we can notice visually and with certainty.

liar to the personal name. The personal name is also the person, at least syntactically. 'I am Jane Mantias' and 'My name is Jane Mantias' mean the same thing, a linguistic convention that holds for numerous languages, as well as for other putatively ostensive conventions.

The Name of Thoreau's

"What's in a name! That which we call a rose
By any other name would smell as sweet"
                    (Juliet, in Shakespeare, *Romeo and Juliet* Act II, scene ii)

Of all the cults, that of the ancestors is the most legitimate, for the ancestors have made us what we are. (Ernst Renan, *"What is a Nation?"*)

The effects of past migrations on distributions of surnames and on distributions of genes must have been similar.[17]

Which is it to be or not to be? The cult of ancestry and genes? Or the recognition of the ruse, of the (mere?) names that make the whole rigamorole possible? Who can listen to the two tormented lovers and not come down on the side that rejects ancestral ties, as do Romeo and Juliet when they renounce the artifice of the kinship ties that doom their romance? Their problem seems a simple semiotic one:

Juliet:
'Tis but thy name that is my enemy;—
Thou art thy self though, not a Montague
What's a Montague? it is nor hand, nor foot,
nor arm, nor face, nor any other part
Belonging to a man. O, be some other name!
                    (Shakespeare, *Romeo and Juliet*, Act II, scene ii)

The lovers are separated by a name, **only** a name and nothing material or natural, such as a hand or a foot. How absurd, how tragic, as when names are used to discriminate against certain families in times of political conflict. The Serbian militia, unable to separate Muslims from Croatians from Serbians by appearance or language, relied on names to determine whom they should execute. And yet Ernst Renan, who is clear about the ways that the nation has been constructed, believes that our familial ancestors have made us who we are, in which case Romeo really *is* a Montague, and not some fellow with that name.

But again, perhaps names are neither constitutive of identities nor emblematic of them. An alternative to either assigning significance to the

[17] Colin Rogers, *The Surname Detective: Investigating Surname Distribution in England, 1086–Present Day* (Manchester and York: Manchester University Press, 1995), p. 5.

name Montague or simply dismissing the relation between one's name and one's essence might be to see the name as fundamentally connected to the underlying person, but to dismiss that aspect of one's identity as an ethical or even sensible site of contention. Even if Romeo truly **is** a Montague, that does not explain why being-a-Montague should matter. A Montague once wronged a Capulet. Likewise, the Croatian Ustazi killed Serbs and Communists during World War Two and a few generations later the Serbs killed the Croatians: " 'Ustasa whore' is particularly commonplace" as an epithet that was used by Serbian soldiers raping Croatian women,[18] for instance. Can this be seen as the misapplication of one's ancestral ties, a faulty sense of intergenerational responsibility and retribution? Or rather, is personal identity (a matter of group membership) always relevant to participants in conflicts between political societies? If notions of intergenerational responsibility imbricate personal identity, then what are the specific practices that link one's synchronic with one's diachronic form of being?

The struggle between the use of the name as purely a signifier and the name as a sign—one that has already sewn up the meaning of the family and nation—is framed by the fact that the allies and enemies are named as such not by hand or foot, or often any other difference among bodies that could be associated with even the possibility of a group with a genetic predisposition toward evil, but by an abstraction, a signifier alone, a proper noun. The phenotype of Montague-ness, Croatian-ness, Jewish-ness, Anglo-ness may or may not be physical appearance but it is, often idiomatically, a personal name. Hence the personal name is not an arbitrary marker, but a form that has a specific and readily apparent content. In the absence of any particular information about a person, someone with a "Serb-sounding name" meeting someone else with a Serb-sounding name thinks the other **is** Serbian, which may prompt a sense of familiarity, even if neither of these people have been to Serbia, are of different classes, and hold very different political views.[19] As William Camden observes in his sixteenth century *Remains Concerning England*, "Sometime the similitude of names doth kindle sparkles of love and liking among meere strangers."[20]

---

[18] Catharine MacKinnon, "Turning Rape into Pornography: Post-Modern Genocide," *Ms.*, July/August, 1993, p. 27.

[19] I have intentionally avoided the question of whether either of these parties "is Serbian" because this depends, to a large extent, on conventions of naming. Part of being Serbian is having a Serbian name, just as part of the constitution of Serbia is the reproduction of a Serbian-named population, all of which is explored in detail below.

[20] *Remains concerning England* (Toronto, Buffalo: University of Toronto Press, 1984), p. 48. Camden is describing the literal similarity of names, as when someone named John bumps into another John, but the principle seems to apply to broader forms of resemblance as well.

The Semiotics vs. the Metaphysics of Personal Names

One response to the above might be to observe that names, however tragically they may be invoked, are still contingent labels. Alexis de Tocqueville might have been named 'Confucius' and he would still have been French. According to this line of thought, pursued by Plato in the *Cratylus* and Frege at the turn of the twentieth century, the paradox of the proper name is largely one of metaphysics.[21] The 'morning star' and the 'evening star' must be different labels for the same star, which does not physically change merely because it is called this or that.[22] Frege's essay "On Sense and Meaning" (*Über Sinn und Bedeutung*) recognizes that the 'morning star' and 'evening star' convey different senses for the same object. Frege thinks that this is a flaw, one that "should not appear in a perfect language."[23] In Frege's "perfect language" words refer to one and only one meaning for any object. If there is more than one sense for an object, we cannot know what the object really is. The idea is that there is a single meaning, one that has what Frege calls "truth-value," and "it is this striving for truth which urges us to penetrate beyond the sense [from the word] to the nominatum."[24] According to Frege, language obscures the truth. His examples then serve to document just how that happens.

The study of semiotics begins with a different view of ontology than that of most metaphysicians. Rather than frustration over the paradoxes of naming, the student of semiotics locates reality as the association between the signifier and the signified: the sign. The analytic distinction between the two resembles what Frege says about the difference between the sense (Sinn) of the sign and its meaning (Bedeutung): The "signs or names 'a' and 'b' name the same thing," but "the sense of 'b' may differ from the proposition expressed by 'a = a'; in that case the two sentences

---

[21] Hermogenes begins by thinking that names are labeling conventions, observing that "we frequently change the names of our slaves, and the newly imposed name is as good as the old. For there is no name given to anything by nature; all is convention and habit of users." But then Socrates points out the ways that names are tools, and that they seem to "distinguish things according to their natures" in "Cratylus," tr. Benjamin Jowett, in *The Collected Dialogues of Plato* (New York: Pantheon Books, 1961), sections 384, 388. Wittgenstein also refers to names as labels that serve as tools, tr. G.E.M. Anscombe, *Philosophical Investigations* (New York: MacMillan, 1958), remarks 11 and 15.

[22] Conversely, something can appear in different states over time and still be called the same name: "Although the man (Nixon) might not have been the President, it is not the case that he might not have been Nixon (though he might not have been *called* 'Nixon' " (Saul Kripke, *Naming and Necessity* [Cambridge: Harvard University Press, 1972]), p. 49.

[23] "On Sense and Nominatum," tr. Herbert Fiegl and Wilfred Sellars, in *Readings in Philosophical Analysis*, ed. H. Fiegl and Wilfred Sellars (New York: Appleton-Century-Crafts, 1949), p. 86, note 2 and p. 96.

[24] Ibid., pp. 90–91.

do not have the same cognitive significance."[25] The signifier exerts an effect on sense that is somewhat independent of the object in the sky. For Frege, evening star = morning star may be true, but qua signifiers the proposition is not true. 'Evening star' ≠ 'morning star'. Frege's formulation of the above leaves intact the possibility of a star that exists independent of our (imperfect) language. Frege does not take account of how intrinsic language is to the very concept of a star, and all other concepts for objects. It is as impossible to consider things absent language as it is to do math without symbols. The properties of the family name are as crucial to intergenerational forms of being as the properties of pi are to the form of a circle.

The History of Names through Families

To trace the details of personal naming conventions and their associations is to discover another dimension of how political society constitutes an intergenerational familial sensibility throughout the nation. The effects of the family name as an expression of national identity develop through highly systematic regulatory practices of political society, regardless of whether the form of rule is tribal, monarchical, or democratic. From the decision to reproduce an Irish birth certificate form on the cover of a book on Irish names,[26] to the reproduction of Irishness through the appropriate registration of the child's "Irish" name, the mechanics of the state (or any other political society) reproducing itself by putting its stamp on its members are not subtle. There are three ways this occurs. The most blatant occurs when legal authorities require certain first or last names and may prohibit others. Until 1993 France had an official list with legal names: Nestor and Achilles were authorized, but Jupiter and Juno were not.[27] Such a list is still in effect in Switzerland.[28] A second practice for determining names is for families to reproduce certain family names, for first names or surnames. And third, people may choose names—for themselves or their children. This usually occurs by drawing from words or names in the language in the nation in which they reside, or the nation they take as their place of origin. Even when the government does not require certain names, the effect of this "choice" is the same. These chosen names will not disrupt the intergenerational reproduction of the nation through the reproduction of "English" men and women, reiterated as such by their

[25] Ibid., p. 102.

[26] Roman Coghlan, *Irish Christian Names: An A-Z of First Names* (London and Edinburgh: Johnston and Bacon, 1979).

[27] "What's in a nom?" *Economist*, July 31, 1993, p. 46.

[28] Article 301 IV CC, in *Introduction to Swiss Law*, ed. F. Dessemontet and T. Ansay, 2d ed. (The Hague, Boston: Kluwer Law International, 1995), p. 52.

distinctively English family names. The infrequently invented names will become absorbed and, like Cleisthenes' invented demes or the children of those who inherit by Roman adoption, come to reproduce a lineage.

Until the Romans, only one name was used for legal purposes—to wit the battle between Mantitheus and "Mantitheus." Although the Greeks relied on personal names for political membership, the Romans were the first to record the *praenomen* [first name], *nomen* [gens, or kinship group], and *cognomen* [family]. Marcus Aurelius (121–80 B.C.) required the "entry of children's names on records before officers thereunto appointed."[29] It was considered an act of good faith for "Lucius Tarquinius" to adopt his Roman name, writes Cicero, "for he had in this manner modified his Greek name, that he might appear to be adopting the customs of his new country in every respect."[30] Ireland is the first nation, after the Roman Empire, to have hereditary surnames. The purpose of the eleventh-century Domesday register in England was to establish the Crown's jurisdiction by designating the lands and people under its control. The first lists were drawn up in Latin but quickly shifted to the colloquial idiom, so that the names adapted from the Domesday register were thought specifically "English."[31]

The practice of using Christian names for last ones, e.g., Johnson, began around the twelfth century. Camden's conjecture is that this occurred from the "desire to continue and propagate their own names to succeeding ages,"[32] although much of his own history is devoted to a description of the juridical imposition of these surnames, designed more to consolidate the ligeance between subjects and the king than between parents and children. The state could have an impact on naming practices in more subtle ways as well. Ever since subjugated populations took on the naming conventions of their colonizers, at least as early as ancient Greece, families have made strategic use of their prerogative to name their children. After the Norman invasion "Guy" was turned into "Guibt" and then, in English, later "Wyatt," so that their children would not be perceived as being from the politically weaker groups of their putatively French parents. Likewise names have been assigned as a form of political resistance, as when the Gypsies in Bulgaria "adopted Islamic, as well as Turkish and Arabic names."[33] Bulgarian authorities responded, in 1968, by requiring all Gypsies

---

[29] Camden, *Remains concerning England*, p. 45. This also suggests, again, that the epochal designations of the Foucauldian analyses mislead: governments, through their regulations, have been producing populations based on family law for thousands of years.

[30] Cicero, *The Republic*, II.xx.35.

[31] Frances Gies and Joseph Gies, *Life in a Medieval Village* (New York: Harper and Row, 1990), pp. 166–67.

[32] Camden, *Remains concerning England*, p. 48.

[33] David Crowe, *A History of the Gypsies of Eastern Europe and Russia* (New York: St. Martin's Press, 1994), p. 23.

to change their names to Boter and Levski, two Bulgarian national heros.[34] The effect of the explicit juridical interventions, as well as their incentives to signify membership through names, is to taxonomize individuals by families and nations. Because of the association of family membership with birth, this practice essentializes both familial and political membership.

Consider the overlay of national differences on **patrinomial** suffixes and prefixes—the father Johnson with his son Johnson and both with the English, while MacIan and his son MacIan are distinctively Irish. To achieve a similar effect early German tribes gave sons names alliterative of their fathers' names, so that it would be easy to recite the family story in rhyme, a practice referred to as one "granting an extension of life, a kind of immortality."[35] By the same convention of patrilineality, one's mother's "maiden name" in the United States is so obscured that it is often used as a secret password for bank accounts and credit cards.

In Europe names were generally passed on through the father, although sometimes this might skip a generation. Camden explains, "[W]omen with us [the English] at their marriage do change their surnames and passe into their husbands names, and justly for that then *Non sant due, sed caro una*: And yet in France and the Netherlands, the better sort of women will still retaine their owne name with their husbands."[36] Camden actually misstates the facts, since this exception held as well in England. A woman also would retain her own name upon marriage in the event that she was from a wealthy family that lacked male heirs. These cases do not fundamentally challenge the practice of patrilineage. Called "parceners," these women inherit so that a father's estate might remain intact even though he had the bad fortune not to have any male children.[37] The daughter's retention of the family wealth and name is a temporary place-holder until **her** son will inherit it. Such an arrangement favors the **wife's** father's name over the father's name of the **husband**, and is not a challenge to patrilineality.

In this period, roughly 1200 to 1700, the parish records served a juridical function similar to the Athenian tribal registries, in that these legal means were used to establish the particularity of an individual. Edward Coke, in a section on contracts and property transfers, advises on the proper source for a signatory's name: "And regularly it is requisite, that the purchaser be named by the name of baptism and his surname, and that special heed be taken to the name of baptism; for that a man cannot have two names

---

[34] Ibid., p. 25.

[35] Henry Bosley Woolf, *The Old Germanic Principles of Name-Giving* (Baltimore: Johns Hopkins Press, 1939), pp. 4, 248.

[36] Camden, *Remains concerning England*, p. 124.

[37] Coke, *Institutes of the Laws of England*, Part One, Sixteenth ed. (London, Dublin, 1809), section 241.

of baptism as he may have divers surnames."[38] The baptismal name was sacred and singular, whereas one could change other names. For some classes and in some places the last name was the equivalent of the contemporary nickname, while the landed aristocracy needed the king's permission to change their names. Camden illustrates this with a story about Baron William Fitz-Gilbert who "obtained license of Henry II, to change his name."[39] Most likely Fitz-Gilbert wanted to change his name because "Fitz" was commonly the prefix given to bastards. The surname functioned as a way of assigning financial responsibility to the father, required by sixteenth-century poor laws.[40] So "Fitz"-gilbert would mean "son of the unwed father Gilbert." For the lower classes the regulation of names seems more lax; in the thirteenth and fourteenth centuries apprentices commonly changed their surnames to those of their masters, and even in the sixteenth century sons changed their names when they left their families,[41] though for many it appears that the surname was "imposed and given unto them by others. . . . For who would have named himselfe, Peaceable, Unready, Without-land, Beauclerke, Strong-bowe, Gagtooth, Blanch-mayne, Bossue, i.e. Crookbacke, but the concurrent voyce of the people, as the women neighbours gave the name to *Obed* in the book of *Ruth*."[42] The 1413 Statute of Additions required the statement of occupation and place next to all Christian names in writs and indictments.[43] The results could be something like a surname Thepunderstepdoghtre, meaning "the punder's step-daughter."[44] Another infelicity in naming occurred when sons had the same or similar names, a common practice that Camden criticizes because of problems in inheritance, it being difficult to distinguish between "Doner and Done."[45] One source for the superfluity of names was the Domesday Book itself. The lines indicating occupation, place of residence, and other information were frequently invoked as "last names," but in no particular order, so that depending on the circumstance the same person might be known as John Miller or John Brown.[46] Again, these confusions occurred only among those who did not own land.

A different problem beset the wealthy. Among noble families only the eldest son assumed the estate surname, but high child mortality rates made

[38] Ibid., I. 3f.

[39] Camden, *Remains concerning England*, p. 121.

[40] Martha Zingo and Kevin Early, *Nameless Persons: Legal Discrimination against Nonmarital Children in the United States* (Westport and London: Praeger, 1994), p. 24.

[41] Smith, *The Story of Our Names* (New York: Harper, 1950), pp. 39, 53.

[42] Camden, *Remains concerning England*, pp. 115–16. Camden suggests the same principle was at work in many surnames as well.

[43] Smith, *Story of Our Names*, p. 38.

[44] Ibid., p. 52.

[45] Camden, *Remains concerning England*, p. 49.

[46] Ibid., p. 44.

it unlikely that any particular son would inherit, and hence two or more sons would have the same name: "Nothing better illustrates the resigned acceptance of the expendability of children than the medieval practice of giving the same name to two living siblings in the expectation that only one would survive."[47] The law of inheritance and feudal estates, in this case, is the set of rules that would determine that a family might have five "Charles."[48]

Names and Nations

When King Edward IV wanted to consolidate his political sovereignty of Ireland, he sought to render the Irish people English nationals, in part by forcing them to change their names. In 1465 Parliament passed the following statute:

> Every Irishman that dwells betwixt or amongst Englishmen in the county of Dublin, Myeth, Vriell and Kildare shall go like to one Englishman in apparel . . . and shall take to him an English surname of one town, as Sutton, Chester, Trym, Skryne, Corke, Kinsale: or colour, as white, blacke, browne: or arte or science, as smith or carpenter: or office, as cooke, butler, and . . . he and his issue shall use this name, under pain of forfeyting of his good yearly.[49]

The place-names and the other nouns referred to in this law are idiomatically "English," not "Irish" and not random signs. Even though the association between the individual and that particular English word might be entirely arbitrary—a baker might have the surname Smith—the name is, to a man of "English apparel," recognizably "English." The stipulation that children must also assume the name again codifies and performs the link of family with nation. The Domesday Book recorded people by "nationality—English, Flemings, French, and Welsch" and sometimes names explicitly designated nationality, as when the official surnames were recorded as "Dorset," "Scot," or "Walsh."[50] Likewise, in 1654 Philip IV required Moors to adopt "Spanish" names, and in 1848 the Hungarian monarchy forced Germans to take on "Hungarian" names.[51]

---

[47] Lawrence Stone, *The Family, Sex, and Marriage in England, 1500–1800* (New York: Harper and Row, 1979), p. 57.

[48] Ibid.

[49] Edward IV. c. 3 (1465), in Great Britain, *The Great Boke of Statutes* (London: Wyllam Meddelton cum priuilegio Regali, 1545), Yale University Beinecke Vault.

[50] Darnby, *Domesday England* (Cambridge: Cambridge University Press, 1977), p. 84.

[51] Smith, *Story of Our Names*, p. 241. The Moors are referred to as such because of the ancient Mauretania, which corresponds approximately to the contemporary territories of Morocco and Algeria. In the eighth century the Moors conquered large portions of Spain, and hence established both the political respect of their peoples and the intermingling amongst them, a fact that is important for explaining the specificity of the origins of the slave trade in southern Africa.

Coke prefaces his 1566 *Institutes of the Laws of England* with a discussion of the recent history of the family name of the author he draws on most heavily, Thomas de Littleton [c. 1481]: "Our author, a gentleman of an ancient and a fair descended family de Littleton, took his name of a town so called, as that famous chief justice sir John de Markham, and divers of our profession, and others, have done."[52] Why the odd-sounding biographical note to preface a tome on English law? (de) Littleton wrote his treatise in French, which Coke was translating. Coke's seems an effort to impute some Englishness to the apparent foreign character of *de* Littleton (by alluding to the good English of those of his profession who were similarly named), the inference being that if something were written by a foreigner it would not be acceptable as English law. It is de Littleton's name alone that Coke fears might taint the jurisprudence as alien.

Similarly, a sixteenth-century lawyer in England, attempting to obtain a mixed jury for his client, against objections she could not prove alien status, stated: "If a party has a foreign name, the officer asks him if he will have a mixed jury, and upon his prayer it is granted to him. He is not asked whether he is an alien or naturalized, but his mere claim is sufficient."[53] Presumably a fellow with a good "English" name such as 'Edward' would not even be asked. Such early dates of invocations of names as marks of national difference suggest that the political familial form has constituted the European concept of the nation for a much longer period than many have recognized, and that this political vocabulary of personal names has shaped idiomatic understandings of the nation. After surnames came to be widely used throughout Europe and their bearers migrated among these countries, it was easy to distinguish between those last names that were "foreign" and those that were not. In the sixteenth century Camden can list the Christian and last names "most usuall to the English Nation, with their significations. For this is to be granted veretie, that names among all nations and tongues . . . are significative, and not vaine, senseless sounds."[54] This, too, dates the specific association of "language" and "nation" much earlier than Benedict Anderson's conjuncture of print-capitalism.

European Jews initially resisted taking surnames, on the principle that none appeared in the Hebrew Bible, and they did not take them *en masse* until governments compelled them to do so, in the late eighteenth and nineteenth centuries. In 1787 Joseph II in Bohemia ordered Jews to take last names but "forbade names after places and 'in the Jewish language.' "[55] Similar laws passed in 1808 in France, 1809 in Frankfurt on the Main,

---

[52] Coke, *Institutes of the Laws of England*, pp. xxix.

[53] Quoted in Constable, *The Law of the Other* (Chicago: University of Chicago Press, 1994), pp. 135–36.

[54] Camden, *Remains concerning England*, p. 94.

[55] Dietz Bering, *The Stigma of Names: Antisemitism in German Daily Life, 1812–1933*, tr. Neville Plaice (Ann Arbor: University of Michigan Press, 1992), p. 27.

and in 1812 in Prussia. These laws were part of Enlightenment campaigns to ameliorate political differences. In Prussia the 1812 "Edict Concerning the Civic Status of Jews in the Prussian State" stated:

> The continuance of this status of denizens and citizens is bestowed on [Jews] ... only under the obligation that they bear firmly fixed surnames, and that not only in keeping their business books, but also in drafting their contracts and legal declaratory acts they should use the German language, and in signing their names no other characters than German or Latin ones.[56]

Jews who resisted were assigned "ugly" names, such as Schwessloch (Sweat-hole) and Kanalgeruch (Sewerstench). These might be changed with a bribe, to names such as Rosenblum or Violetsaft (Violet sap).[57] Napoleon forbade names used in the Hebrew Bible or the names of towns: " 'from the promulgation of the present law onwards, only those names used in the various calendars and those of the famous great men of ancient history may be accepted as first names in the registers of civil status.' "[58] The Nazis provide notorious examples of the use of names to regulate populations. In 1938 the German government produced a list of 185 male names and 91 female names that Jews and only Jews could use. Jews who had other names were required to add "Israel" or "Sarah." France and Norway had similar Nazi-era rules.[59]

The Nationality Effects of Personal Names

The 'morning star' is no more the same as the 'evening star' than 'Mary Doe' is the same as 'Mrs. John Doe' or than 'Alexis de Tocqueville' is the same as 'Confucius', although he might have the same physical body. Personal names, like other signs, do not simply label someone. Depending on the place and the name, they perform nationality, and sometimes race, as well as gender. There are no 'Mr. Mary Doe'-s. In Louisiana a light-skinned Creole "too non-Caucasian to pass for White" is taunted because of her name: "People call her German because her last name is German."[60] If she had another name she would be Black. The German name renders her Creole. The reason names can be said to constitute one's group identity, rather than simply reveal it, is that but for the conventions of these names

[56] Ibid., p. 31.
[57] Ibid., p. 35.
[58] Ibid., quoting from the 1803 General Law on Personal Status.
[59] Frank Nuessel, *The Study of Names: A Guide to the Principles and Topics* (Westport: Greenwood, 1992), p. 164.
[60] Virginia Domínguez, *White by Definition: Social Classification in Creole Louisiana* (New Brunswick: Rutgers University Press, 1986), p. 172.

the contours of these as well as other affiliations wrought through rubrics of intergenerationality would be other than what they now are. The fact that a name is so quickly associated with nationality is a formal characteristic of how nationality is constituted that is itself crucial to the meaning of nationality.

These senses garnered from the utterance of a name, even if they are often mistakes, convey certain heuristic assumptions about personal identity and identities of nation, race, and gender. If the author of *Democracy in America* were to have a non-French-sounding name, that would be meaningful. Certain questions might arise, and not others, such as, Are his parents Chinese? Were his parents influenced by Chinese thought? Did he decide to change his name (and what kind of person changes his name)? The answers to these questions—or even just the fact that they are asked—would tell us something about this man that would distinguish him as someone different from 'Alexis de Tocqueville'.

A personal name has effects that other kinds of names for things do not. Calling the herb 'cilantro', 'coriander', or 'Chinese parsley' may render it unfamiliar to those who know it by other names, but it would not give rise to the same kinds of questions about the identity of the thing that occur if the author of *Democracy in America* were named 'Confucius'. The signifier 'Alexis de Tocqueville' renders a sign that is radically different from that produced if the signifier is 'Confucius'. The signs that result from 'cilantro' and 'Chinese parsley', while different, do not have effects that are all **that** different.

If someone is named Christine Garza, she is thought Hispanic or Latina. Danielle Lavesque is someone thought to be French; Danielle Lavesque-Manty is someone thought to be French and married to someone with a name whose origin is less "obvious," at least in the United States. Miriam Cohen is thought to be Jewish. And I might ask Danielle, "What kind of name is 'Manty'?" to which the idiomatic response would be the name of a political community. "Finnish" would be an idiomatic response, and unidiomatic would be "My husband's favorite food." In each case the last name, also called a "family name," is associated with a nationality, which is one means by which a political society reproduces itself in such a manner as to reproduce the effect of a primordial-seeming nation. The overlay of taxonomies of family and nation in the last name effects a tight metonymic relation between the two, reinforcing the idea that family and nation have a meaningful tie. The link here is not conscious. Most metonymic associations are not. Yet just as the "Marlboro Man" photos effect a link between Marlboro cigarettes and the rugged masculinity of "the West," "Goldman" effects a link between one's Jewish and familial ancestry.

At first it may seem naive to point out that names associate individuals with particular political societies and nations. The congruence may seem both arbitrary and irrelevant, but like other apparently pre-political relations that turn out to be political, names have been deeply imbricated in the reproduction of political societies. Marc Bloch writes, "In Europe, long after the demise of feudal society, the permanent family name, which today is held in common by men often devoid of any feeling of solidarity, was the creation not of the spirit of kinship, but of the institution most fundamentally opposed to that spirit—the sovereign state."[61] The state creates not only families, but the nomenclature to indicate and enforce their familial status. The difficulty of imagining names that are not associated with family or nation suggests how very deeply this practice is embedded, and not just in one society. But there is no reason that individuals' names must connote family or other memberships. For purposes of individual identity, names, logically, could be utterly idiosyncratic or random. In fact, however, the patterns of personal names display highly structured regularities of nation and family that define who we are, and not just what we are called. These personal names are so important because we do not exist without them. Paul Ziff demonstrates this: "'Witchgren' is a proper name. It is the proper name of . . . you cannot complete that sentence."[62] Or at least not without being tautological. Of course one could supply enough details (e.g., 'Ziff's cat on his good mat.') so that there is no question that one is describing . . . Witchgren. This seems to be Ziff's thinking here. 'Witchgren' just won't leave our thoughts, once we know who she is.

Personal Names: Some Unique Features

The semantics of personal names follow from the nomenclature of nations, and are neither "significative" of themselves, as Camden suggests,[63] nor mere ostensive labels, as John Stuart Mill maintains: "Proper names are not connotative; they denote the individuals who are called by them; but they do not indicate or imply attributes as belonging to those individuals."[64] That someone is called Sutton does not mean he lives there, nor do we infer that a Smith works with iron. Ziff dismisses the study of proper names altogether: "Proper names are an important topic in the

---

[61] *Feudal Society*, tr. L. A. Manyon (Chicago: University of Chicago Press, 1961), p. 140. Bloch's formulation of the role of the state in the production of family names is slightly confused. He has just described kinship ties as coextensive with family name. This suggests that the "spirit of kinship" may also have its roots in the "sovereign state" as well.

[62] Paul Ziff, *Semantic Analysis* (Ithaca: Cornell University Press, 1967), p. 87.

[63] Camden, *Remains concerning England*, p. 94.

[64] *A System of Logic: Ratiocinative and Inductive* (New York and Bombay: Longman's, 1900), p. 20.

philosophy of language, but only because their importance has been exaggerated by philosophers and grammarians."[65] Still, Ziff himself recognizes that personal names may be used to distinguish one's nationality from another: "One may not know a single word of Chinese and yet know of Hsieh Ho. 'Hsieh Ho' is a Chinese proper name."[66] If we know that 'Hsieh Ho' is a Chinese transliteration, then we think we know something about Hsieh Ho. This means that names are more than the purely arbitrary nomenclature Mill imagines. They may be overrated for their significance in philosophy and grammar, but they seem very important for political theories of identity. Lamenting the American cultural invasion blamed for two French girls' Kurt Cobain-inspired suicides, their headmaster refers to "the American look; the children with names like Steve and Kevin; the movies and the music and the increasing use in speech of Americanisms."[67] The mayor's proposition that 'Kevin' and 'Steve' are American names, and not British or Irish ones, seems unconvincing. But his practice of associating name with nation is not confusing. We understand him though we may think he is wrong.

Another way to think about how names are used is to imagine that our names really were ostensive labels denoting particular individuals and nothing more. Imagine each individual distinguished only by a randomly assigned hieroglyph. In the case of either arbitrary hieroglyphs or names from a universal register there would be absolutely no associations between nationality and one's personal name. Then it really would be silly to imagine one could infer someone's family-based nationality from a name. Or imagine the initial naming procedures of the Normans were still in place. Imagine everyone had a Latin name. Someone with an English blacksmith for a father would have the same surname 'Faber' as the son of the "French" blacksmith.[68] The system that transmits particularity from a political society to its members would be seriously weakened. Without at least the belief that individual people can be distinguished "by name," as Serbian or Croatian, for instance, it becomes that much more difficult to even think in terms of any internal regulation of identities.[69] That names

---

[65] Ziff, *Semantic Analysis*, p 85.

[66] Ibid., p. 86. This sentence appears in a context unrelated to the point for which it is being used here.

[67] Roger Cohen, "2 'Perfect Little Girls' Stun France in Suicide," *New York Times*, May 30, 1997, p. A4.

[68] Frances and Joseph Gies, *Marriage and the Family in the Middle Ages* (New York: Harper and Row, 1987), p. 166.

[69] The invocation of names in the former Yugoslavia is an excellent example of how personal names evoke nationality. People there believe they can easily distinguish who is Serbian (Eastern Orthodox), Croatian (Roman Catholic), or Muslim by either a first or last name. In recognition of this one of Tito's first gestures was to change his name from the

run in families reinforces the tie of nation and family to the individual. One is thought to be **born**: Neda, Marinka, Jovan, or Josip, so that is who one is, including all of the connotations and puzzles of nationality a name provokes.

This is not to suggest that every time a personal name is used that people conjure images of flags and countries, only that the taxonomies of personal names are, at least idiomatically, far more limited than those for other sites of national taxonomies. The Olympics and other international competitions arbitrarily associate nationality with certain athletic competencies. The result is the "Russian hockey" team and the "Brazilian soccer" team, and therefore, something distinctively sports-relevant about the taxonomy of the nation. If this taxonomy is relevant to practices as important as hockey and soccer, if it matters that baseball is a distinctively "American," "Japanese," and "Cuban" sport, then the existence of all these countries must be as concrete as that of hockey, soccer, and baseball. Still the nomenclature of national difference in sports operates differently from that of names and personal identity.

Imagine the announcement at the Olympic Games that "synchronized swimming" television coverage is about to begin. One asks "What kind of **sport** is that?" Responses might include "a sport in which the different sides display their skills at swimming patterns in unison" or "a sport in which the spectators do not know the score until the judges announce it" or "a relatively new sport." One could respond also that men do not tend to participate in it, or that swimmers from a certain country seem especially good at it. Now suppose someone hears an announcement, "Pradeep Chhibber is the coach" and asks, "What kind of **name** is that?" Idiomatic responses would be confined to those about nationality and gender. The only other possible responses, which would be non-idiomatic, would take the form of responding to "Pradeep Chhibber" as words per se, as in: "Pradeep Chhibber is the kind of name with two words with eight letters in the first word and eight in the second." Or "Pradeep Chhibber is the kind of name of which the first word begins with a p and the second word with a c."

Personal Names and Other Taxonomies

Individuals from "different racial and ethnic groups may employ what are considered to be 'unusual' first names from the perspective of the majority

---

"Croatian" Josip Broz to Marshall (leader) Tito. Josip is "Croatian." The "Serbian" form is "Jovan."

group."[70] This means that the name functions as a Sausserian sign, one that connotes a relation to a certain kind of group. To use a name is to invoke a particular semiotics of difference. Family genealogies are always organized by nation. Historians of names organize them by nation as well.[71] Childrens' names also are taxonomized by nation.[72]

Even if an association is mistaken in particular cases, the fact that we might be prompted to say something such as "My friend Jesus Carlos is not really Spanish" (or of "Hispanic" or "Latino" background) tells us something about the connotations of names. Although it would be grammatically correct, it would be rather unlikely that we would say, "My friend Jesus Carlos is not really Jesus" or "My friend John Smith is not really a blacksmith" because we no longer associate a name with someone's actual occupation.

The other semiotic system in which names function is that of gender. Along with taxonomies of nation, a salient division of names is between boys and girls. That some names may not always easily match in predictable ways follows from the fact that names have underlying associations of gender. Some mistakes are idiomatic and others are not. We do not point at Carol and say, "When you said 'Carol' I thought you meant someone wearing glasses" or "When you said 'Carol' I thought you meant a bald person" since neither optical fitness nor scalp condition are associated with personal names. But we might point at Carol and say "When you said 'Carol' I thought you meant a woman" as we notice Carol is a man. Similar to the nation/name relationship, the gender/name relationship both assigns and produces a status of belonging with social and juridical effects that are naturalized as "gender."

Political societies can also be distinguished by the sources and principles they draw on for naming. It is the practice of the Chukchee, not the Swedes, to name children in a way that will trick the evil spirits into staying away. The spirits are thought not to be interested in children with names such as "dog penis" or "monkey cheek." Hence these are common Chukchee names.[73] A person in England named 'hyena droppings', however, would attract attention.

---

[70] Nuessel, *The Study of Names*, p. 4.

[71] Smith provides a list of the patronymical form of name by nation, *Story of Our Names*, pp. 124–25; and Camden's section on "Christian Names" denotes the country associated with that name—e.g., "Maria" (Spanish), "Mary" (English), in *Remains concerning England*. The following are exemplary titles of books on family histories and names: *Burke's Genealogical and Heraldic History of the Landed Gentry of Ireland* (London: Burke's Peerage, 1958); Edward MacLysaght, *The Surnames of Ireland* (Dublin: Irish University Press, 1973); Joseph Osborne, *Heirlooms of Ireland: An Easy Reference to Some Irish Surnames and Their Origins* (Baltimore: Clearfield, 1995).

[72] E.g., Patrick Wolfe, *Irish Names for Children* (Dublin: Fillard MacMillan, 1992).

[73] Fred Alford, *Naming and Identity* (New Haven: HRAF, 1987), p. 65.

Names and Places

Another way to think about the semiotics of proper names is to reflect on the association of names of places with names of nations, or names of a group of people that are the same as the place: "The adjectives and nouns derived from toponyms are frequently employed to indicate people who are from that area or who currently live there," such as Chicago and Chicagoans.[74] Bloch, for example, writes: "As early as 833 we find the Hungarians, whose name appeared then for the first time, disturbing the settled populations."[75] In the tenth century "Hungarians" take a "permanent settlement in the plains which today bear their name."[76] Geography is the mapping of where particular groups reside in the world. One might recount numerous other instances of this throughout Europe, including the German "tribes,"[77] when German settlement constitutes a germanische territory, but not, yet, the country Deutschland. Describing the nomenclature of early English kings, Edward Freeman writes:

> In everything, in short, belonging to our old days [beginning in the eleventh century] it is the people who stand forth and not mere land. In fact, except in the use of old geographical names like Gaul and Britain, the land can hardly be said to have a being or a name apart from the people. The land is simply called by the name of the people, like Lokroi and Leontini in Greek geography, like Franken and Hessen in Germany.[78]

We think of regions such as "the Congo" as a concrete geological space, but it is a geographical one, existing only in association with the Congolese who live there.

Political societies without governments also have names. Robertson Smith describes "collectives" whose names are those of totemic ani-

---

[74] Nuessel, *Study of Names*, p. 61.

[75] *Feudal Society*, tr. L. A. Manyon (Chicago: University of Chicago Press, 1961), p. 8.

[76] Ibid., p. 9.

[77] An obvious caution is that this nomenclature is itself linguistically specific. 'Germans' refer to themselves as 'Deutsche'. While the pronunciation of "foreign" names may be changed depending on where they are pronounced, the convention is to maintain the spelling—unless of course the name has already been changed by the individual or by the country to which she has emigrated. The German 'Schmidt' is not called 'Smith', although Anglophones do say he is from 'Germany' and not 'Deutschland'. Each country orients its geographies toward itself, which is why there are no maps that label countries so as to conform with the respective self-labelings. If such a map did exist it would be meaningless, since differences in alphabets would render certain names utterly unintelligible.

[78] *The History of the Norman Conquest*, appendix M "King of England or King of the English," rev. U.S. ed. (Oxford, New York: MacMillan, 1873), p. 586.

mals.[79] The important point to bear in mind here is that a nation (or "collective") is always such in relation to a name. The association of a name with a nation is not a result of some linguistic rule, such that each thing necessarily has a unique name. There is no such rule. One might observe a particular crowd and it might or might not have a name. The phrase 'The Rolling Stones' refers to a group, but the phrase 'The people over there' also does this. One might be a member of a specific bridge club and it might have a proper name 'The S.F. Sharks' or it might not have one. It could simply be that one plays with a group of friends. Everyone knows who is in the group and there is no need for a name. Strangers are excluded simply by etiquette, without resorting to nomenclatures of particularity. One cannot, however, belong to a nation that lacks a name. That is, every nation, as the natural seeming manifestation of a political society, has a proper name—one to which political leaders may devote substantial resources establishing and protecting.[80]

Chapters 2 and 3 have established the ways that political societies shape the contours of nationality, by conventions of marriage rules, citizenship, rules about property and territory, and finally, by controlling the nomenclature of its members' personal identities. Chapter 4 shows how the affiliations of race follow from those of the political society/nation, as a naturalized earth becomes the site for designating certain group identities. This political cartography, interpreted as the result of fixed, determinate boundaries rather than aggregations of political boundaries, provides the exterior form for racial identities that are then held in place by political societies that continue to invoke long-standing rules of exclusion to control the membership of the national population.

[79] *Kinship and Marriage in Early Arabia* (1885; rpt. London: Adam and Charles Black, 1907), p. 18. Lévi-Strauss claims the opposite, in his reporting on research by Jürg Gaschē. According to Indian informants in the Northwestern Amazon basin, the words "existed first, without meaning, and it was only by accident [that they came to denote] clans and individuals. It similarly occurs that identical words can designate different things in neighboring dialects" ("Religion, Language, History: Concerning an Unpublished Text by F. Saussure," in *View From Afar*, tr. Joachim Neugroschel and Phoebe Hoss [New York: Basic, 1985], pp. 151–52).

[80] Some of the 'Roma' do not want to be called 'Gypsies'; many 'Hrvatski' resent being referred to as 'Croatian'; and of course various political leaders in twentieth century Africa have changed the names bestowed on their countries by colonialists and previous leaders.

Four

Race and the State

MALE-ORDER BRIDES AND THE GEOGRAPHIES OF RACE

> In his [*New Yorker*] article Philip Gourevitch
> modified one of my statements by having me say,
> "What do I have to do to not be racist? Marry a
> black woman? With AIDS, if possible?"
> However, as my recording of our interview
> shows, I said marry "a black person" ("**un noir**"),
> and not a black woman" ("**une noire**"). My
> expression, on this side of the Atlantic, has an
> obvious ironic meaning that Mr. Gourevitch did
> not pick up. I am sure your readers will catch all
> of its humor.
>
>   (*Jean-Marie Le Pen*[1])

LE PEN'S translation, as an effort at setting the record straight, is quite odd. The reference to "un noir," a Black—as in "a Black person and not a Black woman"—can mean only that Le Pen is speculating about marrying a Black man (a person-not-a-woman). Also, he thinks it important to clarify that talk about marrying a Black woman with AIDS is something we might take seriously, whereas we will catch the humor in his marrying a Black man. Why? What is it about marriage to **un noir** that Le Pen finds so amusing? The "joke" is supposed to be funny because marriage is the kind of contract we just know that Le Pen in particular would only have with a White, French woman sans AIDS. Marriage is thought to suggest love and intimacy, which is why Le Pen thinks mocking his projection of political correctness (marrying a Black man with AIDS) is especially amusing. What Le Pen presumably does not realize is that the reason marriage is his punch line is that the institution does not just passively accommodate the racist prejudices of people such as Le Pen, but actively constitutes "un noir" and "une noire" in the first place.

---

[1] In "The Mail," *New Yorker*, June 2, 1997, p. 6.

In view of the crudely stupid and harmful rhetoric of someone like Le Pen it may seem off the point to pursue precision in racial terminology, if the goal is to establish egalitarian norms and practices. It is easy to observe the unfounded basis of his discriminatory ideology and, using boilerplate liberal precepts, observe the inadequacies—logical and political—of policies that harm individuals based on status and not competencies. And yet, it is precisely because figures such as Le Pen, and organizations in the United States such as the Aryan Nation, are the exceptional manifestations of the more humdrum mechanisms of race that inquiry into the long-standing structures of race is important. It is the ways that race may so often seem to be a harmless sort of difference, especially in liberal ideologies, that allow us to lose sight of the governmental institutions and state forms that always inform racial taxonomies. That races are constituted and sustained by government agencies, and even more importantly, that races are reproduced through explicit and implicit invocations of the state form that comprises political territories of origin, means that there are no cases in which race is apolitical and no possibility for a race to be a form of being with emancipatory possibilities. As opposed to some who argue that racism creates race, the contention here is that race always entails race-ism, just as much as gender differences always entail sexed forms of domination and that class entails exploitation. To see the character of the power particular to racial domination is to note its coincidence with, rather than its independence from, a state form.

Race is the culmination of political society, family, and nation. Calling on the internal rules of political society—especially birth certificates and marriage law—as well as the familial form of nations for the constitution of racialized territories of origin—race dialectically grounds certain modern political societies as naturally different, based on laws (of nature) the state creates.[2] Race follows from these dialectics, as the form that, when these other forms of being (and those of religion) are in flux, makes concrete the political geographical territories and political societies, by tying sub-populations to the apparently fixed dimensions of land and body. The "African" must be a real racial type, it is intuited, because Africa is a real place. While nations might be imagined communities with political borders subject to dispute, Africa is considered immutable.

Although nationality and ethnicity are treated as primordial, these forms of being manifest largely as phenomena of "practices," not phenomena of "physical characteristics." The ancestral differences that give rise to the

---

[2] The only kind of political society that uses race is a state. Other political societies, such as the ancient Greek polis or the Roman empire, did not seem to associate observed physical differences with the contours of a group tied to a geographical territory of origins, which is the definition of race this chapter develops.

possibility of a national or ethnic background are not thought to be revealed by the body, but by effects of family name, language, or style of dress. If someone claims "You look French" and by this means that the person's body is a specifically French body, then France has become racialized. This convention of racializing what are referred to in the United States idiomatically as "national origins" was extremely common until the early twentieth century. John Stuart Mill, for instance, in discussing the cultural characteristics assigned to French, Italians, Irish, English, Swiss, Romans, Teutonics, and Spartans, interchangeably refers to their 'race' and 'national character'.[3] In the United States up through the turn of the century it was common to refer to new immigrants from Europe, such as the Irish and Italians, as members of different 'races' as well as different 'nationalities'. Underlying the collapse of the two terms was the notion that there were distinct bloodlines that distinguished subpopulations in ways that mapped onto sovereign political territories, as nationality and physical appearance were coterminous.

The eventual differentiation between 'race' and 'nationality' corresponds with a moment in the global economy when people were almost as likely as commodities to cross borders. This new mobility may have undermined assumptions about a physiological relation that one might have to a nation. Second- and third-generation emigrants lose obvious traces of their countries of origin, by changing their names and losing their accents. Obviously this is not the case for many. But it is easy to adopt these conventions of assimilation. This fluidity of nationality and citizenship came to be widely recognized (celebrated and denigrated) in the early twentieth century. One implication was that the view of nationality as akin to a birthmark could not be sustained. So old caricatures of physical, visible differences between national groups also lost much, though not all, of their salience. This is not just a story about the fabled United States' "melting pot," but holds for Jews assimilating throughout Europe, the Irish in England, and Latvians in Russia as well.

For race, contrariwise, the display of ancestral difference is for the most part indexed by physiognomy, where degrees of the "Blackness," "Whiteness," or for Mill, "Frenchness," of one's ancestors are inferred from one's present physical appearance. The purpose of pointing out this contrast between ideas about race and those about nationality is not to suggest that there are genuine differences among subpopulations' physiogamies that make it easier to imagine undermining the effects of national, compared to racial, differences. Rather, it is because the form of race is one that exists vis-à-vis discourses about observed physical differences that

---

[3] "The Subjection of Women" (Vermont and London: Everyman's Library, 1985), pp. 278–79.

it seems a more intransigent type of attribute than forms of being associated with discourses of practices. The form of race lends certain meanings to the specific content of certain kinds of observed differences and not to others. Nothing about physical differences among human beings requires the concept of race, as I show below, but the concept of race produces the effect of thinking certain kinds of differences natural, as well as immutable. So, although one is Taiwanese because one's parents are Taiwanese, and one is Asian because one's parents are Asian, the marks of the Taiwanese ancestry are matters of language, dress, and citizenship, whereas the indication that one is Asian is a matter of the observation of certain physiological, embodied traits. The contrast between national and racial forms does not mean that nations are imagined and races are real, but that the indexes of nationality are thought of and experienced as somewhat more contingent than those of race.

Numerous scholars have pointed out the infelicities of inferences about racial determinacy: people may have certain physiological signs of Blackness and no traceable Black ancestors, and vice versa. Virginia Domínguez's work on the history of Louisiana Creole communities[4] shows how the state intervenes to continually (re)organize taxonomic schemes that would otherwise disintegrate due to the centrifugal pressures of "mixed" births, ambiguous appearances, and personal efforts to control who one is.

The rules of kinship generated by the state, however, continue to militate against this disintegration. The certificates naming racial identities at birth, marriage, and death have been used to establish racialized rules for who can reproduce (legitimate) children and inherit. As is the case for affiliations of family and nation, marriage and inheritance rules also overdetermine the nexus of race and property ownership. In 1993 the median **income** of White families was $39,300. The median income for Black families that year was $21,542.[5] This is a dramatic difference, but even more dramatic are the differences in family **wealth**. In 1993 the median net worth for White households was $45,740. For Black households, the median net worth was $4,418.[6] This difference in wealth accounts for the difference between owning a home and having money saved up for college, and not having these. Since wealth flows largely through families, the conventions that form families will also contribute to the formation of wealth. Important to the racial character of these disparities is that the state does not just passively allow pre-political wealthy Whites to pass wealth on to their

[4] *White By Definition: Social Classification in Creole Louisiana* (New Brunswick: Rutgers University Press, 1986).

[5] *Statistical Reference Index. Abstracts* (Washington, D.C.: Government Printing Office, 1995), p. 474.

[6] T. J. Eller and Wallace Fraser, *Asset Ownership of Households: 1993* (Washington, D.C.: Bureau of the Census, 1993), p. 9.

White children but itself has constituted "Whites" and reproduced their wealth as Whites by precluding interracial marriages.

Still, simply observing state interventions in the constitution of a group does not tell us much about race, since many of the identities constituted by the state for purposes of regulating economic relations are not racialized. The certificate to cut hair renders one a "barber," which is a profession, not a race. Without that certificate certain property relations are precluded, but that does not mean the state has constituted a "race" of barbers. Barbers are not distinguished by their appearances. Unlike the belief that one can ascertain who is the "White" person among a crowd of "Asians" we would believe we would be less effective at identifying the state-certified barber in a crowd of other state-certified workers.

One response to the observation about the state's role in constituting race might be that there really are underlying attributes of race, and the government simply names these attributes, albeit sometimes incorrectly. For the government to shuffle around certain labels in a manner that may seem arbitrary or incoherent is just one more sign of bureaucracy's failures and does not mean "race" is something the state invents. For instance, if I mistakenly refer to an object that is really red as "bright orange," no one will propose we abandon the concept of color. Phenomenologically, colors exist. I just erred in saying that something really red was "bright orange." Insofar as race is phenotypical, it might be thought to reveal (or not reveal) a genetic trait, in ways that differ from, say, identities of a French nationality or of barbers. The intuition here is that differences inscribed on the body must speak to genuine, biological distinctions, not artifacts of the state. This belief rests, in turn, on the idea that bodily differences are essential whereas differences of speech, dress, and cuisine are accidental. The assumption is that humans cannot control what their bodies look like, whereas we can determine—in ways that vary according to the whims of taste and fancy—these other habits. The body's appearance is something that appears necessary, while our practices are contingent.[7] Hence, it is reasonable to regard race, more than nationality, as a fixed attribute of a pre-political, biological individual.

Much of the preceding discussion of the meanings of the concept of race—as well as those of political society, nation, and family—touch on

---

[7] That is why gender differences are also thought natural. Of course the transgendered indicate the mutability of our bodies as well. In principle this might be conceived as turning gendered "bodies" into contingent "practices"—the preference for a certain kind of surgery might be considered continuous with adopting a certain accent or eating particular foods. Yet currently surgical interventions are still on a dichotomized body, one which continues to be perceived in rigid binaries. One is more or less male or female, as seen in ways that correspond to or diverge from "natural" males and females (Judith Butler, *Bodies that Matter: On the Discursive Limits of 'Sex'* [New York: Routledge, 1993]).

the ways that different theories of knowledge accompany different theories of these affiliations. One of the difficulties in humanist studies is that, unlike those in idioms of math or other non-historical fields of inquiry, the object being investigated is simultaneously beyond and within the everyday world, as a matter of definition. Physicists do not have to grapple with the ways that gravity impedes human movement in particular, when they conduct their experiments and write their equations to explain the character of weight at the center of the galaxy or the earth. That our everyday intuitions do not easily grasp the concept of zero gravity (or that our intuitions may be simply wrong or untestable) does not give pause to the physicist. That for long periods of time people thought the earth flat in no way falsified the work of those who knew otherwise.

However, if a theory of a concept of race cannot incorporate popular intuitions of the day and account for them, then it is non-idiomatic, arbitrary, and therefore incorrect. Just as the previous chapters have attempted to draw on a mix of historical documents, philosophical debates, and contemporary linguistic idioms to elucidate the meaning of concepts in a way that addresses unresolved theoretical and political questions, this chapter pursues similar lines of inquiry, by using what is right in otherwise misleading contemporary definitions of race, rather than simply presenting one definition as an a priori logical truth.

Toward a Phenomenology of Race

Most discussions of relations between White Americans and Black Americans among social scientists focus on the dynamic of racism, and not race.[8] These studies assume race differences as constitutive of groups, and then provide evidence for how these differences result in certain "racial" or "racist" conditions or attitudes. This work assumes three dominant forms. One view among Whites has been that **social differences reflect important genetic differences between races**, differences that have been "scientifically" shown to render Whites more suited for positions of high social status than Blacks.[9] A second account is that **physical differences**

[8] The initial view of race as referring to problems of "Whites" and "Blacks" is neither arbitrary, nor strictly United States-centric, but follows from a belief Oliver Cox has defended, which is that the concept of race used to define dynamics among other groups is parasitic on the dichotomized concept of race as it emerged during the European slave trade. So although Asians face different obstacles than Blacks or Latinos, and the Asian racial identity means something quite different than others, the notion that "racial" differences imbricate power relations can be explained by the concept's roots in the slave trade (*Caste, Class, and Race* [1948] [New York and London: Monthly Review, 1959]).

[9] For research on how the "Protestant work ethic" is racially coded, see Donald Kinder and Lynn Sanders, *Divided by Color: Racial Politics and Democratic Ideals* (Chicago: University

just happen to provide the site for deeply felt psychological needs
people have to be part of a group that oppresses other groups. The
difference in physical appearance provides a convenient site for people to
invent stories about their differences. American slavery and contemporary
racial discrimination both, in this model, are represented as products of
an innate need to experience who one is through being in a group that
excludes and stigmatizes others. A third explanation of racism is that people
are not born with any innate desires to be close to some people and distant
from others, but that **pressing economic circumstances induce people
to favor their group over others.**[10] Although all of these explanations
capture something about the dynamics of racial group differences, none
of these accounts addresses the question of how individuals come to be
taxonomized into specifically **racial** groups.

The account of innate differences that favor Whites was widely, though
not completely, discredited by and among scientists between World Wars
One and Two.[11] Part of the problem in the work on race were the unending
battles over how to perform racial classifications. Some scientists maintained that there were three races, others, that there were over three
hundred.[12] Also, scientists were challenged by children of so-called mixed
marriages, and could not agree on how to classify them. In the absence
of an obvious classificatory scheme, the assertion of racial group differences

---

of Chicago Press, 1996), pp. 136–50. Margaret Wetherell and Jonathan Potter also show
how "work" is represented as a phenotype of the genotype of "whiteness" (*Mapping the
Language of Racism: Discourse and the Legitimation of Exploitation* [New York, London: Columbia
University Press, 1992]), esp. the chapter "Ideology and Political-Economy," pp. 11–31.
Balibar writes: "[T]he cultures supposed implicitly superior are those which appreciate and
promote 'individual' enterprise, social and political individualism, as against those which
inhibit these things," in "Is There a Neo-Racism," in Balibar and Wallerstein, *Race, Nation,
and Class*, [London: Verso, 1991], p. 25).

[10] Combining features of all three approaches, Michael Banton has developed a rational
choice theory of race: 1) individuals use physical and cultural differences to create groups;
2) this results in racial and ethnic groups; 3) group interactions will change the boundaries
of these groups (*Racial and Ethnic Competition* [Cambridge: Cambridge University Press,
1983], p. 104).

[11] Though W.E.B. Du Bois and many others challenged scientific work on races in the
late nineteenth century, the two anthropologists who most effectively discredited "scientific
racism" from the early twentieth century through World War Two are Franz Boas and his
student Ruth Benedict. In addition to their scholarly publications, both were extremely active
in their professional societies and engaged in broader public debates about race. See Boas,
Race and Democratic Society, collected papers (New York: J. J. Augustin Publisher, 1945); Benedict,
Race and Racism (London: Routledge and Sons, 1945), *Race: Science, and Politics* (New York:
Modern Age Books, 1940). Elazar Barkan believes that their views would have been accepted
much earlier, except that most of those arguing against scientific racism were Jewish. Their
work was held to be self-interested by others in the field (*The Retreat of Scientific Racism*
[Cambridge, New York; Cambridge University Press, 1992], p. 9).

[12] Yehudi Webster, *Racialization of America* (New York: St. Martin's Press, 1992), p. 34.

foundered on the absence of identifiable racial groups. Still, many continue to consider physical differences to be both genetically determined and determinate of social differences. IQ controversies occasionally flare in the United States,[13] and there are occasional Ku Klux Klan marches and Aryan Nation terrorist scares. But now there is the notion that such activities may constitute 'racism', which was not a word before 1930.[14]

The dominant scholarship in the United States now represents the different status of Whites and Blacks in this country as rooted in differences of socio-economic backgrounds, such that income and class background correlate with race so as to render some groups systematically less able to "fit in" with the dominant culture of late capitalist America.[15] The belief has been that some set of vaguely defined cultural differences correlate with race. Not genetic inferiority, but social policies and dominant group prejudices have denied Blacks equal access with Whites to the American dream. The corollary was a prescription to change the environmental factors so that opportunities available to Whites would be open to Blacks as well. This social-scientific response to nineteenth-century prejudices is really an answer to a question about racism, not race. It provides a non-essential explanation of a dynamic whereby one group does not "fit" and therefore is held in low regard by members of a dominant group. This social scientific approach to prejudice addresses the dynamic of racism but reveals little about the meanings of "race." Implicit in this view is a belief that biological differences such as skin color manifest in natural group differences. These differences are not problems unless groups organize according to these biological attributes and, as in the slave trade, one group exploits another with no basis other than these differences.

One flaw in this account, as in all accounts that treat racial groups as given entities, is that the subtle physiological and genetic differences that exist *among individuals* are in fact fine-grained 'clinal' differences that are continuous, not categorical. Gene clusters vary in small degrees. "Race" imputes categorical breaks along what is really a continuum of gene clusters. The researchers who put forth this critique of social scientific studies of

[13] That a book in the 1990s on IQ differences even prompted controversy (and not marginalization) suggests this is still a view thought to be defensible (Richard Herrnstein and Charles Murray, *The Bell Curve: Intelligence and Class Structure in American Life* [New York: Free Press, 1994]).

[14] Barkan, *The Retreat of Scientific Racism* (Cambridge: Cambridge University Press, 1992), p. 3.

[15] The work of sociologist Robert Park, a student of Talcott Parsons, exemplifies this. See *Race and Culture* (Glencoe, IL: Free Press, 1950). The "culture of poverty" work inaugurated among this generation and popularized in the policy recommendations of Senator Daniel Moynihan is still pervasive. One of the most prominent contemporary critics from this school is William Julius Wilson, cf. *When Work Disappears: The World of the New Urban Poor* (New York: Knopf, 1996).

race maintain "race" is not real, but a folk concept.[16] (This critique of the concept of race has so permeated the field of anthropology that a survey of over seven hundred anthropology textbooks in the late 1980s found that most either define "race" as a folk category or do not mention it at all.)[17] Yet even absent categorically obvious genetic differences among individuals, distinct "racial" groups still seem to be recognizable, a fact that the anthropologists' description of "race" as a "folk concept" seems to trivialize.

The next account of race—people have a deep psychological need to distinguish themselves from each other—is also incomplete, although it certainly dominates the academic and even popular literature, in which prejudice is accepted as an irrational, emotional impulse. In a chapter heading, anthropologist Ruth Benedict, a leading scholarly critic of racism in the 1940s and 1950s asks, "Why Then Race Prejudice?" Her answer: "Racist dogma is modern," but it expresses the "old human obsession," that "my group is uniquely valuable and, if it is weakened, all valuable things will perish."[18] The problem with this assertion is that history undermines its largely functionalist assumptions, which leaves the theory no place on which to stand. In the absence of any "racist gene," or babies whose first words are "I am White," the main evidence that people have deep-seated racist fantasies is that people behave in a racist fashion. This observation does not account for the historically specific emergence of the modern concept of race, which arises at the same time that 'race' becomes a word— at the time of the Inquisition and the beginning of the slave trade. (Nor does such a story about the "old human obsession" account for the frequent cosmopolitan, anti-racist movements that in many ways seem more prevalent than their provincial, particularist counterparts.)

Etymology

The *Oxford English Dictionary*'s first overarching definition of 'race' is "a group of persons, animals, or plants connected by common descent or origin." In small print a further explanation follows: "In the widest sense

[16] See for example Anthony Kroch's entry on "racism" in the *Encyclopedia of Anthropology*, David Hunter and Philip Whitten, eds. (New York and London, 1976).

[17] Audrey Smedley, *Race in North America: Origin and Evolution of a Worldview* (Boulder: Westview Press, 1992), p. 2, citing Alice Littlefield, Leonard Lieberman, Larry Reynolds, "Redefining Race: The Potential Demise of a Concept in Physical Anthropology," *Current Anthropology* 23(6) (1982), pp. 641–56. Kwame Anthony Appiah also follows this line of thinking, *In My Father's House* (Oxford, New York: Oxford University Press, 1992) pp. 28–46.

[18] *Race: Science and Politics*, p. 222. For a similar description of racism as part of human nature, see Edward Shils, "Color, the Universal Intellectual Community, and the Afro-Asian Intellectual," in *Color and Race* John Franklin, ed. (Boston: Houghton Mifflin, 1968); and

the term includes all descendants from the original stock, but may also be limited to a single line of descent or to the group as it exists in a particular period." Three refinements of this definition ensue, referring to lines of ancestry. The fourth definition is: "One of the great divisions of mankind, having certain physical peculiarities in common." Then, in small print, the following caveat is offered: "The term is often used imprecisely; even among anthropologists there is no generally adopted classification or terminology." As evidence for this, the following example is used: "1971 R. M. and F. M. Keeling, *New Perspectives in Cultural Anthropology* 51: 'It is at this point that 'race' becomes relevant. Though in popular usage it is emotionally charged and imprecise, it has a straightforward and important meaning in evolutionary biology. A race is a geographically separated, hence genetically somewhat distinctive, population within a species.' "[19]

This popular imprecision in the use of 'race' does not seem to trouble most of those who use the word, according to the experts who document confusing uses of words. *Webster's Dictionary of English Usage* "examines and evaluates common problems of confused or disputed English usage."[20] 'Race' does not appear in this text. 'Mankind', 'native', 'human', and 'man' do appear, as instances of words fraught with political troubles that become expressed in language. About the word 'man' *English Usage* states: "Man in its generic sense 'a human being' has come under considerable attack in recent years by people who feel that because it is so widely understood in its somewhat more recent sense of 'a male person' its generic sense slights women."[21] The *Dictionary of Changes in Meaning* includes 'race', but only the definition that applies to "running a race or moving rapidly." It contains no mention of the other word 'race'.[22] Despite the scientific uncertainty as to the meaning of 'race', we English-speakers apparently continue to use it as though we know what we mean.

The imprecision in the meaning of 'race' may itself be what makes race such an impossible concept for scientists. If by 'race' we mean both a category pertaining to "physical peculiarities" **and** a category referring to a "line of descent," then scientists along with the rest of us cannot help but be confounded when phenotypes and genotypes do not conform. If 'race' referred only to genes or only to appearance, then this problem

John Dollard, *Caste and Class in a Southern Town* (New York: Harper, 1957). Benedict misleads here, because later the book does offer an historical account of race and racism that has nothing to do with this psychological explanation.

[19] *Oxford English Dictionary*, 2d ed. 'Race' as in "running a race" is under a separate heading, and has a separate etymological history.

[20] 1st ed., p. 4a.

[21] Ibid.

[22] Adrian Room, *Dictionary of Changes in Meaning* (London and New York: Routledge and Kegan Paul, 1986).

would be eliminated, but 'race' refers to both. How did we come to have a word whose proper use yields such elusive meanings?

Most etymological dictionaries stop at the Portuguese 'raca' in outlining the history of 'race', indicating that 'raca' is of "obscure origins."[23] But there are efforts to reach further back. Ernest Klein states that 'race' "probably derives from Arabic rā's, head, beginning origin,"[24] which is related to Hebrew 'rōsh' and 'resh'. This is the "twentieth letter of the Hebrew alphabet, from the Mishnaic Hebrew 'resh', literally meaning 'head.' "[25] Klein traces 'resh' back to 'Bereshith', which refers to "the creation; the first book of the Pentateuch," and which is rendered as 'genesis' in Greek. 'Bereshith' is, Klein says, related to the Aramaic 'resh', the Arabic 'rā's', and the Ethiopian 'res', all of which refer to 'head' often meaning 'origin'.[26] None of Klein's entries on the origins of 'race' include any reference to differences in appearance.

According to Eric Partridge, 'race' means "A family, a tribe a people. Probably Latin *ratio*, a species, in medieval Philosophy."[27] Likewise, Leo Spitzer in his etymological essay "Race" argues that 'race' is from a use of the Latin 'ratio', a word that referred to one's spirit, akin to a Platonic form. It was a spiritual principle thought to infuse one's soul, rather than a biological difference among bodies. After showing the "secularization" of spiritual difference suggested in *ratio* (based on a reference by a Dr. Johnson who writes: "I hope her disease is not of the cephalic race."), Spitzer writes:

> What a significant comment this affords on the modern 'racial' beliefs! As these are 'abandoned, forsaken' by God, so the notion of divine participation is lost in the term 'race.' It is not merely a pun if I say that modern racialism is not only 'geistverlassen' . . . but also 'God-forsaken.' And the Augustine who says so often in the much quoted chapter that only the pure religious and charitable mind can approach intuition of those God-willed ideas of things would surely protest against the modern rationalistic anticipation of an 'idea of a race' . . . as an absurd attempt to see with 'bodily eyes' what only spiritual vision may attain to.[28]

Spitzer notes the irony of a word that first marked spiritual differences becoming so debased, such that those labeled in a 'racial' fashion are

---

[23] Jacob and Wilhelm Grimm, *Deutsches Wörterbuch* also stops at the Portuguese 'raca' in its etymological explanation of 'Rasse' (Leipzig: S. Hirzel, 1893).

[24] *Comprehensive Etymological Dictionary: Dealing with the origin of words and their sense development, thus illustrating the history of civilization and culture* (London and New York: Elsevier Publisher, 1966), vol. 1, p. 1294.

[25] Ibid., p. 1333.

[26] Ibid., p. 165.

[27] *Origins* (New York: MacMillan Publishers, 1959), citing Walshe, *A Concise German Etymological Dictionary* (London: Routledge and Kegan Paul, 1952).

[28] "Race," in Spitzer, *Essays in Historical Semantics* (New York: S. F. Vann, 1948), pp. 152–53.

semantically as well as historically beyond the reach of God. Spitzer's etymological thesis is echoed by Joan Corominas's entry, which also states that the Spanish 'raza' is from the Latin *ratio* and initially referred to religious differences, specifically to those who were non-Christian.[29]

Hence, the English word 'race' itself was coined relatively recently. There had been a long history of European contact with Africans, but not until around the fifteenth century did some Europeans speak of Africans as an inferior 'race'.[30] And even then, that judgment was not universally in effect. For instance, Black and White indentured servants initially received the same treatments in the British colonies, until the period between 1680 and 1710.[31] Winthrop Jordan writes that "until the emergence of nation-states in Europe, by far the most important category of strangers was the non-Christian."[32] This seems to suggest that even if people have an inherent propensity to hate "others," they did not always select these others on the basis of differences understood as racial.

"Race" in (Translations of) Antiquity

Clearly kinship networks and nations existed before the seventeenth century; and group-based exploitative economic and political relations certainly were widespread before then as well. Accounts from around the globe tell of tribes that would capture and enslave members of other tribes, as well as attempt to conquer territory. For centuries Christian "just wars" legitimated the enslavement of one's enemy throughout Europe and Asia. But physiological differences were not at the root of how these group differences were represented.[33] What we would call lineage and language, not race, marks off Greeks from "barbarians." 'Barbarian', from the Greek 'barbaros', was used to refer to all non-Greeks. The plural of this was '(hoi) barbaroi', which means "(the) Unintelligibles, the Stammerers" and is also cognate with 'babble'.[34]

In ancient Greece conflict was between different *ethnoi*, characterized by their geographical territories of origin and the language they spoke, though modern English translations anachronistically refer to these as

---

[29] Joan Corominas, *Diccionario Crítico Etimológico Castellano e Hispánico*, vol. 4 (Madrid: Editorial Gredos, 1981), p.800.

[30] Spitzer, "Race," pp. 147–70.

[31] Michael Goldfield, "The Color of Politics in the United States," in Dominick Lacapra, ed., *The Bounds of Race: Perspectives on Hegemony and Resistance* (Ithaca: Cornell University Press, 1991), p. 116; and George Frederickson, "Social Origins of American Racism," *Arrogance of Race* (Middletown: Wesleyan University Press, 1988), pp. 189–205.

[32] *White Man's Burden* (New York, Oxford: Oxford University Press, 1974), p. 337.

[33] Ernst Renan, "What Is a Nation?" (1882), in Homi Bhabha, ed., *Nation and Narration* (London and New York: Routledge, 1990), pp. 8–22.

[34] Partridge, *Origins*, p. 39.

'races'. One English edition of Herodotus's *Histories* includes the following: "The Ionians are an indigenous race . . ." and "Of the Pelasgian language I cannot speak with certainty, but that it was not Greek may be inferred from the language of those of the Pelasgian race now living in Creston . . ." And "[T]hese are a fair sample of the Pelasgian race."[35] In all of these examples 'race' is either simply added—"the Pelasgian race" instead of "the Pelasgian"—or is offered as a translation of *ethnos*. In other phrases, however, the same word is translated as 'nation' or 'people.' The "language of the Pelasgian peoples" and the "Greek peoples," for instance, are both renderings of '*ethnos*'.

When Rome settled the province of what the Romans called "Africa" in 146 B.C. (and "New Africa" in 46 B.C. as they colonized further South and West), there was no difference between the treatment of the indigenous populations of these areas and those in other regions being conquered in Europe:

> The legal distinction between the inhabitants of the metropolitan country and those of the provinces was progressively obscured under the empire, both by the settlement of Roman citizens in the provinces and by the granting of Roman citizenship to subject peoples and individuals. This process was consummated in AD 212, when citizenship was granted to nearly all freeborn inhabitants of the Roman empire. By that time, there had already been many emperors of non-Italian origin, and the current dynasty, the Severi (AD 193-235), hailed from northern Africa.[36]

The encounters of "Blacks" and "Whites" described by Martin Bernal and Frank Snowden indicate mutual interest in differences in skin color, but no specific cultural, caste, or political associations result from this attention. Michael Banton disagrees with this view: "[D]iscrimination against strangers and particularly dark-skinned people" occurred in "antiquity." But the only evidence for this assertion he offers is a quotation from Aristotle, in which Aristotle has observed that some are naturally slaves.[37] There is no reason to consider this a claim about "race" as opposed to one about inferiority. Aristotle does not mention differences in appearance or even that one inherits such traits of inferiority from one's parents, or that entire political societies ought to be regarded as naturally inferior. Banton has projected modern ideas about racial slavery onto the Greeks.[38]

[35] Herodotus. *The Histories*, tr. Aubrey de Sélincourt (Middlesex: Penguin, 1955), p. 61.

[36] R.C.C. Law, "The Roman Empire in Africa," in *Cambridge History of Africa*, J.D. Fage and Rolland Oliver, eds. (Cambridge: Cambridge University Press, 1978), p. 192.

[37] *Politics*, I.2.125261. 7–23.

[38] *Race Relations* (New York: Basic Books, 1967), p. 12. M. I. Finley also discredits Banton's reading of Aristotle, in *Ancient Slavery and Modern Ideology* (New York: Viking Press, 1980).

In the third century skin color had no role in assigning one a place in an empire, even when the metropole was populated by people with a different appearance than those initially inhabiting the periphery. Snowden believes the peaceful relations between Rome's center and Africa "undoubtedly owed not a little to Augustus' foresight and to the diplomatic negotiations of Ethiopian and Roman ambassadors, some of whose names appear in inscriptions dating from 13 B.C. and later."[39] Romans did have slaves from North Africa, but only as prisoners of war, a relation that was reciprocal. Indeed there were at least several hundred years during which dark-skinned people were conquering or enslaving lighter-skinned Europeans. The Moors occupied parts of Spain and Portugal in the tenth and eleventh centuries. They remained politically dominant in some regions until the fifteenth century, about fifty years after Portugal sent ships to the regions of south Africa, new to Europeans, in response to Church writings and proclamations that banned using Christians as slaves, even if they were captured in just wars.

An early Spanish opponent to the slave trade wrote King Philip III (Philip II of Portugal) in 1612:

> Modern theologians in published books commonly report on, and condemn as unjust, the acts of enslavement which take place in the Provinces of this Royal Empire, employing for this purpose the same principles by which the ancient theologians, doctors of canon law, and jurists have regulated legitimate and just acts of enslavement. According to these principles, only infidels who are captured in just wars or who because of serious crimes have been condemned by their Rulers may be held as legitimate slaves, or if they sell themselves, or if they are sold by their own fathers who have legitimate need.[40]

The close contact with the northern Africans had meant that many had converted to Christianity, or shown the propensity to do so. (Of course many, such as the author above, continued to insist that nothing about the slave trade was legitimate.) Hence to appear to adhere to the ban on Christian slaves required ventures with people with whom the Spanish and Portuguese had no previous relations.[41]

---

[39] Snowden, *Before Color Prejudice: The Ancient View of Blacks* (Cambridge: Harvard University Press, 1983), pp. 30–31.

[40] "Proposta a Sua Magestade sobre a scravaria das terras da Conquista de Portugal," Document 7.3.1, no 8 Secao de Manuscritos, Biblioteca Nacional, Rio de Janeiro, Message to King Phillip III, Spain, 1612, in *Children of God's Fire: A Documentary History of Black Slavery in Brazil*, Robert Conrad, tr. and ed. (Princeton: Princeton University Press, 1983), pp. 11–12.

[41] A. C. de C. M. Sanders, *A Social History of Black Slaves and Freedman in Portugal, 1441–1551* (Cambridge, New York: Cambridge University Press, 1982). Ruth Benedict and Oliver Cox offer similar accounts of the origins of "race" through the slave trade.

Hannah Arendt, Martin Bernal, Oliver Cox, and Frank Snowden all date the current understanding of race as one that is recognizable no earlier than the fifteenth century.[42] The most minimal acquaintance with European politics belies two dominant explanations of racism. The fifteenth century was centuries prior to Darwin's natural scientific shroud for the concept, and centuries beyond the time Europeans from the Roman Empire had colonized parts of Africa. Hence, race is not an outgrowth of ideas about natural selection nor an age-old expression of innate differences that result in slavery. Neither the demands of science nor those of conquest account for the concept's emergence in the fifteenth century.

Further, if racism were a natural sentiment, rooted in an inherent need for animosities, then we cannot explain why for hundreds of years large numbers of people have held racism in contempt, out of strong cosmopolitan sentiments. The notion that people have psychologically rooted drives to distinguish themselves from others on the basis of physiological difference[43] does not account for the many people who oppose inequalities based on physical difference, nor the fact that this opposition has been institutionalized in many countries. Of Portugal, Europe's first country to embark on the slave trade, A. C. de C. M. Sanders writes:

> In 1444, for instance, the first slave auction at Lagos was interrupted by the common folk who were enraged at seeing the separation of families of slaves, and even Zurana, the royal chronicler, declared his sympathy for these unfortunates.[44]

What really should prompt us to think about race, instead of racism—for purposes of alleviating structural inequalities of power—is that so many people are actually strongly opposed to racism, even as the concept of race

---

[42] Arendt, *Origins of Totalitarianism*, 2d ed. (New York: World Publishing Co., 1958); Bernal, *Black Athena*, vol. 1 (London: Free Association Books, 1987); Cox, *Caste, Class, and Race*; and Snowden, *Before Color Prejudice*.

[43] Joel Kovel attributes "white racism" to the power of the story of Ham, exiled and made Black because he looked at his father Noah when he was drunk and naked. Kovel argues that there is a specific fear of blackness in the white psyche, since Blackness is a metaphor for feces and hence property—both of which cause Whites anxiety: "Property in the modern Western matrix is filthified matter to be controlled and enjoyed without conscious guilt." Black skin, according to Kovel, triggers an unconscious association among feces, control, and hence the desire for domination. Although I agree with Kovel's repeated connections between property, nationalism, and racism, I find his causal explanation absurd. First, it is not true that property is only fetishized in the "West" and that this is necessary for slavery, since tribes in Africa cared about property and were enslaving each other long before Portugal sent ships there. Second, our own rules for property rights resemble those of Rome, yet Romans did not enslave Africans because of "race." If "Whites" are intrinsically troubled by Blacks, then we would expect the Romans enslave Severi rather than make him the leader of the Roman Empire (*White Racism: A Psychohistory* [New York: Pantheon Press, 1970], pp. 16, 18, 187, 88–89, 26).

[44] Sanders, *Social History*, p. 35.

continues to have resonance in their societies. If a psychological desire like that depicted by Joel Kovel is so deeply rooted that it inspires people to enslave others simply by virtue of physical appearance, then why was there a period when these physical differences did not result in institutionalized slavery, and why have so many people and countries resisted such an impulse?[45]

What Race Is (Not)—I

Not only have linguists and historians been unable to determine a formally consistent meaning of the word 'race', but contemporary scientists are divided about its current meaning. There are no concepts of the word 'race' that are uniformly accepted by the natural scientific community.[46] Social scientific studies that refer to race frequently do not bother to define 'race' or define it very superficially, usually by tautology. Even those who believe in inherent racial hierarchies do not offer a clear definition of race. One would think that such definitions would be especially important to those pursuing racist public policies, but that is not the case. For instance, psychologist Arthur Jensen, a staunch advocate of the belief that IQ tests demonstrated Whites genetically superior to Blacks, states:

> Socially we usually have little trouble recognizing a person's race, based on overall physical appearance. If a group of persons were asked to classify racially the various people they observe on the streets of any large city in the United States, there would undoubtedly be very much agreement among their classifications. And if the persons so classified were asked to state their racial background, there would be high agreement with the observers' classifications. This is the social meaning of race used by the proverbial 'man in the street.' It is also the form of racial classification used in the vast majority of studies of racial differences in IQ.[47]

Jensen himself notes that about 20 to 25 percent of "Black" Americans have "White" genes, so clearly genes alone cannot determine race.[48] Hence part of the literature begs the question of defining race, and part defines race, but does so tautologically. (Potential threshold criteria of "51 percent

---

[45] The racist post-colonial immigration rules highlight one way that during the period of Empire the Indian and English subject had equal mobility. Smith, *New Right Discourse on Race and Sexuality* (Cambridge: Cambridge University Press, 1994), p. 96.

[46] *Oxford English Dictionary*, 2d ed.

[47] Webster, *Racialization of America*, quoting Jensen, p. 72. This is an effort to address the point that those whose birth certificates indicate they are "White" have had children with those whose birth certificates indicate they are "Colored" or "Asian" or "Black."

[48] Ibid.

of a particular gene" or a "plurality of genes from a particular race" are useless, in that the denominator remains unknown. The definition "A White is someone who is 51 percent White" does not further inform us about what counts as "White.")

Here are some alternatives proposed by prominent investigators of this concept.

> **1)** [Race is a] classification based on traits which are hereditary. Therefore when we talk about race we talk about (1) heredity and (2) traits transmitted by heredity which characterize all the members of a related group.[49]

The first part of the definition is over-inclusive, and the second part is tautological, since what characterizes the "related group" as such is precisely what is being defined. The definition is too broad because many traits are inherited but not "racial." For instance, we do not have 'race'-s of people with Type O blood, even though this is an inherited "trait" and everyone who has it could be taxonomized as related by virtue of having this trait (or having in common parents who pass this on).

> **2)** [Race relations are] behavior which develops among peoples who are aware of each other's actual or imputed physical differences.[50]

Here the distinguishing racial taxonomy, which is physical, is also over-inclusive. We do not behave in a specifically racist manner, though we may exhibit shock or prejudice, when we are aware of the "actual or imputed physical difference" of someone we imagine might be blind or near death, or a man wearing a skirt, or a gang of teenagers with pierced body parts and mohawks.

> **3)** [Racism is a] form of status consciousness that arises when one group justifies its dominance of another group on grounds of real or alleged differences in ancestry and/or physical characteristics.[51]

Encountering individuals with especially large ears, or bushy eyebrows, or small hands, all of which may suggest a "real or alleged difference in ancestry and/or physical characteristics" does not lead to a specifically "racial dominance," but possibly ridicule and more likely lack of interest.

> **4)** [Racialization is the] systematic accentuation of certain physical attributes that allocate persons to races that are projected as real and thereby become the basis for examining all social relations.[52]

---

[49] Benedict, *Race: Science and Politics*, p. 11.
[50] Cox, *Caste, Class, and Race*, p. 320.
[51] Frederickson, *Arrogance of Race*, p. 221.
[52] Webster, *Racialization of America*, p. 3.

This definition is partly right, it seems, but far too vague. If the purpose is simply to attend to the fact that invocations of race refer to physical difference, then, like the preceding definitions, it may not be wrong, but it is unhelpful, since it begs the problem of distinguishing between contexts that render some physical characteristics "racial." Not all physical characteristics prompt these invocations, and those that do may or may not lead to a specifically racial observation in all contexts. For instance, a big nose might be mocked as "Jewish" or it might be ridiculed for being a big nose.

> 5) **Race**: The folk category of the English language refers to discrete groups of human beings who are categorically separated from one another on the basis of arbitrarily selected *phenotypic* traits.[53]

This phenomenological definition recognizes the constructed character of racial difference, but it is still over-inclusive. Fat people and thin people have different "phenotypic traits," but this does not lead to "weight" as a racial category, folk or otherwise. And clearly the same thing goes for "males" and "females," who also display some systematic differences in phenotypic traits—and in their genes—that do not, however, constitute them as different "race"-s.

> 6) To be distinguished reliably requires that races differ from others in the incidence of alleles of some genes influencing observable attributes. This criterion can be met with regard to the major subgroups of humanity.[54]

This definition is circular with regard to the "race"-s (the "major subgroups") assumed already to exist. Such a genetic definition is unhelpful. We do not have races of Downs Syndrome-prone people, or races of people who transmit fat genes, or thin genes, or bald genes, or races of men and women,[55] even though these groups have differences in the "incidence of alleles of some genes influencing observable attributes." We do not see a race of fat people dispersed throughout the world, who sometimes intermarry and produce more children with fat genes (and who sometimes marry thin people, in which case the fat gene occasionally will be recessive, just as skin pigmentation may be).

Numerous scholars from several disciplines have long recognized problems with the racial classificatory schemes and justifications outlined above.

---

[53] David Hunter, in *Encyclopedia of Anthropology*, p. 222.

[54] *Encyclopedia of Psychology* (New York and Brisbane: John Wiley and Sons, 1984), p. 200. It should be noted that many scientists pursuing genetic research refer to their work as "population studies," and avoid references to "race" altogether, because about 85–90% of differences are "within population variation" (Stephen Zegura, note responding to Debra Schindler, "Anthropology in the Arctic: A Critique of Racial Typology and Normative Theory," *Current Anthropology*, 26(4) [August–October, 1985], p. 492).

[55] Actually, the *OED*, 2d ed. does record the use of 'race' to refer to "one of the sexes" in 1590, but clearly that use is now obsolete.

And yet they too do not tell us what race is. The most sophisticated books on race tell us only what race is not. For instance, Yehudi Webster shows how biological, historical, cultural and economic explanations all fall short. His plea is for social scientists to stop studying "race," since it does not really exist. Webster believes that social scientific discussions of race are in fact the main culprits of the concept's original and continued salience:

> The realist or social constructionist characterization [as opposed to the biological one] simply allows social scientists to continue to operate with a flawed racial classification. . . . To claim that the expansion of public policies on race relations, and the development of race relations research are unrelated to popular racial thinking is to absolve these institutions of any social responsibility. A radical and philosophically sensitive sociology would investigate the collaboration between government and social scientists in the racialization of society. The reference to 'social meaning' may turn out to be a self-serving legitimization of racial studies.[56]

Webster believes that since race does not really exist, scientists and policy makers should stop talking about it as though it did.[57] They should stop asking questions about one's "race" on surveys, employment and education applications, and the census, he believes. That way our social categories will more accurately reflect reality. The salutary social benefit is that racism will go away once race does, according to Webster.

The State of Race

Another way to think about race is not to accept what one group of experts asserts race is, nor to develop a definition so broad as to allow for, alternatively, fat and thin people, the bald and hirsute, the nearsighted and farsighted, homosexuals and heterosexuals, or men and women, to be considered "race"-s. These other classifications have been used as the basis for invidious (as well as benign) forms of discrimination and they may prompt allegations of correspondences between phenotype and genotype: a bald man may have children who are at greater risk of baldness than

[56] Webster, *Racialization*, p. 82. In a book charting the same intellectual history of "race" as Webster's, Banton defines race as a "folk concept" that has changed over time (*Racial Theories* [Cambridge: Cambridge University Press, 1987]). See also James Davis *Who Is Black?: One Nation's Definition* (University Park: Pennsylvania State University Press, 1991); and Balibar, "Is There a Neo-Racism," p. 19. Another philosophical debunking of "race" is in Jacques Barzun, *Race: A Study in Superstition* (1937; rev. ed. New York, London: Harper and Row, 1966).

[57] Marvin Zimmerman adopts a similar position, arguing that since psychologists cannot state what race is, they should abandon making "racial" comparisons. "Some Dubious Premises in Research and Theory on Racial Differences" (*American Psychologist* [December, 1990], pp. 1297–1303).

children of someone with lots of hair—even as the classifications of what counts as "lots of hair" and "bald" may be subject to dispute. For instance, baldness at death may be regarded as normal, so at what age does it count as a genetic trait? 20? 30? But why not 29? Or 31? The same "problem" of indeterminacy applies to sexuality and gender classifications. If a woman usually has sex with women, but also intercourse with men on occasion, is she "lesbian" or "bisexual"? Foucault's study of hermaphrodites raises questions about gender classifications.[58] There might be sound logical reasons to stop using these categories altogether. One could think (and people have said as much): we have done without the "homosexual" in the past and ought to do so in the future. But in the end we do not eliminate these signs from our language. Just as the atheist's denial of God's existence does not eliminate the reality of that presence for others, Appiah's philosophical rejection of race, as discussed in the Introduction,[59] only impedes our understanding of the concept's meaning and does not eliminate it from our discourse and reality. When God really is dead no one will know about it. Finally, it is not clear why Appiah objects to the concept of "race" but not to that of "Africa," which he celebrates. Both race and Africa seem equally real or impossible. If one is African because of one's parents— Appiah's claim—then Appiah has simply replaced the Darwinian gene pool with the equally divisive and scientifically suspect family tree.

Rather than distinguishing race as a concept whose reality is more tenuous than that of other identities, I want to propose an alternative understanding, one that follows from the work of W.E.B. Du Bois, and also portions of writings by Appiah, David Goldberg, and others who regularly point out the salience of stories of origins for race and also the role of geography in its manifestations. Ultimately, what makes someone Black, for example, at least in the United States, is that we understand that at some point she had ancestors in Africa; what makes someone White is that we understand that at some point she had ancestors in Europe. This also accounts for how it is that someone may "look" White and yet "be" Black (and vice versa), depending on the story one wants to tell. So, out of the tensions in the meanings of "race" as a folk concept, supplemented by a recognition of the importance of geography to regulating our ideas about phenotypical differences as specifically racial, a definition of race can emerge: a subpopulation of human beings with observed or imagined physical characteristics understood to correspond with a geographical territory of origins. Presently the geographical territory of racial origins is understood as a continent. At times the equally artificial boundaries of

---

[58] *Herculine Barbin: Being the Recently Discovered Memoirs of a Nineteenth Century French Hermaphrodite*, introduction (New York: Pantheon Press, 1980).

[59] *In My Father's House: Africa in the Philosophy of Culture* (New York, Oxford: Oxford University Press, 1993), pp. 174–75.

the state-nation are also imagined as outlining territories of "origin"al differences in bodily appearance. This definition recognizes the importance of imputed visible differences attached to a story of origins from a geographical territory.

The phrase "geographical territory of origins" captures the concern with origins that underlies stories of ancestry. To be "originally" from a place implies that one has ancestors who lived in a particular place. At the same time, the emphasis on geography denotes the fixed and contingent character of representations of race better than more vague phenomenologies of familial ancestry or genes alone. This also makes the story of race seem fairly essentialist. From Africa: Black. From Europe: White.

According to the *Dictionary of Human Geography* 'Caucasoid' refers to "one of the primary races of people, found in Europe, N. America, and from the Middle East to northern India. It is the most variable in physical appearance of all the great races." The entry then goes on to describe skin color, eye color, and hair colors and textures of the Caucasoid.[60] 'Mongoloid' is defined as the "peoples of Southeast, East and Central Asia and the American Indians." A physical description follows.[61] Finally, 'Negroid' is defined first by physical characteristics, and then by place of origins: "The majority of Negroids have their origins in Africa."[62] From these entries it seems that "race" refers to a set of physical characteristics attached to one's ties to ancestors from places like Europe, Asia, and Africa.

Africa, Europe, and Asia are geographical places that are naturalized by their correspondence with geologically formed regions of the earth. Insofar as Asia seems natural, it is only natural, given variations in climate and terrain, that groups of people from different geographical regions will differ amongst themselves, supposedly making them racially distinct. But if the story were that simple, then the fetishisms associated specifically with race would be random. With no further explanation it is indeed nonsensical for us to assign arbitrary phenotype and genotype configurations to adaptations made to "geography"—constructing the rubric of race—and not to mutations and adaptations of flat-footedness. What makes Asians? The answer—whatever made Asia—does not lead in the essentialist justification of racial classifications that it first appears. The notion that *geographical* differences lead to differences among people is not the same as saying that "race" is the outcome of *geological* difference.

[60] Brian Goodall, *Dictionary of Human Geography* (Middlesex and New York: Penguin, 1987), p. 157.

[61] Ibid., p. 310.

[62] Ibid., p. 320. For purposes of my analysis it is irrelevant that this definition indicates a "majority" and not all "Negroids" are from Africa. Here I simply want to show the use of geographical designations in definitions of race.

Clinal differences among selected pairings of genotype and phenotype are clustered into races by the contingency of national borders and by geography—our synthetic graphics of the earth—not geology, or what we see when we understand the earth does not change all that much and all that quickly, that relative to an individual's life-span the earth is more or less immutable.[63] The geographical determination underlying the use of "race" rests on another category that is actually far more naturalized (and with far less reason) than race. What is Africa? A continent. What is a continent? According to the *Dictionary of Geography*, a 'continent' is "one of the earth's major constituent land masses," "Africa," "North America," "Central and South America," "Asia," "Europe," "Australia," or "Antarctica," each of which occupy so many millions of square miles, depending on whether or not one includes the former USSR. Calculations are offered for Europe and Asia with and without the USSR, which alone should prompt us to wonder about the natural status of the continents.[64] From the *Dictionary of Geography* we have learned that Africa is a continent. A continent is Africa.

"Nor can I guess for what reason the earth, which is one, has three names, all of women."[65] Herodotus recognizes the political character of these places, the historical contingency of "Africa," "Asia," and "Europe." He does not mistake the apparent givenness of the continents for any essential quality of "Asia"ness or "Africa"ness. They are simply "women's names that . . . have been given." Herodotus next sees fit to investigate the origins of these names and hence these locations, although his speculations do not lead to any firm answers:

> [N]or can I learn the names of those who divided the world, or whence go the names which they gave. For Libya is said by most Greeks to be called after a native women of that name, and Asia after the wife of Prometheus. . . . But as for Europe, no men have any knowledge whether it be surrounded or not by seas, nor whence it took its name, nor is it clear who gave the name, unless we are to say that the land took its name from the Tyrian Europe, having been (as it would seem) till then nameless like the others. But it is plain that this woman was of Asiatic birth, and never came to the land which the Greeks now call

[63] Geological maps are also contingent. Their taxonomic devices change depending on the interests of the scientists or those who commission their work.

[64] F. J. Monkhouse, *A Dictionary of Geography* (Chicago: Aldine Publishing Company, 1970).

[65] Herodotus, Book IV.45 (*The Histories*, tr. A.D. Godley [Cambridge: Harvard University Press, 1921], p. 285). "Racial" differences among the population are never entertained as the explanation. I use this translation here because I find it a more literal rendering, whereas I used the Selincourt translation in note 35 to make a specific point about anachronistic translations of *ethnos* as 'race.'

Europe. . . . Thus far have I spoken of these matters, and let it suffice; we will use the names by which custom has established.[66]

Custom, not nature, makes continents. According to an 1835 speech by Rep. Trimble, a staunch believer in Manifest Destiny, although God had given the world "natural boundaries," societies had not accepted them:

> Man, in his made career of glory, his thirst for dominion, had rejected as useless the great and permanent boundaries of nature, and sought out ideal, perishable limits of his own condition.[67]

Historian Albert Weinberg, considering this speech, writes "The principle of the natural barrier is thus concerned not with the unifying territorial features, but with those which clearly and securely separate peoples."[68] Rivers and mountains do not separate peoples. Governments do. People do not gain their identity from the land. Rather, the land gains its identity from the people who occupy it. "Germany" exists because that is the place where "Germans" live. Borders do not arise from the land, but from the identities of the occupying nations. When Rep. Ingersoll, another believer in Manifest Destiny, referred to political sovereignty as a consequence of the "natural boundaries between the Anglo-Saxon and Mauritanian races"[69] he was making the point that the Anglo-Saxons and Mauritanians make geography (according to where they live), and not the other way around.

Herodotus, in his many descriptions of parts of the world, defines a territory according to the group of people that occupy it. He writes, "I cannot help but laugh at the absurdity of all the map-makers—there are plenty of them—who show Ocean running like a river round a perfectly circular earth with Asia and Europe of the same size."[70] He then offers to straighten out the misconceptions as to what the earth looks like:

> Let me spend a few words in giving a proper notion of the size and shape of these two continents. Persian territory extends southward to the Red Sea, as it is called; north of them are the Medes, and then the Saspires, then the Colchians, who go as far as the northern sea, where the mouth of the Phasis is. These four

[66] *Histories*, tr. Godley, ibid.

[67] Quoted in Albert Weinberg, *Manifest Destiny: A study of nationalist expansion in American history* (Gloucester: P. Smith, 1958), p. 55. I use this quotation here because, as we shall see below, the doctrine of Manifest Destiny was important to the consolidation of the national identity of the United States much later in the century as well. It is relevant, then, to note the theory as being located in a very statist understanding of geography.

[68] Ibid.

[69] Ibid. It is telling that Ingersoll notes this boundary in particular, since contemporary U.S. law treats those from Algeria and Morocco (formerly Mauritanian territory) as White.

[70] Herodotus, *Histories*, Book IV.36.

nations [**ethnoi**] fill the area between the Black sea and the Persian gulf. Thence run westward two great continental promontories, one of which stretches from the Phasis on the north along the Black Sea and the Hellespont to the Mediterranean at Sigeum in the Troad, and again, in the south, along the Mediterranean coast from the Myriandric gulf, near Phoenicia, to Cape Triopium. This branch of the continent contains thirty nations.[71]

A continent is what has nations. A specific continent is such by virtue of the nations there. Asia looks different, depending on what we think about whether it includes the former Soviet Union, not certain rivers and mountains. A continent is also literally named by state-nations. Antarctica exists by an agreement not among the scientists who work there, but the state-nations in which they have citizenship. (A committee of representatives of state-nations designated "Antarctica" a place and stipulated the terms of research and commerce possible there.)[72]

Race and Marriage

Just as the existence of continents is determined by political societies, within political societies racial forms of being are determined by the government. One of the major sites where the government—acting in the name of the state as a membership organization—has intervened to define the meaning of race as well as specific racial identities has been marriage law. Current governmental racial classifications all follow from the legal history of racial classifications. The state does not treat racial identity as amenable to synchronic reassessments. Rather, one's race is the race of one's ancestors, which is always what the state announces was the race of one's ancestors.

Just as the form of political societies is a constitutive unit in the aggregation of the geographical space that race entails, the state constitutes racially specific marriage forms. In the United States courts have construed the correct and hence legal marriage form as simultaneously "Christian" and "European." This collapsed racial/religious rubric articulates the marital relation specific to this state-nation. One of the most famous marriage cases, *Reynolds v. United States* 8 S. Ct. 145 (1878), upholds penalties for polygamous marriage against Mormon assertions of the First Amendment's Free Exercise Clause: "Polygamy has always been odious among the northern and western nations of Europe, and, until the establishment of the Mormon Church, was almost exclusively a feature of the life of Asiatic

[71] Ibid., Book IV.37–38.
[72] "On Map of Antarctica, What Isn't in a Name?" *New York Times*, January 12, 1997, p. A7.

and of African people."[73] In this opinion, Europe is conflated with northern and western Europe, as a racialized experience in contrast with those of "Asiatic and of African people." Obviously the category is confused. Of interest are not the details or logic of the classification, but the formal articulation of a specifically national marriage structure within a framework of a racialized religion. The state's association of marriage with nationality, race, and religion binds the last three in a manner constitutive of a particular kinship form. The form, i.e., the rules and prohibitions for the right kind of marriage follows from an overdetermined nexus of principles imputed to affiliations of a specific religion (Christianity) and a specific race (European), and not utilitarian principles of good child-rearing practices, or deontological arguments about the single most rational marriage form.

The twentieth century anxiety over illegitimacy in the United States is, in part, a consequence of marriage laws with racial overtones. Patriarchal monogamy is not viewed simply as preferable to other marriage arrangements, but as specifically European, while anything else is regarded by the state as Asian or African. Why is the state so invested in marriage? If the state is formally committed to sex equality and has no interest in favoring one inheritance practice over another, one would expect the state to recede from legislating in this area. What is it to the state whether a father is married to the mother of his child, or whether, relatedly, kinship is matrilocal or even matriarchal? In his still-influential *Report on the Negro Family* (1967) Patrick Moynihan admitted the political motives for favoring a patriarchal family:

> There is, presumably, no special reason why a society in which males are dominant in family relationships is to be preferred to a matriarchal arrangement. *However, it is clearly a disadvantage for a minority group to be operating on one*

---

[73] *Reynolds* 165. Current court opinions continue to support a particular form of marriage in the name of "enlightened nations" and "our traditions," so that the cultural specificity of this marriage form is recognized and privileged, but without naming the specific other compared to which "ours" is enlightened. See, for example, *Singer v. Hara*, 522 P.2d 1197 (1974); the current marriage form is justified due to the "prevailing mores and moral concepts of this age," which the court finds rooted in "scriptural, canonical, and civil law," in *Adams v. Howerton* 486 F. Supp. 1119, 1123 (1980); polygamy is a "blot on our civilization" and "contrary to the spirit of Christianity and of the civilization which Christianity has produced in the Western world" in *Mormon Church v. U.S.* 136 U.S. 1 49 (1889); *Moore v. East Cleveland* 431 U.S. 495, 503 (1976); *Caban v. Mohammed* 441 U.S. 397. On the Constitutional status of the specifically Christian form of marriage in this country, Carol Weisbrod writes that "co-option of the state by the church must now be justified by the state in entirely secular terms" ("Family, Church, and State: An Essay on Constitutionalism and Religious Authority," *Journal of Family Law* 26 [1987–88], p. 765). The Supreme Court does not follow this practice consistently, as in the references to Leviticus in *Bowers v. Hardwick* 478 U.S. 191 (1986); and a still influential federal court decision against same-sex marriage holds that the exclusive

principle, while the great majority of the population, and the one with the most advantages to begin with, is operating on another. This is the present situation of the Negro. Ours [i.e., White society] is a society which presumes male leadership in private and public affairs.[74]

That is, most people in this country are White; Whites have power over Blacks; Whites have patriarchal values; therefore, African-Americans should be more patriarchal as well.[75] The explanation is illuminating, especially when pragmatic arguments against the consequences of matrilocal households as well as illegitimacy fail.

In Europe the countries with the lowest rates of marriage and the highest proportions of illegitimate children perform **better** than those with high rates of marriage and low rates of illegitimacy, on a wide array of quality-of-life indicators. In the United States out-of-wedlock births were at 21 percent in 1990. In the Sweden and in Denmark, the figures were 46.4 percent and 41.9 percent, respectively. In Austria 21.5 percent of children were born out of wedlock. These countries outperform the United States in average levels of education and income per capita. They have lower rates of infant mortality and violent crime. Among the countries with far lower rates of out-of-wedlock births are those with largely Catholic populations, including Ireland (7.8 percent), Italy (4.4 percent), and Spain (3.9 percent). These countries fare worse than the United States when it comes to levels of education, income per capita, and rates of infant mortality. They have more violent crimes than do the European countries with high rates of out-of-wedlock births, but not as many as in the United States.[76] The inference is not that marriage or illegitimacy has obvious economic consequences, but that both interact with other practices in ways that stymie simplistic utilitarian inferences about the institution.

In addition to the form of marriage being specifically racialized, the rules of marriage have also been relied on by the state to reproduce racial identities. In an early decision allowing a railroad to have "separate but equal" seating, the Court relied on "the Creator's" thoughts on marriage in particular, to prove it appropriate for the state to recognize racial differences:

---

validity of different sex marriages is as "old as the book of Genesis" (*Baker v. Nelson* 191 N.W. 2d at 186).

[74] "The Negro Family: The Case for National Action" in *The Moynihan Report and the Politics of Controversy*, Lee Rainwater and William Yancey, eds. (Cambridge and London: MIT Press, 1967), p. 75, emphasis added.

[75] For an affirmative statement about this difference, see Karen Sacks, *Sisters and Wives* (Westport: Greenwood Press, 1977).

[76] Source: Michael Wolff, Peter Rutte, and Albert F. Bayers, *Where We Stand* (New York, Toronto, and London: Bantam Books, 1992).

Conceding equality, with natures as perfect and rights as sacred, yet God has made them dissimilar, with those natural instincts and feelings which He always imparts to His creatures when He intends that they shall not overstep the natural boundaries He has assigned to them. The natural law which forbids their intermarriage and that social amalgamation which leads to a corruption of races, is as clearly divine as that which imparted to them different natures ... From social amalgamation [sitting next to someone of a different race on a train] it is but a step to illicit intercourse, and but another to intermarriage.[77]

Importantly, *intermarriage*, not illicit sex, is the furthest one might stray from a Christian God's intention. Children of interracial parents had to be classified as having a father of the same race as the mother, or the parents would be punished.[78] That marriage was a factor in the reproduction of racial affiliations was a point Tocqueville made, when he wrote that "whites and emancipated Negroes face each other like two foreign peoples on the same soil." Tocqueville maintained that "there are only two possibilities for the future: the Negroes and whites must either mingle completely, or they must part." Elaborating on "mingling" he explained that "it is the mulatto who forms the bridge between black and white; everywhere where there are a great number of mulattoes, the fusion of the two races are not impossible."[79] It was, of course, the 'mulatto' that marriage law annihilated—a legal eradication that was reinforced in the "one drop" rule, making 'mulattoes' Colored or White. Current debate over the proposal of a "multiracial" category on the Census and other government documents is the legacy of *Loving v. Virginia* (1967), the United States Supreme Court case that overturned miscegenation laws. Only after the legal prohibitions on interracial marriage are eliminated is it possible to see significant increases in the numbers of "inter-racial" children.

Anti-miscegenation laws prohibited so-called interracial marriage in this country until 1967.[80] The purpose of these laws was to regulate the "White-

---

[77] *West Chester and Philadelphia Railroad Co. v. Miles* Penn. S. Ct., 211 (1867).

[78] Paul Lombardo writes: "Administrative enforcement by minor state bureaucracies also perpetuated the accepted mythologies, especially those involving the miscegenation taboo." He then describes a twenty-year racist correspondence between Virginia's head of the Registrar of Vital Statistics and John Powell, founder of the Anglo-Saxon Clubs of America (ASCA), which began in the early 1920s. "Miscegenation, Eugenics, and Racism: Footnotes to *Loving v. Virginia*," *University of California Davis Law Review* 21 (Winter, 1988), p. 427. See also Robert Sickels, *Race, Marriage, and the Law* (Albuquerque: University of New Mexico Press, 1972), and Raymond Diamond and Robert Cottrol, "Codifying Caste: Los Angeles' Racial Classification Scheme and the Fourteenth Amendment," *Loyola Law Review* 29 (Spring, 1983), pp. 255–85.

[79] *Democracy in America*, tr. George Lawrence (New York: Anchor, 1969), pp. 355, 356.

[80] In another telling portrait of the multiple layers of marriage politics, colonial law in Virginia prohibited "fornication" between "Negroes" and "Christians," again suggesting that religion, race, gender, nationality, and sexuality are always politically intertwined. Nancy

ness" of the country. Marriage regulation was a proxy for physical restraints against interracial heterosexual intercourse, to wit: "Free persons and slaves are incapable of contracting marriage together; the celebration of such marriages is forbidden, and the marriage is void; it is the same with respect to the marriages contracted by free white persons with free people of color."[81] Hence relatively few children were reported as being the offspring of interracial couples, even where the actual identities of the parents were known. With "miscegenation" and "fornication" both against the law, interracial children were either legal nonentities or evidence of a crime.

Another consequence of these laws was that these illegitimate children could not inherit: "Bastard, adulterous or incestuous children shall not enjoy the right of inheriting the estates of their natural father or mother, in any of the cases above mentioned, the law allowing them nothing more than a mere alimony."[82] This law helps explain disparities in the wealth of Blacks and Whites. Legitimate Black children would be the descendants of slaves; illegitimate Black children were precluded from inheritance. States still distinguish between the claims of legitimate and illegitimate children against their parents estates. Parents currently can, of course, will their estates to whomever they please. But the state-issued classifications establish a grammar that produces "illegitimate" and "legitimate" children and hence the norms of attachment and obligation associated with these different classes of children: "Although these code articles do not openly differentiate rights to inherit by race or color, they effectively protect the estate of white families from being passed on to colored relatives."[83] With laws regulating both miscegenation and legitimacy in effect until the 1970s, the disparity in family wealth between Whites and Blacks is completely predictable.

Race and Birth Certificates

States list one's parents "race" on one's birth certificate and hence have sole control over the criteria for determining what counts as one's own race. The consequences of these birth certificates extend beyond the life of the individual, as subsequent generations have their race determined through ancestry, and the mark of one's racial ancestry is indicated on the

---

Cott, "Giving Character to Our Whole Civil Polity: Marriage and the Public Order . . . ," in *United States History as Women's History*, ed. Linda Kerber et al. (Chapel Hill and London: University of North Carolina Press, 1995), p. 388, note 45.

[81] Louisiana Civil Code 1808, page 24, article 8, quoted in Domínguez, *White by Definition*, p. 25.

[82] Louisiana, Article 920 (revised Civil Code of 1870), quoted in ibid., p. 63.

[83] Ibid., p. 73.

earlier birth certificates. The federal forms used to register births require the recording of the race of both parents. The possible designations are: Other Asian or Pacific Islander, White, Black, Indian (includes Aleuts and Eskimos), Chinese, Japanese, Hawaiian (includes part Hawaiian), other non-White, Filipino. The list raises many questions. Why designations for "other Asian" and "other White" but not "other Black"? Why so many national designations for "Asians"? Despite the idiosyncrasy of these categories, the state is adamant on its prerogative to maintain them.

In 1985 the United States Supreme Court let stand a lower-court decision allowing Louisiana state officials to classify their citizens racially.[84] But even if the plaintiff had succeeded, she would not be considered, from the point of view of the state, indubitably White. The procedure for changing birth certificates in Louisiana is to cross out the old designation and then write the new designation in red ink. This means that the old designation is not obliterated but remains in a manner that will continue to raise questions about one's true identity. A crossed-out "Negro" might still be regarded as being Negro, or so thought the plaintiffs who filed suits to have Louisiana issue them "clean" birth certificates when their racial designations had changed.

In one case a previously "White" family had their classification changed, unbeknownst to them:

> Gerard H. Cline Sr. requested a birth certificate for his son, Gerard H. Cline, Jr., for use in enrolling him in school. At that time, he was informed that the boy's race had been changed from white to Negro, and also that the same change was made on the birth certificates of his wife, Elaine Mary Dejean, her sister, Marguerite Estelle Dejean Rosenbohm, their brother, Sidney Dejean, Jr., their children, Lionel Rosenbohm, Jr., Charmain Rosenbohm, Kathleen Rosenbohm, and Sidney Dejean, III, and the birth and death certificates of the children's grandfather, Sidney Joseph Dejean, Sr. The alterations were made by drawing lines through the word "White" which appeared on the original certificates and the word Negro was written in ink to designate their race. These alterations occurred without the knowledge of any of the plaintiffs, and the person who made the changes and the reason therefor are both unknown.[85]

The family was not satisfied when the redesignation was crossed out, but desired new birth certificates, because the alterations, by law, are seen as alterations, prompting them to be interrogated in ways that racial designations on clean birth certificates are not. The law says that "Except for delayed or **altered certificates**, every original certificate on file in the

---

[84] La. App. 4 Cir. 1985. *Doe v. State*, 479 So.2d 369, writ denied 485 So. 2d, appeal dismissed 107 S. Ct. 638.

[85] *Cline v. City of New Orleans* La., 207 So. 2d 856, 858 (1968).

division of public health statistics is prima facie evidence of the facts therein stated."[86] The court and the law acknowledge that the state wants to keep records that will call into question changed designations. Because Cline convinced them that there was no question concerning his family's race, they were issued new records.

In another case, the crossed-out version of the birth certificate was upheld. The plaintiff wanted to have his birth registration changed by

> showing him to be white instead of colored and to change his name from Larry Lille Toledano to Larry Lille Mullet. He alleged that he was born to Idyl D Hall on March 4, 1937, seventy-eight days after his mother's marriage to Chester J. Toledano. He alleged that he was of the white race; that his father is Edwin J. Mullet, who was married to his mother at the time of his conception; that his mother married Chester J. Toledano on January 11, 1937, and that she obtained a divorce from Edwin J. Mullet on December 16, 1953 (obviously the pleader meant 1936 . . .).[87]

In several places in the opinion the Court expressed some doubt about the authenticity of the records Toledano had produced. While not accusing him of lying outright, the judge held that the crossed-out designation of Toledano as "colored" was an accurate portrait of Toledano's race: "It is our opinion that no amount of obliteration or erasure on the birth certificate will erase or change the fact that the plaintiff was registered at birth as colored. . . . To effectively wipe out all evidence of the error, it would be necessary to expunge the records of this case."[88] The state's doubt must remain in the records.

For purposes of recording information on birth certificates, most states now ask hospitals to indicate the parents' race and do not record the child's race, although this is reported for purposes of more detailed records not printed on the actual certificate.[89] But even here the state's role in racial classifications is substantial. Because it is impossible to change the racial designation on a birth certificate, one is at the mercy of one's parents for racial identity. Further, the identification of the parents discussed above is done by hospital employees, not the parents, and may be used to question racial identities at marriage or death. Finally, the classificatory possibilities are predetermined by the state—Asian, Black, Japanese, for instance— based on ideas about physical traits associated with political territories. One may engage in long debates over one's own racial form of being, but the only definition that has force is that of the state birth certificate,

---

[86] Louisiana Revised Statute 40:266, quoted in *Cline* (above, note 84), at 859.

[87] *Toledano v. Drake*, 161 So.2d 339, 340 (1964).

[88] *Toldedano*, 311.

[89] Dominguez, *White by Definition*, p. 3.

and its criteria depend on political-geographical boundaries, not personal, subjective affinities.

Race and the Government

The United States federal government provides the following definitions of various races, for purposes of entitlement programs and affirmative action policies:

(1) **Black, not of Hispanic Origin**: A person having origins in any of the black racial groups of Africa.

(2) **Hispanic**: A person of Mexican, Puerto Rican, Cuban, Central or South American or other Spanish culture or origin, regardless of race.

(3) **Asian or Pacific Islander**: A person having origins in any of the original peoples of the Far East, Southeast Asia, the Indian Subcontinent, or the Pacific Islands. This area includes, for example, China, Japan, Korea, the Philippine Islands, and Samoa.

(4) **American Indian or Alaskan Native**. A person having origins in any of the original people of North America, and who maintain cultural identification through tribal affiliation or community recognition.

(5) **White, not of Hispanic Origin**. A person having origins in any of the original people of Europe, North Africa, or the Middle East. Additional sub-categories based on national origin or primary language spoken may be used where appropriate, on either a national or a regional basis.[90]

These classifications are consistent with the use of national boundaries to equate continents with races. One is Asian if one has "origins" in China, Japan, or Korea for instance. What does it mean to have "origins" in a country? Normally we think of 'origins' as a beginning. To be a member of categories 3 through 5 requires one to have "origins" in an "original people." What is an "original people"? How does one come to have an origin in a nation or a continent? One's parents give one an origin, but they might give one that origin in one place or another, and they might have had their beginning in one place or another and then just move. So it is one's "origins" in contrast to a place of birth that determine race. That covers the immigrants from Europe who have children in Asia, ensuring their children will not be classified as "Asian." How original must the original people be? If it is correct that the human species itself began in what we call Africa, then based on the above definition we are all

---

[90] Paragraph 42.402 Definitions, Subpart F—Coordination of Enforcement of Non-discrimination in Federally Assisted Programs, 28 CFR Ch 1 (7-1-92 edition), p. 692.

African.[91] If no one has "origins" in Europe, then no person can, following government classifications, be labeled White.

The U.S. government seems to recognize the problem of original origins in its tautological first definition: A "Black" person is a person who is of a **black** racial group" in Africa. This appears necessary so that one does not count Whites born in South Africa, for instance, as Black, insofar as they have their origins in Africa.[92] In this case the "Africa" qualification of who is Black is useless, irrelevant. Either everyone with origins at some point in Africa is Black (the definition does not stipulate a time period), which would include everyone; or "Black" refers to skin color alone, in which case the invocation of "Africa" is entirely irrelevant.

These federal classificatory schemes are also challenged by groups who want to readjust categories for the purpose of aggregate data collection, as well as by individuals who feel wronged by the present system. Mustafa Hefny brought a lawsuit against the OMB on the grounds that he was misclassified as White because he immigrated from Egypt: "Hefny says that as a Nubian, his hair is kinkier, his complexion darker and his features more African than blacks such as Detroit Mayor Dennis Archer and retired Gen. Colin Powell."[93] Hefney's challenge relies on a political society to assign race. He simply is redefining his political society of origins. "Nubian" is not a physiological description. A Nubian is a descendant of the Nubians, "an ancient kingdom in Northeast Africa, in what is now Egypt and Sudan."[94] The geographical designation of the ancient kingdom Nubia (a political society and geographical territory) is one Hefny associates with certain physical characteristics ("kinky hair") he thinks mark him Black.

These classifications have changed in the past, and they will, no doubt, change again.[95] Reflecting the tautologies that permeate the system, one

[91] Rebecca Cann, Mark Storekin, Allan Wilson, "Mitochondrial DNA and Human Evolution," *Nature* 325, 1 (January, 1, 1987), pp. 31–36. This article was popularized as the one with the story about an African woman who, between 100,000 and 140,000 years ago, supposedly was the mother of the entire *homo sapiens* species. The basis of this claim is a study of the DNA from 150 placentas from around the world. The authors invoke the statistical principle of parsimony to claim that "[a]ll present-day humans are descendants of that African population," insofar as this hypothesis minimizes the "number of intercontinental migrations needed to account for the geographical distribution of mtDNA types" (pp. 35, 33).

[92] This also speaks to the problem of the "African-American" appellation, rather than "Black." Presumably a light-skinned person from a Dutch-born family who had emigrated to the United States from South Africa would count as an "African-American," which may not be a bad thing, insofar as it causes us to understand the contingency of these supposedly natural classifications.

[93] John Hughes, "Man Sues to Change Federal definitions," *Detroit Free Press*, June 5, 1997, 17A.

[94] Ibid.

[95] The 2000 census will provide people the opportunity of checking more than one box under the heading of "race."

study called for "all blacks to be identified as blacks—not just those whose origins are from the black racial groups of Africa."[96] It is ironic that the discipline that gave us scientific understandings of "race," namely that of anthropology, is now the one telling us that race does not exist, and that insofar as the concept does exist, it is primarily a matter of political organizations and boundaries. Of racial classifications in the Arctic, anthropologist Debra Schindler writes: " 'Race' is a sociological phenomenon associated with oppression by the state, not a physiological boundary defined by specific biochemical criteria."[97] A response states: "It would be productive . . . to focus research upon features suitable for verification of polity differences in the past, beginning with polities indicated in primary Russian data and Aleut folklore."[98] So, while political scientists are busy studying "races" based on illogical typologies that have been repudiated by the people who developed them, anthropologists are deciding that political communities might have something to do with what we call 'race'.

What Race Is (Not)—II

The account of racial taxonomies offered is not definite about the content of any particular race but is very specific as to the form taken by race. Such specificity challenges the notion that race is a diffuse concept, that "racism appeals either to inherent superiority or to differences. These putative differences may be strictly physical, intellectual, linguistic, or cultural."[99] David Goldberg also notes: "It should be obvious from all I have said that race cannot be a static, fixed entity, indeed is not an entity in any objective sense at all. I am tempted to say that race is whatever anyone in using that term or its cognates conceives of collective social relations."[100] Goldberg refers to the "complexity" of the concept of race. Sometimes it is one thing and sometimes something else, depending perhaps on the self-identification of the individual.[101] This is a highly unsatis-

---

[96] Hughes, "Man Sues."

[97] Schindler, "Anthropology in the Arctic," *Current Anthropology* 26, 4 (August/October 1985), p. 483.

[98] Ibid., p. 484. Schindler's essay argues against those anthropologists of the Arctic who persist in using racial typologies. But one of the more striking aspects of this article and the responses to it is the extent to which Schindler is taken to task by these specialists for constructing "straw men," based on the fact that few archaeologists or anthropologists in her field use racial typologies in their work. Only one of the approximately dozen responses actually defends racial typologies, and his defense is a qualified one (Kenneth Weiss, "Discussion," *Current Anthropology* 26, 4 [August/October, 1985], pp. 490–91).

[99] Goldberg, *Racist Culture* (Cambridge: Blackwell, 1993), p. 56.

[100] Ibid., p. 81.

[101] Ibid., pp. 101–3, 86.

fying theoretical position, no more appropriate for a scholarly definition of race than for those of freedom, justice, or anything else.

Goldberg attempts to demonstrate the slippery qualities of the concepts of race, religion, ethnicity, and nationality by asking "What is a Jew?"[102] But the possibility of assigning all of these designations to Jews does not mean these concepts are contingent or vague. Imagine a chair in my living room. "What's that?" is asked by an insurance agent, an interior decorator, and a three year old. The replies: 1) "It's worth about $100"; 2) "A family heirloom that I must hold onto." 3) "That? That's a chair." Goldberg asks "What is a Jew?" notices a variety of answers, and claims this a function of the ambiguity of all of them—race, nation, ethnicity, religion, and so on. This does not follow any more than it follows that because "cost" is one among several possible ways of conceptualizing a response, that "cost," "heirlooms," and "furniture" are ambiguous words or concepts. Each of these is a perfectly clear concept, relevant in different contexts.

Also, it matters that certain answers to "What's that?" won't do. If the response were "Oh, that's the hallway," the interlocutor would know she had been misunderstood, that this reply could not possibly refer to the chair, on the one hand. On the other hand the "heirloom" response could indicate an ostensive mistake, with the respondent thinking that the decorator had been asking about an old chest of drawers directly behind the chair. 'Chair' and 'chest' have something in common that 'chair' and 'hallway' do not share: the possibility of being both furniture.

The same holds for uses of 'race', 'nationality', 'ethnicity', and 'religion'. Races may be located either by reference to individual nations or aggregations of nations, so that the same group may be named as a nation or a race. 'Japanese' or 'Asians' may be thought races. But no racial designation exists independent of the political-geographical designation of both Japan and Asia. This means that 'Japanese' may be a national designation, depending on whether or not physical attributes are associated with the form of being. This is what prompts Goldberg to attribute an insurmountable vagueness to what counts as racial exclusions.[103] Returning to his example, Jews are a *race* when they are a people who are thought to have certain *physical differences* associated with a geographical territory of origins. In this case, the biblically described lands of the "Israelites" count as the place of origins. ('Israelites', not Jews, is the translation of the designation in the Hebrew Bible.)[104] Jews are a *nation* when conceptualized as members of a specific political society; they are Israelites by ancestry, but not necessarily physically distinct from other groups.[105] Jews are an *ethnicity* when consid-

---

[102] Ibid., p. 101.

[103] Ibid., p. 103.

[104] "Jews" are named as such by the Romans, a point discussed in Chapter 6.

[105] Israelites were patrilineal until the Mishnaic period, at which point it is recorded in the Talmud: "Your son by an Israelite mother is called your son, but your son by a heathen

ered as a potential national group within the borders of some place that is not Israel, not their "original" nation.[106] Finally, Jews are a *religious* group when described as a membership organization that distinguishes in particular ways between the sacred and profane. Likewise, Blacks are a racial group when thought of in terms of physical differences associated with a territory of origins, i.e., Africa; and likewise Whites are a racial group when conceptualized as having physical differences associated with origins in Europe.

Are Blacks an ethnic group? When Jesse Jackson organized to have "Blacks" identify as "African-American," he was calling for African-Americans to be just another ethnic group. Ethnic groups designate a people associated with a nation that exists elsewhere. Africa is not a nation, but an aggregation of nations. It is only because Africa has some of the political instruments associated with a nation that the label African-American is even conceivable. The numerous Pan-African conventions, organizations, and agreements[107] consolidate Africa as a political space that makes possible a sense of ancestral ties to that region and not simply one's tribe. However, it is the incommensurability of these African institutions with those of actual state-nations that makes the use of this "ethnic" label both possible and awkward.

The Form of Race and Intergenerationality

So I end where Appiah begins, with his father's house. He writes: "From him I inherited Africa."[108] The inheritance is something protected from his mother's side, from the Anglo political institutions that never domi-

---

woman is not called your son" (*Qiddushin*: 68b. From "Patrilineal Descent," in *Oxford Dictionary of the Jewish Religion*, R. J. Werblowsky and Geoffrey Wigoder, ed. [New York and Oxford: Oxford University Press, 1997]).

[106] It is also true that "ethnicity" is often experienced as a category of exoticism, such as when people refer to "ethnic" food or dress. I want to emphasize the importance of the fact that the underlying reference groups for all of these invocations are forms parasitic on political organizations, and not just any kind of difference. The Beatniks, for instance, inspired the formation of a sub-culture that was exotic vis-à-vis mainstream 1950s United States. But those who associated with Jack Kerouac were not considered to be part of an "ethnic" group. 'Punk', 'queer', 'stock car race fans' and even 'neo-Nazi' name particular sub-cultures in the United States, but they are not idiomatically called 'ethnic'. Again, the taxonomy I have in mind does not require that the political society actually exist, only that it is thought to have existed in the past or aspires to exist as a political society in the future. Insofar as continents are also a function of political societies, an 'ethnic' invocation vis-à-vis Africa or Asia is consistent with my definition. In the latter case, it is the addition of certain state-nations into a continent that forms this political society.

[107] And see Appiah, *In My Father's House*, p. 180.

[108] Ibid., p. viii.

nated the tribal experiences of "funeral, . . . music, . . . dance, and of course
. . . the intimacy of family life."[109] Appiah suggests that in Ghana the
chieftain, not the state courts, "exercise[s] substantial power in matters of
marriage, inheritance, and upbringing, and through all these, wealth."[110]
In repeating the conventional wisdom that associates that which is "African" with that which is "tribal," and both of these with the "intimacy of
family life," on the one hand, and, on the other, connecting the "state
courts" with that which is Anglo and the disruptions of intimate family
life, Appiah obscures the ways that it is the very interventions of the chief
that call into question Appiah's notion of family as all that intimate. If the
contrast between Europe and Africa is itself the basis of Appiah's notion that
African societies are more congenial, more intimate, places than European
ones, that may reveal less about the absence of rules in African tribes than
it does about the role of orientalism in the generation of Third World
beliefs about themselves, generated in contrast to the forms imputed to
other countries.[111] The notion that one inherits certain rituals absent political institutions in Africa is as untenable as the romanticization of these
political rites. Appiah is proud of being African (he begins to publish under
the name "Kwame" Anthony Appiah) and is therefore boasting about the
practices that he feels gave him this sense of who he is. Appiah thinks he
is telling us how he was made, but really he is pointing out the kinship
rules that produce, and reproduce, Africa.

The private family that gives Appiah his personal links to Africa, whether
that family is reproduced by a chieftain or government bureaucrat, functions in a manner inimical to freedom, in that both sustain political societies
characterized by certain roles that interpellate individuals into forms of
being and experiences that are at best irritating restrictions difficult to
challenge, and are at their worst deadly. The ancestral nation, ethnicity,
or race is harmful in itself, and not just one possible basis of harm. Any
group history created by ancestry establishes political taxonomies of imper-
meable exclusions. Race is the culmination of a historical process that
renders nature and people properties negotiated among state-nations. Recall the United States definitions of race and this becomes obvious. One's
race is determined by the existence of "Korea" or other state-nations that
constitute Asia, Europe, or Africa, all in the name of a natural, "original"
relation to the world.

The concept of race functions to affirm the determinacy of the state-
nation, which might otherwise dissolve into the ideals of democracy and
individuality that Kant predicted would lead to the cessation of all wars.

[109] Ibid., pp. 7–8.
[110] Ibid., p. 160.
[111] Edward Said, *Orientalism* (New York: Vintage Books, 1978).

After writing that a republican constitution is the only pure one, Kant says that it

> also provides for this desirable result, namely perpetual peace, and the reason for this is as follows: If (as must inevitably be the case, given this form of constitution) the consent of the citizenry is required in order to determine whether or not there will be war, it is natural that they consider all the calamities before committing themselves to so risky a game.

The risks include doing the fighting themselves as well as paying the costs of war.[112] The reason Kant was wrong, that citizens of republics cheerfully rally around the flag, is not that the populace believes in "trickle down" theories of war bounty, but rather, as Hegel pointed out, that the members of a political society identify themselves as, and therefore exist through, the perpetuation of that political society. One's racial form of being has become a key aspect of this process.

Nationality is a liminal space of contradiction that is as necessary as it is elusive; nationality differs from other discursive objects that are more consistently and idiomatically "natural." Race, in this context, helps makes nationality clear. The idea of race apparently stands above the contingency of the nation, justifying the preservation of borders in a manner resonant of Hegel's monarchical appeals to God. When Christianity's "just wars" no longer yielded justified slaves, the politically remote geography of southern Africa determined a "race," a type of people with observed or imagined physical characteristics associated with a particular geographical place.

Under Appiah's pan-Africanism "We [Africans] share a continent and its ecological problems. . . ."[113] In making this claim, Appiah is not inventing African particularity in an otherwise universalist world but rather countering "Africa" to the equally particularist and kinship-based "Europe," since both continents exist by virtue of the aggregation of state-nations that in turn are constituted by the kinship rules of their respective political societies. This topography yields kinship classifications with the same force as those given us by the geneticists whom Appiah criticizes. Are White colonists and their progeny included in Appiah's pan-African project? Appiah's account of difference, finally, does not abandon ancestral stories of origins that reproduce the hardened sense of racial identities he and others find so troublesome. Furthermore, such intergenerational group forms require hierarchical gender roles, a point pursued in Chapter 5.

---

[112] *Perpetual Peace*, tr. Ted Humphrey (Indianapolis: Hackett, 1983), p. 113.

[113] *Father's House*, p. 180. For further discussions of the possibilities and limits of an African 'philosophy,' see essays by Lucius Outlaw, in *On Race and Philosophy* (New York and London: Routledge, 1996), especially chapters 3 and 4.

Five

Compensatory Kinship Rules

THE MOTHER OF GENDER

> *Matrimonium* is an institution involving a
> mother, *mater*. The idea implicit in the word is
> that a man takes a woman in marriage, in
> *matrimonium ducere*, so that he may have
> children by her.[1]

> Is the book fair based on sodomy? I don't believe
> [homosexuals] have any rights at all. I hope the
> time never comes when we want to reverse
> nature and men bear children.[2]

RATHER than view "anatomical sex differences" as the cause of inequalities between men and women, what if we begin with the fact that one group controls the reproductive abilities of another, to see how this particular kind of control itself constitutes "sex differences" that produce men and women? This chapter documents historical and current exemplary legal episodes in which apparently gender-neutral membership rules of political society constitute crucial sex differences that are relied on for the continued legitimacy of these membership rules.

That gendered kinship rules are important to the maintenance of political societies is expressed in President Robert Mugabe's hysteria, as well as the rhetoric on same-sex marriage in the United States. A gay and lesbian booth at a book fair leads to sodomy. Sodomy's violation of reproductive roles leads to the idea that men will bear children. And, as we shall see in the rhetoric of U.S. politicians, the possibility of gay men having their sexual relations acknowledged by state marriage laws is not just repulsive and immoral but will lead to the downfall of that political society as such.

---

[1] Susan Treggiari, *Roman Marriage: Iusti Coniuges from the Time of Cicero to the Time of Ulpian* (Oxford: Oxford University Press, 1991), p. 5.

[2] Robert Mugabe, quoted in "Zimbabwe Leader Condemns Homosexuality," *New York Times*, August 2, 1995, A7.

Rather than pre-existing sex differences being reflected in and exacerbated by laws, the very definition of matrimony suggests the institution is constitutive of inequity in roles related to reproduction, that marriage is an assymetrical system assuring men access to mothers (*mater*), creating unrecognized and largely unrequited demands on women. It is not that some people give birth and others do not that leads directly to gender roles. Rather, gender is what occurs through very specific rules a political society develops as it reproduces itself. The marked mother, subject to the institution of men taking her for the purpose of having children (matrimony), affects all those who grow up as potential mothers. Perhaps these effects are what we perceive as sex.[3]

Although kinship forms vary across time and place,[4] many people still believe that there is something natural about kinship. From this point of view, the most obvious consequence of kinship rules is that they bring fathers into relations with their children. Absent kinship rules, biological mothers will be connected to their children; kinship rules then make it possible for biological fathers to have a similarly "natural" bond to their children. Under these assumptions "political" kinship forms of membership may be simply passive reiterations of underlying human aspirations for a family, and explicit rules for membership in political society use kinship principles because this is what human beings naturally do.

Locke, for example, writes that desire between the sexes inherently results in biological families and these aggregate into a larger "society," which at a certain point becomes "political" (when, according to Locke, the father becomes a "king"). Ironically, this view of the family as natural seems to affirm Sir Robert Filmer's view of political society, and to pose a problem for those who want to argue against kinship rules as criteria for membership in a political society. Social contract opponents to the kinship model of modern political societies, such as Locke, argue that once political societies have attained a certain size, the membership criterion of birth

---

[3] Butler has demonstrated the mistake of associating 'sex' with biology and 'gender' with culture, as sex, too, is discursive. However, the shift from the use of 'sex' to 'gender' among feminist intellectuals and many in the broader public also suggests that the two are not near synonyms. Here a phenomenological framework that appreciates that different levels of consciousness about what is 'sex' as it is superseded to become 'gender' that is in turn superseded to become 'difference' may negate but not destroy the moments of realization through which they proceed to stage different family dramas. Biology (sense-certainty), culture (perception), and scholarly scrutiny to the interaction of these two moments inevitably recuperate rather than annihilate all of the terms under investigation. 'Gender,' as it is used by post-structuralists, is the realization that 'sex' is experienced as natural and is something else as well.

[4] Kingsley Davis offers a chart of twenty squared kinship possibilities. *Human Society* (New York: MacMillan, 1948), pp. 414–16.

for citizenship may be dismissed as anachronistic remnants from an earlier age. The rules for family membership become distinguished from those of citizenship.

These views imply a dichotomy between the family, which is natural, and political society, which is artificial. Based on the idea that authority in the family is natural and sensible, while order in the state is artificial (and any authority needs justifications), Edward Jenks writes, "The State is the very antithesis of the family, and of all institutions based on kinship."[5] This line of thinking accepts that a political society's rules for membership are arbitrary, but still maintains that families are natural. On this view, political societies may very well appropriate certain practices of kinship to mark some as insiders and others as outsiders, but such invocations ought to be viewed as possibly mistaken, and as separate, in any case, from the otherwise natural dynamics that constitute families.[6] Hence even those writers who see political society as the site of convention may overlook the ways this political society constitutes the family, even as the family continues to be depicted as natural.

Feminist Theories of the Family

Feminists have tremendous stakes in discussions about whether the family is natural, since male roles have virtually always afforded more power and status to their bearers than to corresponding female roles. In the history of European family law, the husband has had more prerogatives than the wife, the son more than the daughter. Debates about whether the family is natural are also often debates about whether male dominance is natural. For feminists, men's advantages from marriage law are themselves evidence of men's (and hence the law's) instrumentality. Marriage law's bias on behalf of men as a class against women as a class, on this reading, may betray men's wiles or even physical dominance, but there is nothing any more "natural" in the political advantages they bestow on themselves than in the advantages the Stuarts had vis-à-vis the rest of the English population.[7] The sheer fact of initial trickery or a winning army does not make the consequent hierarchy natural, or so liberals have argued.

---

[5] *The State and the Nation* (New York: E. P. Dutton, 1919), p. 153, quoted in Martin Sicker, *The Genesis of the State* (New York: Praeger, 1991), p. 49.

[6] Another approach is to suggest that precisely because families are natural, then so too are the larger affinities that develop from them. If nations are but families *writ* large, then a special fellow-feeling within them makes sense because families are just like that, a line of thinking pursued in Chapter 3.

[7] Mary Wollstonecraft, *A Vindication of the Rights of Women* (1792; rpt. London: Rutland, Everyman's Press, 1985), pp. 21–22.

There is some debate over whose interests—men's or women's—marriage serves. Rousseau complains that women's trickery turned noble savages into oppressed husbands; advantageous for women, marriage hinders men. Engels, too, notes the advantages for women of being one man's property rather than the object of group rape.[8] On this view, marriage is an improvement for women. What these theories fail to appreciate are the ways that the very form of kinship rules creates gender roles, even when these laws provide apparent equality to husbands and wives. The very form of a political society controlling reproduction establishes birth, and hence mothers, as objects of state intervention. This objectification genders the state—as the force oppositional to the mother—as paternal. Because maternity and paternity are associated with women and men, respectively, these latter, sexed subject positions develop in the matrix of hierarchical kinship conventions. By rendering membership rules those of birth, a process characterized as "natural," the masculine citizen appropriates maternal power. The seamless overlaps between law and family naturalize the politically constituted family and simultaneously conceal the artifice of membership rules.

The history of marriage as a history of women's oppression is certainly a compelling one, well-documented by several generations of feminist researchers. Drawing on their insights (referenced below) this chapter moves in another direction, attending to the specific effects of these marital discourses on gender status—on what counts as "masculine" and what counts as "feminine." Rather than begin with the idea that already-present sex/gender differences congeal in various status relations, this chapter considers how laws themselves bring about gendered forms of being, even when the laws seem to treat wives and husbands equally.

The focus here is on the United States because it is the country Marx, with good reason, held up as exemplary of the most "completely developed political state," that is, the one with the fewest status requirements for political membership and participation.[9] To show the impact of marriage on gender in the United States is to show the depth and scope of marriage laws in the articulation of sex differences. That Marx's focus was on religious freedom in particular, and that marriage is closely tied to religious discourses, also makes it especially relevant to return to his analysis of the United States.

---

[8] *The Origin of the Family, Private Property, and the State* (1884; rpt. New York: Pathfinder Press, 1972), p. 85; Rousseau, *Discourse on the Origin of Inequality*, tr. Donald Cress (1755; rpt. Indianapolis: Hackett, 1992), p. 39.

[9] Marx, "On the Jewish Question," in *The Marx-Engels Reader*, ed. Robert Tucker (New York: W. W. Norton, 1978), p. 30. Marx could not have been thinking about sex roles when he wrote this. At that time only a very small proportion of women could vote or run for office, a fact that would require a major qualification to his characterizing the United States as "completely developed."

The State of Modern Marriage Law

The Reformation-era notion of the family as pre-political is the one that has continued to inform liberal and radical views of the relation between marriage and the state. Interestingly, though, for the state to institutionalize this view of the family performs the very politicization of the husband-wife relation that Luther and his followers seemed to reject. Of course the situation is not as stark as presented. Luther somewhat inconsistently would argue the prerogatives of the parents against those of the Church and state, but he would also concede the prerogative of the state against that of the Church.[10] These paradoxes appear in Marx's "On the Jewish Question" (1843), an essay that established the grounds for subsequent claims that in modernity economic or other social relations may not be constrained, or even all that deeply affected, by legal ones.[11] Some feminist theorists have used this essay to show that the elimination of legally codified inequalities does not overthrow a social order in which men dominate women. Elaborating Foucault's insights on power as reproduced at the margins rather than descending from a sovereign, still other feminists attempt to enhance women's perspective and agency by focusing on these ostensibly non-statist experiences. For example, Kathy Davis and Sue Fisher introduce *Negotiating at the Margins* by explaining that their essays attend to the:

> discursive micropractices through which power and resistance are negotiated by women who are all too frequently situated at the margins of the social and symbolic orders. These margins provide fertile sites for feminist theorizing as well as for delineating women's power practices. It is here that women routinely engage in struggles ranging from the most mundane to the most heroic.[12]

State interventions such as marriage law, however, remain important for the reproduction of gendered forms of being and the state itself. The meanings of the most apparently "cultural" or "natural" roles of mother and father still are constituted by and through the state.

While other scholars have shown the inconsistency of marriage and liberal theory,[13] or demonstrated the illogic of the requirement of a

---

[10] This is discussed in Chapter 6.

[11] "On the Jewish Question," in Tucker, ed., *The Marx-Engels Reader*, 2d ed., pp. 26–52.

[12] *Negotiating at the Margins: The Gendered Discourses of Power and Resistance* (New Brunswick: Rutgers University Press, 1993), p. 13.

[13] Sara Ketchum, "Liberalism and Marriage Law," in *Feminism and Philosophy*, ed. Mary Vetterling-Brogin, Frederick Elliston, Jane English (New York: Rowman and Littlefield, 1977), pp. 264–76; J. S. Mill, *The Subjection of Women* (1869; rpt. Rutland, Vermont: Everyman's Library, 1985), especially chapter two; Susan Okin, *Justice, Gender, and the Family* (New York: Basic Books, 1989); Carole Pateman, *The Sexual Contract* (Stanford: Stanford University Press, 1988), especially "Feminism and the Marriage Contract," chapter 6; Mary

hierarchical private sphere for women in the construction of an egalitarian public sphere for men,[14] the argument here is that marriage genders the fully developed political state and its citizens, *even when it appears that the state does not have sex-specific requirements for the duties of "husband" and "wife."*[15] So, while gender distinctions are effaced in many other parts of the law,[16] and while there are far fewer explicitly discriminatory laws that regulate marriage than when the state was more explicitly patriarchal, marriage still creates political status roles.[17]

Marx incorrectly defines the fully developed, liberal state as one that has eliminated all political status relations.[18] The modern state has eliminated the "villain," "knight," "lord," "serf" and "peon," but one juridical status relation remains: that of the "husband" married to his "wife."[19] With

---

Shanley, "Marital Slavery and Friendship: J. S. Mill's *The Subjection of Women*," in *Feminist Interpretations and Political Theory*, ed. Carole Pateman and Mary Shanley (Cambridge: Polity Press, 1991); Mary Wollstonecraft, *A Vindication of the Rights of Woman*, pp. 164–80.

[14] Catharine MacKinnon, *Toward a Feminist Theory of the State* (Cambridge: Harvard University Press, 1991), especially chapter eight; Katherine O'Donovan, *Sexual Divisions in the Law* (London: Weidenfeld and Nicolson, 1985).

[15] Older accounts of the gender-specific, exploitative aspects of marriage are still relevant, especially in states with marital rape exemption laws. On the history of marriage as an inegalitarian institution, see Engels, *Origin of the Family, Private Property, and the State*; Gerda Lerner, *The Creation of Patriarchy* (New York, Oxford: Oxford University Press, 1986); Mary Shanley, *Feminism, Marriage, and the Law in Victorian England, 1850–1895* (Princeton: Princeton University Press, 1984); Carol Smart, *The Ties that Bind: Law, Marriage and the Reproduction of Patriarchal Relations* (London, Boston, and Melbourne: Routledge, Kegan, Paul, 1984).

[16] By 'law' I mean simply interpretations of the written documents that outline the scope of state action and restrictions. Law is what announces what the state can do, and not what "the people" or individuals cannot do. I put it this way to emphasize the constitutive aspects of law sometimes lost in analyses of liberal states, on the part of pluralists as well as Foucauldians; see Alan Hunt, in *Explorations in Law and Society: Toward a Constitutive Theory of Law* (New York, London: Routledge, 1993), especially "Foucault's Expulsion of Law: Toward a Retrieval" and "Law as a Constitutive Mode of Regulation."

[17] Other critics of what has been called "heteronormativity" have noted the persistence of state interventions in the construction of sexuality. Among those not previously cited are Richard Collier, *Masculinity, the Law, and the Family* (London and New York: Routledge, 1995); Lisa Duggan, "Queering the State," *Social Text* 39 (Summer, 1994), pp. 1–14; David Evans, *Sexual Citizenship: The Material Construction of Sexualities* (London, New York: Routledge, 1993); Janet Halley, "The Construction of Heterosexuality," in *Fear of a Queer Planet*, ed. Michael Warner (Minneapolis: University of Minnesota Press, 1994), pp. 82–104; Gayle Rubin, "Thinking Sex: Notes for a Radical Theory of the Politics of Sexuality," in *Pleasure/Danger: Exploring Female Sexuality*, ed. Carole Vance (Boston: Routledge and Kegan Paul, 1984), pp. 267–319; Jacqueline Stevens, "Leviticus in America: On the Politics of Sex Crimes," *Journal of Political Philosophy* 1 (2), (June, 1993), pp. 105–36.

[18] Marx, "On the Jewish Question," p. 33.

[19] The state interest in marriage is stated in a late nineteenth century case, *Maynard v. Hill*, 125 U.S. 190 (1888). A frequently quoted passage from that decision maintains that marriage is an "institution, in the maintenance of which in its purity the public is deeply

the appellation "husband," fathers have the prerogatives of paternity that they would lack were the distinctions of marriage not in place. By legally privileging what is "political" (husband-fathers) over what is "natural" (mothers) through marriage, the state engenders parenting roles in a hierarchical fashion. A large number of political and economic benefits go to people who fit the legal definition of the married couple. Many of these flow from the state itself, using this definition in contexts ranging from tax returns to social security benefits to citizenship criteria. The state favors the married couple over any other dyad or individual.

Nonetheless, family law in the United States is far less discriminatory against women than it was as recently as 30 years ago. Indeed, it is the egalitarian quality of much of the juridical marriage relation that renders the exceptions all that more telling. Specifically, court opinions of the United States, with rare exceptions, continue to insist that a husband must be a "man" and a wife a "woman," in the name of nature, the Bible, or of a particular kinship pattern in which women's bodies reproduce children for state-licensed husbands to control.

Court decisions are crucial for an analysis of marriage because law constitutes marriage, as far as the state is concerned. That is, the state does not passively reflect or regulate pre-existing marriage norms. Unlike most other laws, marriage law is what language philosopher J. L. Austin calls "performative" of the actions it is apparently simply regulating. Austin writes that one's utterance is performative when one is "*doing* something rather than merely *saying* something." Austin's first example of this is a marriage ceremony: "Suppose, for example, that in the course of a marriage ceremony I say, as people will, 'I do'—(sc. take this woman to be my lawful wedded wife)."[20] Performatives may "misfire" if the context is inappropriate, for instance, if one attempts to divorce one's wife by "standing her squarely in the room and saying, in a voice loud enough for all to hear, 'I divorce you'. Now this procedure is not accepted . . . at least not in this country and others like it."[21] Of all his examples only marriage requires a specifically legal context for the statement to be felicitous.

Law is not definitive in the same way for other activities that it regulates. It is possible but illegal to drive 90 miles per hour (mph) or to purchase

---

interested, for it is the foundation of the family and of society, without which there would be neither civilization nor progress" (211). Marriage, according to this decision, "is not so much the result of private agreement, as of public ordination" (quoting from *Noel v. Ewing* 9 Indiana 37 [1857]). Unlike other contracts which the state passively enforces, the state itself actively creates the status of husband and wife in its "public ordination" of marriage. More recent constitutional law treats marriage as a "right," as well as a status; see *Loving v. Virginia* 33 U.S. 1 (1967); *Zablocki v. Redhail* 434 U.S. 374 (1977).

[20] "Performative Utterances," in *Philosophical Papers* (Oxford: Clarendon Press, 1961).

[21] Ibid., p. 225.

beer for a nine year old. It is not possible to be married in any way other than that which one's state legislature recognizes. One does not look to law for what counts as "90 mph" or "nine years old." Further distinguishing marriage law from most others is the approach the state uses in defining the practice. It is very common for a law or court decision to rely on dictionaries and to offer rather formal definitions of specific relevant concepts. What is unusual about the definitions of marriage is that the courts quite deliberately and confidently define it on their own authority, because marriage is a practice that only the state, ultimately, is able to define, and the courts reiterate this principle. The judiciary recognizes its own interventions as artifice and accords itself, as the guardian of the state, the epistemological position of being able to decide what counts as marriage.

"On the Jewish Question"

Marx criticized Hegelian philosopher Bruno Bauer's worry that the political recognition of Jews as Jewish citizens (as opposed to German citizens) would reinforce Judaism and undermine a secular state.[22] Bauer thought it fine for Jews to be citizens, but their Judaism would have to be a strictly private affair. Everyone should have political rights, but the German state should recognize only "Germans," not "Jews." Marx writes: "Bauer demands, on the one hand, that the Jew should renounce Judaism . . . in order to be emancipated as a citizen. On the other hand, and this follows logically, that the political abolition of religion is the abolition of all religion."[23] Bauer reasons that if the state rids itself of religion, then religion will vanish, and hence "Jews" and "Christians" and their conflicts will go away as well, leaving a universal, harmonious society of "citizens," and then "men."

Marx disagreed, pointing out that the United States had done the most to separate the state from religious practices, and yet no other country had more religious believers and sects:

> There is not, in the United States, either a state religion or a religion declared to be that of a majority, or a predominance of one religion over another. The state remains aloof from all religions. . . . And yet 'no one in the United States

---

[22] "Die Jüdenfrage" (Braunschweig, 1843). A typescript English translation is *The Jewish Problem*, tr. Helen Lederer (Cincinnati: Hebrew Union College-Jewish Institute of Religion, 1958). An intriguing discussion of the legacy of this essay is Enzo Traverso, *The Marxists and the Jewish Question: The History of a Debate, 1842–1943*, tr. Bernard Gibbons (Atlantic Highlands: Humanities Press, 1990).

[23] Marx, "On the Jewish Question," p. 29.

believes that a man without religion can be an honest man.' And North America is pre-eminently a country of religiosity, as Beaumont, Tocqueville, and the Englishman [Thomas] Hamilton, assure us in unison.[24]

Clearly the state's removal of religion from its purview could not be associated with a decline of popular expressions of religion.

Marx argues that law may provide conditions for equality that go unrealized in daily life. He shows this by describing two spheres that exist in relation with each other: *political society* (relations constituted by the state and its laws) and *civil society* (all other relations). Political society and civil society do not exist autonomously, according to Marx. Civil society is not the equivalent of a Lockean "state of nature." Rather, political society and civil society require each other. All social relations defined as "non-political" are created by the state. For instance, the "right" to practice one's religion is constituted by a legal document (the Constitution, in the United States) that is interpreted by state agents (the Supreme Court). The relation of husband to wife, constituted by the state through marriage laws, is another example of the state's creation, through law, of a sphere of "private" relations ostensibly outside the "public" realm.

The grounding for these rights is not the Bible or some other ostensibly pre-political sentiment. They are not the result of a persuasive utilitarian treatise on the relation between religious choice and the happiness of individuals. Rather, we know religion is a right because Marx can refer us to the 1791 and 1793 versions of the French republican "Declarations of the Rights of Man" and to Articles from the eighteenth century state constitutions of Pennsylvania and New Hampshire.[25] Marx points out that the political discourse of rights and liberties does not point to genuine freedom. This can be found only in a uniquely "human emancipation," not in political or civil society: "To be *politically* emancipated from religion is not to be finally and completely emancipated from religion, because political emancipation is not the final and absolute form of human emancipation."[26] That the state asserts what counts as a right, or what counts as freedom, renders that freedom contingent and illusory. One needs to abolish the civil society/political society distinction—the difference between one's legal status as equal and one's daily experiences as oppressed—before real, human emancipation is possible.

The success of religious sects in civil society highlighted the possibility for oppressive economic relations to flourish in civil society, under capitalism. A liberal state does not mandate specific labor roles of "capitalist"

[24] Ibid., p. 31, quoting Gustave de Beaumont, *Marie ou l'esclavage aux Etats-Unis Bruxelles* (Bruxelles, 1835), p. 217.

[25] Ibid., pp. 41–42.

[26] Ibid., p. 32.

and "proletariat," but the dynamics of exploitative capitalist relations in civil society prevail. The worker is no less tied to the cycles of capital accumulation for want of an oath of fealty than the (e)state-named serf who was tied to the labor patterns of feudal accumulation. Universal suffrage and hence equality in political society implies no consequences for civil society. Everyone may be a citizen, but not everyone can be a capitalist, Marx reasons.

On the Marriage Question

The modern, liberal state and its laws seem gender neutral. Legislation does not specify who must do the housework any more than it specifies who may accumulate capital. Nonetheless, men have more power and authority than women in our society. How does this come about? Wendy Brown, in her essay on abortion rights, uses Marx to explain this: "The *political* emancipation of women (suffrage, equal rights, etc.) leaves intact the fact of sexism with regard to reproductive relations just as 'political emancipation from religion leaves religion in existence.' "[27] Similarly, Catharine MacKinnon writes that the apparent gender neutrality of the liberal state serves the hierarchies of civil society: "civil society, the domain in which women are distinctively subordinated and deprived of power, has been placed beyond reach of legal guarantees. Women are oppressed socially, prior to law, without state acts, often in intimate contexts."[28] Brown's and MacKinnon's observations seem to make sense, since women in the United States have the same individual political rights as men. These are rights that some in the 1920s thought would be the first step in the alleviation of gender inequalities. Yet women continue to suffer from various forms of violence, exploitation, and discrimination, especially in the "private" realms of family and market.

Part of the problem in the analysis above is that civil society is not a private sphere present from when proto-*homo sapiens* rose from the muck, a point often undeveloped in the writings of many who use Marx. Rather than leave women alone, in some pre-legal limbo, juridical discourse itself constitutes certain activities as "private." That is, through law the state creates the private realm in which sexual and other violence is permitted. When men in the past have gotten away with beating their wives, the reason has often been that the state positively excuses certain domestic

[27] "Reproductive Freedom and the Right of Privacy," in *Families, Politics, and Public Policy: A Dialogue on Women and the State*, ed. Irene Diamond, (New York and London: Longman, 1983), p. 327, quoting from Marx, "On the Jewish Question," p. 31.
[28] *Toward a Feminist Theory of the State*, p. 165.

forms of violence. Marriage law makes this especially clear: the British common law did not ignore wife-beating, but articulated its "reasonable bounds";[29] marital rape exemptions did not ignore rape within marriage but explicitly *required* the state to protect this form of violence. Sir Matthew Hale wrote:

> the husband can not be guilty of a rape committed by himself upon his lawful wife, for by their mutual matrimonial consent and contract the wife hath given herself in this kind unto her husband and which she can not retract.[30]

This is not a passive acknowledgment that men use force against women; it is a positive exemption from state punishment for men who are husbands and use force against their wives.

The marriage relation also creates public, that is, politically relevant forms of being: "Marriage is commonly thought to lie in the realm of private decision making, but . . . the institution of marriage is and has been a public institution and a building block of public policy."[31] The modern state cannot leave marriage alone, any more than could the Athenian one:

> One might go so far as to say that the institution of marriage and the modern state have been mutually constitutive. As much as (legal) marriage does not exist without being authorized by the state, one of the principal means that the state can use to prove its existence—to announce its sovereignty and its hold on the populace—is its authority over marriage.[32]

[29] William Blackstone, *Commentaries on the Laws of England*, 8th ed. (Oxford, 1775), pp. 444–45, quoted in Henry Kelly, *"Rule of Thumb and the Folklore of the Husband's Stick,"* *Journal of Legal Education*, 44 (September, 1994), pp. 351–52. Some feminist theorists have suggested that common law permitted a husband to beat his wife as long as the rod was no wider than the husband's thumb. The origins of this legal "rule of thumb," however, are more complex. It was first popularized, according to Kelly, when the judge who made such a decision was ridiculed in some eighteenth century cartoons. However, American courts (mis)took this phrase to be one based on a dense web of common law, and moved between endorsing and overturning this "precedent" (ibid). See also Ann Jones, *Next Time She'll be Dead* (Boston: Beacon Press, 1994), and Susan Schechter, *Women and Male Violence* (Boston: South End Press, 1982).

[30] 1 M. Hale, *Historia Placitorum Coronas* 628, 629, quoted in Sandra Ryder and Sheryl Kuzmenka, "Legal Rape: The Marital Rape Exemption," *John Marshall Law Review* 24 (Winter, 1991), pp. 394–95; see also O'Donovan, "Sexual Divisions," pp. 119–45; and Robin West, "Equality Theory, Marital Rape, and the Promise of the Fourteenth Amendment," *Florida Law Review* 42 (1990), pp. 45–79. On the engagement of the law in this area, Aryeh Neier says the "law cannot be neutral on this issue. It either protects the victims of rape or it protects the rapist. If the law exempts husbands from rape charges, the implication is that it condones husbands raping wives"; quoted in Ryder and Kuzmenka, p. 419.

[31] "Giving Character to Our Whole Civil Polity: Marriage and the Public Order in the Late Nineteenth Century," in *United States History as Women's History: New Feminist Essays*, ed. Linda Kerber, Alice Kessler-Harris, Kathryn Sklar (Chapel Hill and London: North Carolina University Press, 1995), p. 107.

[32] Cott, "Giving Character," p. 109.

This seems on its face a curious statement. Presumably the state announces its sovereignty everytime it enforces **any** law. Likewise, law is not the only institution in which marriage is relevant. Discourses of economics, religion, and science, for instance, may "prove their existences" when they offer statements on marriage as well. However, the juridical relation to marriage may be distinguished from that of other regulative practices in one highly significant realm: its use in the creation of the state's citizens. Marriage continues, now as before, to reproduce the state in three ways. First, marriage provides the *legitimacy* that renders some children citizens and others aliens. Second, marriage is a *form* of kinship relations that defines the particularity of that state against others. Third, marriage is the bench-mark of *full citizenship*. The juridical privileging of a certain kinship struc-ture marked by marriage—in tax law, health and welfare policy, educational policy and immigration law—continues to render the married couple as the ultimate unit worthy of the fullest political rights. Nancy Cott shows how marriage was crucial to the regulation of race relations and religious affiliation, and as constitutive of the modern state. But rather than simply conclude that the state uses kinship rules for the purposes of establishing membership, Cott emphasizes the impact marriage has on sex roles: "[H]eterosexual marriage" is the "most direct link of public authority to gender formation."[33]

While marriage laws might have legislated inequalities in the nineteenth century, that is no longer the case. Gender neutrality in law seems to be becoming the norm, as many of the more obvious inequalities associated with the status roles of "husband" and "wife" no longer exist. Most states lack any gender-specific language in matters of property ownership, di-vorce, alimony and adultery. Marital rape exemptions have been abolished in at least nineteen states:[34]

> [D]uring the 1970s there were successful attempts in most states to make laws
> gender neutral. Such campaigns were particularly significant in the family law
> area, where gendered rules had been the norm. Feminists concerned with law
> reform considered the push for degendered rules a symbolic imperative, even
> when they recognized that such rules might actually result in removing an
> arguable advantage for women, as in the case of maternal preference rules for
> deciding custody cases.[35]

[33] Ibid., p. 121.

[34] Ryder and Kuzmenka, "Legal Rape," p. 417.

[35] Martha Fineman, *The Illusion of Equality* (Chicago: University of Chicago Press, 1991), p. 80. In her more recent work, Fineman recognizes the "sacred" character of marriage, but sees this as an extension of—not in tension with—the view of the nuclear family as "natural." Fineman thus understands the challenge to the "natural" family as emanating strictly among feminists, and not the Courts and the state, as this chapter contends. Fineman proposes two policy reforms. The first is to "abolish marriage as a legal category"; the second is to privilege

These trends might suggest that the state may be withdrawing from the regulation of marriage. The state's regulation of marriage now appears to be a matter of merely heuristic, and not political, interest, since marriage implies an absence of dynamics of power between husband and wife. The consequences of the state's actions in this realm seem so minimal as to be almost irrelevant. Its interest in marriage seems anachronistic, a display of nostalgia that tells us something about the state's sentimentality—that it even bothers with the practice seems quaint—and little about sexism. The trend suggests that at some point, the state will abandon its hollow echoes of traditions no longer in effect and walk away from regulating marriage.

The gender dynamic that Cott associates with the state does not appear to harm women per se. It disadvantages those people, both male and female, who want state recognition—in the sense of those full political rights—of non-monogamous unions. Would-be polygamists experience discrimination. The status rules marginalize those women, and of course men, who are not White and hence denied the White privileges reproduced through the racialized, nationalist exclusions of birth and marriage criteria for citizenship. Marriage indirectly hurts Black, Latina, and Asian women, but as "minorities" constituted as abject forms of being, and not as women, it might seem. The absence of legal barriers to employment and other opportunities and resources in the United States does not mean this racialized inequality is now "cultural" or merely an expression of accumulated disadvantages. The political spirit that associates non-Whites with historically second-class individuals situates "them" as the exception, the other. "They" are the ex-disenfranchised, whose entitlement is not based on belonging but on someone else including them. In this sense, the political imprint of difference may be indelible. It may fade, but it is always there. Another group clearly affected by sex-specific spousal roles are those in same-sex relations. Same-sex couples are denied spousal employment benefits, social security benefits, marital "privacy" (the courts accord more Fourth Amendment and Fifth Amendment protections for married than unmarried couples), favorable immigration status, and many other "rights" enjoyed by married couples.

All this is to say that it may seem that women are not the ones singled out for oppression when marriage is construed strictly as a relation between husbands-as-men and wives-as-women, as long as both are treated the same in law. Some might argue, for instance, that the exclusion of homosexual marriage from kinship possibilities renders marriage an institution that

---

the "Mother/Child dyad" as a "caregiving family . . . entitled to special, preferred treatment by the state." She adds the caveat that "men could and should be Mothers" and that the Child "stands for all forms of inevitable dependency" (*The Neutered Mother, the Sexual Family, and Other Twentieth Century Tragedies* [New York, London: Routledge, 1995]), pp. 146–47; 155; 172–73, note 36; 228; 230–31; 234–35.

reproduces "heterosexuality" but not necessarily "gender." The state does not determine the content of the female "wife"-s and male "husband"-s roles. Perhaps a fully developed political society has managed to break the logic of what Gayle Rubin calls the "sex/gender system," in which heteronormativity requires women-as-property, for purposes of exchange relations among men.[36] If heterosexuality is institutionalized in a completely egalitarian form, then a certain form of sexuality seems not to entail gendered power relations. Perhaps, then, Cott would be more correct in saying that "[h]eterosexual marriage" is the "most direct link of public authority" to **sexuality** formation, but not, as she claims, to "**gender** formation."[37] If now all that is expected for marriage is a "man" and a "woman," with no other gendered attributes required of these partners, then the state seems not to be filling in the blank of what it means to be a (male) husband and a (female) wife. Any sex-specific roles would seemingly emerge from extra-juridical contexts.

The reason that marriage still constitutes gender difference is that the political statuses "husband" and "wife" are not as identical as they appear. As long as kinship rules exist, this is inevitable. Marriage statutes, as interpreted by the courts, position women as part of nature and men as part of political society. Marriage constitutes men's control over women's labor when it gives "husbands" custody rights that biological fathers per se lack.[38] The state, then, awards men control over the labor of women's bodies (children) by virtue of the political conventions of marriage. When married to a woman, a man is always the legal father of children he conceives with her, and often the presumptive father of any child she bears. Her relation to the child is by birth (natural), while his is by marriage (political). 'Matrimony' is the naming of the mother. This form suggests that mothers are just there, by nature, and it is the legal convention of marriage that constitutes fathers. To paraphrase Sherry Ortner, mothers are to nature as fathers are to politics.[39]

[36] "The Traffic in Women: Notes on the 'Political Economy' of Sex," in *Toward an Anthropology of Women*, ed. Rayna Rapp Reiter (New York: Monthly Review Press, 1975), pp. 157–210.

[37] Cott, "Giving Character," p. 121.

[38] By positioning children as the objects of women's labor, the state defines children as property. Though this contributes to an alienated concept of personality (as children "belong to" their parents, not themselves), that alienation is not the focus of this chapter.

[39] Sherry Ortner, "Is Female to Male as Nature is to Culture?" in *Women, Culture, and Society*, ed. Michelle Rosaldo and Louise Lamphere (Stanford: Stanford University Press, 1974), pp. 67–88. As examples of the devaluation of females, Ortner writes: "female exclusion from a most sacred rite or the highest political council is sufficient evidence." The fact that the state constitutes the sacred quality of marriage, one that excludes women from the sacred position of "husband," similarly situates women in the realm of nature and men in the realm of politics. Ortner writes: "[M]y thesis is that woman is being identified with—or, if you

The politics/nature distinction has sometimes been gendered in an apparently opposite fashion as well. Rousseau's work is an example of this, as was the temperance movement in the late-nineteenth and early-twentieth centuries in the United States. During that period women's and Christian organizations figured the state as an institution that would domesticate the savage sexuality of its male citizens. It was also a "maternalist" institution that would protect its weaker members.[40] Law as a feminine, maternal force underscores the compensatory character of the state's masculinity. This conjunction may suggest that when men appropriate birth, qua "father"-s, their control of birth remains an ultimately feminine, i.e., maternal, activity.[41] They cannot **be** the mother, but through matrimony, they can have her. The state itself, by controlling reproduction, appropriates the reproduction for which mothers are otherwise responsible. The state is at once fatherly (political) and maternal (in charge of birth).[42] In its insistence on controlling marriage, the state positions itself as constitutive of intergenerational forms of being. It is the prerogative of the state to distinguish, and hence to constitute, the difference between what is **profane** (sex as "fornication," children as "illegitimate") and what is **sacred** (sex within marriage, legitimate children).[43] Not just United States custody law, but all kinship systems depend on the negation of mothers. As Kingsley Davis noted, the primary function of kinship systems is to bring men into a relation with children. Political societies reach out to give men authority they would otherwise lack.

A possible revisionist criticism of this view might point to examples of matrilineal societies. That is, some scholars might infer from matrilineal practices that kinship rules do not necessarily subjugate women to men. These matrilineal societies actually might be instances in which a high regard for maternity resulted in a higher status for women than for men.[44]

---

will, seems to be a symbol of—something that every culture defines as being of a lower order of existence than itself." This realm, according to Ortner, is nature, or the profane. But whereas Ortner develops an essentialist argument about women's "natural procreation functions" as the root of this identification, mine is a phenomenological argument about the juridical rendering of this dichotomy.

[40] Theda Skocpol, *Protecting Soldiers and Mothers: The Political Origins of Social Policy in the United States* (Cambridge: Harvard University Press, 1992).

[41] Norman O. Brown makes this point, in *Love's Body* (New York: Random House, 1966).

[42] Another parallel worthy of note is the state's monopoly on the legitimate imposition of death. This appropriation of the power over life and death reflects that maternal relation to her newborn child, who depends on her for survival.

[43] See also Fineman, *Neutered Mother*, pp. 146–47.

[44] These women-as-agent accounts take two forms. One shows instances of matrilineal societies that are also matriarchal; the other re-reads the significance of the roles women play in societies that appear to be juridically dominated by men. For examples of the former, see Ladislav Holy, *Strategies and Norms in a Changing Matrilineal Society* (Cambridge and New York: Cambridge University Press, 1986); Michael Peletz, "The Exchange of Men in

Still, as long as paternity is regulated, and even when **mothers** seem to be at the center of what is sacred, figured as such by matrilineal rules of descent, kinship forms still adversely affect women, because matrilineality has no necessary relation to matriarchy. The main arguments that women have power in these and other contexts are largely heuristic, asserting that we "could" interpret events differently. For instance, Michelle Rosaldo urges that scholars represent women's status as highly variable and contingent. These representations are best suited to challenge the conservatism born from "faith in ultimate and essential truths, a faith sustained in part by cross-cultural evidence of widespread sexual inequality." And yet Rosaldo does little to dispute the observation that sexual inequality *is* universal, noting her own impatience with the "many anthropologists who argue for the privileged place of women here or there." "My reading of the anthropological record," she continues, "leads me to conclude that human cultural and social forms have always been male dominated."[45] To criticize certain representations that seem persuasive, even to the critic, on the grounds that they make inequality seem "natural," is disingenuous. The problem here is a confusion of "universal" with "essential," or "necessary." The solution requires an uncoupling of these terms, not the effacing of certain facts.

Also, as Rosaldo suggests, evidence of matriarchal power is quite weak. Karen Sacks's attention to women's productivity does not contravene the fact that these contributions result in little status for them. Michael Peletz's argument that a "traffic in men" was undertaken by women fails because he does not recognize the significance of men's continued political power, which is never the case for women who are exchanged by men. In societies in which the terms of kinship and all other functions of the community are controlled by men, the bare fact that wealth goes through the line of the mother does not speak to the relative power of women. The very fact that paternity exists for men already figures mothers as relational (to husbands) and not autonomous.

Malinowski's oft-quoted statement on paternity is instructive:

The most important moral and legal rule concerning the physiological side of kinship is that no child should be brought into this world without a man—and

---

19th-century Negeri Sembilan (Malaya)," *American Ethnologist* 14 (3) (August, 1987), pp. 449–69; and Karla Poewe, *Matrilineal Ideology: Male-Female Dynamics in Luapula, Zambia* (London and New York: Academic Press, 1981). The latter, by far the more popular approach, includes Eleanor Burke Leacock, *Myths of Male Dominance: Collected Articles on Women Cross-Culturally* (New York and London: Monthly Review Press, 1981); Sherry Ortner, "Gender Hegemonies," *Cultural Critique* 14 (Winter, 1989–90), pp. 35–80; Michelle Rosaldo, "The Use and Abuse of Anthropology: Reflections on Feminism and Cross-Cultural Understanding," *Signs* 5(3), (1980), pp. 389–417; Karen Sacks, *Sisters and Wives: The Past and Future of Sexual Equality* (Westport, London: Greenwood Press, 1979).

[45] Rosaldo, "Use and Abuse," p. 393.

one man at that—assuming the role of sociological father, that is, guardian and protector, the male link between the child and the rest of the world.[46]

The passage is of interest because it is not true, and yet, despite a vast amount of evidence to the contrary, views such as Malinkowski's remain widely held. Anthropologists writing before and after his classic essay have presented numerous counter-examples. In the article immediately following Malinowski's, in the same book, V. F. Calverton observes that the "Votyaks honor the illegitimate mother," and "[a]mong the Nandi a girl cannot marry until she has born at least one illegitimate child."[47] Further, Evans-Pritchard has shown that among the Nuer, a husband may be another woman. He writes:

> What seems to us, but not at all to Nuer, a somewhat strange union is that in which a woman marries another woman and counts as the pater of the children born of the wife. Such marriages are by no means uncommon in Nuerland, and they must be regarded as a form of simple legal marriage, for the woman-husband marries her wife in exactly the same way as a man marries a woman.[48]

The requirement of an illegitimate child violates the notion that societies value a recognized tie between a father and his genetic child. The requirement of illegitimacy indicates that the control of mothers takes many forms, and that it is universally a major project of a political society to instruct its members on these practices.

Any kinship system exists in relation to an otherwise unregulated process of reproduction. That is, kinship suggests the possibility of species reproduction absent kinship. Marking the activity as subject to certain distinctions imposed by a political society bestows certain meanings on these practices. When a political society takes charge of maternity, it performs associations between the maternal and the natural, not because kinship systems are necessary, but rather because they serve certain purposes that seem necessary but on closer inspection are not. Kingsley Davis and others have insisted on the opposite, Davis maintaining that "reproduction can be carried out in a socially useful manner only if it is performed in conformity with institutional patterns."[49] Elsewhere Davis writes that "every family is actually a biological group," but after noting tremendous variation among kinship forms, he observes, "The structure of the human family is rooted not in biology, but in the folkways and mores."[50] One way to reconcile these claims is to note, as Davis does, that the human species is

---

[46] Malinowski, "Parenthood," *New Generation: The Intimate Problems of Modern Parents and Children*, ed. V. F. Calverton (New York: Macauley, 1930), p. 137.

[47] "The Illegitimate Child," in *New Generation*, p. 201.

[48] *Kinship and Marriage among the Nuer* (Oxford: Clarendon Press, 1951), p. 108.

[49] Davis, "Illegitimacy and Social Structure," *American Journal of Sociology* 45 (1939), p. 259.

[50] Davis, *Human Society* (New York: MacMillan, 1949), pp. 387, 399.

one that "interbreeds" and so, depending on the remoteness of ties one traces, it can be said that we are "all biologically related," which simply illustrates the uselessness of biological arguments about kinship. If biology means we are all interrelated, then it cannot be the basis of kinship forms that establish an "us" distinct from "them."

Why is reproduction regulated by political societies per se? One argument, put in practice in Rome and in modern Italy, Germany, and the nineteenth-century United States (among other places), is that augmenting the legal family unit will increase the population.[51] The so-called "bachelor taxes" under Augustine and current tax credits for children born to married couples associate marriage with species reproduction. Yet other writers construed marriage as an impediment to reproduction. Eighteenth-century French thinkers argued that one way to increase the population was to make divorce easier and marriage generally less restrictive.[52]

It is true that reproduction is necessary for the species to survive. It is not true that reproduction must be gendered. Many activities are necessary for humanity's sustenance. People need shelter, food, and water. The production and collection of all of these has been in certain places and times gendered. Why is it more difficult to imagine that yam collection need not be gendered than that child production need not be gendered? Just as yam collection may be but need not be associated with kinship roles, the same holds true for childbirth. Rules specifying roles in kinship systems themselves mark these practices as gendered. They do not follow from something like the-practice-in-itself. Kinship regulations are not in place because of "givens" such as human nature or biology.

We regulate kinship because of beliefs such as this:

> We have seen that throughout history civilizations that have allowed the traditional bonds of family to be weakened—those civilizations have not survived. America has, and always should be, a nation that prioritizes traditional family values and the tradition of a one man and one woman marriage.[53]

Yet of course weakened civilizations have died, but the human species survived well enough for Rep. Ron Packard to cast his vote. The marriage form exists to maintain ongoing political communities, not humanity itself. It is not a coincidence that Packard invokes both history and the tradition

---

[51] In Rome, "all celibates above . . . a certain age" and all widowers who did not remarry could not inherit or receive legacies. "Similar penalties were imposed upon married but childless persons, while to those who had children, especially three or more, quicker advancement in their public careers was offered" (Cary and Scullard, *A History of Rome Down to the Reign of Constantine*, 3d ed. [London: MacMillan, 1975], p. 328).

[52] Traer, *Marriage and the Family in Eighteenth Century France* (Ithaca: Cornell University Press, 1980), pp. 57–59.

[53] Congressman Ron Packard (R-Oceanside), Press Release, July 11, 1995.

of marriage to make his arguments. Marriage in the United States assures the preservation of a U.S. American intergenerational identity, without which there will be humans, but not U.S. Americans, and therefore no U.S. American history. A group must be confident that it will stretch into the future in order to know that it may look back, if its history is to be secure. Only a small fraction of the groups mentioned in the Hebrew Bible or various texts by Herodotus survive as such today. What is the history of the Temanites? The Halicarnassians? Even as we know who some of these groups became, the merging has meant, for the Temanites and the Halicarnassians, the same loss of national identity as that experienced earlier this century by women who married aliens. The Temanites vanish into the Yemenites.

Family Court

It is through the operation of marriage law that particular political societies reproduce as such. In the United States the marital status of "husband-father" trumps a biological father's claim to his children, and it also trumps a mother's "natural" status—as the laws on surrogacy, discussed below, make clear. A woman's right to make decisions about her children is substantially undermined if she is married to the father. Not biological paternity but marriage creates this form of dependence for her.

Insofar as the courts associate women with nature, the state's articulations of the maternal relationship appropriate and displace this feminine status. Luce Irigaray writes:

> Historically, the obligation for women, to give birth to children within their husbands' genealogy corresponds to the beginnings of *non-respect for nature*, to the establishment of a notion or concept of nature that is substituted for the fertility of the earth . . . Paradoxically, the cult of the mother often goes hand in hand, in our cultures, with scorn for or neglect of nature.[54]

Explicitly and in the more nuanced metonymic associations that follow from its interventions, the state's control of reproduction through marriage disempowers mothers by associating them with a view of nature that is itself constituted by the grammar of the dichotomy of political society/nature imposed by the very form of political societies.

The court decisions most constitutive as well as illustrative of the politicization of fatherhood consider child, really infant, custody. In these cases, which include surrogacy cases, adoption cases, and cases of artificial

[54] "The Necessity for Sexuate Rights," in *The Irigaray Reader*, ed. Margaret Whitford (Oxford and Cambridge: Blackwell, 1991), p. 200.

insemination, the biological parents are not married.[55] According to most statutes and court decisions, when parents are unmarried, and when the father has demonstrated no interest in either the mother or the pregnancy, the mother has the prerogative to determine whether to allow the child to be adopted. The permission of the father is not required. Apparent exceptions to this rule are emerging, although all are cases in which the father has shown an interest in the pregnancy and in the child. In these cases the courts have named an equivalence between the mother who bears a child and the father who, for instance, establishes a trust fund in the child's name. On this basis, biological fathers have custody rights similar to those of married fathers. In all of these cases the state holds the prerogative not simply to enforce "the law," nor to use the law to enforce contracts and status relations decided in civil society. Rather, the state assigns status. "Wife," "Husband," "Father," and "Mother" are all state creations. As Judge Montgomery said: "We know what a child is. But what is a father, mother, or parent? It is time to redefine such once simple words from a perspective of the law. . . . [W]hat exactly *is* a daddy? Is it a noun or a verb?"[56]

In addressing similar questions the courts have established the following system of custody rights. Marriage statutes are largely the work of state legislatures, which means they vary, but every state has laws defining marriage.[57]

In their decisions the courts have established certain equivalences among different status relations. In *Caban v. Mohammed* 441 U.S. 380 (1979), a

---

[55] See *Child Custody and the Politics of Gender*, ed. Carol Smart and Selma Sevenhuijsen (London and New York: Routledge, 1989). Smart points out that the rhetoric on the child's need for the father aligns the father and child against the mother: "The more men's interests and children's interests are seen to coincide, the more mothers are disempowered" (p. 10); Nancy Erikson, "The Feminist Dilemma over Unwed Parents' Custody Rights," *Law and Inequality* 2 (1984), pp. 447–72; Kathryn Katz, "Ghost Mothers: Human Egg Donation and the Legacy of the Past," *Albany Law Review* 57 (1994), pp. 733–80. For a review of cases focused on problems of illegitimacy, see Martha Zingo and Kevin Early, *Nameless Persons: Legal Discrimination Against Non-Marital Children in the United States* (Westport and London: Praeger, 1994).

[56] "Child Abuse and Changing Definitions," address at the annual meeting of the Child Abuse and Neglect Committee, published in *Texas Bar Journal*, 57 (September, 1994), p. 886.

[57] One difference is the person or organization designated to signify that a wedding has been performed. Most states require a religious official or state magistrate; but some states exclude certain minister-by-mail "denominations." A few allow anyone to sign the form. Also, some of what follows is taken from state supreme court opinions, and these also reveal discrepancies. When it is relevant, I have provided information on the frequency of certain policies, such as surrogacy laws. These decisions are on cases the courts themselves deem "unique," "exceptional," or "unusual," and so one might wonder whether they help us understand the daily practices of most citizens. However, it is law that renders these situations marginal, not the parental disputes per se; without marriage law there is no "unique" marriage arrangement. In prompting a careful consideration of the "logic" of marriage rules, these cases provide insights that otherwise normalized understandings of marriage preclude.

Biological Fathers' Rights to Custody

	Father has custody rights	Father lacks custody rights
Biological parents unmarried, father does not contribute financially or show legal interest in pregnancy[a]		X
Biological parents unmarried and father contributes financially and shows interest during pregnancy[b]	X	
Biological parents unmarried and father shows financial and emotional commitment to child, but mother's husband wants custody[c]		X
Biological parents married and father shows no commitment to child and provides no financial support[d]	X	

[a] *Lehr v. Robertson*, 463 U.S. 248 (1983); *Caban v. Mohammed*, 441 U.S. 380 (1979); *re Adoption of Reams* 557 N.E.2d 159 (1989).

[b] *Abernathy v. Baby Boy*, 437 S.E. 2d 25 (1993); Michael Azzariti, "Domestic Law," *South Carolina Law Review* 46 (1994), pp. 48–54; Norman Allen, "*Adoption of Kelsey S.:* When Does an Unwed Father Know Best?" *Pacific Law Journal*, 24 (1993), pp. 1633–1680.

[c] *Michael H. v. Gerald D.* 491 U.S. 110 (1989).

[d] This is the presumption that inheres in the "best interest" standard, Weitzman, p.49; see also *re: Matter of Baby M.* 537 A.2d 1227 (1988).

frequently cited decision, the majority ruled that paternity per se does not entail custody rights: "The mother carries and bears the child, and in this sense her parental relation is clear. The validity of the father's claim must be gauged by other measures. By tradition, the primary measure has been the legitimate familial relationship he creates with the child by marriage with the mother."[58] In *Lehr v. Robertson*, 463 U.S. 248 (1982) the Court ruled that the "mere existence of a biological link" does not merit protection of paternal rights, so that an unwed mother may allow her child to be adopted without the father's consent.[59] Only her consent, and that of her husband, if any, is required.

[58] E.g., *Caban v. Mohammed* 441 U.S. 380, 397 (1979), cited in *Lehr v. Robertson* 463 U.S. 248, 260 (1983).

[59] *Lehr.* States vary in requirements of paternal consent. In New York consent is not required, a law that Lehr said deprived him of a fundamental right. The Court disagreed.

The mother's biological link to the child is assumed to be of a different character. Hence the Court did not recognize that her unmarried status yielded an equal protection claim for an unmarried father. The defense of this position is that the mother, not the father, has a "continuous custodial responsibility."[60] In this case the mother had this responsibility because she did not allow the father to visit or to assume any other responsibility. According to the facts of the dissenting opinion, Lehr visited the hospital when the baby, Jessica, was born and tried to maintain contact. However, after the mother was released from the hospital, she "threatened Lehr with arrest unless he stayed away and refused to permit him to see Jessica."[61] The majority discounted Lehr's interest because it did not take the proper, i.e., legal, form, which required him to follow New York guidelines for signing up on the "putative father registry."[62] The dissent emphasizes the importance of the biological tie and the actual interest shown,[63] while the majority emphasizes the importance of sticking to the rules—holding that the state, not biology or personal desire, constitutes the family.

The importance of the marriage tie is announced in *re Adoption of Reams* 557 N.E. 2d 159 (1989) and other surrogacy situations that require the surrogate *husband*'s consent before the child may be declared that of the biological father.[64] As the court stated in *Reams*, "[L]egal parentage, not to be confused with biological parentage, must be established before the issuance of custody can properly be decided. . . . "[65] The husband of the

[60] *Lehr* at 267–68. In two high profile custody disputes in the 1990s the "return" of children to biological parents was ordered only after the father established the marital status of "husband" to the mother. These were cases in which biological fathers were initially unaware that they had children. Had the fathers simply claimed that they had not been informed and that they wanted the respective children, they would have had no standing. Karl Clausen had to marry the biological mother before he could file his custody claim. *Re: Baby Girl Clausen*, 1993 (No. 96366, Nos. 96411, 96531, 96532), text from LEXIS (© Reed Elsevier Inc.) on-line database.

[61] *Lehr* at 269.

[62] *Lehr* at 248.

[63] *Lehr* at 268–76.

[64] As of 1992, 18 states had some regulations of surrogacy practices. Of these, 11 explicitly voided surrogacy contracts; 4 allowed surrogacy contracts, but held the surrogate's husband as the putative father, so that his consent for adoption was necessary; one made the father the legal parent (Arkansas); and one simply said that surrogacy contracts should not be considered "child selling" (West Virginia). I have relied for these numbers on the information provided in the appendix of Alice Hofheimer, "Gestational Surrogacy: Unsettling State Parentage Law and Surrogacy Policy," *New York University Review of Law and Social Change*, 19 (1992), pp. 613–16. The states voiding the contracts have the same implications as those requiring the husband's consent for adoption, since if the contract is not recognized, the husband will be considered the legal father.

[65] *re Adoption Reams* 557 N.E. 2d 159 (1989) at 162.

inseminated woman is, in all but one or two states,[66] legally the father. This has been held when either the father/sperm donor wants custody,[67] or the mother wants to arrange adoption without paternal consent.[68] The apparent state interest here is in the protection of the husband's custody rights over his wife's children, against those of a biological father.

In the case of *Reams*, where a woman was artificially inseminated with sperm belonging to neither the prospective adoptive father nor her own husband, her husband's consent was necessary for the adoption to proceed: "even though Norma Stotski [biological mother] and Leslie Miner [biological father] executed consent forms which they thought to be valid, neither could relinquish legal custody of Tessa to Mr. Reams through the adoption process" because "Mr. Stotski, by virtue of the fact that he is married to Norma Lee Stotski, **shall be treated in law and regarded as the natural parent** of Tessa Reams. Thus, it is Mr. Stotski's consent, in addition to Mrs. Stotski's consent, that is required to effectuate an adoption of Tessa Reams."[69] The biological father's consent is irrelevant.[70] By dubbing political men ("husbands") "natural fathers" when recognizing someone else is the biological father, the state commits a telling semantic mistake. On the one hand, the courts maintain that a political relation is always, in marriage law, privileged over a natural one. On the other hand, the courts regard this legal status as "natural." The courts constitute this privileged relation by naming those who are husbands (fathers by law) as "natural." Legal "husband-fathers" have the recognition that natural "natural-fathers" lack.

In *Michael H. v. Gerald D.* 491 U.S. 110 (1989), in which Michael D. inseminated Carol, who was separated from her husband, Gerald, Michael and Carol signed a statement stipulating that "Michael was Victoria's natural father." After she reconciled with her husband, Carol "instructed her attorneys not to file the stipulation."[71] Michael, supported by a court-appointed advocate for the daughter Victoria, sought visitation rights and was granted them, until Gerald intervened on the grounds that as the

---

[66] Arkansas law is clear on this, but the statute in New Hampshire is not. On the one hand, it says that the husband is the putative father, but on the other hand, it says that "the paternity presumption is rebuttable" (ibid, p. 615). This seems to suggest an easy case for a biological father with a paternity test, but marriage trumps the "rebuttable presumption."

[67] *Matter of Baby M.*

[68] *Lehr.*

[69] *Reams* at 165, 164, emphasis added.

[70] The Uniform Parentage Act, adopted by eighteen states as of 1993, says: "If, under the supervision of a licensed physician and with the consent of her husband, a wife is inseminated with semen donated by a man not her husband, the husband is treated in law as if he were the natural father of a child thereby conceived." quoted in Hollace Swanson, "Donor Anonymity in Artificial Insemination: Is it Still Necessary?" *Columbia Journal of Law and Social Problems* 27, (fall, 1993), p. 162.

[71] *Michael H. V. Gerald D.* 491 U.S. 110 (1989) 115.

husband he was the "presumptive father." Michael had no grounds on which to file for visitation rights.[72] The United States Supreme Court decision begins, "California law, like nature itself, makes no provision for dual fatherhood."[73] This being the case, the Court must decide who the father will be. This is purely a status decision, one in which individual rights cannot be pressed until one subject position achieves a legal, not natural, recognition.

The question before the Court, then, is who is the father? The husband or the father? The answer: the husband. The reason is, according to Justice Scalia, for centuries our laws have protected the custody claims and responsibilities of husbands and ignored those of biological fathers.[74] Elaborating on the family rights "traditionally protected by our society," Scalia writes:

> The family unit accorded traditional respect in our society, which we have referred to as the 'unitary family,' is typified, of course by the marital family, but also includes the households of unmarried parents and their children. Perhaps the concept will be expanded even beyond this, but it will bear no resemblance to traditionally respected relationships—and thus will cease to have any constitutional significance if it is stretched so far as to include the relationship established between a married woman, her lover, and their child during a three-month period when, if he happened to be in Los Angeles, he stayed with her and the child.[75]

That "nothing in older cases" suggests the "power of a natural father to assert parental rights over a child born into a woman's existing marriage with another man" requires that Michael note other places in which this power is "so deeply embedded within our traditions as to be a fundamental right. . . . "[76] Scalia finds none.

The majority argument advances in three steps. First, Scalia asserts that a child may have only one father—the biological one or the legal one. Second, Scalia assesses the different rights at issue for the biological father, as opposed to those of the husband: "Here, to *provide* protection to an adulterous natural father is to *deny* protection to a marital father, and vice-

[72] The California statute reads: "[T]he issue of a wife cohabiting with her husband, who is not impotent or sterile, is conclusively presumed to be a child of the marriage." Cal. Evid. Code Ann. Para. 621a. Michael's case was dismissed when Gerald was ruled the father, on the grounds that to do otherwise would "impugn the integrity of the family unit." Supp. App. to Juris. Statement, A–91, quoted in *Michael*, 115. Michael appealed on the grounds that this decision violated his procedural and substantive due process rights, and was supported by Victoria's advocate, *Michael*, 115, 116.

[73] *Michael*, 115.

[74] *Michael*, note 3.

[75] *Michael*, note 3.

[76] *Michael*, 123, 124.

versa. If Michael has a 'freedom not to conform' (whatever that means), Gerald must equivalently have a 'freedom to conform.' "[77] Third, a legal choice must be made, even when it is conceded that "multiple fatherhood" would be most beneficial to the child: "[W]hatever the merits of the guardian ad litem's belief that such an arrangement can be of great psychological benefit to a child, the claim that a State must recognize multiple fatherhood has no support in the history or traditions of this country."[78]

The child advocate believes such a ruling would deny Victoria a relationship with her biological father that "legitimate" children enjoy. This, held the guardian, would deny her right to equal protection. This claim is rebutted by Scalia: "Illegitimacy is a legal construct, not a natural trait," and under California law Victoria is "legitimate" (the daughter of her mother's husband). In other words, the "natural" relation of paternity can be overridden by a legal definition. The Court develops a self-consuming argument in which biological paternity (natural) is the model of "single fatherhood." This determines the necessity of a single legal father. Once in place, the natural father model is trumped by the legal father model.

In this country the state's interest in regulating birth through marriage appears to require rules that denigrate women's control and that discriminate against same-sex couples. Only heterosexual marriage guarantees paternal rights. The very representation of a mother's "natural" relation with the infant requires a legal system that performs a comparable relation for the husband, if paternity is to be politically institutionalized. The effect of this is to sacralize paternity in comparison with the apparent materiality and determinacy of maternity. The singularity of the totem—of the Durkheimean nation-state and the paternal name—requires exclusions. If women could marry women and men marry men, or if a plurality of forms of parenting were recognized, then gendered paternity would have no privileged place in law, and hence no privileged place in our kinship system.

The history of patrilineality suggests that fatherhood in an ongoing family line is extremely important in this society. Preventing same-sex couples from marrying affirms the sex-specificity in the husband and wife relation and hence the sacred character of the husband-father's relation to the child. If roles were not sex-specific, the kinship system as a whole would produce sacred/profane membership rules. As is the case among the Nuer, the sex-specific "husband-father" would not be among them. A husband might be a woman. Another way to think about this is that "paternity" suggests exclusions, as do all relations. The "father" requires the "not-father." If this father is to be sacred for males, associated with

[77] *Michael*, 130.
[78] *Michael*, 130.

masculinity per se, then husbands—the sacral fathers—must be men. Were women eligible to become husbands, the determinacy of the gender (marital role)/sex (who gives birth) mapping fades. Again, there is no biological basis for this rule of exclusion; it is part of the same system that places the paternity rights of husbands over those of fathers.

Marriage law in this country may change, and the change may begin in Hawaii. The arguments that proved successful in *Baehr v. Lewin*, 852 P.2d 44 (1993) were the same ones that failed in other states. One possible explanation for the different results for the same arguments is that Hawaii has a fairly recent experience with non-Christian marriage roles and practices. Although the Christian missionaries have left their mark and many in Hawaii oppose same-sex marriage, the Sovereign People's movement has endorsed the possibility of same-sex marriages on the grounds that this was "traditional" to the pre-colonial peoples of Hawaii. In *Baehr* the court held that same-sex couples should be allowed to apply for marriage licenses, that "husband" and "wife" need not be sex-specific roles—unless the state could prove that the "sex-based classification is justified by compelling state interests and the statute is narrowly drawn to avoid unnecessary abridgements of the applicant couples' constitutional rights."[79] The court drew on the state's Equal Rights Amendment, holding that if a man could be a husband, then it might well be unconstitutional discrimination to prevent women from applying to be husbands as well, and vice-versa. The State Attorney General is appealing this ruling, attempting to show that Hawaii has a "compelling interest" in maintaining its current marriage laws, so same-sex marriages are still prohibited,[80] but the responses to the possibility are instructive. Numerous state legislatures are considering or have passed laws that prohibit recognition of same-sex marriages performed elsewhere. These will invite Constitutional scrutiny, since the Full Faith and Credit section in the U.S. Constitution has been interpreted to require states to recognize marriages performed in other states. The possibility that the legalization of marriage in Hawaii might have implications for the nation has prompted Rev. Lou Sheldon of the Traditional Values Coalition to call for amending the Constitution: " 'If you destroy the heterosexual ethic, then you are destroying a major pillar of Western civilization' "—a move, he threatens, that may prompt conservatives to

---

[79] *Baehr* at 59, 60. For an analysis of the history and possibilities of same-sex marriage law, see Paula Ettelbrick, "Wedlock Alert: A Comment on Lesbian and Gay Family Recognition," *Journal of Law and Policy*, 5 (1), (1996), pp. 107–66.

[80] On November 3, 1998, Hawaiians voted to amend the state constitution to specify that the legislature has the power to reserve marriage to different-sex couples; however, the *Baehr* case is still in litigation.

attempt to "strike down the 'full faith and credit' provision of the U.S. Constitution."[81]

Is the United States so frail that same-sex marriage would prompt its demise, not to mention that of Western civilization? Why does Rev. Sheldon care about this, anyway, so long as he is free to take advantage of the First Amendment and save those unfortunate souls who might be enticed to pursue same-sex relations? After all, recognizing same-sex marriage at best makes this contract a possibility, not a requirement, so that religious leaders are as free as they ever were to proselytize and in this way save Western civilization. The reproducing state has an enormous investment in controlling kinship rules; further, religious leaders, too, avail themselves of kinship rhetorics in a manner that is both auxiliary to and in tension with the dialectics of political society and family. It is this last point that Chapter 6 explores.

[81] Quoted in Elaine Herscher, "When Marriage Is a Tough Proposal," *San Francisco Chronicle*, May 15, 1995, A1, A10.

Six

The Religious Future

> And God said to him, "Your name is Jacob; no
> longer shall you be called Jacob, but Israel shall
> be your name." So his name was Israel. And God
> said to him, "I am God Almighty: be fruitful and
> multiply; a nation and a company of nations shall
> come from you, and kings shall spring from you.
> The land which I gave to Abraham and Isaac I
> will give to you, and I will give the land to your
> descendants after you."[1]

> Tell us, then, what you think. Is it lawful to pay
> taxes to Caesar, or not? . . . "Show me the
> money for the tax." And they brought him a
> coin. And Jesus said to them, "Whose likeness
> and inscription is this?" They said "Caesar's."
> And Jesus said to them, "Render therefore to
> Caesar the things that are Caesar's, and to God
> the things that are God's."[2]

RELIGIOUS forms of being seem to have much in common with those of
nation, ethnicity, and race. Indeed, at times it seems all these strands of

---

[1] Unlike my practice in the previous chapters, all Bible passages in this chapter are quoted
from the Holy Bible, revised standard version, from the University of Virginia's Electronic
Text Library.

The passage above is from Genesis 35:10–11 (etcbin/toccer-new?id=RsvGene2&
images=images/modeng&data=/lv2/english/relig/rsv&tag=public&part=35&division=div). I
quote this entire web-site location to document the newly impermanent semiotics of information, because, as I discuss below, the form of the original, inalterable written page is a
hallmark of religious doctrine, while electronic texts are notable for the ease by which they
may be simultaneously revised and re-circulated to large international audiences. In the past,
oral traditions would change their stories, but often slowly. Modern telecommunications
make possible changes that are instantaneous. Also, as is the case for, say, radio or television
broadcasts, this enables their obliteration, as the image is here one instant and gone the
next. Cybertexts of letters are also immediate, but still offer the form of authority and
authenticity (parasitic on the printed word), and yet they may easily disintegrate or change.
Hence, to follow the cyber-impulse of Donna Haraway's imagination, present/future forms
of communication through electronic media may unsettle the possibility of regarding the
content of the information conveyed with the reverence now associated with religious texts.

[2] Matthew 22:17–21.

affiliation run together into one inseparable clump, such that the respective forms of being are intertwined: the Buddhist Asian Japanese, the Catholic European Irish, the Muslim Arab Egyptian. While the Introduction through Chapter 5 have shown that the interconnections of family, nation, ethnicity, race, and gender share a political theoretical logic of ancestral ties and invocations of birth, this chapter argues that religious affiliations should be conceptualized quite differently. The religious form of affiliation bears a family resemblance to these other affiliations, while expressing its differences in direct, albeit oppositional, tandem with them. It is precisely the materialist, propertarian logic of political society's family form against which religious commitments and institutions develop, "so that, he who marries his betrothed does well; and he who refrains from marriage will do better,"[3] to quote one from among innumerable religious texts that privilege celibacy over family as the true sign of religious devotion, in some cases even when one is married.

Unlike membership in the neighborhood bridge club, the religious form of group membership speaks in clear counterpoint to the ancestral rhythms of the nation, ethnicity, race, and family roles. The bridge club has nothing to do with ancestral forms. Strictly religious groups—to be distinguished from religious-political amalgamations with overt political investments (discussed below)—stand in a direct challenge to family ties. The main distinction between ancestral and religious forms is that the former exist by virtue of the past, whereas one comes to religion through attempting a relationship to the future. Of course such a motion implies its opposite, which is to say that just as a nation concerns itself with the future when it attempts to reproduce the past—to preserve and carry forth the terms of its imagined birth—religion is intricately engaged with ancestral forms of membership. In its purest form religious opposition to political society is not that of hostility toward the government (though that may be present as well) but is characterized by religions' always-present, if tacit, simple effacement of the familial ties that make possible nations, races, and family roles.

Perhaps the best evidence that religious discourses concern death and the future are not the rants of their followers, but rather the ravings of the reluctant insane. I quote from the memoir of a psychotic atheist not only to illustrate the ways that Daniel Paul Schreber associates the end of the world with God, which is telling in itself, but to contextualize questions about religion in a framework that elaborates tensions between individual quirks, individual faith, mass delusion, and mass faith[4]:

---

[3] I Corinthians 7:38.

[4] This is all to say that we would be well-advised to be circumspect as to the ease of distinguishing the believer from the lunatic. Freud ends his account of Schreber's case as

Other rays [that had permeated Schreber's consciousness] ... carried names such as 'the Lord of Hosts', 'the Good Shepherd', 'the Almighty', etc. etc. Connected with these phenomena, very early on there predominated in recurrent nightly visions the notion of an approaching **end of the world**, as a consequence of the indissoluble connection between God and myself.[5]

Schreber has made a mistake, one that most will have avoided. God will not end the world due to Schreber's resistance (or acquiescence) to the rays' sexual advances. Yet the terms of Schreber's distress are familiar ones—the Lord of the Hosts, the Good Shepherd, the Almighty—embraced by the devout and regarded as mistaken as Schreber's persecution fantasies by atheists. The institutions that sustain religious practices, I want to suggest, exist by virtue of a grammar that requires certain shared beliefs that are not natural in the form of their acceptance (as are contemporary ideas about the family, for instance), but still viewed as necessary, by virtue of the always-present imminence of death.[6] While the experience of birth generates intergenerational forms of being of nationality, ethnicity, and race, the recognition of death is responsible for religion.

Just a Millenerian Computer Glitch?[7]

It was in the year 5735 or 35, depending on whether the calendar in use was a Hebrew one or that of the Atomic Era,[8] when Stanley Oscar Brown started eating his Kozy Kitten cat (and people) food at work in Florida. Brown said that eating cat food was part of his "personal religious creed" and that "Kozy Kitten People/Cat Food ... is contributing significantly to [his] state of well being ... and therefore to [his] overall work perfor-

---

follows: "It remains for the future to decide whether there is more delusion in my theory than I should like to admit, or whether there is more truth in Schreber's delusion than other people are as yet prepared to believe" ("Psycho-analytic Notes on an Autobiographical Account of a Case of Paranoia [Dementia Paranoides]" [1911], *Standard Edition*, tr. James Strachey, vol. 12 [London: Hogarth Press, 1958], p. 79).

[5] Daniel Paul Schreber, *Memoirs of My Nervous Illness*, tr. and ed. Ida Macalpine and Richard Hunter (1903; rpt. London: W. M. Dawson, 1955), p. 84, emphasis in original. Schreber was a highly ranked German politician in the late nineteenth century. He resided, against his will, in mental institutions for several years following episodes of delusional behavior. Schreber thought his "nervous illness" (Nervenkranken) a consequence of his resistance to God (the rays) attempting to impregnate him, and recorded his experiences. Schreber's *Memoir* was the case study Freud used to establish the belief that sexual disorders are the root of psychosis.

[6] That these views are widely held can be confirmed, at least in a preliminary fashion, by their illogical reiteration by the psychotic.

[7] For the past few years computer experts have been warning of massive computer failures, as software unable to accommodate the impending 00 of the year 2000 will crash.

[8] http://www.panix.com/~wlinden/calendar.shtm

mance"[9] by "increasing his energy."[10] Perhaps the Israelites would take umbrage. Cat food, simply by virtue of being "cat food," is not kosher, but Oscar Brown had a different religion, and Kozy Kitten food it was. Alas, his co-workers would have preferred the cat-food averse Oscar Mayer (who was Jewish). The boss, however, told Brown the concern was about his noxious behavior, not his efficiency. Brown was told to stop eating the Kozy Kitten food, but he stood by his principles and was fired. That is when Brown went to work. First he filed a claim with the Equal Employment Opportunity Commission (EEOC), and when that was dismissed, he went to court.

Kozy Kitten cat food is produced by the H. J. Heinz Corporation, which produces many other foodstuffs, including Heinz 57 Ketchup (sometimes used to imitate human or animal blood for Halloween parties and in films). Brown was fired not for eating a Heinz product, but for eating a Heinz product labeled as "cat food." The label had to be a mistake, though. Stanley Oscar Brown, a person, was happily eating the stuff, which is why he referred to it in his letter to the EEOC as "Kozy Kitten People/Cat Food." He might also have had in mind that "Kozy Kitten" is partly a person. The Kozy Kitten Corporation is part of the H. J. Heinz Corporation, and a corporation is a person. According to the United States government, "The term 'person' includes one or more individuals, governments, governmental agencies, political subdivisions, labor unions, partnerships, associations, **corporations**, legal representatives, mutual companies, joint stock companies, trusts, unincorporated organizations, trustees, trustees in cases under Title 11, or receivers."[11] If a corporation is a person, then Kozy Kitten Corporation is a person. That would make Kozy Kitten both food and a person, so maybe that is why Brown called it "people food," though for Brown's purposes it is probably a good thing that the court did not think Kozy Kitten a person. If the court that heard Brown's case thought for a second that Brown was eating a person instead of cat food, then perhaps it would have treated Brown's case as a serious one. Instead the court found that his "appeal *sub judice* is frivolous," and that cat food consumption was not a protected religious activity. But if Brown could have shown that his cat-food eating was required by certain religious dietary rules, then he would have had a legal chance to continue eating his preferred lunch. It is perfectly fine to fire someone because one is repulsed by humans eating cat food, but only when the motive is secular, not religious, disgust.

At the same time, if a person acts based on religious beliefs, then others cannot interfere by threatening loss of employment. Brown might have

---

[9] *Brown v. Pena*, 441 F. Supp. 1382 (1977).
[10] *Brown* at 1384.
[11] 42 U.S.C. Chapter 21, 2000e.

cited John Locke, who wrote that magistrates cannot "compel anyone to his religion . . . because no man can so far abandon the care of his own salvation as blindly to leave to the choice of any other, whether prince or subject, to prescribe to him what faith or worship he shall embrace."[12] Title VII of the 1964 Civil Rights Act states the same thing: "It shall be an unlawful practice for an employer to fail or refuse to hire or discharge any individual, or otherwise to discriminate against any individual with respect to his compensation, terms, conditions, or privileges of employment, because of such individual's race, color, religion, sex, or national origin." Following this reasoning, Brown drafted his own letter on toleration and submitted it to the Florida EEOC.

30 years before La Prime 1-358-557, the date that results when one subtracts Gregorian years from the Galactic Mileau calendar, Brown received a discouraging response. The Miami District Office said that Brown had "failed to establish a religious belief generally accepted as a religion."[13] Maybe Stanley Brown was a Christian, and the court found no evidence that Christians had to eat Kozy Kitten cat/people food, or, possibly Brown was without any religion. Maybe Brown was just goofing around, eating his cat food and pretending to be religious.

Religious Differences

The sections below review the ways that religion is distinguished in United States statutory and constitutional law from the ancestral forms of the various groups discussed in the previous chapters. I move among the contemporary legal discourse on religions, and their foundational texts, and current understandings among contemporary adherents and scholars, so as to connect various experiences of religion with its legal status. By seeing how **behaviors** are emphasized in religious cases and texts, while the nominal **identity** of a form of being is at stake for cases of discrimination on grounds of sex, race, ethnicity, and nationality, one can understand the ways that religious affiliations differ from those that depend on intergenerationality.

Alone among the list of "suspect classifications" in the United States statutory code, a religion is the only one that one easily might not even have. One's race, color, sex, or national origin might be ambiguous, but to be persuasive about lacking any of these would be a noteworthy event. Even when classifications are liminal and contested, the parties do not argue that they do not have these identities at all, but rather that their identities are ones other than what the government or citizens recognize.

---

[12] "Letter on Toleration," transcribed by William Popple, gopher://vt.edu:10010/02/116/2.
[13] Brown at 1384.

The Roma who are being denied citizenship in the Czech Republic do not claim they are not Roma, that they lack a nationality, but that the Roma should be given the status of Czech citizens.

When Mustafa Halefy sued to have his racial designation changed, his assertion was not that he did not have a race.[14] His claim was that the government had misclassified his race. Likewise, the transgendered sue and are sued not because they lack a sex, but because there are questions about which sex they have. Michael T., for example, was born "Marlene T." and held by a court in which he was being sued by his former "wife" as "indeed a female."[15] Nonetheless, the court held Michael T. responsible for child support payments, even though the marriage was "fraudulent" and New York's Domestic Relations Law recognized parents only in "biological terms." Rather than claim that, because the case was confusing, Michael did not have a sex, the court said that he did have a sex, "indeed a female" one, even though this particular sex was clearly at odds with the decision against him, which held him to be the child's father: "The actions of this respondent in executing the Agreement above referred to certainly brought forth these offspring as if done biologically.... This Court finds that under the unique facts of this case, respondent is indeed a 'parent' to whom such responsibility attaches."[16] Still, although the court detached Michael's sex from its normally understood biological basis, the decision never said that Michael or Marlene lacked a sex.

One is born into these other forms of being mentioned in Title VII, but one's religion might be a choice and might be acquired later. Unlike these other affiliations, the First Amendment protects only the right to have a religion, and offers no similar "right" to a race, color, national origin, or sex. Inscribing these into the Constitution would be like saying one had the right to breathe, which, like a race, color, national origin, and sex one seemingly simply possesses, without willing it. People might dispute their right to choose to be this or that sex, claim national origins in this or that country, or belong to this or that race, but no one claims the prerogative to a practice on the general grounds that she is a sexed, national-ized, or racialized individual. Helen Reddy's Top 40 song in the 1970s proclaimed, "I am woman, hear me roar," not "I am gendered. . . . "

Unlike these other forms of being, religion need not be tied to discourses of ancestry. Unlike the success of the ancestry quiz for resolving doubts

[14] Chapter 4 reviewed arguments against the existence of the concept of race, but as that chapter showed, these views are not hegemonic, persuasive, or legally recognized.

[15] *Karin T. v. Michael T.* 484 NYS 2d 780, 782 (1985).

[16] *Karin T.* at 784. When Michael took on the legal responsibility of a parent by agreeing to raise the children as Karin's husband, which was a legal status the state would not recognize, Michael effectively took on a biological status that the court would recognize, that of a "parent."

about a person's nationality or race, the question, "What is the religion of your parents?" is not definitive for the religion of the child. When one is pressed on the issue whether one is really a Christian, the response that "My parents are Christians," is not dispositive. A substantial number of Hare Krishna followers had Christian parents. These children are Hare Krishna converts, and not themselves Christians. The claim that "I found God at the laundromat" would be taken as better evidence of one's religious status than the religiosity of one's parents.[17] The history of Christianity is a history of the battle for the individual's soul, which, for most of the history of the Church, was thought independent of the body and therefore, not tied to one's parentage. Each soul had to be saved separately, and with the active participation of the believer, precisely because its ultimate status was not inherited and already established.

Christians debate infant baptism, weighing the advantages of saving a pre-conscious soul in the event of early death against the disadvantages of asserting a Christian form of being its bearer did not actively choose.[18] Amidst the impassioned exchanges, the argument that infants should be baptized because they simply inherited the religion of their parents is not offered. It is precisely Christianity's lack of interest in the body and lineage that has resulted in the religion's missionary zeal. The child of Christian parents is no more or less amenable to or worthy of salvation than the child of Muslim or Jewish parents, from the point of view of Christianity.

The failure of intergenerationality to determine religious affiliation is clearly the case for Christianity, but not always true for Judaism, Confucianism, and Hinduism. For instance, the Acting Chairman of the Union of Orthodox Rabbis in the United States and Canada has announced that Reform and Conservative Jewish synagogues are not really Jewish. Nonetheless, he reassured Jewish people that this had no implications for their individual identities: "[A]ny person born by a Jewish mother is a Jew. We only said that the Reform and conservative doctrines, that their Judaism is not Judaism, because there is only one Judaism."[19]

To be Hindu is to have an ancestor who is Hindu, since, like Judaism and Confucianism, Hinduism is tied to a national form of being.[20] The

---

[17] I am assuming that these statements are truthful—that the person's parents are Christians and that the individual found God at the laundromat.

[18] Kurt Aland, *Did the Early Church Baptize Infants?*, tr. G. R. Beasley-Murray (London: SCM Press, 1963); Jochim Jeremias, *The Origins of Infant Baptism: A Further Study in Reply to Kurt Aland* (Naperville: A. R. Allenson, 1963).

[19] Rabbi Hirsh Ginsberg, quoted in Lynn Cohn, "Infighting," in *Detroit Jewish News*, April 4, 1997, p. 3.

[20] Partha Chatterjee describes the historical development of Hinduism in concert with the formation of a specifically Indian nationality, in *Nation and Its Fragments: Colonial and Postcolonial Histories* (Princeton: Princeton University Press, 1993). Muslim forms of being have a similar double relation to nationality, insofar as the religion originated through specifically

Jews were the Israelites.[21] Hinduism is the religion associated with the national origins of India. Among the "Brief Guidelines" for "Who Is a Hindu?" are the criteria: "He who considers India his Dharmasbhumi, that is, his Land of Religion no matter what his adopted nationality is, is a Hindu." From what follows below it seems that the author is referring to those of Indian ancestry who have adopted a nationality of, say Canada, and not a Canadian non-Indian person who simply decided to become Hindu. Here, as in Judaism, religion is the forward-looking set of sacred/ profane distinctions that may be mapped precisely onto a distinctly national form of being.[22] Other criteria: "He who calls himself the follower of that religion whose founder, primal prophet was born in India, is a Hindu." And finally, "With the conviction that 'Hinduism' is not a religion, but only a cultural heritage, he who recognizes and respects the religions that come within its orbit, is a Hindu."[23] Emphasizing the congruence of religion and nationality, by lineage, the author of the popular text *Daddy, Am I a Hindu?* responds to the question, "Does Hinduism believe in conversion?" with "Not at all. A true Hindu never proselytizes. On the contrary, the Gita urges everyone to follow the religion in which he/she was born. A MAN IS BORN AS A HINDU, NEVER CONVERTED INTO HINDU-

---

national forms of being and political conflicts in the seventh century, when Mohammed emigrated from Mecca to Medina. The Koran refers as well to an intergenerational set of ties that reach back to the Israelites: "He has picked you out and has not placed any constraint on you concerning religion, the sect of your forefather Abraham. He has named you Muslims both previously and right now, so the Messenger may be a witness for you, and you may act as witness for mankind" (*The Qur'an*, 22:77 [tr. from T. B. Irving, first American version (Brattleboro: Amana, 1985)]). Conversions to Islam were frequent during the Ottoman Empire, as those in conquered territories faced clear financial incentives based on Koranic rules on taxation.

[21] To those who did not live in the territory of Israel all twelve tribes eventually became known as "Jews," named as such after the tribe of Yehuda—Judah. The tribe of Judah occupied the territory to which all Israelites migrated following the second destruction of the temple and the defeat of the House of David: "While the name 'Jew' became common usage outside the Land of Israel, the Hebrew speaking Jews within the land were particular to call themselves 'Israel.'" The fact that Judas Iscariot is the one held responsible for the death of Christ meant further diabolical associations of the "Jew," as "Judas was linked with the devil (Luke 22:3), and the result was the evil triangle of devil-Jew-Judas" (*Encyclopedia Judaica*, s.v. "Jew").

[22] One of the antagonisms among Jews concerns precisely this question of the status of Israel as a political project. The Hasidim believe Zionism violates the spirit of the Torah's instruction that a Messiah will precede the consolidation of Israel as a nation. Nonetheless, as is the case for other anti-Zionist Jews as well, the origins of the Jews through a political kinship system, rather than via a charismatic leader, means the identity will always have overtones of a nation, if not because of the present, or the post-World War II past, then from the Hebrew origins story.

[23] Her Holiness Majadevi Jagadguru Mate, *Who Is a Hindu?* (Bandalore: Viswakalyana Mission, 1989), p. 152. For a more critical account of Indian identity, see Chatterjee, *The Nation and Its Fragments*.

ism."[24] It is the national character of both Jewish and Hindu forms of being that makes possible the distinction between the indisputable identities of the people as Hindu or Jewish alongside the theological debates over the rituals and doctrine associated with these.[25]

Whereas disputes over religious practices aligned with national identities may be settled without the losing group being cast off, religious groups with the membership criteria of faith in a specific doctrine regularly divide into smaller sects and practice excommunication. It is therefore predictable that the grounds for Jews "disowning" family members is marriage to a non-Jew—on the grounds that this will violate rules of intergenerational continuity. For Catholics and other Christian sects, marriage outside of the congregation—a violation of ritual—is simply grounds for excommunication, but there is no doctrine that requires one's family to do likewise. Internecine quarrels among self-identified Christians took the form of Augustine labeling the Donatists heathens. If one did not practice Christianity the right way, then one was just calling oneself Christian, but was not truly Christian. For Hindus and Jews, the deviants were still Hindus and Jews but were practicing their faith in misguided ways.

The acceptance of individuals into a religion whose practices they do not observe results in a paradox: why bother claiming these nominally affiliated individuals if their practices bear little relation to certain key rituals thought to be associated with that religion? The answer, from the first Rabbi of Israel: "In a world that is filled with so much *sinat chinam*, hatred for the Jew with no reason, we must counteract with *ahavat chinam*, love for every Jew, even when there is no reason."[26] The apparent expansiveness of the Rabbi's embrace of all Jews entails a more insidious distinction that simultaneously enables the specifically nationalist fervor of "Chosen People-hood" associated with the Jewish form of being, which is an ancestral as well as a religious form. It is precisely when the ideological dimensions of a group are ignored that the formal invocations of identity purely for the sake of identity—the hallmark of the ancestral group—are set in place.[27]

[24] E. D. Viswanathan. *Daddy Am I a Hindu?* (Bombay: Bharatiya Vidya Bhavan, 1988), p. 4, capitals in original.

[25] None of the above rudimentary discussions of membership criteria specific to Judaism or Hinduism are meant to denote definitive sets of rules, but merely to illustrate that insofar as it is suggested that birth is required to belong, these groups take the form of a nation, while those groups that depend on individual choice and that require the performance of certain rituals oriented toward visions of a sacral future, are religious.

[26] Quoted in Rabbi Mitchell Wohlberg, "It's Apparent: We're All God's Children," *Detroit Jewish News*, April 11, 1997, p. 30.

[27] The long-standing debate in Israel over the group that will control the definition illustrates the ways that Judaism is tied to intergenerational political societies. The recognition of Reform and not exclusively Orthodox converts to Judaism, as well as patrilineage and not

Quasi-"National" Religions

Ancestry often seems to influence one's religious denomination, even when strict theological principles do not suggest that one is born into a particular religion. That is, it may seem that Judaism and Hinduism are not the only religions that have nationalist overtones, which might prompt the mistaken belief that the religious form is simultaneously an ancestral one. National and religious affiliations frequently overlap, as when it is claimed that the United States is a Christian country (despite the fact that many founders were Deists and thought Christianity and its conventions foolish).[28] The overlap of religious and national identities seems especially obvious for religions identified by a national name, to wit, the denominations Russian Orthodox, Serbian Orthodox, Greek Orthodox, Roman Catholic, and Anglican. Religions also have a political overlay when particular parties develop by invoking their ties to a transnational religion. Just as the label and concept of "Canadian whiskey" does not mean whiskey is analytically a part of nationality, the presence of religious rhetoric in political campaigns does not mean that religions are inherently tied to specific political societies. Although a political society may take on a particular religion from above (e.g. Constantine's Rome) or from below (e.g., Khomeini's Iran), the effect is always that religions are absorbed by a political society, and not vice-versa. Iran becomes Muslim, rather than Islam becoming Iranian. Within the political societies, then, religions may become absorbed by the very state-nation that at various points opposed them. First Pontius Pilate crucified Jesus Christ, and then came the oxymoronic "Roman" Catholicism. Luther was a criminal, and then in Germany the law became Lutheran.

Religion, the Nation, and the Individual

Just as the ability of Jews to remain Jews by virtue of ancestry alone diminishes the religious significance of the tenets of Judaism to that form of being, when a political society takes on the mantle of religion, that

---

just matrilineage, would not be regarded as especially "enlightened" by the Palestinians in the area, as the simple formulation of a "Jewish state" is not undermined.

[28] Deist Thomas Paine believed that simple noise control concerns outweighed the prerogative of churches to use bells, a standard of respect for the "right" to religion far below that of contemporary legal practices: "As to the bells, they are a public nuisance. If one profession is to have bells, and another has the right to use the instruments of the same kind or any other noisy instrument, some may choose to meet at the sound of cannon, another at the beat of drum, another at the sound of trumpets and so on, until the whole becomes a

simple form of alliance itself diminishes the spiritual possibilities of that religion. Kierkegaard is right to note how religions have become profaned, trivialized matters of prestige and habit, not devotion.

> There is no good calling upon a Holger Danske or a Martin Luther; their day is over and at bottom it is only the individual's laziness which makes a man long to have something cheap, second-hand, rather than to buy the highest of all things very dear and first-hand.[29]

Once religious worshipers coalesce into groups, say a parish or a particular sect, Kierkegaard believes these groups often take on a separate life of their own, detracting from whatever spiritual ecstasy a way of worship might have held for its early adherents.

When referring to the tendency of Christians to "found society after society,"[30] Kierkegaard could have had in mind the Puritans, as he describes the humor of the streetfight in which one of the three men who had ganged up on a fourth is knocked down by the crowd and beaten: "The avengers had, in fact, applied precisely the same rules as the offenders."[31] Or maybe Kierkegaard anticipated the Roman Catholic Croatians and Serbian Orthodox Christians, the descendants of those who resisted the Ottoman Empire's conversion incentives, and then punished Muslims (descendants of ex-Christians) because of their religion. The Roman Catholics, like the participants in the street brawl, do not see, as Kierkegaard puts it, the "humor in the situation."

> I went up to one of the avengers and tried by argument to explain to him how illogical his behaviour was; but it seemed quite impossible for him to discuss the question: he could only repeat that such a rascal richly deserved to have three people against him.[32]

The Croatian Catholics who take over the homes of Croatian Muslims intellectually understand the parallels with their expropriations a few hundred years earlier. This comprehension, however, only makes them indignant over the actual injustices committed against them, and defensive about the military necessity that requires their control of previously Muslim neighborhoods.

---

scene of general confusion" ("Citizen Representative," Worship and Church Bells, http://www.infidels.org/library/historical/thomas_paine/worship_and_church.htm).

[29] Tr. Alexander Dru, "The Present Age," in *The Present Age and Of the Difference between a Genius and an Apostle* (New York: Harper and Row, 1962), p. 58.

[30] Ibid.

[31] Ibid., p. 55.

[32] Ibid.

We remain in Kierkegaard's "present age" of religious (national) societies battling religious (national) societies. Religious activity for the individual, which is Kierkegaard's definition of a true religion, appears impossible:

> [S]o far the dialectic of Christendom tends toward representation (the majority
> sees itself in its representative and is set free by the consciousness that it is the
> majority which it represented, in a sort of self-consciousness).[33]

The formal difference between religion and ideas about group affiliation
and representation, according to Kierkegaard, is that the former makes
possible a particular relation between the individual and a higher power
whereas the latter is about the present age, the mundane, from *mundus*,
"the earth." A strictly religious practice takes one outside the "present
age," which is always a historical period and hence always circumscribed
by a particular political order. (The most obvious manifestation of this is
the measure of time imposed by the calendar.)[34]

As the practices of religious individuals become institutionalized, they
take on the conventions of the present age, which, to recall the work of
Hayden White and Hegel, is a specifically national age and time, even
when the calendrical dating system may be uniform across countries. The
current Gregorian calendar, introduced by Pope Gregory XIII in 1582,
was a modification of the Julian calendar, adopted by the Church and
dated so that the zero point is supposed to coincide with Christ's birth.
The calendar was embraced immediately by Catholic countries, but Protestant ones hesitated.[35] The specifically religious significance of the seven-
day week is less revealing of the calendar's meaning than the form it takes,
which is to represent an intergenerational time line consistent with the
demands of political society. The Church might announce a new calendar,
but its implementation depended on the decisions of political, not religious, leaders.

---

[33] Ibid., p. 52.

[34] Heidegger writes: "*In analysing the historicality of Dasein we shall try to show that this entity
is not 'temporal' because it 'stands in history' but that, on the contrary, it exists historically and can
so exist only because it is temporal in the very basis of its Being*. Nevertheless, Dasein must also
be called 'temporal' in the sense of Being 'in time'. Even without a developed historiology,
factical Dasein needs and uses a calendar and a clock ... Thus the time which any Dasein
has currently interpreted and expressed has as such already been *given a public character* on
the basis of that Dasein's ecstatical Being-in-the-world. . . . [This is the] time which we know
as astronomical and calendrical *time-reckoning*" (tr. John Macquarrie and Edward Robinson,
Being and Time [1926] [Harper and Row, 1962], pp. 428–29, 463–64, emphasis in original).

[35] "Great Britain and its colonies did not adopt the new calendar until 1752. . . . The
calendar was not accepted by Russia until the Bolshevik Revolution" (Anthony Aveni, *Empires
of Time: Calendars, Clocks, and Cultures* [New York and Tokyo: Kodansha, 1989], pp. 117–18).
The purpose of the new calendar was to set the date of Easter consistently, a goal first
pursued through the Council of Nicea in 325, as a means of uniting the Eastern and Western
Holy Roman empires (ibid., p. 115).

The present age is anchored to the past by the zero point of its calendar. A calendar places a group in and through time together, but the religious impulse carries people beyond the group. The past denotes the birth of one's group and is largely political, while contemplation of the future imagines the death of the individual and is more consistently mentioned in relation to religious forms of membership. Whereas the political-national community asks its individuals to make sacrifices, including death, for the sake of that group, a religion asks the group to make its sacrifices for the good of each discrete soul. The soldier dies for his country, the exorcised child for her soul in particular. Christ instructs his followers to exchange wealth predicated on the intergenerational political-state form for the ecstasy of devotion. The followers of Jim Jones in Guyana and the Heaven's Gate community in San Diego committed group suicide so that each might individually reach heaven, just as Christian and Islamic martyrs count on the salvation of their individual souls.

The millinerian character of religious fundamentalisms also conveys a sense of orientation rooted in action toward the future, rather than celebrations of the past. God's plan articulates one's destiny, and the past is simply not that important.[36] Once a state-nation appropriates a religious idiom that speaks beyond generations, that religious practice ceases to be strictly religious, Kierkegaard claims:

> No society or association can arrest that abstract [leveling] power, simply because an association is itself in the service of the levelling process. Not even the individuality of the different nationalities can arrest it, for on the higher plane the abstract process of levelling is a negative representation of **humanity pure and unalloyed**. The abstract levelling process, that self-combustion of the human race, produced by the friction which arises when the individual ceases to exist as singled out by religion, is bound to continue like a trade wind and consume everything.[37]

Once one's spirituality is practiced because of the brute fact of membership in a society by birth (a nation), the content of the practice has irrevocably lost its distinctiveness. Rather than allowing for individual redemption, a religion practiced because one belongs to a group has levelled the individual into the nation, hence foreclosing that person's distinctive possibilities of divine contemplation or worship, Kierkegaard believes.

---

[36] John Garvey points out the common emphasis on a creator's imminent plans for a cataclysmic future in the writings of Sikh, Christian, Jewish, and Muslim fundamentalists, in "Fundamentalism and Politics," in Martin Marty and Scott Appleby, eds., *Fundamentalisms and the State: Remaking Polities, Economies, and Militance* (Chicago and London: University of Chicago Press, 1993), p. 18.

[37] Kierkegaard, *The Present Age*, pp. 55–56, emphasis in original.

Religion in Opposition to the Individual

But now we have to ask whether it is just national religions that ruin religion, or whether there are any religions that enable individual actions as such? Kierkegaard seems to have romanticized religion so that it fits the spirit of his bourgeois romantic age, whereas religions have very little to do with the individual Kierkegaard celebrates. A religion, like a nation, always requires the very form of institutionalization Kierkegaard decries. As the court ruled in the case of the Kozy Kitten cat food eater, a "personal religion" is an impossibility:

> The Fifth Circuit has identified three major factors which enter into a determination of whether a belief is religious: the 'religious nature of a belief depends on (1) whether the belief is based on a theory of 'man's nature or his place in the Universe,'(2) which is not merely a personal preference but has an institutional quality about it, and (3) which is sincere.[38]

The court used these criteria and decided that "Plaintiff's 'personal religious creed' concerning Kozy Kitten cat food can only be described as such a mere personal preference and, therefore, is beyond the parameters of the concept of religion as protected by the Constitution or, by logical extension, by 42 U.S.C. 2000e." The implication is that if Kozy Kitten eating had been part of a religion as defined by Judge King's three criteria, King might well have decided in Brown's favor.

To count as religious, a set of practices needs to be more than weird—a colloquial word for the phenomenology of taxonomies of purity and contamination, sacred and profane, that distinguish religious practices from mere quirks. Most people, most of the time, do not observe religious rituals. That is what distinguishes them, makes them sacred. Religious practices that violate a law or deserve protections are ones that require their observers to taxonomize the world and behaviors in unconventional ways:

> All winged insects that walk upon all fours are detestable to you. But among the winged insects that walk on all fours you may eat those that have jointed legs above their feet, with which to leap on the ground. Of them you may eat: the locust according to its kind, the bald locust according to its kind, the cricket according to its kind, and the grasshopper according to its kind. But all other winged insects that have four feet are detestable to you.[39]

The instruction requires a certain attention to insects that, but for one's religion, one would not pursue. At the same time, more than "special

---

[38] *Brown*, note 9.
[39] Leviticus 11:20.

concern" for certain activities is necessary for the practice to be religious. If many people follow certain prohibitions, then these rules are thought religious; if only one person does, that is madness. The above passage from Leviticus might now be classified as obsessive compulsive behavior, if it were just Stanley Brown's idea to divide insects in this manner during his lunch break. Imagine how one might regard a man who each morning, before he did anything else, felt compelled to say "Thank God I am not a woman." What would it mean, if each morning he simply could not do anything before he said these words? That the mantra is required by certain interpretations of Jewish law makes it archaic, patriarchal, and insulting. But the person who says it is thought "religious"—possibly ludicrous— but not insane.

'Religion' comes from the Latin *ligare*, to bind, and *re-*, again.[40] One can have idiosyncratic ideas about salvation—that it comes from eating cat food, for instance—but then they are just that, and not religious. What distinguishes the peculiarities of personal habit from those of religious ritual is that the latter are binding upon one and bind one to others: a group of people follow practices with the consciousness that others also think these distinctive and necessary.[41]

Kierkegaard seems not to recognize that the tension between individual faith and the group mentality he has in mind is not just between religion (for individual freedom) and nation (for group practice), but within religion itself:

> Simply in order to put a passing whim into practice a few people add themselves together, and the thing is done—then they dare do it. For that reason not even a pre-eminently gifted man can free himself from reflection, because he very soon becomes conscious of himself as a fractional part in some quite trivial matter, and so fails to achieve the infinite freedom of religion.[42]

What is this infinite freedom of religion? Can there be a specifically religious private ecstasy? 'Ecstasy' is from the Greek *stēnai*, "to stand," and *ec-*, "out" and meant "[standing] out of place."[43] Ecstasy refers to an experience of otherness, a standing apart from others associated with the kind of out-of-body experience that has ruptured the intergenerational community that locates itself in the association of a single body of people

---

[40] Eric Partridge, *Origins: A Short Etymological Dictionary of Modern English*, 2d ed. (New York: MacMillan, 1959), p. 345.

[41] When people refer to certain habits as 'religious', as in "I watch 'Seinfeld' religiously," the meaning is parasitic on the idiomatic use of 'religion' as an activity that one does as a member of a community of faith, as though compelled, as though without the possibility of choice that one conventionally associates with television-viewing behavior and not church attendance.

[42] Kierkegaard, *The Present Age*, p. 53.

[43] Partridge, *Origins*, p. 663.

in and through time. Chapters 1 and 2 mentioned the anti-materialism and anti-family rhetorics of early Christianity. Other religions have similar ecstatic values. For instance, Buddhists' quest for "nibbana does entail a distinctive form of action, one that generates neither positive nor negative merit, but results instead in 'detachment' from the world."[44] The injunctions of Christ to break with the family, to leave the body politic for a life of religion poses a challenge. What kind of paradox is the religious body, the ecstatic community, the out-of-body body that violates the rules of metonymy that the political body seems so effortlessly to reproduce?

Religion and Other Rights[45]

The First Amendment was passed as one among the first ten amendments to the United States Constitution, collectively referred to as the Bill of Rights.[45] The Bill of Rights may be regarded as exemplary of a balance between the authority of the sovereign and the negative liberty of its subjects that has come to be identified as "liberal." The language of the Declaration of Independence and the Bill of Rights has been taken to refer to "inalienable rights" that people have by virtue of being human. The Constitution creates a certain political association that is in formal tension with the kind of individual such an alliance entails. In addition to the paradox of the state announcing what counts as a pre-political individual

---

[44] Charles Keyes, "Buddhist Economics and Buddhist Fundamentalism" in *Fundamentalisms and the State*, ed. Marty and Appleby, p. 371.

[45] Other than the court decisions cited in the text, the cases I have drawn on to recount the history of interpretations of the religious Free Exercise Clause of the First Amendment include *Romney v. United States*, 136 U.S. 1 (1889), holding that the Church of Jesus Christ of Latter-Day Saints is obligated to follow Utah's laws regarding marriage, which are justified by that state legislature's belief in the Lord's intentions; *Cantwell v. Connecticut*, 310 U.S. 296 (1940), holding that religious practices are synonymous with religious beliefs and deserve protection from state interventions; *Everson v. Board of Education*, 330 U.S. 1 (1946), holding that public funds used to bus students to private Catholic schools does not violate the establishment clause; *Sherbert v. Verner*, 374 U.S. 398 (1963), holding that workers may not be denied unemployment compensation if fired for practicing their sabbath; *Walz v. Tax Commission*, 397 U.S. 664 (1969), holding that tax exemptions to religious organizations do not violate the establishment clause; *Wisconsin v. Yoder*, 406 U.S. 205 (1972), holding that the Amish may not be forced to send their children to public schools; *McDaniel v. Paty* 435 U.S. 618 (1978), holding that church ministers may hold political office; *Hobbie v. Unemployment Appeals Commission of Florida*, 480 U.S. 136 (1986), maintaining that withholding unemployment benefits from a Seventh-day Adventist who was fired for refusing to work on Fridays and Saturdays was unconstitutional; *Ansonia Board of Education v. Philbrook*, 479 U.S. 60 (1986), holding that employers have to "reasonably accommodate" an employee's religious practices, under Title VII, but that this does not mean that they must review all possible accommodations to that religious practice.

right, discussed in Chapter 5, the right to the free exercise of religion entails other conundrums. As Justice Scalia and others have noted in decisions adjudicating this right to religion, the government is in an impossible position when it comes to protecting religious freedom. Take the famous case of the peyote ingesting Native Americans, fired from their jobs as drug counselors for using illegal drugs and denied unemployment compensation.[46] If the government upholds this denial of unemployment benefits, then it is discriminating based on religion. The state that allows Catholics to drink wine as a sacrament[47] but prohibits Native Americans from peyote consumption in their religious rituals, seems to assist in the establishment of one religion and to penalize another. But if the government questions the state's ability to fire them, it is also discriminating based on religion. To allow Native Americans to consume peyote while imprisoning atheists for the same practice discriminates against atheists and others who simply want to use peyote.

Paraphrased, the First Amendment is telling the government "Ignore religion!" The instruction is violated the moment it is heeded. When the Court attends to a practice as "religious" in pursuit of its protection and when the Court exercises vigilance against the state establishing a religion, the government is intervening in religious practices.[48] The Free Exercise Clause is intrinsically at odds with the Establishment Clause: " 'The Free Exercise Clause . . . , by its terms, gives special protection to the exercise of religion.' "[49] If the courts do not issue special protections for religious

---

[46] *Employment Div., Department of Human Resources of Ore. v. Smith*, 494 U.S. 872 (1990).

[47] Even during Prohibition, Congress exempted the consumption of sacramental wine in communion.

[48] Scalia's decision in *Smith* clearly limited the right to engage in certain practices because they are religious. But it was a close (5–4) decision and, although it has been applied subsequently by lower courts, it has not been accepted as precedent by the entire Supreme Court. Justices Souter, Breyer, and especially O'Connor have voiced their concerns about the merits and procedures used in *Smith*. In her dissent in *City of Bourne v. P. F. Flores, Archbishop of San Antonio* (1997), O'Connor wrote: "Contrary to the Court's holding in [*Smith*] the Free Exercise Clause is not simply an anti-discrimination principle that protects only against those laws that single out religious practice for unfavorable treatment. . . . Rather, the Clause is best understood as an affirmative guarantee of the right to participate in religious practices and conduct without impermissible governmental interference." She rejects its *stare decisis* value because "*Smith* is demonstrably wrong [and] . . . a recent decision." Souter, in his dissent in the same case, adds his "doubts about the precedential value of *Smith*" because it was made "without briefing and arguments." By consistently raising these questions the Justices make it possible for the Court to reverse itself. (The same questions were raised by the same Justices in *Church of Lukumi Babalu Aye, Inc. v. Hialeah*, 508 U.S. 520 [1993], when the Court overturned a law banning Santerian animal sacrifices in the Church of Lukumi.)

[49] *Thomas v. Review Bd. of Indiana, Employment Security Div.*, 450 U.S. 707, 713 (1981), quoted in *Church of Lukumi*.

practices, then it seems they are not enforcing the First Amendment; if they do, then they are favoring religion over non-religion, and this seems to violate the Establishment Clause: "The Court must not ignore the danger that an exception from a general obligation of citizenship on religious grounds may run afoul of the Establishment Clause."[50] In response to this dilemma the current popular consensus seems to be that religion has a legitimate role to play in public, juridical life. One refrain, voiced in an extended argument by Stephen Carter, is that religious reasoning is one among many kinds of approaches to moral thought.[51] Not only should the courts protect the free exercise of religion, but they should recognize the legitimacy of religious justifications for particular pieces of legislation. People bring their religious training to public policy decisions, Carter observes. This is not intrinsically a problem, as long as the effects of the legislation do not pose disproportionate burdens for people of different religions.[52]

The cause of this especially perplexing problem of balancing the Free Exercise Clause against the Establishment Clause does not arise for any of the other restrictions on government power in the Bill of Rights. The reason is that the right to religious observation is the only one that requires a group in order to be practiced. While all rights depend on the government that announces them, the right to religion also entails the recognition of a larger group and not just the individual's preferences. In addition to the intrinsic tension between the Establishment Clause and the Free Exercise Clause, the First Amendment seems to guarantee an individual "right" to a group. An individual can decide to worship according to the rules of this or that group, and an individual can practice civil disobedience in accordance with this or that principle, but an individual qua individual cannot be religious. Kierkegaard's aspiration to "free reflection"—what one has absent belonging to an institutionalized group—is, before the law, merely a "personal preference." The idea of an individual right to religion obscures the group form that makes religion possible.

The right to free speech, to bear arms, to have one's home protected from arbitrary police searches, to be protected from cruel and unusual

---

[50] *Wisconsin v. Yoder*, 406 U.S. 205, 220–1 (1972).

[51] *Culture of Disbelief: How American Law and Politics Trivialize American Devotion* (New York: Basic, 1993).

[52] Scalia recognizes the possible consequences of majorities adversely impinging on the religious practices of minorities but says they are outweighed by the dangers of the opposite: "It may fairly be said that leaving accommodation to the political process will place at a relative disadvantage those religious practices that are not widely engaged in; but that unavoidable consequence of democratic government must be preferred to a system in which each conscience is a law unto itself or in which judges weigh the social importance of all laws against the centrality of all religious beliefs" (*Smith* at 890).

punishment by the state and so forth are all rights that one has as an individual. People disagree on the extent to which the government should protect these rights, and they form interest groups to concentrate their political power. Laws regulating access to abortion clinics may pit the American Civil Liberties Union against Operation Rescue. Gun control legislation may have the National Rifle Association advancing arguments against the views of Handgun Control, Inc. These groups do not claim that their positions should be protected by virtue of membership in any one of them, but because of the constitutional force of their arguments about the state and individual. The right to ingest peyote, to donate money in bankruptcy proceedings to the Mormon Church, to build on church property otherwise controlled by zoning laws, however, does not follow from the right to do any of these things per se—ingest peyote, donate money, or erect buildings. These cases arise because the activities may be protected against government intervention if they can be shown to maintain a religion—in other words, if the practices follow from one's membership in a religious group. In general, debtors are required to attend to their prior commitments; some notion of the individual property rights of creditors prevents debtors from sheltering their assets with friends or other family members, and they are prohibited from making significant purchases. Under regular bankruptcy proceedings, one cannot claim a right to give money to the Lion's Club or the American Cancer Society. But when Bruce and Nancy Young donated $13,450 to the Crystal Evangelical Free Church, and were sued by creditors who had liens on their assets because of bankruptcy proceedings, the United States Attorney General's office decided that the couple's donation was constitutionally protected.[53] The Second Amendment, interpreted as guaranteeing individuals the right to own guns, can be invoked simply because one is an individual citizen, whereas these other practices are protected because the people are members of a religious group.

The courts have recognized that they provide protections to religious activities not available to secular practices. One of their justifications for this is that it is unfair to punish people who behave in certain ways because they have the strong conviction that if they do otherwise they will be "condemned to hell" or suffer some other-worldly punishment: "Religion is morality, with a sanction drawn from a future state of rewards and punishments."[54] The reasoning that respects such beliefs is based simply on what people believe, and not ontological facts about the universe. The

[53] Gustav Niebuhr, "Justice Department Withdraws Brief in Tithing Case," *New York Times*, September 16, 1993, B18.

[54] *McAlister v. Marshall*, Pa., 6 Bin. 338, 350, 6 Am Dec. 458, quoted in *Words and Phrases*, vol 36 (St. Paul: West Publishing, 1940), p. 461.

courts are not announcing that if a Quaker is prevented from wearing a hat in a courtroom he definitely will burn in hell. The decisions protecting this behavior in the midst of secular rules prohibiting the conduct are saying that if someone really attaches religious significance to clothing, putting him in circumstances that would cause him to make a choice between punishment for not following certain courtroom etiquette and eternal damnation is unfair, a violation of the right to a religion. One ought to have the right to have potentially incorrect beliefs guide one's behavior. Since certain religious observances are mutually exclusive, the courts recognize that the Sabbath is not ontologically Friday, Saturday, **and** Sunday, and yet judges are willing to write opinions on behalf of those who have a strong belief that it is any one of these. From the point of view of a state protecting religious rights, the judges have no choice but to do so. The only way the government may treat all religions equally is if the courts maintain a nonsectarian perspective.[55]

Religious Behavior and Other Classifications

Whereas religious freedom is a distinctive right in the Constitution, one's religious form of being has an equally peculiar profile in the interpretation of statutory laws protecting civil rights. Religion is not a typical individual right, and it requires protections different from other kinds of group forms with which it is clustered. Under United States law, invoking one's membership in a particular sex, nation, or race does not protect unusual behaviors. One could not claim that it was necessary for a prison to provide diets without pork for their female inmates because as a woman one needs to avoid high-caloric foods to suit certain ideas of femininity. That many women do not subscribe to these norms of beauty, or that pork is not really fattening, are not grounds for rejecting the comparison.[56] Not only do the courts avoid professions of objectively assessing the truth claims

[55] Of course when it comes to certain behaviors, especially those involving sexual conduct, the courts have in the past used specifically Christian rhetoric to justify decisions ranging from the ban on polygamy to sodomy laws. The courts are at their most anti-Establishmentarian when the cases they adjudicate bear directly on religious freedom questions, whereas the decisions not directly speaking to the First Amendment are more likely to rely on Christian rhetoric to support their line of reasoning. For an argument on the legitimate use of Christianity for interpreting law, see Sidney Buchanan, "Morality, Sex, and the Constitution: A Christian Perspective," *University of Dayton Law Review*, 10 (1985), pp. 541–62.

[56] One cannot even claim that pregnancy discrimination is a violation of one's civil rights as a woman. The activities associated with child-bearing pertain to the class of "pregnant persons," whom the civil rights laws and Supreme Court decisions do not specify as a suspect classification.

about the correlations between certain practices and one's prospects in the afterlife, they also do not refer to conflicting assessments of these rituals among practitioners. Not all self-identified Jews or Muslims avoid pork; it is a certain interpretation of dietary rules that results in this behavior. Even among Jews and Muslims, no one knows whether avoiding pork is something with which God is really concerned. That knowledge would require one to be (a) god, and not just prefer to worship one. Written texts are not dispositive. The Hebrew Bible requires patrilineality and animal sacrifices,[57] practices that no organized Jewish sect currently follows. The courts do not inquire into the relevance of particular practices to the exercise of a religion:

> It is no more appropriate for judges to decode the "centrality" of religious beliefs before applying a "compelling interest" test in the free exercise field, than it would be for them to determine the "importance" of ideas before applying the "compelling interest" test in the free speech field. . . . Repeatedly and in many different contexts, we have warned that courts must not presume to determine the place of a particular belief in a religion or the plausibility of a religious claim.[58]

The United States courts are not Talmudic scholars who will debate the true meaning of a biblical injunction. The judges expect only to be shown that some portion of a sect believe these practices are related to the exercise of that religion.

Constitutional and other legislative protections against discrimination based on sex, national origins, or race serve the ostensible purpose of eliminating purely formal and irrational distinctions among **individuals**. Some religious discriminations may also be based purely on the status of another person: "I won't hire a Catholic because I hate Catholics." This is prohibited by the same law that prohibits discrimination based on race, color, sex, and national origin. Such cases are extremely rare. The controversial cases involving religion are those that putatively are not caused by the formal status of the individual, but by the practices associated with that form of being, so that the employer is in the position of saying: "I have nothing against Native Americans; I just do not want my employees using peyote." The difference between invocations of race, color, national origins, and sex on the one hand, and religion on the other, is that the former protect individuals who have what are thought to be immutable identities that themselves yield no important, work-relevant information about that person.[59] Therefore these identities should not be considered

---

[57] Leviticus, for example, 4–12.

[58] *Smith*, 887.

[59] Cass Sunstein shows the trajectory of these decisions, in making the argument for including sexual orientation as a suspect classification. "Sexual Orientation and the Constitu-

in making employment decisions, for instance. In cases involving religious discrimination, the opposite is the case. Rather than contending that who they are is irrelevant and the observant persons were not hired, fired, or otherwise affected because of their form of being, religious protection cases claim that religious status per se is central to the issue being adjudicated—that but for that religious affiliation the law or act of discrimination is permissible, but that if one has a certain form of being, then implementation of the law or criteria is suspect. For cases of alleged religious discrimination, one's nominal identity is not incidental to, but at the heart of, the legal protections. It is not the fact that one might or might not refuse pork for a variety of reasons that prompts the Free Exercise Clause and related protections in civil rights law. The reasoning is that it is only because one is Jewish or Muslim that these practices have meaning and deserve protection. So whereas attention to racial identities (negative or affirmative) may be legally suspect because such concerns are regarded as empty excuses for prejudice, religious identities are deemed to deserve protection because of the meaningful status of the practices associated with them.

The arguments advanced for protecting religious individuals from discrimination then, are quite different from those for other Title VII claimants. A prisoner has the right to certain kinds of protections of devotional rituals that do not depend on a history of religious discrimination. A prisoner has a right not just to an affiliation (as Muslim) but also to certain practices, even if there is no history of discrimination against those practices, or interest in a prison's religious diversity. The current trend in court decisions, even in matters of race and sex-based discrimination is to reject diversity arguments.[60] Rather than entertaining arguments about the benefits of affirming diversity, the courts and some states seem to be retreating to a narrower view of forms of being, one that discounts the relevance of race and sex to employment or educational institutions. In voting rights cases the trend is to be "race neutral" rather than have the state enable or prohibit race-based drawing of congressional districts.

Religion and Democracy

Until *Smith*, the decisions protecting religious activities depended on the degree of harm the Courts anticipated would follow from protecting certain practices. The Court was not going to prevent someone from being

---

tion: A Note on the Relationship Between Due Process and Equal Protection," *University of Chicago Law Review* 55 (fall, 1988), pp. 1161–79.
    [60] *Hopwood v. State of Texas*, 78 F.3d 932 (1996).

prosecuted for murder on the grounds that her religion required human sacrifice: "We have never held that an individual's religious beliefs excuse him from compliance with an otherwise valid law prohibiting conduct that the State is free to regulate."[61] Invoking religion simply changed the approach from a categorical one to one of balancing the harm from these specific individuals ingesting peyote, for instance, against the harm of restricting religious practices. Only if the challenge is a religious one will the courts pursue this balancing. If I went to court to complain that the law prohibiting opium use was fine for others, but that no legitimate public health interest was served by restricting **my** use, I would be punished for using illegal narcotics. Legislators know that laws may be overinclusive and courts respect the implicit judgment that the marginal harm I might suffer because I cannot smoke opium is outweighed by the harms that would result if this behavior were not prohibited for everyone, including me.

The *Smith* decision, while taking much of the force away from the Free Exercise Clause, has by no means entirely eviscerated it. One of the criteria a more recent case announced for assessing whether a facially neutral law violated religious freedom was whether exemptions were available for some secular groups, but not for religious ones.[62] The law banning animal sacrifices on grounds of cruelty is an example of this:

> Killings for religious reasons are deemed unnecessary, whereas most other killings fall outside the prohibition. The city, on what seems to be a *per se* basis, deems hunting, slaughter of animals for food, eradication of insects and pests, and euthanasia as necessary . . . one of the few reported Florida cases decided under 828.12 that the use of live rabbits to train greyhounds is not unnecessary.[63]

While of course there is no reason to think cutting the carotid artery of a guinea pig for religious purposes is more cruel than a rabbit being eaten by greyhounds, it is also true that the courts have singled out religions as the groups able to require the government to demonstrate a "compelling governmental interest." If a private individual can show a law is underinclusive, that does not undermine the constitutionality of the law. But a law that affects religious practices and that fails tests of "neutrality" and "general applicability . . . must be justified by a compelling interest, and must be narrowly tailored to advance that interest" for the enforcement of the Free Exercise Clause.[64] This means that religious behaviors have protections that non-religious behaviors lack.

---

[61] *Smith*, at 878–79.
[62] *Church of Lukumi Babalu Aye, Inc. v. City of Hialeah*, 508 U.S. 520 (1993).
[63] Ibid.
[64] Ibid., Part II.

Religious Freedom "Restored"

In 1993, disappointed with Scalia's decision in *Smith*, Congress overwhelmingly passed the Religious Freedom Restoration Act (RFRA).[65] RFRA's essence was to codify those Supreme Court decisions that had granted the most weight to enforcing the Freedom of Exercise Clause and to dismissing concerns about how that might conflict with enforcing the Establishment Clause. RFRA's proponents believed that Scalia's decision marked a misstep in the jurisprudence on religious freedom: "Many criticized the Court's reasoning, and this disagreement resulted in the passage of RFRA. Congress announced . . . 'governments should not substantially burden religious exercise without compelling justifications.' "[66] Backed by everyone from the practitioners of Santeria to the Pope to the ACLU, RFRA posed an unusual challenge to majoritarian institutions. In passing RFRA, Congress did not separate a specific religious activity as exempt from its regulations—as it has in some laws regulating education and sex discrimination. Instead, RFRA instructed the courts to look kindly on religious groups whenever Congress or various states passed laws impinging on religious activities. This is another twist in United States law that distinguishes legal protections of religion from those of sex, nationality, or race. "Religious practices" are the only ones Congress had instructed courts specifically to protect from the preferences of a majority, **by virtue of laws endorsed by this same majority**. By strengthening an amendment in the Bill of Rights, Congress took the unusual step of weakening its own ability to pass inclusive laws. Unlike other statutory laws protecting minorities—for instance, tax exemptions for certain kinds of corporations, or minority hiring requirements for companies doing business with the federal government—Congress was not just legislating on behalf of **substantive** goals for certain minorities, but legislating against the **procedural** prerogatives of the majority.

The First Amendment of the Bill of Rights, supposedly there to protect against government zealotry, had become a creature of government zealots. The majoritarian Congress instructed the Court to step in to protect various religious minorities. Although the standard RFRA imposed was higher than Scalia's standard, the reasoning was the same: the rights-interested Court and the majoritarian Congress both insisted that religions are special and need special protections. The purely formal nature of religious membership, not the activity, initially prompts Constitutional scrutiny of an action or a law by the courts. Hence a certain Kierkegaardian bemusement here is prompted by a majoritarian institution voting away its majoritarian capacities. Although this is the irony of a bully bullying

---

[65] It passed by a voice vote in the House and a vote of 97–3 in the Senate.
[66] *City of Boerne* (1997), http://supct.law.cornell.edu/supct/html/95-2074.ZD1.html.

itself into no more bullying, rather than the humor of bullies bullying other bullies.

Religion and Sex

Against the view that sees religion as separate from the intergenerational forms of other groups, one might note the concern among various religions to control marriage ceremonies, as well as the underlying discourses of family roles that yield genders. While many religions seem to do this to some extent, they have done so in a manner dialectially connected to the imperatives of political society—as a means of sustaining a competing (though often accommodated) rhetoric that uses intergenerationality for the purpose of meta-generationality, for going beyond the ideas of beginnings and repetitive cycles of reproduction to a discursive site of otherworldliness. That certain religious sects seem to focus on marriage rules as the discursive center of the religion does not mean that sex roles are inherently central to religious discourse, but rather, that religious movements seeking secular authority have astutely noticed the hallmark of political society, which is that terms of membership are regulated through control of the family.

The twentieth-century use of religion to strengthen the role of fathers within families reinforces a tendency Luther criticized, which was the medieval church's use of marriage rhetoric to garner specifically political power. Chapter 2 argued that in Western antiquity political societies' regulation of the family was overtly discussed—in plays, dialogues, and court cases—as serving the interests of that political society, and not natural imperatives or religious ones. The second type of relation between political society and the family emerges through the rhetoric of medieval canonists attempting to wrest authority of the family from political society. Here the argument that families are natural and part of God's divine plan are advanced. The third stage begins shortly thereafter, as political societies in Europe appropriate the natural model of the family to justify the legitimacy of their own hereditary sovereignty, hence naturalizing the family from the point of view of a state (instead of the Church) that continues to legally regulate all aspects of family life. The post-French Revolution populist view of citizens' membership in a state-nation as natural is consistent with this idiom, only this family is not a patriarchal metonym, but the alliance of fratricidal brothers who have killed off the father, an image that seems apt for other republics as well, including the United States.[67]

---

[67] This is the argument Michael Rogin puts forth to describe the populism of Andrew Jackson's presidency, in *Fathers and Children* (New York: Knopf, 1975). Carol Pateman makes a similar argument for Locke's England, while Lynn Hunt uses this approach to describe

This fourth form of the relation between the family and political society begins to emerge in the Reformation, when Luther and others challenge the legitimacy of the state enforcing a particular church's doctrine regulating marriage. Luther argued that marriage was a primarily secular affair and that the government should not be privileging the institutions of one sect over another by enforcing a particular set of rules:

> No one can deny that marriage is an external, worldly matter, like clothing and food, house and property, subject to temporal authority, as the many imperial laws enacted on the subject prove. Neither do I find any example in the New Testament where Christ or the apostles concerned themselves with such matters, except where they touch upon consciousness, as Peter in I Corinthians 7.[68]

Luther's key attacks on the Church are all criticisms of the way that various policies regulating marriage (and celibacy for monks and nuns) are unjust power grabs by the Pope, abetted by weak imperial governments. During the Reformation, the concept of the family is used by rebel Christian theologians to disrupt the legitimacy of monarchs clinging to the gown-tails of church fathers, who are attempting to exercise what is effectively political power. Lutheranism deprived the frequently corrupt Church of its prerogative to be the ultimate institution for blessing marriages—the key to its authority—and gave it to parents. Luther did this not by saying that marriage was natural, but by arguing that it was the province of the state.[69] While Luther succeeded in demoting the Church's role in political society, the religious rhetoric naturalizing the family as part of a separate, private sphere proved more resilient.

Twentieth-Century Fundamentalisms

The key to understanding "fundamentalist" religious movements is not the respective texts, or even the zealotry of their members, but rather, the specifically political character of their goals and institutional engagements. Garvey specifies two types of political causes spurring fundamentalists:

---

revolutionary France and the French Republic, in *The Family Romance of the French Revolution* Berkeley: University of California Press, 1992).

[68] "On Marriage Matters" [1530], *Luther's Works*, tr. Frederick Ahrens, vol. 46 (Philadelphia: Fortress, 1955), p. 265. Luther goes on to characterize the Pope as having "seized worldly matters as his own to the point where he has become nothing but a worldly lord over emperors and kings . . . As soon as we begin to act as judges in marriage matters, the teeth of the mill-wheel will have snatched us by the sleeve and will carry us away to the point where we must also render judgment about the body and goods, and by this time we are down under the wheel and drowned in the water of worldly affairs" (ibid., pp. 265–66). Luther recognizes the specifically political character of marriage, marking it as the point at which its regulation is at once the regulation of political society.

[69] Luther presents the Church as a extortionist ring, establishing rules simply to charge large amounts of money for them to be ignored: "Here they have forbidden marriage up to

[T]he first are movements reacting to a change (or a threat of a change) in national identity. These include the Sunni Muslims in Pakistan, the Sikhs in Punjab, the Free Presbyterians in Ulster, and . . . both Gush Emunim and the haredim in Israel. In the second are movements reacting to government efforts to expand the public sphere in an existing nation-state.[70]

The form, thus, that energizes fundamentalist movements as such is that which corresponds to the contours of political society—either as it impinges on the shape of a national identity or threatens the scope of behaviors religious leaders prefer to control, to keep secure from secular influences. That mechanisms of intergenerationality are such a central activity of political society helps explain why it is the case that these religious movements challenging the state are especially interested in emphasizing themes of sex roles and other family relations. The Taliban in Afghanistan, the Muslims in Algeria, the Promise Keepers in Colorado, all use a discourse of religion to argue for restrictions on women's opportunities, movement, and dress, and for enhancements of men's power in the family.[71]

The increase in the use of the sex/religion discourse in the late twentieth century resembles much earlier appropriations of religious rhetoric for nationalist causes, including those in the Middle East during the periods of colonization by France and Britain.[72] Controlling the family has always been a means by which particular political communities resist occupations and assert their identities. Current efforts to launch social movements that can break the grip of the membership rules of political society are versions of the Lockean exit option, exercised through a refusal to think in secular idioms. Ann Mayer describes Islamic fundamentalists as using a religious framework to challenge "Western-style law and legal systems" perceived to be remnants of their previous colonization.[73] In Iran and elsewhere there was a "fundamentalist takeover of a revolution that was fought primarily for

---

the third and fourth degrees of consanguinity. If in this situation you have no money, then even though God freely permits it you must nevertheless not take in marriage your female relative with third and fourth degrees. . . . But if you have the money, such a marriage is permitted. Those hucksters offer for sale women who have never been their own" ("The Estate of Marriage" [1522], Walter Brandt, tr., *Luther's Works*, vol. 45., [Philadelphia: Fortress Press, 1955], p. 22).

[70] Garvey, "Fundamentalism and Politics," p. 20.

[71] The religion/sex discourse seems to be one that motivates the elites of these movements, but it is the provision of needed social services such as schools, hospitals, and food distribution that is a powerful mainstay of their popular support, at least in Egypt and in Algeria in the early 1990s.

[72] Nikki Keddie, and L. Beck, eds., *Women in the Muslim World* (Cambridge: Harvard University Press, 1978).

[73] "The Fundamentalist Impact on Law, Politics, and Constitutions in Iran, Pakistan, and the Sudan," in *Fundamentalisms and the State*, ed. Marty and Appleby, p. 111.

secular political and economic goals."[74] The same holds true, according to Keyes, of Buddhist "fundamentalism" in Burma, now Myanmar:

> Because Burmese nationalist movements in the 1920s and 1930s looked to reform Buddhism for the ideological rationale for radical opposition not only to the colonial state but also to the secularist premises of the state, the nationalist movements assumed a recognizably fundamentalist character.[75]

Although the instrumental accounts show how political movements can adopt the guise of religion, they do not grapple with the fact that it is the religious form, not a secular movement, political parties, or other non-religious organizations or clubs that seem to have proved most useful for those wishing to fundamentally challenge the state, and one wonders what—if spirituality is not moving them—the religious form offers that is absent in other possible vehicles of protest (or consolidation of authority). One possibility is that it is the very difference of the religious form from any of the other affiliations of the secular, material, mundane world that provides the vivacity that sustains these groups when, by worldly criteria, they are initially so impoverished.

The "New World" has already been taken. The new frontiers for those who chafe under the rule of their political leaders are the religious societies of local neighborhoods, as well as cyberspace. These provide an opening, a way to gather forces against the routinized social sphere. It is enormously difficult to start meaningful new political societies. Those who attempt this usually are labeled cranks or terrorists. But it is easy (and inexpensive) to occupy the long-standing spaces of Judaism, Christianity, Islam, and Hinduism. It is also fairly easy to develop "new" religions in the image of these older ones. Though they take a theological form, these religions are not quelling but prompting activity in politics. If at one time religion was the opiate of the masses, religion is now turning people into political speed demons.

The use of religion for arguments about the family does not follow from the content of any particular religious text. The New Testament on the whole says relatively little about sex roles.[76] The emphasis in the Christian text is on helping the poor and powerless, in challenging the craven leaders who protect the wealthy—"You cannot serve God and mammon"[77]—and in challenging norms of punishment and political enmity with those of compassion and empathy.

[74] Ibid., p. 115.

[75] "Buddhist Economics and Buddhist Fundamentalism," in *Fundamentalisms and the State*, ed. Marty and Appleby, p. 368.

[76] The Hebrew Bible, addressed to the primarily nationalist Israelites, has much more to offer on sex roles and kinship rules than the more spiritually oriented New Testament.

[77] Matthew 6:24.

You have heard that it was said, "An eye for an eye and a tooth for a tooth."
But I say to you, Do not resist one who is evil. But if anyone strikes you on
the right cheek, turn to him the other also. . . . Give to him who begs from
you, and do not refuse him who would borrow from you. . . . You have heard
that it was said, "You shall love your neighbor and hate your enemy." But I say
to you, Love your enemies and pray for those who persecute you. . . . For if
you love those who love you, what reward do you have? Do not even the tax
collectors do the same? And if you salute only your brethren, what more are
you doing than others? Do not even the Gentiles do the same?[78]

The tax collectors and the Gentiles are the money-grubbers who depend
on the state whose values Christ will question, even while he will not
directly oppose it. The repeated theme throughout the New Testament
is the importance of forsaking property rights, associated with families, in
order to follow God. In the same section in which Christ tells his disciples
how "hard it will be for a rich person to enter the kingdom of heaven"
he says salvation can be found for "everyone who has left houses or brothers
or sisters or father or mother or children or fields, for my name's sake,
[they] will receive a hundred-fold, and will inherit eternal life" (Matthew
19:23–27). This speech and others associate the family form with the
acquisition of wealth, for which Christ can more than compensate by
providing an alternative lifestyle and form of inheritance.

The Hebrew God strikes down those who seek to build one community:

Now the whole earth had one language and few words. And as men [descendants
of Shem] migrated from the east, they found a plain in the land of Shinar and
settled there. And they said to one another . . . "Come, let us build ourselves a
city, and a tower with its top in the heavens, and let us make a name for ourselves,
lest we be scattered abroad upon the face of the whole earth." . . . And the Lord
said: "Behold, they are one people, and they have all one language; and this is
only the beginning of what they will do. . . . Let us go down, and there confuse
their language, that they may not understand one another's speech."[79]

The people wanted to remain one community, but the Hebrew God
divided them into nations. For Christ, however, the separation of nations
is not what needs to be created, but what needs to be overcome:

Before him will be gathered all the nations, and he will separate them one from
another as a shepherd separates the sheep from goats. . . . Then he will say to
those at his left hand, "You that are accursed, depart from me into the eternal
fire prepared for the devil and his angels; for I was hungry and you gave me no
food, I was thirsty and you gave me nothing to drink, I was a stranger and you

[78] Matthew 5:38–47.
[79] Genesis 11:1–8.

did not welcome me, naked and you did not give me clothing, sick and in prison and you did not visit me." Then they also will answer, "Lord, when did we see thee hungry or thirsty or a stranger or naked or sick or in prison, and did not minister to thee?" Then he will answer them, "Truly I say to you, as you did it not to one of the least of these, you did it not to me." And they will go away into eternal punishment, but the righteous into eternal life.[80]

Here Christ rejects the many subdivisions of nations in favor of a transcendent division into the accursed and the righteous. Many churches and religiously motivated individuals act on these principles, lobbying the state to assist the poor, unnaturalized immigrants, the sick, and those in prison. Paradoxically, while the New Testament instructs Christians to overlook national boundaries, and to help those the state has imprisoned, various Christians have used the form of religion to successfully press the state to implement certain values in the name of religion. It is no longer, for these religious movements, a matter of being left alone, but rather, in the name of religion, of appropriating the instruments of the very state that Christianity initially opposed.

The State of Religion

Sometime around the Thelemic year 36 BTE[81] Oscar Brown was all set to do battle with Goliath, except that he didn't have any money. He had been fired, after all, and needed money to hire an attorney. He attempted to gain a motion to "proceed *in forma pauperis*,"[82] a phrase from a language that no one has spoken in over several thousand Lilian days. The court stated that Brown should not be allowed to pursue his battle because his claim was "frivolous." On the topic of frivolity, the court had this to say: "The term frivolous, being at least arguably subjective, has been open to extensive interpretation." As the Brown decision continues, we see that frivolity is a serious matter: "The Eighth Circuit, for example, has developed a substantiality test: whether there 'exists substantiality as to such a claim, of justiciable basis and of impressing reality.' "[83] Brown's claim was found not justiciable, but frivolous.

In making this pronouncement, the court distinguished the frivolity of Brown thinking that it was religious faith that convinced him that cat food would improve him and make him a better person, from the "impressing reality" of the Jehovah's witnesses' belief that the "act of saluting the

---

[80] Matthew 25:32–47.
[81] http://www.panix.com/~wlinden/calendar.shtm
[82] *Brown* at 1384.
[83] Ibid., citing *Carey v. Settle*, 351 F. 2d 483, 484–5 (1965).

flag would violate the command of God."[84] Atheists might scoff at this concession, but then they might also laugh at the requirement that anyone should be expected to salute a piece of cloth. Is there a purpose served by the separation of "Mexicans" from "United States" citizens, signified by allegiance to a flag (or the nation for which it stands), that is any more fair and just, or even instrumental and worldly, than the fetishistic distinction between four-legged winged crickets and the other four-legged winged detestable creatures not to be eaten?

[84] *State v. Davis* 120 P.2d 808, 810 (1942).

Conclusion ⸻

POLITICAL societies develop birth practices so as to provide a connection between the current population and those of the past and future, via laws and related regimens of intergenerationality. The connection between birth and specific laws of intergenerationality does not follow from any ontological facts about the biological process of species reproduction, but rather from a set of conceptual associations in dialectical movement with the form of objects grasped by what Hegel termed sense-certainty. That is, birth is experienced as palpable and irreducible, so that any form of being tied to birth would also convey a sense of that form's immediacy and necessity. Intergenerationality as a criterion for membership establishes a group form that demands two interrelated things that have little basis in biology: history and kinship rules. Without history human beings would reproduce, but their heritage would have no more meaning than the bare genealogies of a pedigreed greyhound. One may trace the particular ancestry of an animal, just as one can chart fruit-fly divisions, but that is not history. By the same token, absent kinship rules, the human species would not have even this semblance of particularized continuities (e.g., nations, races, families) but would reproduce as Rousseauan savages. In this case the concept of birth would lack connotations any more poignant than those associated with other routine biological events. Absent particular groups, one's birth and death would have no more relevance to the rules of political association than the current political significance of falling asleep and awakening.

The purpose of positing the conditions of history and kinship rules for considering the salience of birth is neither to claim that birth's current invocations are mistaken, nor that humans might live without history and kinship rules. Rather, the above discussion reveals the specific contexts that render birth such a crucial practice for political societies to control. Of special interest to political societies is not that birth is natural, but that the very form of natality is intrinsically political. For this reason, numerous historical, political, and theoretical arguments against the claim that kinship rules follow from nature have not fundamentally disturbed intuitions to the contrary. Therefore, it is necessary to advance an argument that will more resolutely absorb and surpass these entrenched beliefs. It is important to realize that what can only amount to a pretense of knowledge of whether the family form is natural or artificial (since true consciousness does not fix objects in such an either-or fashion) does not help us understand any of the puzzles of these relations, nor would addressing this question illuminate anything else about the human condition. Mathematical proofs associated with (the concept of) pi, for instance, do not depend on hypotheses of whether this mathematical entity is natural or necessary. What is important about understanding the dialectics of the laws of birth is consciousness of what birth does, i.e., how it shapes a population's appeals to history and its use of the determinacy of ancestry.[1] The announcement of kinship ties by political societies is one of its chief creations, and also a site that has constituted some key meanings of birth.

Political societies institutionalize the relation between birth, history, and kinship rules in ways that make concrete the attachments of parents and children. Immigration laws, laws regulating personal names, the taxonomy of the earth through the aggregation of state-nations, the taxonomy of populations by reference to these places of origins as racial, and the political constitution of maternity (and matrimony) as natural all borrow from the birth connotations wrought through political societies to constitute and regulate certain forms of being.

The summary of the arguments herein prompts three questions that can be described here, but not fully answered. First, why is birth the site of this dense network of laws that determine membership? Second, why insist that the exclusions of birth are especially harmful? And finally, what, if anything, might be done to challenge the prevailing laws of familial taxonomies, to dislodge the centrality of birth to membership in political societies and their related forms of affiliation?

Why Birth?

The first two chapters noted that the impulse to associate based on birth per se is not present in all group forms, raising the question of why political societies in particular are those that paradigmatically use the decision rule of birth for membership. Up until this point, the representations of

---

[1] Related to the observation above is a more fundamental critique of political theoretical concerns about nature, which is that they slip in ethical and empirical judgments that cannot be sustained logically or in practice. Think of the formulaic assumption underlying defenses of the sexual status quo: "X is bad because X is unnatural." It is not coincidental that the paradigmatic concepts of this reasoning have an investment in kinship roles, and yet once one substitutes words that denote challenges to nature that have no bearing on these patterns, the comedic aspects of the syllogism are obvious: plumbing, airplanes, and highrise buildings do not occur "in nature," but they do not come in for criticisms from the groups condemning homosexuality on the grounds that it is a "crime against nature." Further, the very fact that people are engaging in same-sex relations would seem to belie the assertion that the activity is not natural. Finally, there are no human practices that can qualify as natural, by virtue of the fact that there are no human practices that exist outside of discourse. Thanks to Don Herzog, who provided me the above formulation of X and the unnatural.

affiliation herein could be read as furthering a strictly heuristic political project, one that has organized the categories through which certain affiliations are investigated. The Foucauldian sensibility that eschews inquiry into causal or foundational questions about these categories has been respected, for the most part. The importance of the historical form, to the frame of birth and death, to shaping knowledge and consciousness has been noted (against an anticipated Foucauldian resistance to incorporating this observation), but only as an investment of others that requires some attention. This kind of regard for the truth has not been a concern here, until now. What if we defy Foucault and his father Nietzsche? What if we search for some truths about birth and forget for the moment that such a quest is unseemly?

If we allow ourselves a quick peek under the veil of Nietzsche's truth embodied as a woman,[2] what we discover is the phantasmatic pregnant woman. She is the omnipotent one with the power of life and death, the one the boy fears he can never be or have (unlike girls, whose phantasmatic life develops around other denials, but not the overwhelmingly distressing prohibition against being a subject who can give birth). The phallic mother has a womb that has been repressed and fetishized as a penis. This is the young boy's projection of his own phallic ambitions. The mother is the image that dominates the unconscious, even as she is transmogrified through a semiotics of compensatory masculinity into an abject other in the Lacanian symbolic order. Wherever one finds all manner of family laws, colonialism, or war, for instance, one sees structures of pregnancy envy. Every little fascist loves a mommy.

Chapter 2 contains a footnote (note 11) stating that one of the earliest moments of gender development for infant boys is the realization (long before the Oedipal complex), that what distinguishes them from their mothers is that the boys will never give birth. The preceding statements contain several contested theoretical and empirical assertions. Here is not the place to defend them but the place to appeal for psychoanalytic research, on the grounds that the anti-universalist orthodoxies of the late twentieth century may have foreclosed (or at best, delegitimated) too abruptly certain lines of inquiry. Every political society bases rules of inclusion and exclusion on invocations of birth, and every political society has a sex/gender system that exists via its kinship rules—although often specific details may vary, respectively. Although sociology and anthropology have much to offer investigations of these phenomena, especially the structures of variation,

---

[2] Nietzsche writes: "We no longer believe that truth remains truth when the veils are withdrawn. . . . One should have more respect for the bashfulness with which nature has hidden behind riddles and iridescent uncertainties. Perhaps truth is a woman who has reasons for not letting us see her reasons?" "Contra Wagner," in *The Portable Nietzsche*, tr. Walter Kaufmann (New York: Viking Press, 1968), pp. 682–83.

psychoanalytic engagements with Hegelian (as opposed to Lacanian) themes of infant development are especially well suited to accommodating study of such an overdetermined nexus. And yet as a result of a Foucauldian-inspired impatience with psychoanalytic theory among humanists, and the long-standing resistance to psychoanalytic theory among social scientists, the field is in disrepute. Still, the fact is that the political membership rule of birth has withstood infinite variations of time and place. Hence it seems important to be able to draw on approaches that tend toward theories of the universal rather than the particular—while understanding that such an incitement may be vigorously challenged.

Why Challenge Birth Taxonomies?

A psychoanalytic inquiry at best might provide some of the reasons for the widespread existence of certain structures of interpellation, but psycho-analytic theory cannot decipher the meaning of political society's failures. Why insist on referring to the form of political societies' reproductive laws as "failures"? What about those communitarians who find in ancestral forms of being a noble way of life, of determining one's relation to the world? What about hopeful possibilities for birth narratives, such as those suggested by Heidegger and explored by Arendt?

Arendt refers to a discourse of birth, which she often renders as 'natality', as paradigmatic of human action. To the argument that the identities that follow from birth in a particular community create inevitable constraints, Arendt offers two rejoinders. The first is the rather formal Heideggerian notion that the primordial experience of birth is constitutive for remem-brance and beginnings: "[T]he decisive fact determining man as a con-scious, remembering being is birth or 'natality,' that is, the fact that we have entered the world through birth."[3] The fact of birth marks a point before which one had no consciousness. This provides, Arendt believes, the template for our ideas about beginnings, a model which is used when noticing that the flow of events beyond one's individual life-span also have beginnings, origins. The individual human life cycle is a pattern super-imposed on history, as those who have preceded us appear simultaneously "younger" and "older." They are younger because we came later. If we are at the end of history, then they must have been around at its first missteps, at the beginning. They were fumbling children while we are now wise adults. But they are also older because they were here first. The paradox is one of generationality. The child is at once diachronically older but synchronically younger. The child will outlive the parent, and hence

---

[3] Arendt, *Love and St. Augustine*, ed. Joanna Scott (Chicago and London: University of Chicago Press, 1996), p. 51.

chronologically see beyond her, but at any particular point the parent's date of birth renders her older than the child.

On this account, the present age is experienced as the enactment of the previous one's aspirations, just as an adult aims to fulfill her childhood desires. Unlike the individual afflicted by the condition of mortality, in a political society each point in history is both a culmination of previous ones and on the verge of being another generation's past: " '[T]he very fact of memorable continuity of these beginnings in the sequence of generations guarantees a history which can never end because it is the history of beginners whose essence is beginning.' "[4] This is one of the crucial differences between Arendt and Heidegger's view of history, on the one hand, and, that of Hegel, on the other hand, who really did think himself, with the crowning "achievements" of Europe's political and cultural development, to be the last old man. Arendt shows us an alternative way to imagine cycles of birth and death. Implicit in the condition of natality is its role as an object lesson in how to start again, so that natality is a moment of "beginnings." Arendt writes:

> Action has the closest connection with the human condition of natality; the new beginning inherent in birth can make itself felt in the world only because the newcomer possesses the capacity of beginning something anew, that is, of acting
> . . . since action is the political activity par excellence, natality and not mortality, may be the central category of political, as distinguished from metaphysical, thought.[5]

Leave death to Heidegger and metaphysics; Arendt will claim birth for her political theory. As we saw, Arendt herself notes that because natality is about beginnings, it is also about remembrance, about how the past will be carried into the future. When describing natality as "what makes man a political being,"[6] this aspect of continuity is neglected. One might infer—based only on this idea that birth signals beginnings—that the condition of natality is one that would result in a completely different political society each time someone is born or dies.

Though such a possibility may seem to hold exciting challenges of indeterminacy and authenticity, Arendt's intention here is the opposite. Her second defense of using the concept of birth to articulate a theory of political societies is that birth practices insure that new members will not disrupt the stability of any particular political society. Comparing U.S.

[4] Arendt, "Understanding and Politics" *Partisan Review* 20 (1953), p. 390, quoted by Patricia Bowen-Moore, in *Hannah Arendt's Philosophy of Natality* (New York: St. Martin's Press, 1989), p. 25.

[5] *The Human Condition* (Chicago, London: University of Chicago Press, 1958), p. 9.

[6] Arendt, "On Violence," in *On the Crises of the Republic* (New York: Harcourt, Brace, Jovanovich, 1969), p. 179.

American with Roman political institutions, Arendt says both show a concern with cultivating authority, by reproducing respect for foundings in
each generation. Arendt says the root of 'authority' means "to augment."
For Rome, authority "depended upon the vitality of the spirit of foundation,
by virtue of which it was possible to augment, to increase and enlarge the
foundations as they had been laid down by the ancestors."[7] The ideal
method for taking in new members does not rejuvenate and change the
political society with every birth, as Thomas Jefferson preferred. Rather,
Arendt admires the United States for having emulated the trinitarian use
of religion, authority and tradition the Roman Empire relied on to protect
its public space from the potential disruptions genuinely new beginnings
might incur.[8] Arendt refers to the decision honoring these conventions as
the "most important single notion which the men of the Revolution
adopted, not by conscious reflection, but by virtue of being nourished by
the classics and of having gone to school in Roman antiquity."[9] So this
great moment of political birth is delivered by apparently brainwashed
schoolboys, though a few lines later Arendt restores their agency: "They
thought of themselves as founders because they had *consciously* set out to
imitate the Roman example and emulate the Roman spirit."[10] For purposes
of consciousness, deviations from the past are always possible, but they
would not be manifest through so-called empirical details of the putative
differences and similarities between the past and the present. It is the
consciousness—in law and other texts—of the present age's differences
and similarities vis-à-vis the past that is the most important aspect of the
reproduction of that past. In either Arendtian version (unconscious or
conscious reiterations of a previous era's practices), the birth of the United
States is one scripted by the past. Political natality can be about beginnings,
Arendt seems to be suggesting, as long as the beginnings are not too new—
as long as they preserve the form and content of their origins, their past.

This preservation offers stability: "Authority, resting on a foundation
in the past as its unshaken cornerstone, gave the world the permanence
and durability which human beings need precisely because they are mor-
tals—the most unstable and futile beings we know of."[11] Whereas natality
is the condition of newness and breaks, Arendt also thinks it the requirement of a public sphere that will outlive the individual's birth and death.
Arendt, following Heidegger, believes that we need a society that takes the
inevitable form of a past and future, consistent with primordial narratives

[7] *On Revolution* (New York: Penguin, 1963), p. 201.
[8] Ibid.
[9] Ibid, pp. 201–2.
[10] Ibid., p. 203, emphasis added.
[11] "What Is Authority?" *Between Past and Future* (New York: Viking, 1968), pp. 95; see
also p. 125.

wrought of the human conditions of birth and death. On the one hand birth is the potential of the infant to be anyone at all, the inspirational possibility for a political society to start over. On the other hand, birth is just what political society draws on to affirm its origins, its traditions, its institutional permanence.

Arendt thinks this model of authority one that protected the individual, that it was a way of safe-guarding the public realm for human distinction. This way of life has been overtaken by various practices of the modern age, expressed in totalitarianism, mass society, and the nuclear threat, according to Arendt. Yet the same foundational Roman Empire that inspired the American revolutionaries' ardor for the authority Arendt admires, was used by Italian fascists. Maria Quine describes how fascist Italy recalled the membership policies of ancient Rome:

> The demographic campaign inspired major changes in the law, perhaps the most famous of which was the regime's decision in December 1926 to impose a bachelor tax on unmarried men. As in other policy areas, fascism looked to Italy's imperial past to justify this initiative. The regime presented its "celibacy tax" as a direct borrowing from the golden age of Emperor Augustus in Late Antiquity.[12]

What Arendt seems not to recognize is that the membership practices of the political societies she admires are not antithetical to, but rather of a piece with, the natality policies associated with fascist quasi-genocidal policies. Arendt's strictly emancipatory aspirations for a birth narrative cannot be realized. The freedom of natality as a moment of beginnings is also caprice, while the comfort of the birth form's determinacy—as a model for historical grounding—depends on conventions of physical annihilation and psychic suffocation that are anathema to the value of action Arendt holds so dear.

In addition to the dynamics of material deprivations previously discussed, another problem with intergenerational affiliations is that the rules by which political societies reproduce create conditions of alienation, from the Latin *aliengena*, meaning "a stranger, a foreigner by birth."[13] The *Oxford English Dictionary* first notes use of the word in 1330 and offers as one definition of 'alien': "belonging to another person, place, or family; strange, foreign, not one's own." Another major definition: "a person belonging to another family, race, or nation; a stranger, foreigner." This

---

[12] Quine documents how European liberal democracies had eugenics policies that in many respects were indistinguishable from those of their fascist counterparts (*Population Politics in Twentieth Century Europe: Fascist Dictatorships and Liberal Democracies* [London and New York: Routledge, 1996], p. 40).

[13] Partridge, *Origins*, 2d ed. (London: Routledge and Kegan Paul, 1959) and E. A. Andrews, *A Latin Dictionary*, rev. Charlton Lewis and Charles Short (Oxford: Clarendon Press, 1969).

is the same root for the German fremde (alien or strange), which is the root of Hegel's and Marx's Entfremdung (alienation).[14] The problem with political society's laws of intergenerational reproduction is not that these laws result in alienation per se, but that they make determinate an unfortunate form of alienation—one that ties being to a form of consciousness that holds forth only a false promise of reconciliation.

The quintessential moment of alienation is birth, since birth is the first moment of one's material and conscious existence as an individual. A fetus is a part of a whole. At birth the condition changes, so that a new being emerges that becomes separate from its mother, although still dependent on her. The condition of an initial connection to, indeed identity with, one's mother, is one side of how one becomes other, from oneself (as identical with the mother) and one's mother (as she begins to be experienced as other). That is why, from ancient Greek tragedy through twentieth-century psychoanalytic texts,[15] the experience of birth prompts the question that only sometimes explicitly refers back to birth for an answer: "Who am I?" Oedipus's journey toward self-discovery takes a paradoxical form, emblematic of the fact that individuation manifests an umbilical cord that can be cut but never erased or forgotten. On the one hand, Oedipus's first moment of consciousness is his parturition from Jocasta. On the other hand, the political backdrop to the drama implies that his quest(ion) is tied to other dynamics of alienation as well, as Oedipus is not simply removed from his mother but is brought up, politically, as an alien to his kinship group. Essentially, Oedipus is seeking to be rejoined to the condition of his initial separation, his moment of individuation from Jocasta in particular.

Oedipus is removed from a particular political society in which his father is the king. Such a political society exists by virtue of the intergenerational kinship rules that are in a relation of negation to the principle of origins located in the strictly binary relation to his mother (through birth) along with the irrelevance of the father to Oedipus's arrival at consciousness. That is, the rules of a political society's reproduction—insofar as they require rules of matrimony to bring fathers into relations with children—

---

[14] Both Hegel and Marx also use Entäußerung, which also has been translated as 'alienation', though Hegel confines his use of this term to contexts involving the process by which individuals objectify their work. Hegel, when using 'Entäusserung' to characterize the relation between individuals and their property writes, that it "would be better to speak here of a mode of externality. Alienation [Entäußerung] is giving up something which is my property and which is already external, it is not to externalize." (tr. note 16 in *Philosophy of Right*, tr. T. M. Knox [London and New York: Oxford, 1967], p. 322, quoting from *Hegels eigenhändige Randbermerkungen zu seiner Rechtsphilosophie*, ed. G. Lasson [Leipzig, F. Meiner, 1930], p. 29). The stem of Entäußerung is 'außer', meaning "outer."

[15] Freud insisted the gulf was almost nonexistent. For an extended essay arguing this point, see Bruno Bettelheim, *Freud and Man's Soul* (New York: Knopf, 1983).

negate the tie to the *mater*, the mother, which they also reproduce in establishing a kinship-based society (by mimicking the interpellated natural tie, of the mother). Even as it is reproducing the mother-son tie, a political society, by virtue of these rules, is also negating it. In the case of Oedipus the negation is particularly vivid—his removal from his mother literally entails being transplanted to a different political society and becoming a different person in this way as well—but the kinship rules that diminish the mother-child relation are present more generally as well, even for those who are not forced to become aliens from their political societies of birth.

To use these insights about birth and individuation to proceed to discuss Hegel's work—which dramatizes the conjoined political and psychological dynamics of alienation—does not reduce a great philosopher to his infant imagination but rather helps us elucidate the complicated ways that Hegel's texts produce insights about consciousness in general, and alienation in particular. Studies of birth are crucial to such a project.[16] The dynamic of infant separation and childhood development into adulthood are two of the trajectories that Hegel explicitly foregrounds—along with the development of institutions, philosophical outlooks, and epochal worldviews—as key forms inhabited by the dialectics of spirit:

> The child is man implicit. At first it possesses reason only implicitly; it begins by being the potentiality of reason and freedom, and so is free only in accordance with its concept. Now what exists purely implicitly in this way does not yet exist in actuality. Man is implicitly rational, but he must also become explicitly so by struggling to create himself.[17]

At the same time that Hegel analogizes the development of the child's subjectivity with the development of consciousness in general, he also represents the child as an object, from the point of view of its parents. The relationship between the husband and the wife

> has its actual existence not in itself but in the child—an 'other' [Ander], whose coming into existence is the relationship, and is also that in which the relationship itself gradually passes away; and this alternation of successive generations has its enduring basis in the nation [Volk].[18]

---

[16] Although some audiences will find Hegel's vocabulary off-putting, I engage it here because Hegel's formulations brilliantly exemplify a range of popular and highly theoretical intuitions and hypotheses about the relation between alienation and the development of the state.

[17] *Philosophy of Right*, p. 228.

[18] *Phenomenology of Spirit*, tr. J. Sibree (New York: Dover, 1956), p. 273; *Phänomenologie des Geistes* (Frankfurt: Suhrkamp, 1970), p. 336.

Hegel's work astutely interweaves the overlapping dynamics of intergenerational consciousness (child, parent, nation) into a dialectic that reveals the interconstitutive forms of childhood and nation, mediated by family law, not as an ontological claim about parallels among these entities, but as a recapitulation of the fluidity of how consciousness experiences the forms of philosophy, childhood, nation, family, and law. The sub-divisions in academic approaches to these activities, concepts, and institutions (each is all of these) are wrought more from conditions of professionalization than from the character of human development.

Hegel insists that the child, by virtue of being a potential adult, is not a material object. The epitome of Roman law's failings is that it treated children as family property.[19] And yet as Chapter 1 showed, Hegel does not understand children as autonomous beings in their own rights. Rather, Hegel represents them as the "oneness" (Einzelheit) and "substantive being" (substantielles Dasein) of the parents' connection and love.[20] For children to individuate, to become conscious beings and not merely the superficial incarnation of their parents' love, is always, according to Hegel, relational to the larger context of laws and culture into which children are born.

Specifically, Hegel elaborates a process by which individuals, through objectification, become one with the state. As opposed to the social contract theorists who proclaimed an initial tension between the freedom associated with the condition of being pre-political and pre-cultural on the one hand, and obligated to and conditioned by political society on the other, Hegel asserts that freedom lies in the development of the individual will and consciousness that is at one with that of a fully developed state. It is the moments of this process whereby the individual sees himself in the context of work and culture that he does not initially will that are the moments of alienation he must overcome.

The first moment of individuation in Hegel refers to two kinds of political activities that are also formative of the essence of who one is. One dynamic is that of work (Arbeitung), the other culture (Bildung). According to Hegel, although consciousness manifests itself dialectically through various attempts to know the world, the alienation of the servile consciousness through work is the first significant step toward the moment of self-consciousness able to experience freedom:

> Through work ... the bondsman becomes conscious of what he truly is ...
> For, in fashioning the thing, the bondsman's own negativity, his being-for-self,
> becomes an object for him only through his setting at nought the existing *shape*

[19] Hegel, *Philosophy of Right*, p. 41.
[20] Ibid., p. 117; *Grundlinien der Philosophie des Rechts* (Frankfurt: Suhrkamp, 1970), p. 325.

confronting him. But this objective *negative* moment is none other than the alien [fremde] being before which it has trembled. . . . Through this rediscovery of himself by himself, the bondsman realizes that it is precisely in his work wherein he seemed to have only an alienated existence that he acquires a mind of his own.[21]

At first the bondsman sees himself as an object, as subservient to the lord, but by creating a form separate from himself yet under his own control, the bondsman sees himself as a conscious being. His own alienated existence is the condition of his coming into consciousness. The thing he creates is separate but not entirely other, "but [self-consciousness] is certain that this independent object is for it not something alien."[22] It is the process of creating that which is both external to one but not experienced as entirely separate that Hegel documents as the development of individuality.

The second significant moment by which self-consciousness is alienated and overcomes this alienation occurs when the individual is confronted by a culture that is apparently not of his own making:

> The process [Bewegung] in which the individuality [Individualität] moulds itself by culture [Bildung] is, therefore, at the same time the development of it as the universal, objective essence, i.e. the development of the actual world. Although this world has come into being through individuality, it is for self-consciousness immediately an alienated world which has the form of a fixed and solid reality over against it.[23]

Hegel is observing that there is a formal difference between the individual and his political society, such that one might imagine the ethos of the institutions of his political society express norms other than one's own.

This sense of alienation is overcome, Hegel believes, when self-consciousness

> grasps the fact that its certainty of itself is the essence of all the spiritual masses [geistegen Massen]. . . . [T]he world is for it simply its own will, and this is a general will. And what is more, this will is not the empty thought of will which consists in silent assent, or assent by a representative, but a real general will, the will of all *individuals* [Einzelnen] as such . . . so that each, undivided from the whole, always does everything, and what appears as done by the whole is the direct and conscious deed of each.[24]

The main difference between this formulation of the general will and that of Rousseau is Hegel's emphasis on the ways that the state institutionalizes

---

[21] Hegel, *Phenomenology*, pp. 118–19.

[22] Ibid., p. 211.

[23] Hegel, *Phenomenology*, p. 299; *Phänomenologie*, p. 365.

[24] Hegel, *Phenomenology*, pp. 356–57; *Phänomenologie*, pp. 432–33.

this sense of individuality, rather than allow it to be a matter left to the private judgment of each individual.

The ultimate indication of the unity of the individual with the state is not simply individuals thinking about what is best for one's political society over one's selfish interests, or even hindsight that one's preferences were incorrect and the majority was right, but rather, the willingness of the individual to face the loss of his own life on behalf of the state. War, that is, death, provides the principle that Hegel sees as the ultimate grounding of a political society:

> This destiny whereby the rights and interests of individuals are established as a passing phase, is at the same time the positive moment, i.e., the positing of their absolute, not their contingent and unstable, individuality. This relation and the recognition of it is therefore the individual's substantive duty, the duty to maintain this substantive individuality, i.e. the independence and sovereignty of the state, at the risk and the sacrifice of property and life, as well as of opinion and everything else naturally comprised in the compass of life.[25]

Hence, by seeing an organic connection between oneself and one's political society, the initial experience of alienation is overcome; oneness and freedom are now possible.

But is consciousness—which Hegel describes as divided in so many spheres until its unity is achieved in the institutionalization of absolute spirit that envelops one's sense of belonging to a state—actually unified at this point? The principle by which the rational is the actual would seem to condemn Hegel's analysis in at least two respects. First, the principle of ethical universality for the individual has not been realized. There is a vibrant tradition of individualism that has nothing to do with Hegel's concept of the individual but is expressed in the United States militia movement, whereby individuals insist that because they never consented to join this government the laws of the United States government do not obligate them.[26] Hence these people experience themselves as aliens and therefore as alienated from the political society of the United States that would claim otherwise.

Another possible shortcoming of Hegel's analysis comes from his opposite claim, which is that it is birth that binds one to a political society. Here the problem is that the birth principle may be experienced as binding one to an ethnic community that follows from a political society other than the one into which that person was born. When this occurs, when a

---

[25] Hegel, *Philosophy of Right*, p. 209.

[26] In a more philosophical register this sense of individuality is expressed as a problem of agency, as a question about how to figure individual decisions into structural analyses.

Jew, for instance, sells Department of Defense secrets to Israel out of an experience of a superior bond to that country over that of the United States, then Hegel's vision has also failed. Jonathan Pollard, convicted of espionage, is also alienated from the political society that has formally claimed him as its citizen. Noting, however, the appearance of individualism and ethnic commitments in the context of current political institutions does not seriously undermine Hegel's main theses. Hegel may still be right, a defender of his might claim, and the episodes discussed above reveal only that the state and its possibilities have not yet been fully realized.

The most persuasive evidence that Hegel's telos is unattainable and not simply incompletely achieved are the ways that the state-nation form is historically and theoretically consistent with a kind of cosmopolitanism to which Hegel adamantly objected. From groups in civil society such as Amnesty International to organizations such as the United Nations and the international tribunals in the Hague, to the incarnation of those institutions in the relations of work and desire formed across borders, we see that the apotheosis of the individual's will and hence freedom is not restricted to the state-nation. While some laws and forces press for oneness, completeness, and hence freedom at the level of the individual's self-realization through the state-nation, still other laws and forces press in a competing, cosmopolitan direction.

Hegel decries cosmopolitanism as a false invocation of universalism rooted in the idealism of the Enlightenment, an ideology that would set the individual in "opposition to the concrete life of the state."[27] Yet just as the unity of the Hegelian state depends on the plurality of forms of being in civil society, the unity of a cosmopolitan humanity depends on the plurality of states. It is as impossible to be a citizen of the world without states as it would be to be a citizen of a Hegelian state without a differentiated civil society. Insofar as Hegel does not recognize the dynamic that leads toward the overcoming of the particularism of the state-nation, he does not recognize the ways that the state-nation constitutes the premise of a form of alienation that remains unresolved in his philosophy. The consciousness that sees itself as complete in its unity with a state-nation remains alienated—differentiated between two competing principles that remain in tension. The very dichotomy Hegel sought to overcome in Kant, between desire or sentiment on the one hand and law and principle on the other, reappears in Hegel's artificial, premature announcement that the state-nation is the end of history, for there are no uncontested philosophical, political, moral, or empirical justifications for Hegel's assertion that the particularism of the state must triumph over all other commitments, including those to the state's framework of universality.

[27] Hegel, *Philosophy of Right*, p. 134.

Hegel's competing ideologies of cosmopolitanism and nationalism do not exhaust the range of practices and sentiments that might challenge alienation. In addition, one might envisage existential self-affirmation or subtle non-institutional attempts to develop cultural competencies that would assuage the sense of being separate from who one is. But these engagements with alienation too will fail, as the secret to alleviating the pains of alienation is not to destroy it or supercede it, but to see how this particular action of aufheben (overcoming) is not the cure but itself a serious affliction. Freedom lies not in overcoming alienation, but in the realization, through desire as well as work, that alienation does not have to be overthrown, because that would be an end; that would be death.

At the heart of alienation is the fact that birth makes us strangers to ourselves. This we cannot vanquish from being, but alienation can be expressed and experienced in ways that are more or less self-conscious. This is not a matter of individual psychology, but, as the etymology of 'alienation' suggests, of overcoming the rigid boundaries of that moment, of the form of the alien that depends on notions of hard and fast differences. The purpose of this self-consciousness is the realization that the mother from which one separates and the family, nation, and so forth into which one develops are all manifest as dynamics of individuation and differentiation that always contain possibilities for movement away from the lure of determinate one-ness. Again, this is true not because expressions of oneness do not exist, but because true consciousness knows that oneness is not all that exists, that the dynamic of reunification exists in tension with the awareness that this movement is only part of the story of human activity and self-consciousness.

What Is to Be Done?

This is a question that is necessary to both acknowledge and to disavow, as it is impossible to answer it in this context. This has been a book largely about the heuristics of certain forms of being. Of course there are political implications to the arguments. The most obvious is not the anarchist's call for overthrowing government altogether, but rather efforts to think through ways of reproducing political societies so that kinship principles would play a diminished role. Two means for accomplishing this would be the elimination of any state involvement in marriage and the curtailment of citizenship requirements based on birth or ancestry.

Bibliography

Aland, Kurt. *Did the Early Church Baptize Infants?* Tr. G. R. Beasley-Murray. London: SCM Press, 1963.

Alford, Fred. *Naming and Identity: A Cross-Cultural Study of Personal Naming Practices.* New Haven: HRAF, 1987.

Allen, Norman. "*Adoption of Kelsey S.*: When Does an Unwed Father Know Best?" *Pacific Law Journal* 24 (1993): 1633–80.

Althusser, Louis. *For Marx.* Tr. Ben Brewster. London: Verso, 1969.

———. "Ideology and State Apparatuses." In *Lenin and Philosophy*, trans. Ben Brewster. New York: Monthly Review Press, 1971, pp. 127–88.

———. *Spectre of Hegel: Early Writings.* Tr. G. M. Goshgarian (London: Verso, 1997).

Anderson, Benedict. *Imagined Communities: Reflections on the Origin and Spread of Nationalism.* London: Verso, 1983.

Appiah, Anthony. *In My Father's House: Africa in the Philosophy of Culture.* Oxford: Oxford University Press, 1993.

———. "Identity, Authenticity, Survival: Multicultural Societies and Social Reproduction." In *Multiculturalism: Examining the Politics of Recognition*, ed. Amy Gutmann and C. Taylor. Princeton: Princeton University Press, 1994, pp. 149–64.

Arendt, Hannah. *Between Past and Future.* New York: Viking, 1968.

———. *On the Crises of the Republic.* New York: Harcourt, Brace, Jovanovich, 1969.

———. *The Human Condition.* Chicago: University of Chicago Press, 1958.

———. *Love and St. Augustine.* Ed. Joanna Scott. Chicago and London: University of Chicago Press, 1996.

———. *The Origins of Totalitarianism.* 2d ed. New York: World Publishing, 1951.

———. *On Revolution.* New York: Penguin, 1963.

Aristophanes. *Ecclesiazusae.* In *Complete Plays of Aristophanes.* Tr. Jack Lindsay. New York: Bantam, 1962.

Aristotle. *Politics.* In *The Complete Works of Aristotle.* Tr. B[enjamin] Jowett. 2 vols. Princeton: Princeton University Press, 1984.

Augustine, St. *Concerning the City of God Against the Pagans.* Tr. Henry Bettenson. Middlesex: Penguin, 1972.

Austin, J. L. *How to Do Things with Words.* Oxford: Clarendon Press, 1962.

———. *Philosophical Papers.* Oxford: Clarendon Press, 1961.

Aveni, Anthony. *Empires of Time: Calendars, Clocks, and Cultures.* New York and Tokyo: Kodansha, 1989.

Avineri, Shlomo. *Hegel's Theory of the Modern State.* Cambridge: Cambridge University Press, 1972.

Bachrach, Peter. *The Theory of Democratic Elitism: A Critique.* Boston: Little, Brown, 1967.

Balibar, Etienne, and Immanuel Wallerstein. *Race, Nation, Class: Ambiguous Identities.* London: Verso, 1991.

Banton, Michael. *Racial and Ethnic Competition*. Cambridge: Cambridge University Press, 1983.

Banton, Michael. *Racial Theories*. Cambridge: Cambridge University Press, 1987.

Baran, Paul, and Paul Sweezy. *Monopoly Capital*. New York: Modern Reader Paperbacks, 1968.

Barber, Benjamin. "Spirit's Phoenix and History's Owl **or** The Incoherence of Dialectics in Hegel's Account of Women." *Political Theory* 16 (February, 1988): 5–28.

Barkan, Elazar. *The Retreat of Scientific Racism*. Cambridge: Cambridge University Press, 1992.

Barnhart, Robert, ed. *The Barnhart Dictionary of Etymology*. New York: H. H. Wilson, 1988.

Barzun, Jacques. *Race: A Study in Modern Superstition*. New York: Harcourt, Brace, 1937; rev. ed. New York, London: Harper and Row, 1966.

Bauer, Bruno. *The Jewish Problem*. Tr. Helen Lederer. Cincinnati: Hebrew Union College-Jewish Institute of Religion, 1958. Typescript.

Beier, A. C. *Masterless Men: The Vagrancy Problem in England, 1560–1640*. London and New York: Methuen, 1985.

Benedict, Ruth. *Race and Racism*. London: Routledge and Sons, 1945.

———. *Race: Science and Politics*. New York: Modern Age Books, 1940.

Bentham, Jeremy. *A Fragment on Government*. Cambridge: Cambridge University Press, 1988.

Bering, Dietz. *The Stigma of Names: Antisemitism in German Daily Life, 1812–1933*. Ann Arbor: University of Michigan Press, 1992.

Bernal, Martin. *Black Athena: The Afroasiatic Roots of Civilization*. 2 vols. New Brunswick: Rutgers University Press, 1987.

Bettelheim, Bruno. *Freud and Man's Soul*. New York: Knopf, 1983.

Béza, Theodore de. *Concerning the Rights of Rulers over Their Subjects and the Duty of Subjects towards Their Rulers*. Tr. Henri-Louis Gonin. Capetown: NV Drukkerij v.h. C. de Baer Jr., 1956.

Bhabha, Homi, ed. *Nation and Narration*. London and New York: Routledge, 1990.

Bloch, Marc. *Feudal Society*. Tr. L. A. Manyon. Chicago: University of Chicago Press, 1961.

Boas, Franz. *Race and Democratic Society: Collected Papers*. New York: J. J. Augustin, 1945.

Boswell, John. *Christianity, Social Tolerance, and Homosexuality: Gay People in Western Europe from the Beginning of the Christian Era to the Fourteenth Century*. Chicago: University of Chicago Press, 1980.

———. *Same-sex Unions in Premodern Europe*. New York: Villard Books, 1994.

Bourne, Henry Fox. *The Life of John Locke*. 3 vols. Darmstadt: Scientia Verlag Aalen, 1969.

Bowen-Moore, Patricia. *Hannah Arendt's Philosophy of Natality*. New York: St. Martin's Press, 1989.

Braudel, Ferdinand. *Civilization and Capitalism, 15th - 18th Centuries*. Tr. Susan Reynolds. 3 vols. New York: Harper and Row, 1981.

Braverman, Harry. *Labor and Monopoly Capital: The Degradation of Work in the 20th Century*. New York: Monthly Review Press, 1974.

Brimelow, Peter. *Alien Nation: Common Sense about America's Immigration Disaster.* New York: Random House, 1995.

Brown, Norman O. *Love's Body.* New York: Random House, 1966.

Brown, Peter. *The Body and Society: Men, Women and Sexual Renunciation in Early Christianity.* New York: Columbia University Press, 1988.

Brown, Wendy. "Reproductive Freedom and the Right of Privacy." In *Families, Politics, and Public Policy: A Dialogue on Women and the State*, ed. Irene Diamond. New York and London: Longman, 1983, pp. 322–38.

———. *Wounded Attachments: Power and Freedom in Late Modernity.* Princeton: Princeton University Press, 1995.

Brubaker, Rogers. *Citizenship and Nationhood in France and Germany.* Cambridge: Harvard University Press, 1992.

Brundage, James. *Medieval Canon Law.* New York: Longman, 1995.

Butler, Judith. *Bodies That Matter: On the Discursive Limits of 'Sex'.* New York: Routledge, 1993.

———. *Gender Trouble: Feminism and the Subversion of Identity.* New York: Routledge, 1990.

———. "Imitation and Gender Insubordination." In *Inside/Out: Lesbian and Gay Theories*, ed. Diana Fuss. New York: Routledge, 1991, pp. 13–31.

———. "Merely Cultural," *Social Text* nos. 52–3 (Fall/Winter, 1997): 265–78.

Calverton, V. F. "The Illegitimate Child." In *New Generation: The Intimate Problems of Modern Parents and Children*, ed. V. F. Calverton. New York: Macauley, 1930, pp. 189–206.

Camden, William. *Remains Concerning England.* Toronto: University of Tornoto Press, 1984.

Cann, Rebecca, Mark Storekin, and Allan Wilson. "Mitochondrial DNA and Human Evolution." *Nature* 325, no. 1 (January, 1987): 31–36.

Carnoy, Martin. *The State and Political Theory.* Princeton: Princeton University Press, 1984.

Carter, Stephen. *Culture of Disbelief: How American Law and Politics Trivialize American Devotion.* New York: Basic: 1993.

Cary, M., and H. Scullard. *A History of Rome Down to the Reign of Constantine.* 3d ed. London: MacMillan, 1975.

Certeau, Michel de. *Writing History.* Tr. Tom Conley. New York: Columbia University Press, 1988.

Chatterjee, Partha. *The Nation and Its Fragments: Colonial and Postcolonial Histories.* Princeton: Princeton University Press, 1993.

Cicero. *The Republic.* Tr. Clinton Keyes. Cambridge: Harvard University Press, 1928.

Clark, Lorenne. "Who Owns the Apples in the Garden of Eden?" In *The Sexism of Social and Political Theory: Women and Reproduction from Plato to Nietzsche*, ed. Lorenne M. G. Clark and Lynda Lange. Toronto: University of Toronto Press, 1979, pp. 16–40.

Clastres, Pierre. *Society against the State: Essays in Political Anthropology.* Tr. Robert Hurley. New York: Zone Books, 1989.

Clignet, Remi. *Death, Deeds, and Descendants: Inheritance in Modern America.* New York: Aldine de Gruyter, 1992.

Coghlan, Roman. *Irish Christian Names: An A-Z of First Names*. London and Edinburgh: Johnston and Bacon, 1979.

Cohen, Jean, and Andrew Arato. *Civil Society and Political Theory*. London and Cambridge: MIT Press, 1992.

Coke, Edward. *The First Part of the Institutes of the Laws of England: Or a Commentary Upon de Littleton, Not the Name of the Author Only, But of the Law Itself*. 16th ed.; rev. and corr. ed. London: L. Hansard and Sons, 1809.

Collier, Richard. *Masculinity, the Law, and the Family*. London and New York: Routledge, 1995.

Constable, Marianne. *The Law of the Other: The Mixed Jury and Changing Conceptions of Citizenship, Law, and Knowledge*. Chicago: University of Chicago Press, 1994.

Cornell, Timothy. "Rome: History of an Anachronism." In *City-States in Classical Antiquity and Medieval Italy*, ed. Anthony Molho et al. Ann Arbor: University of Michigan, 1991, pp. 53–70.

Cott, Nancy. "Giving Character to Our Whole Civil Polity: Marriage and the Public Order in the Late Nineteenth Century." In *United States History as Women's History: New Feminist Essays*, ed. Linda Kerber et al. Chapel Hill and London: University of North Carolina University Press, 1995, pp. 107–24.

Cox, Oliver. *Caste, Class, and Race: A Study in Social Dynamics*. Garden City: Doubleday, 1948.

Crenshaw, Kimberlé. "Mapping the Margins: Intersectionality, Identity Politics, and Violence against Women of Color." In *Critical Race Theory: The Key Writings that Formed the Movement*, ed. Kimberlé Crenshaw. New York: New Press, 1995, pp. 357–83.

Crowe, David. *A History of the Gypsies of Eastern Europe and Russia*. New York: St. Martin's Press, 1995.

Cunningham, William. *Alien Immigrants to England*. London and New York: MacMillan, 1897.

Dahl, Robert. *Who Governs: Democracy and Power in an American City*. New Haven: Yale University Press, 1961.

Daly, James. *Sir Robert Filmer and English Political Thought*. Toronto: University of Toronto Press, 1979.

Danielson, Caroline. "Citizen Acts: Citizenship and Political Agency in the Works of Jane Addams, Charlotte Perkins Gilman, and Emma Goldman." Dissertation, University of Michigan, 1996.

Darnby, H. C. *Domesday England*. Cambridge: Cambridge University Press, 1977.

Davis, James. *Who Is Black? One Nation's Definition*. University Park: Pennsylvania State University Press, 1991.

Davis, Kingsley. *Human Society*. New York: MacMillan, 1949.

———. "Illegitimacy and Social Structure." *American Journal of Sociology* 45 (1939): 215–33.

Davis, Uri. "Jinsiyya vs. Muwatana: The Question of Citizenship and the State in the Middle East." *Arab Studies Quarterly* 17, nos. 1/2 (Winter/Spring, 1995): 19–50.

Demosthenes. "Mantitheus against Boeotus in Regard to the Name" (39, I); and "Mantitheus against Boeotus Regarding His Mother's Marriage Portion" (40,

II) in *Private Orations*, tr. A. T. Murray, vol. IV (Cambridge and London: Harvard University Press, 1936), notes on pp. 444–46; and 452–53.

Diamond, Raymond, and Robert Cottrol. "Codifying Caste: Los Angeles' Racial Classification Scheme and the Fourteenth Amendment," *Loyola Law Review* 29 (Spring, 1983): 255–85.

Dirks, Nicholas, Geoffrey Eley, and Sherry Ortner, eds. *Culture/Power/History: A Reader in Contemporary Social Theory*. Princeton: Princeton University Press, 1994.

Domhoff, William. *Who Really Rules? New Haven and Community Power Re-examined*. New Brunswick: Transaction Books, 1970.

Domínguez, Virginia. *White By Definition: Social Classification in Creole Lousiana*. New Brunsick: Rutgers University Press, 1986.

Dow, Unity. *The Citizenship Case*. Gabarone, Botswana: Lentswe La Lesedi, 1995.

Dowdall, H. C. "The Word 'State'." *Law Quarterly Review* 39 (1923): 98–125.

Du Bois, W.E.B. "The Conservation of Races." In *W.E.B. Du Bois: A Reader*. New York: MacMillan Press, 1971, pp. 19–30.

———. *Dusk of Dawn: An Essay toward an Autobiography of a Race Concept*. New Brunswick: Transaction Books, 1992.

Duggan, Lisa. "Queering the State." *Social Text* 39 (Summer, 1994): 1–14.

Dummett, Ann. "The Transnational Migration of People Seen within a Natural Law Tradition." In *Free Movement: Ethical Issues in the Transnational Migration of People and Money*, ed. Brian Barry and Robert Goodin. London: Harvester Wheatsheaf, 1992, pp. 167–80.

Durkheim, Emile. *Elementary Forms of Religious Life*. Tr. Joseph Swain. New York and London: Free Press, 1965.

Edwards, Richard, et al. *Segmented Work, Divided Workers: The Historical Transformations of Labor in the United States*. Cambridge and New York: Cambridge University Press, 1982.

Eisenstein, Zillah. *Capitalist Patriarchy and the Case for Socialist Feminism*. New York: Monthly Review Press, 1979.

Eller, T. J., and Wallace Fraser. *Asset Ownership of Households: 1993*. Washington, D.C.: Bureau of the Census, 1993.

Engels, Frederick. *The Origin of the Family, Private Property, and the State*. 1884; rpt. New York: Pathfinder, 1972.

Enloe, Cynthia. *Bananas, Beaches, and Bases: Making Feminist Sense of International Politics*. Berkeley: University of California Press, 1990.

Erikson, Nancy. "The Feminist Dilemma over Unwed Parents' Custody Rights." *Law and Inequality* 2 (1984): 447–72.

Ettelbrick, Paula. "Wedlock Alert: A Comment on Lesbian and Gay Family Recognition." *Journal of Law and Policy* 5, no. 1 (1996): 107–66.

Euripides. *"The Bacchae" and Other Plays*. Tr. Philip Vellacott. London: Penguin, 1973.

Evans, David. *Sexual Citizenship: The Material Construction of Sexualities*. London and New York: Routledge, 1993.

Evans, Peter, Dietrich Rueschemeyer, and Theda Skocpol, ed. *Bringing the State Back In*. Cambridge: Cambridge University Press, 1985.

Evans-Pritchard, E. *Kinship and Marriage among the Nuer*. Oxford: Clarendon Press, 1951.

Falk, Richard. *On Humane Governance: Toward a Global Politics*. University Park: Pennsylvania State University Press, 1995.

Falk, Richard, Robert Johansen, and Samuel Kim, eds. *Constitutional Foundations of World Peace*. Albany: State University of New York Press, 1993.

Fiegl, Herbert. "Positivism in the Twentieth Century." In *Dictionary of the History of Ideas*, vol. 3. New York: Charles Scribner's Sons, 1973, pp. 545–50.

Fields, Barbara, "Slavery, Race and Ideology in the United States of America." *New Left Review*, no. 181 (May/June, 1990): 95–118.

Filmer, Robert. "Patriarcha." In *Two Treatises of Government, With a Supplement, Patriarcha by Robert Filmer*. New York: Hafner, 1973, pp. 250–308.

Fineman, Martha. *The Illusion of Equality*. Chicago: University of Chicago Press, 1991.

―――. *The Neutered Mother, the Sexual Family, and Other Twentieth Century Tragedies*. New York and London: Routledge, 1995.

Fisher, Sue, and Kathy Davis. *Negotiating at the Margins: The Gendered Discourses of Power and Resistance*. New Brunswick: Rutgers University Press, 1993.

Fortes, Mayer, and E. E. Evans-Pritchard, eds. *African Political Systems*. Oxford: Oxford University Press, 1970.

Foucault, Michel. *Archaeology of Knowledge*. Tr. M. Sheridan Smith. New York: Pantheon, 1972.

―――. *Language, Counter-Memory, Practice: Selected Essays and Interviews*. Ed. D. F. Bouchard. Tr. D. F. Bouchard and Sherry Simon. Ithaca: Cornell University Press, 1977.

―――. *Herculine Barbin: Being the Recently Discovered Memoirs of a Nineteenth Century French Hermpahrodite*. Tr. Richard McDougall. New York: Pantheon, 1980.

―――. *History of Sexuality*. Tr. Robert Hurley. 3 vols. New York: Vintage, 1980.

―――. *This Is Not a Pipe*. Tr. James Harkness. Berkeley: University of California Press, 1983.

Fraser, Nancy. "From Redistribution to Recognition? Dilemmas of Justice in a 'Post-Socialist' Age." *New Left Review*, no. 212 (July/August, 1995): 68–93.

Frederickson, George. *Arrogance of Race*. Middletown: Wesleyan University Press, 1988.

Freeman, Edward. *The History of the Norman Conquest*. Rev. American ed. New York and Oxford: MacMillan, 1873.

Frege, Gottlob. "On Sense and Nominatum." In *Readings in Philosophical Analysis*, ed. Herbert Fiegl and Wilfred Sellars, tr. Herbert Fiegl and Wilfred Sellars. New York: Appleton-Century-Crafts, 1949, pp. 85–102.

Freud, Sigmund. "Analysis of a Phobia in a Five-Year-Old Boy" [1909]. In *Standard Edition*, tr. James Strachey, vol. 10, pp. 5–147.

―――. "Psycho-analytic Notes on an Autobiographical Account of a Case of Paranoia (Dementia Paranoides)" (1911). In *Standard Edition*, tr. James Strachey, vol. 12.

―――. *The Standard Edition of the Complete Psychological Works of Sigmund Freud*. 24 vols. Tr. James Strachey et al. London: Hogarth Press, 1955.

Geertz, Clifford. *The Interpretation of Cultures*. New York: Basic Books, 1973.

Gellner, Ernest. *Nations and Nationalism*. Oxford: Blackwell, 1983.

Gies, Frances, and Joseph Gies. *Life in a Medieval Village*. New York: Harper and Row, 1990.

Gilman, Sander. *Difference and Pathology: Stereotypes of Sexuality, Race, and Madness*. Ithaca: Cornell University Press, 1985.

Goldberg, David. *Racist Culture: Philosophy and the Politics of Meaning*. Cambridge: Blackwell, 1993.

Goldfield, Michael. "The Color of Politics in the United States." In *The Bounds of Race: Perspectives on Hegemony and Resistance*, ed. Dominick Lacapra. Ithaca: Cornell University Press, 1991, pp. 104–33.

Goody, Jack. *The Development of Family and Marriage in Europe*. Cambridge: Cambridge University Press, 1983.

———. *The Logic of Writing and the Organization of Society*. Cambridge: Cambridge University Press, 1986.

Gough, J. W. *The Social Contract: A Critical Study of Its Development*. Oxford: Clarendon Press, 1957.

Gramsci, Antonio. *Selections from the Prison Notebooks*. Tr. Quintin Hoare and Geoffrey Smith. New York: International Publishers, 1971.

Grant, Rebecca, and Kathleen Newman, eds. *Gender and International Relations*. Bloomington: Indiana University Press, 1991.

Green, Philip. *Retrieving Democracy: In Search of Civic Equality*. Totowa: Rowman and Allanheld, 1985.

Greenfield, Liah. *Nationalism: Five Roads to Modernity*. Cambridge: Harvard University Press, 1992.

Grimm, Jacob, and Wilhelm Grimm. *Deutsches Wörterbuch*. Leipzig: S. Hirzel, 1893.

Grossberg, Michael. *Governing the Hearth: Law and the Family in Nineteenth-Century America*. Chapel Hill: University of North Carolina Press, 1985.

Grotius, Hugo. *The Most Excellent Hugo Grotius: His Three Books Treating of the Rights of War*, Book I. London: Basset, 1682. Microfiche.

Halley, Janet. "The Construction of Heterosexuality." In *Fear of a Queer Planet*, ed. Michael Warner. Minneapolis: University of Minnesota Press, 1994, pp. 82–104.

Haney-López, Ian. *White by Law: The Legal Construction of Race*. New York: New York University Press, 1996.

Hardin, C. L. *Color for Philosophers: Unweaving the Rainbow*. Indianapolis: Hacket, 1988.

Harrison, A.R.W. *The Law of Athens: The Family and Property*. Oxford: Clarendon Press, 1968.

Harrison, William. *The Description of England*. Ithaca: Cornell, 1968.

Hartmann, Heidi. "Capitalism, Patriarchy, and Job Segregation by Sex." In *The Signs Reader: Women, Gender, and Scholarship*, ed. Elizabeth Abel and Emily Abel. Chicago and London: University of Chicago Press, 1983, pp. 193–226.

Haslanger, Sally. "Gender and Race: (What) Are They? (What) Do We Want Them to Be?" Paper presented at the Institute for Social Research, University of Michigan, Ann Arbor, September, 1997.

Hegel, G[eorg] W[ilhelm] F[riedrich]. *Grundlinien der Philosophie des Recht, oder Naturrechts und Staatswissenschaft im Grundrisse*. Frankfurt: Suhrkamp, 1970.

———. *Phänomenologie des Geistes*. Frankfurt: Suhrkamp, 1970.

Hegel, G[eorg] W[ilhelm] F[riedrich]. *Phenomenology of Spirit.* Tr. A. V. Miller. Oxford: Oxford University Press, 1977.

———. *Philosophy of History.* Tr. J. Sibree. New York: Dover, 1956.

———. *Philosophy of Right.* Tr. T. M. Knox. London and New York: Oxford University Press, 1967.

Heidegger, Martin. *Being and Time.* Tr. John Macquarrie and Edward Robinson. New York: Harper and Row, 1962.

———. *Hegel's Phenomenology of Spirit.* Tr. Parvis Emad and Kenneth Maly. Bloomington and Indianapolis: Indianapolis University Press, 1988.

Herodotus. *The Histories.* Tr. Aubrey de Sélincourt. Middlesex: Penguin, 1955.

———. *Histories.* Tr. A. D. Godley. Cambridge: Harvard University Press, 1921.

Herrnstein, Richard, and Charles Murray. *The Bell Curve: Intelligence and Class Structure in American Life.* New York: Free Press, 1994.

Herzog, Don. *Happy Slaves: A Critique of Consent Theory.* Chicago: University of Chicago Press, 1989.

Hignett, Charles. *A History of the Athenian Constitution.* London and Oxford: Oxford University Press, 1952.

Hill, Christopher. *Reformation to Industrial Revolution.* Middlesex: Penguin, 1969.

Hobbes, Thomas. *Leviathan.* London: Penguin, 1985.

———. "A Discourse upon the Beginning of Tacitus." In *Three Discourses: A Critical Modern Edition of Newly Identified Work of the Young Hobbes,* ed. Noel Reynolds and Arlene Saxonhouse. Chicago: University of Chicago Press, 1985, pp. 31–70.

Hofheimer, Alice. "Gestational Surrogacy: Unsettling State Parentage Law and Surrogacy Policy." *New York University Review of Law and Social Change* 19 (1992): 407–17.

Holy, Ladislav. *Strategies and Norms in a Changing Matrilineal Society.* Cambridge and New York: Cambridge University Press, 1986.

Homans, George Caspar. *English Villagers of the Thirteenth Century.* New York: Russell and Russell, 1960.

Homo, Leon. *Roman Political Institutions: From City to State.* London: Routledge, 1962.

Hull, Isabel. *Sexuality, State, and Civil Society in Germany, 1700–1815.* Ithaca: Cornell University Press, 1996.

Humana, Charles. *World Human Rights Guide.* Oxford: Oxford Univeristy Press, 1992.

Hume, David. "Of the Original Contract." In *Essays: Moral, Political and Literary.* Indianapolis: Liberty Press, 1978, pp. 465–87.

———. *A Treatise of Human Nature.* New York: Dolphin Press, 1961.

Hunt, Alan. *Explorations in Law and Society: Toward a Constitutive Theory of Law.* New York: Routledge, 1993.

Hunt, Lynn. *The Family Romance of the French Revolution.* Berkeley: University of California Press, 1992.

Huntington, Samuel. *American Politics: The Promise of Disharmony.* Cambridge: Belkap Press, 1981.

———. "The Clash of Civilizations?" *Foreign Affairs* 72 (Summer, 1993): 22–49.

Husserl, Edmund. *Ideas: General Introduction to Pure Phenomenology.* Tr. W. R. Boyce Gibson. London: Collier, 1931.

———. *Phenomenology and the Crisis of Philosophy*. Tr. Quentin Lauer. New York: Harper, 1965.

Hutchison, E. P. *Legislative History of American Immigration Policy, 1798–1965*. Philadelphia: University of Pennsylvania Press, 1985.

Hyppolite, Jean. *Genesis and Structure of Hegel's Phenomenology of Spirit*. Tr. Samuel Cherniak and John Heckman. Evanston: Northwestern University Press, 1974.

Ingram, Martin. *Church Courts, Sex and Marriage in England, 1570–1640*. Cambridge: Cambridge University Press, 1987.

Inwood, Michael. *A Hegel Dictionary*. Oxford and Cambridge: Basil Blackwell, 1992.

Irigaray, Luce. "The Necessity for Sexuate Rights." In *The Irigaray Reader*, ed. Margaret Whitford. Oxford and Cambridge: Blackwell, 1991, pp. 198–203.

Isaacs, Harold. *Idols of the Tribe: Group Identity and Political Change*. New York: Harper and Row, 1975.

Joint Association of Classical Teachers (JACT). *The World of Athens: An Introduction to Classical Athenian Culture*. London and Cambridge: Cambridge University Press, 1984.

Jaggar, Alison. *Feminist Politics and Human Nature*. Sussex: Harvester Press, 1983.

Jeffords, Susan. *The Remasculinization of America: Gender and the Vietnam War*. Bloomington: Indiana University Press, 1989.

Jeremias, Jochim. *The Origins of Infant Baptism: A Further Study in Reply to Kurt Aland*. Naperville: A. R. Allenson, 1963.

Jessop, Bob. *State Theory: Putting Capitalist States in Their Place*. University Park. Pennsylvania State University Press, 1990.

Jones, Ann. *Next Time She'll Be Dead*. Boston: Beacon Press, 1994.

Jones, Kathleen. *Compassionate Authority: Democracy and the Representation of Women*. New York: Routledge, 1993.

Jordan, Winthrop. *White Man's Burden: Origins of Racism in the United States*. Oxford: Oxford University Press, 1974.

Justinian. *Justinian's Institutes*. Tr. Peter Birks and Grant McLeod. Ithaca: Cornell University Press, 1987.

Kant, Immanuel. *Critique of Pure Reason*. Tr. Norman Smith. New York: St. Martin's Press, 1965.

———. *Perpetual Peace*. Tr. Ted Humphrey. Indianapolis, Hackett, 1983.

Kantorowicz, Ernst. *The King's Two Bodies: A Study in Medieval Political Theology*. Princeton: Princeton University Press, 1957.

Katz, Kathryn. "Ghost Mothers: Human Egg Donation and the Legacy of the Past." *Albany Law Review* 57 (1994): 733–80.

Kaufmann, Walter, ed. *Hegel's Political Philosophy*. New York: Atherton, 1970.

Keddie, Nikki, and L. Beck, eds. *Women in the Muslim World*. Cambridge: Harvard University Press, 1978.

Kelly, Henry. "*Rule of Thumb* and the Folklore of the Husband's Stick." *Journal of Legal Education* 44 (September, 1994): 341–65.

Ketchum, Sara. "Liberalism and Marriage Law." In *Feminism and Philosophy*, ed. Mary Vetterlin-Brokin, Frederick Elliston, and Jane English. New York: Rowman and Littlefield, 1977, pp. 264–76.

Kettner, James. *The Development of American Citizenship, 1608–1870*. Chapel Hill: University of North Carolina Press, 1978.

Kierkegaard, Soren. *The Present Age and Of the Difference between a Genius and an Apostle*. Tr. Alexander Dru. New York: Harper and Row, 1962.

Kinder, Donald, and Lynn Sanders. *Divided by Color: Racial Politics and Democratic Ideals*. Chicago: University of Chicago Press, 1996.

Kittay, Eva Feder. "Womb Envy: An Explanatory Concept." In *Mothering—Essays in Feminist Theory*, ed. Joyce Trebilcolt. Totowa: Rowman and Allanheld, 1983, pp. 94–128.

Klein, Ernest. *Comprehensive Etymological Dictionary: Dealing with the Origin of Worlds and Their Sense Development, Thus Illustrating the History of Civilization and Culture*. London: Elsevier, 1966.

Kovel, Joel. *White Racism: A Psychohistory*. New York: Pantheon Press, 1970.

Kripke, Saul. *Naming and Necessity*. Cambridge: Harvard University Press, 1972.

Kristeva, Julia. *Strangers to Ourselves*. Tr. Leon Roudiez. New York: Columbia University Press, 1991.

Kymlicka, Will. *Liberalism, Community, and Culture*. Oxford: Clarendon Press, 1989.

Laclau, Ernesto, and Chantal Mouffe. *Hegemony and Socialist Strategy: Towards a Radical Democratic Politics*. London: Verso, 1985.

Leacock, Eleanor Burke. *Myths of Male Dominance: Collected Articles on Women Cross-Culturally*. New York, London: Monthly Review Press, 1981.

Lefkowitz, Mary, and Maureen Faust, comps. *Women's Life in Greece and Rome*. Rev. ed. Baltimore: Johns Hopkins University Press, 1982.

Lerner, Gerda. *The Creation of Patriarchy*. New York and Oxford: Oxford University Press 1986.

Lévi-Strauss, Claude. *The Elementary Structures of Kinship*. Tr. James Bell et al. Boston: Beacon Press, 1969.

———. "Religion, Language, History: Concerning an Unpublished Text by F. Saussure." In *View From Afar*. Tr. Joachim Neugroschel and Phoebe Hoss. New York: Basic, 1985, pp. 148–56.

Livy. *The Early History of Rome*. Tr. Aubrey De Selincourt. London: Penguin, 1971.

Locke, John. *Two Treatises of Government*. Ed. Peter Laslett. Cambridge: Cambridge University Press, 1960.

Loraux, Nicole. *The Children of Athena: Athenian Ideas about Citizenship and the Division between the Sexes*. Tr. Caroline Levine. Princeton: Princeton University Press, 1993.

Lukács, Gyorgy. *History and Class Consciousness*. Tr. Rodney Livingston. Cambridge: MIT Press, 1983.

Luther, Martin. *Works*. Philadelphia: Fortress Press, 1955.

Luxemburg, Rosa. *Crisis of the German Social Democracy*. New York: Socialist Publication Society, 1919.

———. "The National Question and Autonomy." In *The National Question*, ed. Horace Davis. New York: Monthly Review Press, 1976, pp. 101–288.

Machiavelli, Niccolò. *The Prince and the Discourses*. Tr. Luigi Ricci. New York: Modern Library, 1950.

MacIntyre, Alasdair. *After Virtue*. 2d ed. Notre Dame: University of Notre Dame Press, 1984.

MacKinnon, Catharine. *Toward a Feminist Theory of the State*. Cambridge: Harvard University Press, 1989.

Malinowski, Bronislaw. "Parenthood." In *New Generation: The Intimate Problems of Modern Parents and Children*, ed. V. F. Calverton. New York: Macauley, 1930, pp. 113–68.

Marable, Manning. *How Capitalism Underdeveloped Black America: Problems in Race, Political Economy, and Society*. Boston: South End Press, 1983.

Marshall, T. H. *Citizenship and Social Class*. London and Concord: Pluto Press, 1992.

Marty, Martin, and Scott Appleby, eds. *Fundamentalisms and the State: Remaking Polities, Economies, and Militance*. Chicago and London: University of Chicago Press, 1993.

Marx, Karl. *Capital*. Tr. Samuel Moore and Edward Aveling. 3 vols. London: Lawrence and Wishart, 1974.

———. "Critique of Hegel's Doctrine of the State." In *Early Writings*, tr. Gregor Benton. New York and London: Penguin Books, 1975, pp. 57–198.

———. *The Grundrisse*. Tr. Martin Nicolaus. New York: Vintage, 1976.

———. "On the Jewish Question." In *The Marx-Engels Reader*, 2d ed., ed. Robert Tucker. New York: W. W. Norton, 1978, pp. 26–52.

———. "Marx's Remarks on the Programme and Rules of the International Alliance of Socialist Democracy" [pamphlet published December 15, 1868]. In Marx-Engels, *Collected Works*, vol. 21 (New York: International Publishers, 1985), pp. 207–11.

Marx, Karl, and Frederick Engels. *The German Ideology*. Moscow: Progress Publisher, 1976.

Mate, Her Holiness Majadevi Jagadguru. *Who Is a Hindu?* Bandalore: Viswakalyana Mission, 1989.

McClintock, Anne. *Imperial Leather: Race, Gender and Sexuality in the Colonial Context*. New York: Routledge, 1995.

McDowall, David. *A Modern History of the Kurds*. London and New York: I. B. Tauris, 1996.

McMurtry, John. *The Structure of Marx's World-view*. Princeton: Princeton University Press, 1979.

Miliband, Ralph. *The State in Capitalist Society*. London: Wiedenfeld and Nicolson, 1968.

Mill, John Stuart. *The Subjection of Women*. Rutland: Everyman's Library, 1985.

———. *A System of Logic: Ratiocinative and Inductive*. New York and Bombay: Longman's, 1900.

Mills, C. Wright. *The Power Elite*. New York: Oxford University Press, 1959.

Monkhouse, F. J. *A Dictionary of Geography*. Chicago: Aldine Publishing Company, 1970.

Montesquieu, Charles. *The Spirit of the Laws*. Tr. Anne Cohler, Basia Miller, and Harold Stone. Cambridge: Cambridge University Press, 1989.

Moss, Helen. "Accessing Different Types of Lexical Semantic Information: Evidence from Priming." *Journal of Experimental Psychology* 21, no. 4 (July, 1995): 863–83.

Mosse, George. *Nationalism and Sexuality: Respectability and Abnormal Sexuality in Modern Europe*. New York: H. Fertig, 1985.

Moynihan, Patrick. "The Negro Family: The Case for National Action." In *The Moynihan Report and the Politics of Controversy*, ed. Lee Rainwater and William Yancey. Cambridge: MIT Press, 1967, pp. 39–124.

Mulier, Eco O. G. Haitsma. *The Myth of Venice and Dutch Republican Thought in the Seventeenth Century.* Tr. Gerald Mora. Assen: Van Gorcum, 1980.

Nicholson, Linda. *Gender and History: The Limits of Social Theory in the Age of the Family.* New York: Columbia University Press, 1986.

Nietzsche, Friedrich. "Nietzsche Contra Wagner." In *The Portable Nietzsche,* tr. Walter Kaufmann. New York: Viking Press, 1968, pp. 661–83.

Nuessel, Frank. *The Study of Names: A Guide to the Principles and Topics.* Westport: Greenwood, 1992.

O'Brien, Mary. *The Politics of Reproduction.* Boston: Routledge and Kegan Paul, 1981.

O'Donovan, Katherine. *Sexual Divisions in the Law.* London: Weidenfield and Nicolson, 1985.

Ogg, David. *England in the Reigns of James II and William III.* Oxford: Oxford University Press, 1955.

Okin, Susan. *Justice, Gender, and the Family.* New York: Basic Books, 1989.

O'Leary, Síofra, and Tija Tiilikainen, eds. *Citizenship and Nationality in the New Europe.* London: Sweet and Maxwell, 1998.

Oliver, Kelly. "Antigone's Ghost: Undoing Hegel's *Phenomenology of Spirit.*" *Hypatia* 11, no. 1 (Winter, 1996): 67–90.

Ortner, Sherry. "Gender Hegemonies." *Cultural Critique* 14 (Winter, 1989–90): 35–80.

———. "Is Female to Male as Nature Is to Culture?" In *Women, Culture, and Society,* ed. Michelle Rosaldo and Louise Lamphere. Stanford: Stanford University Press, 1974, pp. 67–88.

Outlaw, Lucius. *On Race and Philosophy.* New York: Routledge, 1996.

Ozment, Steven. *When Fathers Ruled: Family Life in Reformation Europe.* Cambridge: Harvard University Press, 1983.

Pagels, Elaine. *Adam, Eve, and the Serpent.* New York: Random House, 1988.

Park, Robert. *Race and Culture.* Glencoe: Free Press, 1950.

Partridge, Eric. *Origins: A Short Etymological Dictionary of Modern English.* 2d ed. New York: MacMillan, 1959.

Pateman, Carole. *The Sexual Contract.* Stanford: Stanford University Press, 1988.

Peletz, Michael. "The Exchange of Men in 19th-century Negeri Sembilan (Malaya)." *American Ethnologies* 14, no. 3 (August, 1987): 449–69.

Peterson, V. Spike, ed. *Gendered States: (Re)visions of International Relations Theory.* Boulder: Lynne Rienner, 1992.

Pitkin, Hanna. *The Concept of Representation.* Berkeley, London, and Los Angeles: University of California Press, 1967.

———. "Obligation and Consent—I." *American Political Science Review* 59 (December, 1965): 990–1000.

———. *Wittgenstein and Justice.* Berkeley, Los Angeles and London: University of California Press, 1973.

Plato. *Cratylus.* In *The Collected Dialogues of Plato,* tr. Benjamin Jowett. New York: Bollingsworth, 1961.

———. *Laws.* Tr. J. Saunders. Middlesex: Penguin, 1970.

———. *Phaedrus.* In *Collected Dialogues of Plato,* tr. R. Hackforth. New York: Bollingsworth, 1961.

———. *Republic*. In *Collected Dialogues of Plato*, tr. Paul Shorey. New York: Bollingen, 1961.

Pollock, Frederick, and Frederic Maitland. *The History of English Law before the Time of Edward I*. 2d ed. 2 vols. Cambridge: Cambridge University Press, 1911.

Poewe, Karla. *Matrilineal Ideology: Male-Female Dynamics in Luapula, Zambia*. London, New York: Academic Press, 1981.

Pritchard, E. E. *Kinship and Marriage among the Nuer*. Oxford: Clarendon Press, 1951.

Quine, Maria. *Population Politics in Twentieth Century Europe: Fascist Dictatorships and Liberal Democracies*. London: Routledge, 1996.

Quine, Thomas. *Ontological Relativity and Other Essays*. New York and London: Columbia University Press, 1969.

Rawls, John. *A Theory of Justice*. Cambridge: Harvard University Press, 1971.

Razi, Zvi. *Life, Marriage and Death in a Medieval Parish: Economy, Society and Demography in Halesowen, 1270–1400*. Cambridge: Cambridge University Press, 1980.

Reich, Robert. *Work of Nations: Preparing Ourselves for the 21st Century*. New York: Knopf, 1991.

Renan, Ernst. "What Is a Nation?" In *Nation and Narration*, ed. Homi Bhaba. London: Routledge, 1990, pp. 8–22.

Reynolds, Susan. *Kingdoms and Communities in Western Europe, 900–1300*. Oxford: Clarendon Press, 1984.

Rich, Adrienne. *Of Woman Born: Motherhood as Experience and Institution*. New York: Norton, 1976.

Rogers, Colin. *The Surname Detective: Investigating Surname Distribution in England, 1086 - Present Day*. Manchester and York: Manchester University Press, 1995.

Rogin, Michael. *Fathers and Children: Andrew Jackson and the Subjugation of the American Indian*. New York: Knopf, 1975.

Room, Adrian. *Dictionary of Changes in Meaning*. London: Routledge and Kegan Paul, 1986.

Rosaldo, Michelle. "The Use and Abuse of Anthropology: Reflections on Feminism and Cross-Cultural Understanding." *Signs* 5, no. 3 (1980): 389–417.

Rousseau, Jean-Jacques. *Discourse on the Origin of Inequality*. Tr. Donald Cress. Indianapolis: Hackett, 1992.

———. *The Social Contract*. Tr. Maurice Cranston. New York: Penguin, 1968.

Rowbotham, Sheila. *Beyond the Fragments: Feminism and the Making of Socialism*. Boston: Alyson Press, 1981.

Rubin, Gayle. "Thinking Sex: Notes for a Radical Theory of the Politics of Sexuality." In *Pleasure/Danger: Exploring Female Sexuality*, ed. Carole Vance. Boston: Routledge and Kegan Paul, 1984, pp. 267–319.

———. "The Traffic in Women: Notes on the 'Political Economy' of Sex." In *Toward an Anthropology of Women*, ed. Rayna Rapp Reiter. New York: Monthly Review Press, 1975, pp. 157–210.

Ryder, Sandra, and Sheryl Kuzmenka. "Legal Rape: The Marital Rape Exemption." *John Marshall Law Review* 24 (Winter, 1991): 393–421.

Sacks, Karen. *Sisters and Wives: The Past and Future of Sexual Equality*. Westport and London: Greenwood Press, 1977.

Said, Edward. *Orientalism*. New York: Vintage, 1978.

Sanborn, F. B. *Henry D. Thoreau*. Boston: Houghton, Mifflin and Co., 1882.

Sanders, A. C. de C.M. *A Social History of Black Slaves and Freedmen in Portugal, 1441–1551*. Cambridge: Cambridge University Press, 1982.

Saussure, Ferdinand. *Course on General Linguistics*. Tr. Wade Baskin. London: P. Owen, 1960.

Saxonhouse, Arlene. *Fear of Diversity: The Birth of Political Science in Ancient Greek Thought*. Chicago: University of Chicago Press, 1992.

Schecter, Susan. *Women and Male Violence*. Boston: South End Press, 1982.

Schindler, Debra. "Anthropology in the Arctic: A Critique of Racial Typology and Normative Theory." *Current Anthropology* 26, no. 4 (August/October, 1985): 475–84.

Schochet, Gordon. *The Authoritarian Family and Political Attitudes in 17th-Century England: Patriarchalism in Political Thought*. New Brunswick: Transaction Books, 1988.

Schreber, Daniel Paul. *Memoirs of My Nervous Illness*. Tr. and ed. Ida Macalpine and Richard Hunter. London: W. W. Dawson and Sons, 1955.

Schuck, Peter, and Rogers Smith. *Citizenship without Consent: Illegal Aliens in the American Polity*. New Haven: Yale University Press, 1985.

Scott, James. *Seeing Like a State: How Certain Schemes to Improve the Human Condition Have Failed*. New Haven, London: Yale University Press, 1998.

Sealey, Ralph. *Women and the Law in Classical Greece*. Chapel Hill and London: University of North Carolina Press, 1990.

Shanley, Mary. *Feminism, Marriage, and the Law in Victorian England, 1850–1895*. Princeton: Princeton University Press, 1984.

———. "Marital Slavery and Friendship: J. S. Mill's *The Subjection of Women*." In *Feminist Interpretations and Political Theory*, ed. Carole Pateman and Mary Shanley. Cambridge: Polity Press, 1991, pp. 164–80.

Sheehan, Michael. *Marriage, Family, and Law in Medieval Europe: Collected Studies*. Toronto: University of Toronto Press, 1996.

Sickels, Robert. *Race, Marriage and the Law*. Albuquerque: University of New Mexico Press, 1972.

Sicker, Martin. *Genesis of the State*. New York: Praeger, 1991.

Skinner, Quentin. "The State." In *Political Innovation and Conceptual Change*, ed. Terrence Ball, James Farr, and Russell Hanson. Cambridge and New York: Cambridge University Press, 1989, pp. 90–131.

Skocpol, Theda. *Protecting Soldiers and Mothers: The Political Origins of Social Policy in the United States*. Cambridge: Harvard University Press, 1992.

Slater, Philip. *The Glory of Hera: Greek Mythology and the Greek Family*. Boston: Beacon Press, 1968.

Smart, Carol. *The Ties that Bind: Law, Marriage and the Reproduction of Patriarchal Relations*. London: Routledge, Kegan, Paul, 1984.

Smart, Carol, and Selma Sevenhuijsen, eds. *Child Custody and the Politics of Gender*. London: Routledge, 1989.

Smedley, Audrey. *Race in North America: Origin and Evolution of a Worldview*. Boulder: Westview Press, 1992.

Smith, Anna Marie. *New Right Discourse on Race and Sexuality: Britain, 1968–1990*. Cambridge: Cambridge University Press, 1994.

Smith, Eldson. *The Story of Our Names*. New York: Harper, 1950.

Smith, Rogers. *Civic Ideals: Conflicting Visions of Citizenship in U.S. History*. New Haven: Yale University Press, 1997.

Smith, W. Robertson. *Kinship and Marriage in Early Arabia*. London: Adams and Charles Black, 1903.

Snowden, Frank. *Before Color Prejudice: The Ancient View of Blacks*. Cambridge: Harvard University Press, 1983.

Sophocles. *The Oresteian Trilogy*. Tr. Philip Vellacott. London: Penguin, 1959.

Soysal, Yasemin. *Limits of Citizenship: Migrants and Post-national Membership in Europe*. Chicago: University of Chicago Press, 1994.

Spitzer, Leo. *Essays in Historical Semantics*. New York: S. F. Vann, 1948.

Spivak, Gayatri. *In Other Worlds*. New York and London: Methuen, 1987.

———. *The Post-Colonial Critic: Interviews, Strategies, Dialogues*. New York: Routledge, 1990.

Sprengnether, Madelon. *The Spectral Mother: Freud, Feminism, and Psychoanalysis*. Ithaca: Cornell University Press, 1990.

Stanbrook, Ivor, ed. *British Nationality*. London and Brussels: Clement, 1982.

Stevens, Jacqueline. "Leviticus in America: On the Politics of Sex Crimes." *Journal of Political Philosophy* 1, no. 2 (June, 1993): 105–36.

———. "The Politics of Identity: From Property to Empathy." Dissertation. University of California at Berkeley, 1993.

———. "The Reasonableness of John Locke's Majority." *Political Theory* 24 (August, 1996): 423–63.

Stoler, Ann. "Making Empire Respectable: The Politics of Race and Sexual Morality in Twentieth Century Colonial Cultures." In *Dangerous Liasons: Gender, Nation, and Post-Colonial Perspectives*, ed. Anne McClintock. Minneapolis: University of Minnesota Press, 1997, pp. 344–73.

———. *Race and the Education of Desire: Foucault's History of Sexuality and the Colonial Order of Things*. Durham: Duke University Press, 1995.

———. "Racial Histories and Their Regimes of Truth," *Political and Social Theory* 11 (1997): 183–206.

Stone, Lawrence. *The Family, Sex, and Marriage in England, 1500–1800*. New York: Harper and Row, 1979.

Strathern, Marilyn. *The Gender of the Gift: Problems with Women and Problems with Society in Melanesia*. Berkeley, London and Los Angeles: University of California Press, 1988.

Sunstein, Cass. "Sexual Orientation and the Constitution: A Note on the Relationship between Due Process and Equal Protection," *University of Chicago Law Review* 55 (Fall, 1988): 1161–79.

Swanson, Hollace. "Donor Anonymity in Artificial Insemination: Is It Still Necessary?" *Columbia Journal of Law and Social Problems* 27 (fall 1993): 151–90.

Taylor, Charles, *Multi-culturalism and the Politics of Recognition: An Essay*. Princeton: Princeton University Press, 1992.

Teichman, Jenny. *Illegitimacy: A Philosophical Examination*. Oxford: Blackwell, 1982.

Tel Aviv Faculty of Law. *Israel Yearbook on Human Rights*. Vol. 23. Tel Aviv: Tel Aviv Faculty of Law, 1993.

Theweleit, Klaus. *Male Fantasies*. Tr. Stephen Conway. Minneapolis. University of Minnesota Press, 1987.

Thoreau, Henry. *Walden and Civil Disobedience*. New York: Penguin, 1983.

Tickner, Ann. *Gender in International Relations*. New York: Columbia University Press, 1992.

Tilly, Charles. "War Making and State Making as Organized Crime." In *Bringing the State Back In*, ed. Evans, Peter, Dietrich Rueschemeyer, and Theda Skocpol. Cambridge: Cambridge University Press, 1985, pp. 169–91.

Tocqueville, Alexis de. *Democracy in America*. Tr. George Lawrence. New York: Anchor, 1969.

Traer, James. *Marriage and the Family in Eighteenth Century France*. Ithaca: Cornell University Press, 1980.

Traverso, Enzo. *The Marxists and the Jewish Question: The History of a Debate, 1842–1943*. Tr. Bernard Gibbons. Atlantic Highlands: Humanities Press, 1990.

Trebilcot, Joyce, ed. *Mothering: Essays in Feminist Theory*. Totowa: Rowman and Allanheld, 1983.

Treggiari, Susan. *Roman Marriage: Iusti Coniuges from the Time of Cicero to the Time of Ulpian*. Oxford: Oxford University Press, 1991.

Truman, David. *The Governmental Process: Political Interests and Public Opinion*. New York: Knopf, 1951.

United Nations. *Statistical Yearbook*. No. 39. New York: United Nations, 1993.

———. Department of Public Information. *These Rights and Freedoms*. 1st ed. New York: United Nations Department of Public Information, 1950.

United States Department of Commerce. Bureau of the Census. *World Population Profile*. Washington, D.C.: GPO, 1996.

———. Bureau of the Census. 1990 Census of Population and Housing. *Geographic Mobility*. CD-Rom (SSTF) 15.

———. *Statistical Reference Index, Abstracts*. Washington, D.C.: GPO, 1995.

Venkataramiah, E. S. *Citizenship: Rights and Duties*. Naga: Proprietrix, 1988.

Vincent, Joan. *Anthropology and Politics: Visions, Traditions, and Trends*. Tuscon: University of Arizona Press, 1990.

Waldron, Jeremy. "John Locke: Social Contract Versus Political Anthropology." *Review of Politics* 51, (Winter, 1989): 3–28.

Waltz, Kenneth. "Anarchic Orders and Balances of Power." In *International Politics: Anarchy, Force, Political Economy and Decision-Making*, ed. Robert Art and Robert Jervis. 2d ed. Toronto: Little, Brown and Co. 1984, pp. 8–28.

Waltz, Waldo Emerson. *The Nationality of Married Women: A Study of Domestic Policies and International Legislation*. Urbana: University of Illinois, 1937.

Walzer, Michael. *Spheres of Justice: A Defense of Pluralism and Equality*. Oxford: Martin Robertson and Co., 1983.

Weber, Max. *Economy and Society: An Outline of Interpretive Sociology*. Tr. Ephraim Fischoff et al. 2 vols. Berkeley, Los Angeles and London: University of California Press, 1978.

Webster, Yehudi. *The Racialization of America*. New York: St. Martin's Press, 1992.

Weinberg, Albert. *Manifest Destiny: A Study of Nationalist Expansion in American History*. Cloucester: P. Smith, 1958.

West, Robin. "Equality Theory, Marital Rape, and the Promise of the Fourteenth Amendment." *Florida Law Review* 42 (1990): 45–79.

Whetherall, Margaret, and Johathan Potter. *Mapping the Language of Racism: Dis-*

course and the Legitimation of Exploitation. New York: Columbia University Press, 1992.

White, Hayden. *The Content of the Form: Narrative Discourse and Historical Representation.* Baltimore and London: Johns Hopkins University Press, 1987.

Wills, Gary. *Under God: Religion and American Politics.* New York: Simon and Schuster, 1990.

Wilson, William Julius. *When Work Disappears: The World of the Urban Poor.* New York: Knopf, 1996.

Wittgenstein, Ludwig. *Philosophical Investigations.* Tr. G.E.M. Anscombe. 3d ed. New York: MacMillan, 1968.

Wolff, Michael, Peter Rutte, and Albert F. Bayers, *Where We Stand.* New York, Toronto, London: Bantam Books, 1992.

Wollstonecraft, Mary. *A Vindication of the Rights of Women.* 1792; rpt. London: Rutland, Everyman's Press, 1985.

Woodhouse, A.S.P., ed. *Puritanism and Liberty: Being the Army Debates (1647–1649) from the Clarke Manuscripts with Supplementary Documents.* Chicago: Chicago University Press, 1951.

Woolf, Henry Bosely. *The Old German Principles of Name-Giving.* Baltimore: Johns Hopkins Press, 1939.

Woshinsky, Oliver. *Culture and Politics: An Introduction to Mass and Elite Behavior.* Englewood Cliffs: Prentice-Hall, 1995.

Wuthnow, Robert. *Communities of Discourse: Ideology and Social Structure in the Reformation, Enlightenment, and European Socialism.* Cambridge: Harvard University Press, 1989.

Young, Iris Marion. *Justice and the Politics of Difference.* Princeton: Princeton University Press, 1990.

Yuval-Davis, Nira, and Floya Anthias, eds. *Woman-Nation-State.* London: MacMillan Press, 1989.

Zaidman, Louis, and Pauline Schmitt Pantel. *Religion in the Ancient Greek City.* Tr. Paul Cartledge. Cambridge: Cambridge University Press, 1992.

Ziff, Paul. *Semantic Analysis.* Ithaca: Cornell University Press, 1967.

Zimmerman, Marvin. "Some Dubious Premises in Research and Theory on Racial Differences." *American Psychologist 45* (December, 1990): 1297–1303.

Zingo, Martha, and Kevin Early. *Nameless Persons: Legal Discrimination against Non-Marital Children in the United States.* Westport and London: Praeger, 1994.

Žižek, Slavoj. *On the Sublime Object of Ideology.* New York and London: Verso, 1989.

About the author ───────────────────────

JACQUELINE STEVENS is an Assistant Professor of Political Science and Women's Studies at University of Michigan, Ann Arbor, on leave of absence as Robert Wood Johnson Health Policy Scholar at Yale University, 1997–1999.